SQL Server 2 Administrator's Guide – Second Edition

A definitive guide for DBAs to implement, monitor, and maintain enterprise database solutions

Marek Chmel

Vladimír Mužný

BIRMINGHAM—MUMBAI

SQL Server 2019 Administrator's Guide – Second Edition

Commissioning Editor: Sunith Shetty

Acquisition Editor: Devika Battike

Senior Editor: Roshan Kumar

Content Development Editor: Tazeen Shaikh

Technical Editor: Sonam Pandey

Copy Editor: Safis Editing

Project Coordinator: Aishwarya Mohan

Proofreader: Safis Editing

Indexer: Pratik Shirodkar

Production Designer: Jyoti Chauhan

First published: December 2017
Second edition: September 2020

Production reference: 1110920

Published by Packt Publishing Ltd.
Livery Place
35 Livery Street
Birmingham
B3 2PB, UK.

ISBN 978-1-78995-432-6

www.packt.com

To my family, friends, colleagues, students, and readers.

– Vladimír Mužný

*Thanks to my family for continuous support, and to my friends
and colleagues for their inspiring ideas and insights.*

– Marek Chmel

`Packt.com`

Subscribe to our online digital library for full access to over 7,000 books and videos, as well as industry leading tools to help you plan your personal development and advance your career. For more information, please visit our website.

Why subscribe?

- Spend less time learning and more time coding with practical eBooks and Videos from over 4,000 industry professionals

- Improve your learning with Skill Plans built especially for you

- Get a free eBook or video every month

- Fully searchable for easy access to vital information

- Copy and paste, print, and bookmark content

Did you know that Packt offers eBook versions of every book published, with PDF and ePub files available? You can upgrade to the eBook version at `packt.com` and as a print book customer, you are entitled to a discount on the eBook copy. Get in touch with us at `customercare@packtpub.com` for more details.

At `www.packt.com`, you can also read a collection of free technical articles, sign up for a range of free newsletters, and receive exclusive discounts and offers on Packt books and eBooks.

Contributors

About the authors

Marek Chmel is a senior cloud solutions architect at Microsoft for data and artificial intelligence, a speaker, and a trainer with more than 15 years' experience. He's a frequent conference speaker, focusing on SQL Server, Azure, and security topics. He has been a Data Platform MVP since 2012. He has earned numerous certifications, including MCSE: Data Management and Analytics, Azure Architect, Data Engineer and Data Scientist Associate, EC Council Certified Ethical Hacker, and several eLearnSecurity certifications. Marek earned his MSc degree in Business and Informatics from Nottingham Trent University. He started his career as a trainer for Microsoft courses and later worked as principal sharepoint administrator and principal database administrator.

Vladimír Mužný has been a freelance developer and consultant since 1997. He has been a Data Platform MVP since 2017, and he has earned certifications such as MCSE: Data Management and Analytics and MCT. His first steps with SQL Server were done on version 6.5, and from that time on, he has worked with all following versions of SQL Server. Now Vladimir teaches Microsoft database courses, participates in SQL Server adoption at various companies, and collaborates on projects for production tracking and migrations.

I would like to thank my loving and patient family for their continued support, patience, and encouragement throughout the long process of writing this book.

About the reviewers

Tomaž Kaštrun is an SQL Server developer and data scientist with more than 15 years of experience in the fields of business warehousing, development, ETL, database administration, and query tuning. He also holds more than 15 years of experience in data analysis, data mining, statistical research, and machine learning. He is a Microsoft SQL Server MVP for Data Platform and has been working with Microsoft SQL Server since version 2000. Tomaz is a blogger, an author of many articles, a frequent speaker at community and Microsoft events, an avid coffee drinker, and is passionate about fixed gear bikes.

Arjun Sivadasan has over 12 years of experience working in various data-focused roles, developing and maintaining mission-critical applications in transactional and analytical environments. After completing his bachelor's in computer science engineering at Kerala University, he started his career as a full-stack developer in Bangalore and soon switched focus to databases. He has since tried to gain expertise in all aspects of data management. He presently works as a data architect for a global product company based in Sydney, Australia. Arjun is passionate about Microsoft data products. He is also an avid blogger and speaks at local user groups. In his spare time, he likes to cook meals for his wife or explore the world on two wheels.

Packt is searching for authors like you

If you're interested in becoming an author for Packt, please visit `authors.packtpub.com` and apply today. We have worked with thousands of developers and tech professionals, just like you, to help them share their insight with the global tech community. You can make a general application, apply for a specific hot topic that we are recruiting an author for, or submit your own idea.

Table of Contents

Section 2:
Server and Database Maintenance

3
Implementing Backup and Recovery

4
Securing Your SQL Server

Section 3: High Availability and the Cloud with SQL Server 2019

7

Planning Migration and Upgrade

8

Automation – Using Tools to Manage and Monitor SQL Server 2019

9

Configuring Always On High Availability Features

10

In-Memory OLTP – Why and How to Use it

11

Combining SQL Server 2019 with Azure

12

Taming Big Data with SQL Server

Other Books You May Enjoy

Index

Preface

SQL Server is one of the most popular relational database management systems developed by Microsoft. This second edition of *SQL Server Administrator's Guide* will not only teach you how to administer an enterprise database, but also help you become proficient at managing and keeping the database available, secure, and stable.

You'll start by learning how to set up your SQL Server and configure new and existing environments for optimal use. The book then takes you through designing aspects and delves into performance tuning by showing you how to use indexes effectively. You'll understand certain choices that need to be made regarding backups, implement security policy, and discover how to keep your environment healthy. Tools available for monitoring and managing a SQL Server database, including automating health reviews, performance checks, and much more, will also be discussed in detail. As you advance, the book covers essential topics such as migration, upgrading, and consolidation, along with the techniques that will help you when things go wrong. Once you've got to grips with integration with Azure and streamlining big data pipelines, you'll learn best practices from industry experts for maintaining a highly reliable database solution.

Whether you are an administrator or are looking to get started with database administration, this SQL Server book will help you develop the skills you need to successfully create, design, and deploy database solutions.

Who this book is for

This book is for database administrators, database developers, and anyone who wants to administer large and multiple databases single-handedly using Microsoft's SQL Server 2019. A basic awareness of database concepts and experience with previous SQL Server versions is required.

What this book covers

Chapter 1, *Setting Up SQL Server 2019*, offers an overview of the SQL Server technology stack, tooling, and several recipes on how to install technologies and features of SQL Server the right way.

Chapter 2, Keeping Your SQL Server Environment Healthy, provides a plethora of follow-up activities once SQL Server is configured, including post-installation configuration, to follow best practices for maintenance and operations.

Chapter 3, Implementing Backup and Recovery illustrates the importance of data reliability and accessibility as the key responsibilities of every database administrator. It also explains all aspects of proper recovery strategies as well as all the knowledge needed to configure backup and restore strategies properly.

Chapter 4, Securing Your SQL Server, outlines the options for securing the server from a number of perspectives, starting with service accounts, authentication, auditing, and other important tasks for overall security management.

Chapter 5, Working with Disaster Recovery Options, outlines the list of options available to help overcome any disaster when operations go down.

Chapter 6, Indexing and Performance, provides an overview of performance monitoring techniques. As a part of performance optimization, indexing is also explained here.

Chapter 7, Planning Migration and Upgrade provides practical information on how to plan a migration and upgrade the older version of the SQL Server environment to the current version.

Chapter 8, Automation – Using Tools to Manage and Monitor SQL Server 2019, shows how to proactively use tools to manage SQL Server 2019 and to monitor its health, together with an in-depth look at techniques and tools used for automation on SQL Server.

Chapter 9, Configuring Always On High-Availability Features, shows practical information and examples of how to plan, configure, and manage Always On configuration for your SQL Server environment and also provides information on the High Availability/Disaster Recovery technology that is required for SQL Server.

Chapter 10, In-Memory OLTP – Why and How to Use It, illustrates the strong features of In-Memory OLTP in terms of dramatically increasing the throughput of transactions in SQL Server databases by describing how and in which cases to implement, use, and monitor In-Memory OLTP.

Chapter 11, Combining SQL Server 2019 with Azure, illustrates how cloud solutions have become common in many cases by explaining how Azure can help with several scenarios and also provides an overview of SQL technologies offered by Azure.

Chapter 12, Taming Big Data with SQL Server, incorporates a new feature for managing big data workloads, called big data clusters, but that's not the only option as regards how to work with big data, and in this chapter you'll find out how to tame the monster.

To get the most out of this book

Software/hardware covered in the book	OS requirements
SQL Server 2019	Windows OS, Windows Server, Linux
Azure SQL Database	

If you are using the digital version of this book, we advise you to type the code yourself or access the code via the GitHub repository (link available in the next section). Doing so will help you avoid any potential errors related to the copying and pasting of code.

Download the example code files

You can download the example code files for this book from your account at www.packt.com. If you purchased this book elsewhere, you can visit www.packtpub.com/support and register to have the files emailed directly to you.

You can download the code files by following these steps:

1. Log in or register at www.packt.com.
2. Select the **Support** tab.
3. Click on **Code Downloads**.
4. Enter the name of the book in the **Search** box and follow the onscreen instructions.

Once the file is downloaded, please make sure that you unzip or extract the folder using the latest version of:

*   WinRAR/7-Zip for Windows
*   Zipeg/iZip/UnRarX for Mac
*   7-Zip/PeaZip for Linux

The code bundle for the book is also hosted on GitHub at https://github.com/PacktPublishing/SQL-Server-2019-Administrator-s-Guide. In case there's an update to the code, it will be updated on the existing GitHub repository.

We also have other code bundles from our rich catalog of books and videos available at https://github.com/PacktPublishing/. Check them out!

Download the color images

We also provide a PDF file that has color images of the screenshots/diagrams used in this book. You can download it here: `https://static.packtcdn.com/downloads/9781789954326_ColorImages.pdf`.

Conventions used

There are a number of text conventions used throughout this book.

`Code in text`: Indicates code words in text, database table names, folder names, filenames, file extensions, pathnames, dummy URLs, user input, and Twitter handles. Here is an example: "`ActiveDirectory` is automatically managing the account password without any service disruption."

A block of code is set as follows:

```
-- bringing data back
alter table MovieRatings set (remote_data_archive (migration_
state = inbound))
go


-- leaving data in Azure
alter table MovieRatings set
(remote_data_archive = off_without_data_recovery
(migration_state = paused))
go
```

When we wish to draw your attention to a particular part of a code block, the relevant lines or items are set in bold:

```
use [AdventureWorks]
exec sp_replicationdboption @dbname = N'AdventureWorks',
    @optname = N'publish',
    @value = N'true'
GO
```

Any command-line input or output is written as follows:

```
EXEC sp_configure 'backup compression default', 1
GO
RECONFIGURE
GO
```

Bold: Indicates a new term, an important word, or words that you see on screen. For example, words in menus or dialog boxes appear in the text like this. Here is an example: "Once **Replication** is enabled for the database, you can create the publication and add the snapshot."

> **Tips or important notes**
> You may find many errors in the error log of your SQL Server, which will lead you to the required `TLS1.2` hotfix installation.

Get in touch

Feedback from our readers is always welcome.

General feedback: If you have questions about any aspect of this book, mention the book title in the subject of your message and email us at `customercare@packtpub.com`.

Errata: Although we have taken every care to ensure the accuracy of our content, mistakes do happen. If you have found a mistake in this book, we would be grateful if you would report this to us. Please visit `www.packtpub.com/support/errata`, selecting your book, clicking on the Errata Submission Form link, and entering the details.

Piracy: If you come across any illegal copies of our works in any form on the internet, we would be grateful if you would provide us with the location address or website name. Please contact us at `copyright@packt.com` with a link to the material.

If you are interested in becoming an author: If there is a topic that you have expertise in, and you are interested in either writing or contributing to a book, please visit `authors.packtpub.com`.

Reviews

Please leave a review. Once you have read and used this book, why not leave a review on the site that you purchased it from? Potential readers can then see and use your unbiased opinion to make purchase decisions, we at Packt can understand what you think about our products, and our authors can see your feedback on their book. Thank you!

For more information about Packt, please visit `packt.com`.

Section 1: Provisioning the SQL Server Environment

The objective of this section is to walk you through the SQL Server technology stack, its complete installation on different operating systems, and initial post-installation configuration.

This section contains the following chapters:

- *Chapter 1, Setting Up SQL Server 2019*
- *Chapter 2, Keeping Your SQL Server Environment Healthy*

1
Setting Up SQL Server 2019

Microsoft SQL Server is not just a database engine; over the years, it has become a very complex and robust technology set for data management, analysis, and visualizations. As the progress of technologies incorporated into SQL Server grows, it has become more complicated to decide which specific technology is needed, how to prepare the environment for its installation, and which configuration properties administrators should be aware of. With the rising popularity of cloud services, we also have a great option to host database services in Microsoft Azure as well. This chapter offers an introduction to the SQL Server technology stack in on-premises environments and helps you to accomplish its proper installation to start your work with SQL Server.

In this chapter, we will study what the SQL Server technology set contains and the purpose of each technology. We will also get familiar with the prerequisites and pre-installation steps, and will find out which settings are important and which post-installation steps are recommended during the installation of Windows. Using a step-by-step approach, we will learn to install SQL Server on Linux using Ubuntu. In this chapter, we will also understand the process of SQL Server provisioning in containers.

In this chapter, we will cover the following topics:

- Overview of the Microsoft SQL Server 2019 technology
- Preparing the SQL Server 2019 installation on Windows
- Installing SQL Server 2019 on Windows
- Installing SQL Server 2019 on Linux
- Installing SQL Server 2019 on containers

Overview of the Microsoft SQL Server 2019 technology

Microsoft SQL Server offers a powerful end-to-end data processing platform. In other words, we can gain data from an extensive set of sources, securely and reliably managed, transformed, processed, analyzed, and visualized under an all-in-one license.

The following diagram shows what the bigger picture of the SQL Server technology set looks like:

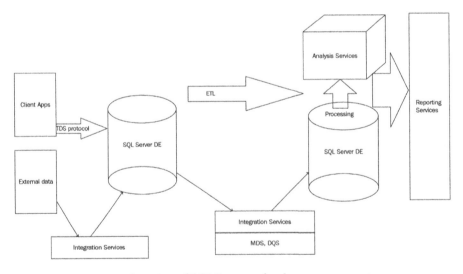

Fig. 1.1 – Overview of SQL Server technology set on-premises

The preceding diagram shows one of the many possible ways in which technologies within SQL Server can cooperate. **SQL Server Database Engine** (**DE**) is depicted twice in the diagram because it possibly plays two major roles within the data processing platform, as follows:

- **Line-of-Business (LOB) application contention**: In the diagram, at the left occurrence of SQL Server DE, SQL Server provides data ingestion from client applications or other external sources of data.

- **Business Intelligence (BI) contention**: In the diagram, at the right occurrence of SQL Server DE, the SQL Server instance manages data warehouses, that is, databases used for Analysis Services data model processing or for reporting purposes.

As seen in the preceding diagram, SQL Server contains many technologies used and maintained by just one person. So, the following list shows how specific roles use such technologies:

- **Database Administrators** (**DBAs**): DBAs work with SQL Server and **SQL Server Agent** services, ensuring the continuity of operations, security, **disaster recovery** (**DR**) strategies, and similar tasks.

- **SQL developers**: SQL developers are responsible for the content of databases, from database design and transaction handling to the quality and accuracy of data stored in databases.

- **Extract, Transform, Load (ETL) developers**: ETL developers' playground lies mainly in **SQL Server Integration Services** (**SSIS**) services. ETL developers create a whole ETL workflow and ensure the quality and integrity of data extracted from sources and uploaded to targets of the ETL flow.

- **BI developers**: BI developers work mainly with reports on **SQL Server Reporting Services** (**SSRS**) and with multidimensional data models hosted on **SQL Server Analysis Services** (**SSAS**).

Although our attention is focused on DBAs, it is still useful to have a brief idea of other user roles within the same huge technology set. The DBA is mainly responsible for assisting all users.

Now, we will explain all components, including SSIS and SSRS, in more detail in the following sections.

Understanding SQL Server DE

The core service in the SQL Server technology set is the SQL Server DE service. This service covers the following three responsibilities, apart from storing and manipulating data:

- **Handling recovery**: This responsibility means that after any sudden or a planned breakdown of the service or database, the service will recover every database to its last consistent state without any undone transactions.

- **Handling transactions**: A transaction is mentioned as a single unit of work, and SQL Server DE guarantees that transactions will be durable and isolated and correctly finished with COMMIT or ROLLBACK.

- **Handling security**: SQL Server DE resolves every request for authentication and authorization and decides if a user or application is known (authenticated) and if a user or application has permission for certain actions (authorization).

SQL Server does not provide its capabilities to end users only. Still, it's necessary to keep in mind that SQL Server DE serves as a base service for almost every other service in the SQL Server technology stack and note the following important points:

- Every BI service, such as Analysis Services or Reporting Services, is actually a client of SQL Server DE.

- Some services, such as Machine Learning Services, can be installed within or independently of SQL Server DE.

- **SQL Server Agent** (not seen in the previous diagram) plays an exceptional role in the SQL Server ecosystem. This service exists as an indivisible part of every SQL Server DE application. SQL Server Agent hugely helps administrators, as well as other services or components, to automate routine tasks.

Why do we need this information? It's one of the crucial moments when planning a SQL Server installation. For example, Analysis Services is a heavily resource-consuming service, and its deployment along with SQL Server DE could lead to big performance problems and user disappointment with regard to responses on their requests. From a different perspective, installing SQL Server services on separated operating systems leads to increased license expenses and more complex administration efforts.

The following sections will describe each SQL Server service in detail.

SSIS

SSIS is basically used as a data pump of SQL Server. SSIS is used to maintain data movements and transformations between a wide scale of heterogeneous data sources and destinations, as well as migrating or transforming data between several instances of SQL Server. A very common use case of SSIS is in data warehousing to extract, transform, and save data from **online transactional processing** (**OLTP**) databases to a data warehouse.

The working unit of this technology is the `SSIS` package. This is an executable unit of integration services, and we can think of it as a simple application. Its definition consists of two main parts: **control flow** and **data flow**. Control flow contains tasks such as creating a temporary folder (`Filesystem task`), accessing a **File Transfer Protocol** (**FTP**) site (FTP task), and many others. One of the most crucial tasks in control flow is called the data flow task. This data flow task contains a definition of the path that data goes through, from data source to data destination.

The integration service itself is not mandatory for `SSIS` package execution, but the service is used for integration services packages management. It's installed for backward compatibility with older versions of the `SSIS` packages deployment model. `SSIS` packages are now commonly placed into a database called **SSISDB**. The database is not often accessed directly by users or administrators; it is maintained using the **Integration Services Catalog**.

From an administrator's point of view, the SSIS service installation could be omitted if all existing `SSIS` packages are deployed to the Integration Services Catalog, which can be created anytime just by a few clicks in **SQL Server Management Studio (SSMS)**.

Integration services often cooperate with two features for data cleansing, validating, and deduplicating. These services are called **Master Data Services** (**MDS**)and **Data Quality Services** (**DQS**).

MDS

MDS is a technology that provides a very efficient way to manage data that has to be maintained centrally for more applications (for instance, an organizational structure or chart of accounts) or data that should be cleansed and validated before it is sent to other data destinations such as a data warehouse. From an administrator's perspective, it's a database usually called `MDS`, `MDM`, or `master_data_services` (the administrator can choose the database name) and a website created on **Internet Information Services** (**IIS**). `MDS` is not installed within an SQL Server installer; a graphical tool called **Master Data Services Configuration Manager** is used for its installation and configuration.

Loading data into a MDS database is often done using SSIS. Then, the data is optionally cleansed by data stewards. Clean and consolidated data could be subscribed via **subscription views**. Definitions of these views are created through the management of the IIS website and stored in the MDS database.

DQS

DQS is a technology providing you with a way to **deduplicate** and correct data that originates from several sources. Actually, DQS is not a service installed within the SQL Server installer, but it's created by an independent application.

The `SSIS` package has a special control flow task called the **DQS cleansing task** that is used when some of the DQS knowledge base (a set of rules created by the data steward) has to be used for data cleansing before the data is written to a target.

Developing solutions with SSIS, and optionally with MDS and DQS, needs complex developers' expertise not primarily needed by SQL Server administrators. From the administrator's perspective, SSIS, along with MDS and DQS, is just another database maintained by SQL Server.

SSAS

SSAS is a very robust and scalable service that steps behind relational database limits by pre-calculating data that has been read from a relational data source. SSAS stores the data in multidimensional storage called a **storage model**.

This approach is even more efficient for further analysis and visualizations than just the usage of relational data because the multidimensional format allows users to drill down and pivot actions as well as advanced aggregations or period-to-date queries. From this perspective, SSAS forms the core component of corporate as well as self-service BI solutions.

Analysis Services can be installed within SQL Server installer, but it is not always a good idea to have both the SQL Server DE and SSAS service installed on the same computer. We must remember that SSAS is an extremely complicated engine with a lot of physical **input/output (I/O)** operations when accessing a storage mode. A lot of memory cache is used for data processing and data querying and entails significant **central processing unit (CPU)** consumption for computations. One more important thing is that results from SSAS are often consumed in applications such as decision support, management reports, and so on, and it's crucial to get responses fast without waiting.

As mentioned previously, in many cases SSAS has to be installed on its own computer. The only disadvantage is that separate installations of SQL Server services lead to separate licensing and more complex maintenance needs. In other words, *the more computers that are used to spread SQL Server technologies across an infrastructure, the more licensing expenses will grow.*

SSAS can be installed in two distinct modes, as follows:

- **Multidimensional mode**: This mode is used for centrally created data cubes and mining models.

- **Tabular mode**: This mode is also called **in-memory** mode. It's used to host PowerPivot models.

If both modes are needed, the SQL Server installer must be executed twice, and two instances of SSAS have to be installed.

Multidimensional mode of SSAS installation

The **multidimensional mode** is used for corporate BI scenarios. IT departments develop dimensions, data cubes, and mining models.

The multidimensional mode requires regular data processing, so its approach is for bigger centralized analysis, trend predictions, longitudinal studies, and more. The multidimensional mode is seen as a bigger, robust, and scalable mode, but often with data delay. (An existing storage model called **Relational online analytical processing (ROLAP)** can be used for real-time analysis but has a lot of constraints. An overview of a real-time operational analysis scenario will be described later in this book.)

Tabular mode of SSAS installation

SQL Server, as well as other Microsoft technologies, supports BI solutions created by business users. This approach is intended for users who are subject matter experts more than IT experts, who have simple but strong enough tools to create their own analysis and visualizations. The toolset is known as **Power BI**. A part of Power BI is the **PowerPivot** technology—compressed and somehow pre-calculated data used to build data models similar to data cubes.

For the possibility of sharing our own data models with other users in a well-managed and secured environment, the PowerPivot mode of SSAS was originated. Data models can be deployed with almost no adjustments to the server environment and can then be accessed by authorized users.

One big advantage of PowerPivot mode is that data models are held in memory, and when some additional data is needed to fulfill user requests, it can be read from the data source directly.

Although a detailed description of how analysis services work is beyond the scope of this book, we must know that combining analysis services—no matter which installation mode—with other SQL Server services leads to big performance problems.

SSRS

Data, either relational or multidimensional, does not have its own visible face—data is not visual. To have a complete end-to-end data management platform, Microsoft offers a service called SSRS as a part of the SQL Server technology set. This service is designated to access data from a variety of sources and visualize the data to users. SSRS is a favorite service for centralized and managed reporting.

From an architectural point of view, SSRS is a Windows (or newly Linux) service that offers HTTP/HTTPS endpoints for human-readable as well as web service content consuming. The human-readable endpoint is called **Report Portal**. It is just a web application for report consumption and management (formerly, Report Portal was called **Report Manager**).

SSRS has many useful features, including report deployment, report previews, subscriptions, or report exports to formats such as MS Excel or PDF.

> **Note**
> SQL Server 2019 Reporting Services installation is no longer a part of the SQL Server installer. From now, SSRS is installed and versioned separately. Linking to the installer is accessible from the **SQL Server installation center** or the setup wizard step with **Feature Selection**.

When SQL Server 2016 was up to date, it had two installation modes for reporting service—**Native mode** and **SharePoint mode**. However, in SQL Server 2019, **SharePoint mode** is no longer offered.

When installing SSRS, the web installer allows only installation of the service itself without creating the `ReportServer` and `ReportServerTempdb` databases for services metadata, as illustrated in the following screenshot:

Fig. 1.2 – Reporting Services installation step

In production environments, it is a better option to install an instance of SQL Server DE on its own computer and then install SSRS on its own computer as well. Metadata databases are created later by a visual configuration tool called **Reporting Services Configuration Manager**.

Machine Learning Services

Predictive analysis profits from efficient and enlarged languages such as Python or R. SQL Server 2016 was the first version of SQL Server that incorporated new features called **R Services**. This feature is not seen in SQL Server 2019 installation anymore because it was renamed as **Machine Learning Services**. The renaming reflects the new Python support in SQL Server 2017. SQL Server 2019 offers Java as a third usable language in Machine Learning Services.

Machine Learning Services can be installed via **in-server** mode. In this installation mode, Java, Python, and R support is incorporated directly into SQL Server DE. When the in-server mode is selected, developers can call the SQL Server stored procedure, sp_execute_external_script, with an R command, a Java command, or a Python command as a parameter.

The second possible mode of installation is the Machine Learning standalone server, which is an independent server consuming and executing R as well as Python scripts and visualizations.

SQL Server Agent

SQL Server Agent's installation is done along with the SQL Server DE installation. The only exception is that SQL Server Express Edition does not allow us to use the SQL Server Agent service.

From an administrator's point of view, SQL Server Agent is a service to plan, execute, and monitor regular tasks (jobs). But the service is used by many other components and services of SQL Server; for instance, SSRS uses SQL Server Agent jobs to deliver reports to end users and more. The first approach that we could consider is the planning and execution of regular administration tasks such as those contained in maintenance plans (backups, reindexing, and so on). However, SQL Server and its services also need to execute other automated actions—for example, the following:

- MDS jobs for the internal maintenance of the MDS database
- Reporting Services jobs for regular subscriptions, report snapshots, and report cache housekeeping
- SQL Server replications internally represented as sets of jobs
- When data collection diagnostics are configured, collection jobs are created and executed

> **Note**
> We will discuss the features of SQL Server Agent throughout this book.

In this section, we have seen the application of and the need for certain SQL Server services and features. We have also seen why it is important to install the servers on different operating systems. Now, let's go on to prepare our computers to start the SQL Server 2019 installation on Windows.

Preparing the SQL Server 2019 installation on Windows

The previous section described the whole set of services and features contained in SQL Server. From now on, we will pay attention to on-premises SQL Server DE installed on Windows only.

In this section, we will discuss the following topics:.

- Which edition of SQL Server to buy with respect to the features and performance capabilities
- How to prepare our Windows operating system and other prerequisites
- Installation options such as installation wizard, Command Prompt, and the sysprep utility

Edition comparison

Microsoft provides SQL Server in several editions. Each edition has its supported features, and with these features, the allocation of resources will differentiate. This can be seen in terms of performance, price, runtime, and service availability. A complete edition comparison matrix is published at `https://docs.microsoft.com/en-us/sql/sql-server/editions-and-components-of-sql-server-2017?view=sql-server-ver15`. The core editions are as follows:

- **Enterprise edition**: Intended for big enterprise environments.
- **Standard edition**: Contains almost all services (except MDS and DQS) but has some limited hardware resource consumption as well as some internal limits in SQL Server DE.
- **Developer edition**: Edition containing all enterprise features, but for development purposes only! Must not be provisioned to the production environment.
- **Express edition**: The Express edition of SQL Server is published for free but with many limitations; for example, Analysis Services, Integration Services, and SQL Server Agent are not contained in this edition.

Pre-installation tasks

When planning to install SQL Server 2019, there are three important points to be considered, as follows:

- Amount of memory
- Disk set
- Security consequences

Planning memory

Every edition of SQL Server has its limit of maximum consumable memory. It's needed to set up the accessible memory correctly because SQL Server consumes as much memory as possible. Every request to SQL Server needs memory. When preparing the server for SQL Server installation, we must consider two main memory usages, as follows:

- **Interpreted queries**: This is the traditional approach where SQL Server processes user requests. Data is stored on disk, and when some portion of data is needed by any query, it's cached to a memory area called the buffer cache. The buffer cache, with many other memory portions such as the procedure cache, user connections, and others, is a matter of memory limit given by the edition of SQL Server.

- **In-Memory OLTP**: In-memory OLTP (with original code name Hekaton, which is still used in articles and books sometimes) is a relatively new SQL Server DE technology that was introduced with the SQL Server 2014 Enterprise edition. Later, in SQL Server 2016 SP 1, In-Memory OLTP has ceased to be an Enterprise feature, and now its memory capacity depends on memory limit determined by certain editions. For example, SQL Server Standard Edition has maximum memory set to 128 GB, and In-Memory OLTP capacity is set to 1/4 of maximum SQL Server memory per database, which means 32 GB of memory up to the regular limit for each database that uses In-Memory OLTP. The In-Memory OLTP area is used for memory-optimized tables—tabular structures for extremely fast access, especially in conjunction with natively compiled stored procedures. If any application needs to use In-Memory OLTP technology, be aware of this extra memory requirement.

When planning the amount of memory, we must keep in mind any concurrent service or application that will be present on the same server.

Planning disk capacity

No simple formula exists to calculate disk capacity. We can just estimate the amount of disk space needed from similar applications or older databases. Disk space needs to be described on MSDN as sufficient for an empty SQL Server installation, not for the production environment.

When preparing disks, we should consider the following points:

- Using directly attached disks is a very common approach. The only possible issue is that the server itself does not have a sufficient number of controllers, so disks don't have enough space for large-scale, real-world production databases. Directly attached disks are a good option when the server should be quickly provisioned—for instance, in production halls where hardware lifetime is shortened by a dusty environment.

- Usually, the best way is to use **storage area network (SAN)** storage, which has a sufficient number of controllers and allows you to spread every database across more disks.

- Let its own disk be present for the `tempdb` database; this database is used internally by SQL Server as well as explicitly by developers as an optimization helper for complicated queries (however, this is not the best practice).

- If the server has a low amount of memory (less than 64 GB) and more memory is needed, especially for read-intensive OLTP databases, the administrator can set up a **buffer pool extension (BPE)**. This is a file supplying more memory space for so-called clean pages. SQL Server enhances the buffer cache and stores data pages intended to be read-only from the database to this file. A best practice is to place the BPE on its own **solid-state drive (SSD)** disk.

- Data files and log files of databases should always be separated. SQL Server uses write-ahead logging. This means that SQL Server caches data from data files, and, at the same moment, describes to the transaction log file what will be done with the data. When data and log files are not separated, overhead could occur on the disk controller.

- Even if many databases consist just of two files (primary data file and transaction log file), larger databases can be divided into more data files. As per the performance requirements, data files can be placed to more disks. This possibly causes the need for more physical disks. Dividing a database into more files will be described in further chapters.

Software and other requirements

When installing SQL Server 2019 on Windows, only a 64-bit system is supported. Supported versions of the operating system start from Windows Server 2012 and above for non-Enterprise editions; desktop operating systems—such as Windows 8.1 or Windows 10 (including Home edition)—are supported as well.

SQL Server uses the .NET Framework for some features. The .NET Framework of versions 2.0 and 3.5 SP 1 must be present before installation.

The easiest way to check whether everything is in place is to start the **SQL Server Installation Center**. It starts automatically when installation media is added to the server, or it can be reached from Windows Explorer by clicking on the setup.exe file. The **SQL Server Installation Center** provides a central point from where to find resources about SQL Server as well as tools needed for a standalone installation, cluster installation, adding or removing SQL Server components, and so on. The installation center is divided into sections, and every section contains a list of links. The first section, when the installation center starts, is called **Planning**. There is a link to a tool called **System Configuration Checker** (**SCC**). This section is shown in the following screenshot:

Fig. 1.3 – SQL Server Installation Center

The SCC is a tool that checks all prerequisites needed for the successful installation of SQL Server. The following screenshot shows how it looks when every requirement is fulfilled:

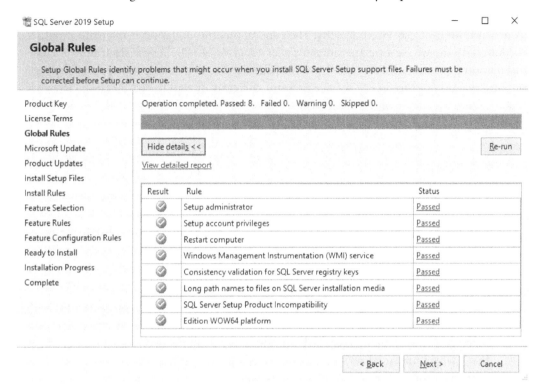

Fig. 1.4 – SCC successful result

Besides the requirements, the SCC checks the overall state of the server and other prerequisites, such as whether the installation is running with administrator's privileges or whether a restart is needed.

Security accounts for SQL Server

SQL Server, as well as other technologies within the SQL Server technology set, needs to log in to the operating system. From a security point of view, it is important to set an account for every service correctly. The general recommendation is to create a login account with the weakest permissions for every service of SQL Server separately. As the installation process itself is run in the administrator's security context, the installer will set local permissions for every service account correctly during the installation. The following are the most common scenarios:

- **Built-in service accounts**: This type of account provides less control from the administrator's side, and it's good enough for small, standalone installations of SQL Server. In a wider domain environment, it's not recommended at all.

- **Dedicated domain account**: This option means that the domain administrator prepares dedicated domain accounts with regular user rights (no elevated permissions are needed or recommended), and during installation (or after the installation), prepared domain accounts are set. A big concern is that such domain accounts must fulfill security policies—namely, password expiration—and SQL Server as a machine cannot create its own password for, say, every 3 months.

- **Managed service accounts**: Managed service accounts are domain accounts similar to regular domain accounts. Unlike domain accounts, managed service accounts create and change their passwords without any action needed from administrators. That's why a managed service account is usually the best approach to setting security accounts for SQL Server and its services.

Installing SQL Server 2019 on Windows

Microsoft provides several options to install SQL Server and its technologies as simply as possible. Almost everything is done through the **SQL Server Installation Center**, which is opened via the autorun property of the installation media. The next chapter describes typical scenarios of installation and first post-installation checks and configurations.

Installation options

The **SQL Server Installation Center** provides several ways to install SQL Server. The most common method of installation is to use the wizard for a standalone installation as well as for a cluster installation of SQL Server.

For situations where more SQL Servers are propagated into the environment (for example, new departments or sales points are often created, and every department or sales point has its own SQL Server), SQL Server provides an option to be installed through the command line, which is also the only installation approach possible for installations on core editions of Windows servers, or sysprep installation.

Installation wizard

The installation wizard starts from the **SQL Server Installation Center** from the second tab, called **Installation**. There are several wizards (shortened), as follows:

- New SQL Server standalone installation
- Install SQL Server Reporting Services (new since SQL Server 2017; the version 2016 installation of SSRS was added to SQL Server's installation wizard directly)
- Install SQL Server Management Tools (means SSMS; beginning in version 2016, management and data tools are not installed within the SQL Server installation process; they are downloaded, installed, and versioned separately)

The first option, called **New SQL Server standalone installation**, is the right way to install SQL Server on a clean machine just with the operating system. When a user clicks on this option, the wizard starts. The installation wizard consists of many steps. The way through each step is this:

1. **Global Rules**: This is an automated installation step that checks the state of the operating system.

2. **Product Updates**: This step is also automated and checks if any available updates of SQL Server exist.

3. **Install Setup Files**: The runtime environment is prepared for further installation. This step also does not need any interaction with the administrator.

4. **Install Rules**: This step checks the registry keys' consistency. It also checks if the computer is a domain controller (installation of SQL Server is not allowed on domain controllers), and it also checks for firewall rules. If any of the checks fail, the setup process is corrupted, and the issues reported by **Install Rules** must be corrected.

5. **Installation Type**: On this page of the setup wizard, we can decide if we want to install a new instance of SQL Server, or add features to an existing instance of SQL Server.

6. **Product Key**: This step asks for a license key. If we do not have the key, we can select one of the free editions (Evaluation, Express, or Developer edition).

7. **License Terms**: We should read through and accept the **end-user license agreement (EULA)**.

8. **Feature Selection**: The following screenshot shows the tree of SQL Server features:

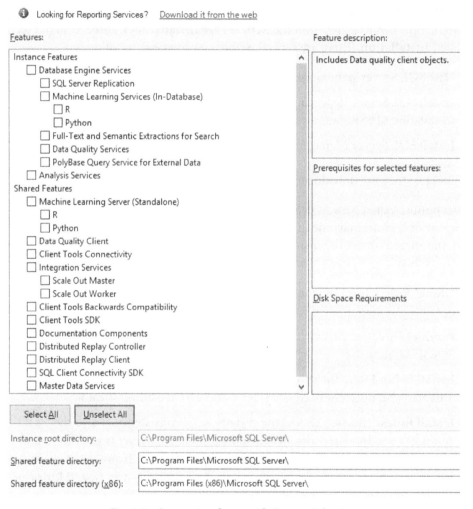

Fig. 1.5 – Setup wizard step with Feature Selection

As shown in the preceding screenshot, the setup wizard offers a wide set of features to be installed at once. For administrators who already installed previous versions of SQL Server, the setup step writes an information message about **SQL Server Reporting Services**. This service is installed separately from the SQL Server installation.

When Installing SQL Server DE, the administrator selects the following options:

- **Database Engine Services**: This is the core component, DE itself.

- **Optionally SQL Server Replication**: For the ability to set up replication scenarios.

- **Optionally Full-Text and Semantic Extractions for Search**: Full text is a strong feature provided by SQL Server DE, and it could be very useful for users.

> **Note**
>
> Other options, such as **Machine Learning Services** (provides support to run external scripts on SQL Server), can be installed later or in a standalone separated setup. Features such as PolyBase are beyond the scope of this book.

In the bottom part of this setup step, the user decides where to place program files, not data files. Lets take a look at these steps:

1. **Instance Configuration**: In this step, the administrator decides if the default or named instance of SQL Server will be installed. SQL Server can run in multi-instance mode. This means that more than one instance of SQL Server could be installed on the same machine. It is a good example of a side-by-side upgrade when it is done on the same operating system.

   Another scenario for several instances could be when some application needs its own SQL Server configuration (for instance, SharePoint Server). That's why SQL Server provides an ability to install **default instances** and **named instances**. The default instance has no special additional name provided by the administrator during installation, whereas every named instance must have its own additional name that is unique on a certain computer. When connecting to the default instance, clients just use the computer's name or IP address (such as MYSQLSERVER01); when connecting to a named instance, users must provide the instance name (for example, MYSQLSERVER01\MYADDITIONALNAME).

2. **Server Configuration**: **Server Configuration** is divided into two tabs. Don't forget to go through both! The first tab, **Service Accounts**, is to set user accounts for SQL Server and all other installed features. The second tab is called **Collation**. The following two screenshots show both tabs on this installation step:

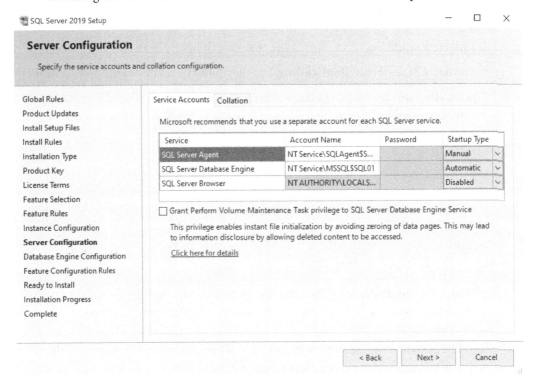

Fig. 1.6 – Server Configuration, Service Accounts tab

The preceding screenshot shows the first **Service Accounts** tab of the **Server Configuration** installation step. The tab is the place where accounts are selected for each SQL Server service. The step also contains a **Grant Perform Volume Maintenance Task privilege to SQL Server Database Engine Service** checkbox. If the checkbox is checked, the service account use by SQL Server will be allowed to grow data files without the need to fill newly obtained space in the files with zeros. This privilege speeds up the growth operations of data files. Lets look at the **Collation** tab in the following screenshot:

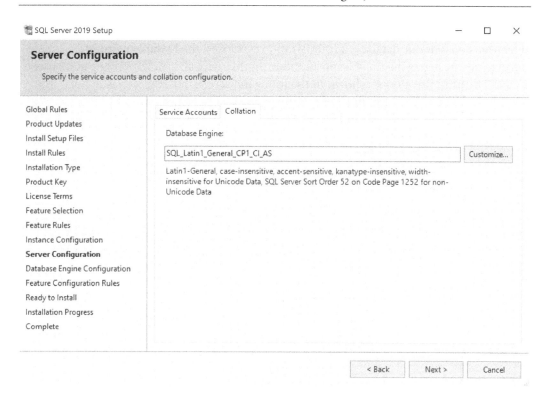

Fig. 1.7 – Server Configuration, Collation tab

The preceding screenshot shows the **Collation** tab. The **Collation** setting defines which code page, sort rules, and case sensitivity will be used as the server's default way of handling string characters. This server default is inherited by databases as a database default collation, and every character column in the database has its own collation inherited from the database default collation. On the database as well as on the column level, the collation setting could be overridden, but it's not a good practice. It is crucial for the proper working of SQL Server to set the server default collation correctly. It's not simple to say which collation is the correct one. The only idea is that, if you're not sure, a better approach is to use an **American National Standards Institute (ANSI)**-compatible collation with case insensitivity in a combination of unicode SQL Server data types such as nchar or nvarchar.

> **Note**
> Collations contain only a configuration value that cannot easily be changed after installation! When mismatched, it leads to a reinstalling of system databases.

The next steps could vary—their set and order depend on features selected in the **Feature Selection** step. For our database administration purposes, the **Database Engine Configuration** step is the most important one. In this step, all crucial configurations are done by an administrator. As shown in the following screenshot, the step is divided into tabs (don't forget to go through all of them!):

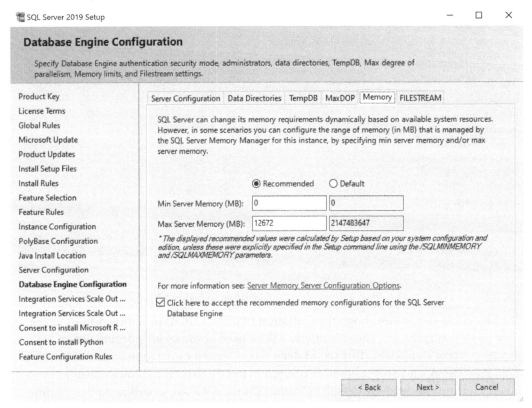

Fig. 1.8 – Database Engine Configuration

The preceding screenshot shows the **Database Engine Configuration** step of the SQL Server installation wizard. Let's look at the different tabs present on the wizard, as follows:

- **Server Configuration** contains basic settings for SQL Server security from a client's perspective. The first setting is **Authentication Mode**. It has two options, as follows:

    a) **Windows authentication mode**: In this mode, logins to SQL Server can be established in a trusted way only. This means that only logins created from Windows (domain or local accounts of groups) can connect to SQL Server.

b) **Mixed mode**: For cases when every user comes with its domain identity, SQL Server can manage **Standard logins** or **SQL logins**—logins with passwords managed directly by SQL Server. This was considered a minor security risk, but since SQL Server 2005 (this was the first version of SQL Server able to consume **Group Policy Objects** (**GPOs**)), this is not a problem anymore.

When the administrator selects **Mixed mode**, they must provide a strong password for standard system SQL Server login called **sa**. This is the standard administrator login on SQL Server.

Authentication mode is the configuration value that can be changed later during a SQL Server instance's lifetime. Still, it needs restarting, so it's a better approach to set it directly during installation.

In the last part of this tab is a list of **sysadmin server role members** of the SQL Server instance being installed. Add yourselves to the list and add other users to the list of principals who will have administrator access to the SQL Server.

- **Data directories** tab is important as well. It's a set of paths to the filesystem where system databases, user databases, and backups are placed when the user does not provide their actual paths, listed as follows:

  a) **Data root directory**: This is the base path to all data files (with `.mdf` or `.ndf` extensions). All system databases are placed on this path (with the exception of the `tempdb` database). It is not recommended to use the default path to the program files, as was explained in the *Planning disk capacity* section; the best practice is to have a disk prepared just for data files.

  b) **User database directory**: This is the default base directory for user database data files. For certain data files, this path can be overridden.

  c) **User database log directory**: In this, all log files (with the `.ldf` extension) of every database are placed. Never mix data and log files in the same place.

  Users, as well as system databases, could be moved to different locations.

- **TempDB** pre-calculates the best configuration settings for the `tempdb` database. The `tempdb` database has a very special position in SQL Server, as well as for developers using it in some optimization tasks. The optimized execution of the `tempdb` database roughly depends on the following:

  a) Number of data files

  b) Their location

  c) Their symmetric growth

The number of data files is calculated from the number of CPUs. A best practice is to have 1/4 to 1/2 data files to the number of CPUs (even logical CPUs). The best location of data files is on a fast separate disk. In the case of `tempdb` failure due to a disk failure, `tempdb` is regenerated every time SQL Server starts.

The symmetric growth of all data files is carried out by the SQL Server engine automatically. Unlike the prior versions that had trace flags set in startup parameters, this is not needed from SQL Server 2016.

- **MaxDOP** allows us to limit the maximum number of CPUs used for parallelism at the instance level. This configuration value can be adjusted later during the instance's lifetime, without the need to restart the service. We can leave **MaxDOP**'s default value as 0. Still, SQL Server tends to overutilize CPUs in highly parallelized queries, which can lead to inaccessible CPUs for other tasks on SQL Server (this situation is known as SOS_SCHEDULER_YIELD wait). **MaxDOP** is also configurable at the database level, but this configuration is not part of the installation process.

- The **Memory** tab is new for the SQL Server 2019 installation wizard, which is why it is also shown in the preceding screenshot. Even if we can set minimum and maximum memory consumption for our instance of SQL Server later, the installation wizard helps us to estimate the right amount of maximum memory. We can select between the following two options:

  a) **Recommended**: The estimation of **Max. Server Memory (MB)** configuration. The max. server memory value limits the amount of memory used by SQL Server. Using the **Recommended** option also allows us to adjust **Min. Server Memory (MB)**. This is the amount of memory that, once consumed by SQL Server, is not brought back to the operating system.

  b) **Default**: If the max. server memory estimation offered by the installation wizard is not used, max. server memory stays at the default value, which is unlimited.

- **FILESTREAM**: The **FILESTREAM** is a type of storage for binary data such as documents or pictures saved in the database. If you have no idea about saving **FILESTREAM** data at the moment of installation, the **FILESTREAM** should remain disabled. It can be enabled and configured later, without the need to restart SQL Server.

After the database engine configuration, additional wizard steps could occur, depending on other features selected in **Feature Selection**.

> **Note**
>
> Maybe some readers are concerned about where the SQL Server Agent configuration is. SQL Server Agent doesn't have any special settings in the installation process, and its installation is automatically done along with every instance of database engine installation.

- **Ready to install**: This step of the installation wizard is basically the summary of selected options for review before the installation begins, but this step also contains a text field called **Configuration file path**. This text field contains a complete path to the configuration file. The file is very useful as a template when more instances of SQL Server need to be installed.

The installation wizard is almost complete now, and the setup operation starts and shows its progress.

Installing SQL Server from the command line

Installing SQL Server directly from the command line is possible, but when searching the *Install SQL Server from the Command Prompt* topic on MSDN, the user will obtain a huge set of options that need to be added to the Command Prompt (or to the `.bat` file) directly. This leads to a big risk of misspellings and other mistakes.

A better approach is to use configuration files for Command Prompt installations. This approach contains the same options as Command Prompt, but we can find very good working examples from any setup already run from the wizard. When the wizard setup finishes, it leaves the setup log and configuration on disk. If SQL Server is installed in the default location, the path is `C:\Program Files\Microsoft SQL Server\150\Setup Bootstrap\Log`. In this location is a file called `Summary.txt` that contains the actual path to the `ConfigurationFile.ini` file. The configuration file can be copied and adjusted as needed and then run using the following command from Command Prompt:

```
setup.exe /ConfigurationFile=<path to my config file>.ini /
IACCEPTLICENCETERMS
```

The SQL Server installation wizard allows you to prepare a configuration file without installing. When the administrator goes through the wizard, everything is saved in the newly created configuration file. In the summary step of the wizard, the path to the configuration file is shown. So, the administrator can cancel the wizard without the actual installation of SQL Server.

> **Note**
>
> `ConfigurationFile` could be edited. However, we can set different instance names or service account names, for instance, but it is still needed to add the `/IACCEPTLICENCETERMS` command parameter to the command line.

Checking the completed installation

We have taken all the necessary steps to install a standalone instance of SQL Server DE. The next step is to check if the installation was successful and if the instance is up and running.

If any error occurs during installation, additional diagnostics are needed. Every single task of the setup process is described in the setup log (in the case of the default installation path, the log is placed on the `C:\Program Files\Microsoft SQL Server\150\Setup Bootstrap\Log` path).

However, it is still a good practice to check whether everything works as expected. Those simple post-installation checks could be done using **Sql Server Configuration Manager**, as illustrated in the following screenshot:

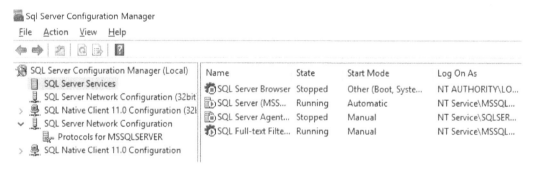

Fig. 1.9 – Sql Server Configuration Manager

Sql Server Configuration Manager is the only visual client tool actually installed in the SQL Server setup. **Configuration Manager** is a snap-in to **Microsoft Management Console** and consists of two main sections, as follows:

- **SQL Server Services**: When selected in the left pane, the right detail pane shows every SQL Server service or feature installed with its **Name, State, Start Mode**, and **Log On As** account. These settings can be changed by right-clicking on a certain row and selecting **Properties** from the pop-up menu. The **Modal Properties** dialog appears, and we can go through it to correct any setting as needed.

- **SQL Server Network Configuration (32-bit)**: In this section, administrators view a list of instances (the MSSQLSERVER instance name seen in the preceding screenshot is the internal name for the default instance of SQL Server), and when any instance on the left is clicked on, a list of network protocols appears in the right pane.

There are also other nodes in the tree shown in the left pane of **Sql Server Configuration Manager** such as **SQL Native Client configuration**, which provides the ability to set client aliases for SQL Server instances (for example, when SQL Server is accessible only via its IP address, which is almost non-readable to users). Still, the preceding two sections are the most important ones.

SQL Server services configuration node

The administrator can call for a pop-up menu from every record shown in the right pane. Special attention should be focused on SQL Server itself and SQL Server Agent.

SQL Server may be shown in several records because every instance has its own configuration, so the first good thing is to select the right record. The following screenshot shows the **Properties** dialog box:

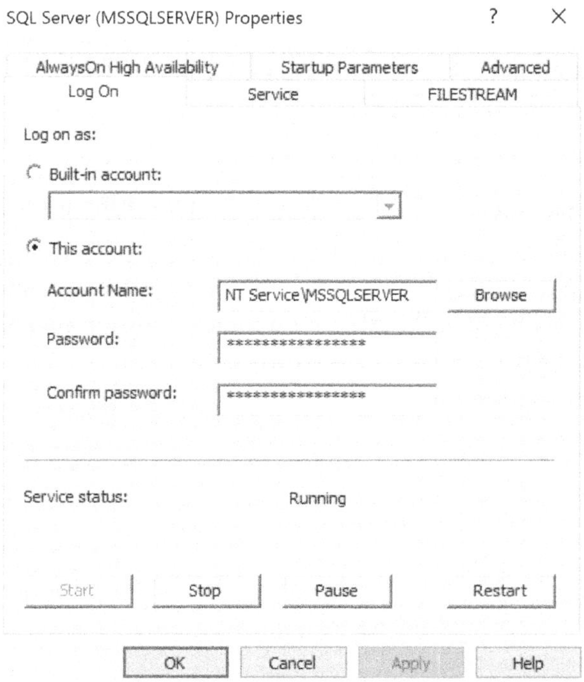

Fig. 1.10 – SQL Server instance properties

As shown in the preceding screenshot, the **Properties** dialog box allows you to set the following:

- **Log On** tab: The context of the Windows account that will be used by the instance to log in to the operating system. This configuration needs restarting if changed.

- **Service** tab: The only setting enabled on this tab is **Startup mode**, which should be set to **Automatic**.

- **FILESTREAM** tab: This tab contains **FILESTREAM** settings. As described earlier, **FILESTREAM** is a special kind of storage for binary data such as pictures or documents stored in relational data directly to a database. From an administrator's point of view, **FILESTREAM** must be enabled for at least T-SQL Access. When enabled, databases can contain **FILESTREAM** file groups, which are actual representations of the binary storage. There's an enhancement called **File Tables** for which the second two textboxes (**allow for I/O...** and **enable remote clients...**) must be switched on.

- **Startup Parameters** tab: This tab contains three startup parameters as default, as follows:

  a) d: The location of the primary data file of the database master (must be reconfigured when the master database is moved).

  b) l: The location of the log file of the database master (must be reconfigured when the master database is moved).

  c) e: The default path for error logs written by SQL Server.

  d) Additional parameters such trace flags and others can be added if needed.

- **AlwaysOn High Availability** tab: AlwaysOn is an advanced concept of data availability and reliability built on top of **Microsoft Cluster Service** (**MSCS**). When certain instances attend to the AlwaysOn group, it must be enabled on this tab. MSCS must already be present before this configuration is done.

- **Advanced** tab: This tab actually has no advanced settings, just error reporting and user feedback to Microsoft.

Special attention should be given to SQL Server Agent. SQL Server Agent is installed with every single instance of SQL Server. In other words, every instance of SQL Server has its own SQL Server Agent instance. Immediately after installation, SQL Server Agent is set to **Manual Startup** mode, which is not good enough for production environments.

That's why one of the first post-installation configurations should be to change SQL Server Agent's startup mode to **Automatic**. This is because the SQL Server Agent is an invaluable service for a lot of regular administrator tasks as well as automated tasks done by SQL Server itself (for example, data collection, strong diagnostics tool, and collecting performance statistics using SQL Server Agent jobs).

Understanding the SQL Server network configuration node

SQL Server communicates with clients on its own network
application protocol called **Tabular Data Stream** (**TDS**). Under this network application layer, **TCP/IP** and **Named Pipes** (now deprecated) network protocols are supported. The third option, called **Shared Memory**, is always enabled and allows communication between server and client when the client is running locally on the same machine as SQL Server.

SQL Server supports both 32-bit and 64-bit protocols, so configuration for both modes is the same. Under the **SQL Server Network Configuration** node (even if it's the 32-bit node), network protocols for every instance of SQL Server already installed on the machine are placed. The administrator selects certain instances (for example, Protocols for MSSQLSERVER, which is the default instance), and in the right pane of the **Sql Server Configuration Manager**, selects the property window for certain network protocols by right-clicking on **Properties**.

The most complex configuration has to be made on the TCP/IP protocol. When SQL Server 2019 is installed, the protocol is enabled, so the administrator just checks whether the proper TCP ports are used. The default TCP port used for SQL Server communication is port number 1433. For additional named instances, ports starting with numbers 1450, 1451, or similar are often used. The ability and the port number have to be set for every variant of the IP address of every network interface.

After this configuration is done, the instance of SQL Server needs to be restarted.

Testing connection to a fresh SQL Server

As mentioned earlier, SQL Server does not contain a client management toolset in its installation. It's a good idea to install **SQL Server Management Studio** directly on the server where the SQL Server service is already running because a lot of the administrator's tasks will be done directly on the server, but for a quick check whether SQL Server is accessible to clients, Command Prompt can be used. Its name is sqlcmd , and it's the only client tool installed with SQL Server directly. This tool is very useful in the following scenarios:

- When **SQL Server Management Studio** is not present or cannot be used (for example, when restoring the master database)
- When the Express edition of SQL Server was installed, and SQL Server Agent cannot be used (when planning regular tasks, it can be done by PowerShell or by sqlcmd in conjunction with **Windows Task Scheduler**)

The simplest way to use sqlcmd is shown in the following code example:

```
sqlcmd
```

When running sqlcmd as shown in the preceding code example, it tries to connect the local default instance of SQL Server using the current user's Windows account. When successfully connected, rows in the Command Prompt window start to be numbered.

A better approach is to call sqlcmd with parameters precisely set, as follows:

```
sqlcmd -E -S localhost
```

In a domain user context or with a SQL login context, you would run the following code:

```
sqlcmd -U <user name> -P <password> -S localhost
```

Let me elaborate on each of the parameters, as follows:

- The E parameter (beware that all parameters of all command-line tools provided by SQL Server are case-sensitive) says to the connection that Windows login context of the user currently logged in the desktop will be used.
- The U and P parameters are used when the user wants to connect via a mixed **Authentication mode** of SQL Server. Then, the user and password created on the SQL Server are used, not the Windows identity.
- The S parameter is used for the name of the server. If connected locally on a default instance of SQL Server, shortcuts such as . or (localhost) could be used.

All the preceding examples start the `sqlcmd` tool in interactive mode. When successfully connected, rows start numbering, and the user can start to write queries. The GO keyword must follow every query. This keyword (sometimes called **batch terminator**) causes the text written to the console to be sent to SQL Server and then processed.

Results returned back to the console are not so readable that the `sqlcmd` could be started with the command parameter, o, followed by the path to the output file. The output file is just a text file catching all results from all queries sent by the user in the session.

When the user wants to run `sqlcmd` in unattended mode, the i parameter followed by the path to the input file may also be very useful. A complete example is shown in the following snippet:

```
--    content of demo.sql file
use master
go
select @@version as VersionOfMySQL
go
```

The first piece of the snippet shows the correctly created input file (for example, demo. sql).

The `use master` line establishes the correct database context in the connection, and it is highly recommended to never commit this row because very often, the database context is not the default database context set for login.

The third line is just an example of doing something meaningful.

When an administrator wants to run a script file like this, they can add the following command to Command Prompt:

```
sqlcmd -E -S (localhost) -i "c:\demo.sql" -o "c:\demo_output.
txt"
```

The command will run, and it will save all results (even if an error occurs) to the file called demo_output.txt.

There are more useful command parameters for `sqlcmd`, but this set, especially the first three examples, is sufficient to test an instance's accessibility locally.

For remote testing of accessibility, a very common way is to use **SQL Server Management Studio**. Common issues (followed by **Error No. 40 - Network Related Error**) are as follows:

- **SQL Server instance is not running**: In **Sql Server Configuration Manager**, this error is seen if the service is running or not. When it's not running, we can try to start it up manually and diagnose additional errors.

- **TCP/IP protocol is disabled**: This issue may be corrected by **Sql Server Configuration Manager** (requires restart after reconfiguring).

- **Other than default TCP port number is used**: This can be corrected on the user's side by adding the port number after the server name (for example, MYSQLSERVER:12345).

- **Firewall rules are not set**: This must be resolved on the firewall's side by enabling certain ports for communication.

Installing SQL Server 2019 on Linux

Since SQL Server 2017, Microsoft decided to offer its distribution on Linux. SQL Server's Linux distribution helps administrators to use familiar operating systems as well as install SQL Server to containers. This section is a step-by-step walkthrough example of the sample SQL Server installation process on Ubuntu 18.04.

Preparing the test environment

For many administrators and DBAs strongly bound to Microsoft operating systems, the world of Linux seems very strange and confusing. That's why the first step is a preparation of the **Hyper-V virtual machine** (**VM**). Microsoft provides a Hyper-V option called **Hyper-V Quick Create**. Its usage is very simple and straightforward, as follows:

1. In the **Start** menu, find the **Hyper-V Quick Create** application.
2. In the opened window, select **Ubuntu 18.04**.
3. Click the **Create Virtual Machine** button.
4. Follow the installation instructions.

The whole installation process is almost self-managed and takes up to 15 minutes. When your Ubuntu is ready, turn it on and connect to it using **Hyper-V Manager**. If everything works, you are prepared for SQL Server 2019 installation on Linux.

Installing SQL Server

The installation process of SQL Server on Linux differs from the Windows installation because of the following three points:

- It uses the Linux shell.

- All services such as SQL Server Agent or **SQL Server Integration Services** are installed separately.

- Not every service is supported on Linux (for instance, SSRS).

Our task is to install just the database engine of SQL Server, but the process of installation of other services is very similar.

First of all, we need to look for the Linux shell. At the bottom-left corner of **Ubuntu PC** is an icon that looks similar to the Windows **Start** button. When this icon is clicked, the main screen appears, showing all installed applications. One of these applications is **Terminal**. Click on it and take the following steps:

1. Execute the following command in **Linux Terminal**:

    ```
    wget -qO- https://packages.microsoft.com/keys/microsoft.
    asc | sudo apt-key add -
    ```

    The command imports the public repository key needed for validity checks of the downloaded build of SQL Server.

2. The second command registers the MS SQL Server Ubuntu repository from which the installation will be downloaded. The following command does the registration:

    ```
    sudo add-apt-repository "$(wget -qO- https://packages.
    microsoft.com/config/ubuntu/18.04/mssql-server-2019.
    list)"
    ```

    The sudo command from the preceding code snippet says to the operating system that the command itself will be executed with elevated permissions. So, it's possible that you will be asked to write your password into the command line.

3. Once the repository is registered, the following two commands will install SQL Server:

    ```
    sudo apt-get update
    sudo apt-get install -y mssql-server
    ```

4.   After installation, you need to go through a simple configuration. You will be asked for a password and an edition of the freshly installed instance of SQL Server. The following command runs the configuration:

```
sudo /opt/mssql/bin/mssql-conf setup
```

5.   The last step is to check if SQL Server runs and if a connection can be established to it. Checking the service status can be done using the `systemctl` command, as follows:

```
systemctl status mssql-server
```

6.   The preceding command should show status Active (running). If not, execute the following command:

```
systemctl start mssql-server
```

This command starts the SQL Server service. If anything is not correct, the result of the command will show part of the SQL Server error log with a certain error.

Testing connection to SQL Server on Linux

We should test the connection to our fresh SQL Server installation from inside as well as from outside of the Linux computer. The Linux distribution of the SQL Server service does not contain client tools, or even the `sqlcmd` command line. So, the first step is to install the `sqlcmd` command line. The process of installation is very similar to the installation of SQL Server. The following script shows all commands leading to the `sqlcmd` installation:

```
wget https://packages.microsoft.com/config/ubuntu/16.04/prod.
list | sudo tee /etc/apt/sources.list.d/msprod.list
sudo apt-get update
sudo apt-get install mssql-tools unixodbc-dev
echo 'export PATH="$PATH:/opt/mssql-tools/bin"' >> ~/.bashrc
source ~/.bashrc
```

When all the preceding commands are executed, we can call the `sqlcmd` command line with the following parameters:

```
sqlcmd -U sa -P <strong sa password>
```

If the preceding command succeeds, lines in the Terminal window start to be numbered, and we can try any SQL command such as SELECT @@VERSION.

If everything works from inside, we can make the same connection test from outside of our Linux computer. During this walkthrough, we used the Hyper-V virtualization environment, so we can install Management Studio and try to connect to the SQL Server on Linux using both Management Studio or the sqlcmd command.

> **Note**
>
> When testing the connection to the virtual computer, use the IP address rather than the computer's name.

SQL Server on Linux works the same way as on SQL Server on Windows. From this moment, we will use SQL Server on Windows primarily, but if you wish to, enjoy your Linux distribution of SQL Server.

Installing SQL Server 2019 on containers

Virtualization of computers hosting SQL Server is very common nowadays. Containers provide the next level of virtualization. A container itself is a lightweight computer hosted by the container environment. The question is: why use containers over virtual machines? Containers provide a simple way to prepare the environment that is often destroyed or moved between hosts. It is useful, for instance, during the development phase, when developers need to refresh their server environment frequently.

The basis of containers adopted by Microsoft lies on a Linux-based technology called **Docker**. It's also a prerequisite when we'd like to try provisioning. We need to have **Docker Engine 1.8** or higher installed on our Linux computer, or we can install Docker for Windows as well.

> **Note**
>
> Installing Docker for Windows needs the Hyper-V feature of Windows installed, because Docker itself is then running on the Linux VM.

The provisioning of SQL Server to containers is a scripting task. We can use **bash** or **PowerShell**, depending on the hosting environment. The following walkthrough example will provision SQL Server on Docker for Windows, so all commands are written using PowerShell:

1. As a first step, the SQL Server 2019 container image is downloaded from the Docker Hub with the following command:

    ```
    docker run -e "ACCEPT-EULA=Y" -e "SA_PASSWORD=<strong
    enough password>" -p 1433:1433 -d "mcr.microsoft.com/
    mssql/server:2019-CU3-ubuntu-18.04"
    ```

    The preceding command downloads the image to the local computer. Consider the following facts:

    a) The `SA_PASSWORD` parameter must follow the SQL Server default password policy (at least eight characters, special symbols, and numbers). Otherwise, the installation fails.

    b) The `-d` command parameter allows different versions of the SQL Server image to be selected. All images are accessible at `https://hub.docker.com/_/microsoft-mssql-server`.

2. We can check the list of all downloaded containers using the following command:

    ```
    docker ps -a
    ```

If we see our SQL Server container in the list retrieved by the preceding command, we can connect the SQL Server instance using any of our preferred tools.

Summary

The SQL Server ecosystem provides you with a wide set of technologies. The first problem is to know what is the responsibility of every single technology of SQL Server. In the first section of this chapter, we cleared what is necessary to install, which helped us recognize what we need.

In the second section, we prepared our operating system and the complete infrastructure to install SQL Server. The most important decision before starting the installation is which technologies to install and how many computers will be needed to distribute SQL Server services appropriately across an infrastructure. Before installing SQL Server DE itself, we need to ensure that a sufficient set of disk storage is in place, appropriate security accounts are prepared, and all software prerequisites are fulfilled.

The installation described in the *Installing SQL Server 2019 on Windows* section of this chapter is quite a straightforward process, but we should still consider some settings. Even if many of the settings can be adjusted after the installation completes, the SQL Server installation wizard helps us with the correct setting. In this section, we also highlighted settings (namely, **Collation**) that cannot be changed after the installation of the SQL Server.

After installation, it's highly recommended to check whether SQL Server is running, and, if not, check logs in the `Setup Bootstrap` folder. When SQL Server is successfully running, we need to check SQL Server's accessibility locally and remotely.

Last but not least is a check of the SQL Server Agent state because, for administrators, this service is an invaluable helper when performing day-to-day administrative tasks. SQL Server Agent should have the startup mode set to automatic and should be running all the time SQL Server DE is.

It is very useful to do more configuration after installation. The next chapter talks about these configuration settings and discusses more on how to keep SQL Server healthy.

2
Keeping Your SQL Server Environment Healthy

In the first chapter, we saw that SQL Server is a complex software suite consisting of many services that work together. Based on the deployment scenario, we can have even more instances of SQL Server services running on the same host. SQL Server Database Engine is usually a key service in the Enterprise environment because many other applications and tools depend on SQL Server for their primary data storage. It's a crucial task to keep our SQL Server environment healthy, not only with proper maintenance and monitoring but also with proper post-installation configuration. Installation, as we have seen in the first chapter, is not just about configuring many of the settings and keeping the default values. A default configuration might not be ideal for your production environment, and it's important to understand the benefits of any modifications to the default values. The goal of this chapter is to provide the basic post-installation configuration steps for adjusting the SQL Server deployment to your needs.

This chapter will cover the following topics:

- Understanding SQL Server patching

- Configuring SQL Server post installation

- Creating a performance baseline

Understanding SQL Server patching

Once you install SQL Server, you need to watch for future updates released by Microsoft. You can confirm which updates were installed to your server by checking the build number of the SQL Server deployment. You can find the build number in **SQL Server Management Studio (SSMS)**, as you can see in the following screenshot, or via the `SELECT @@VERSION` command:

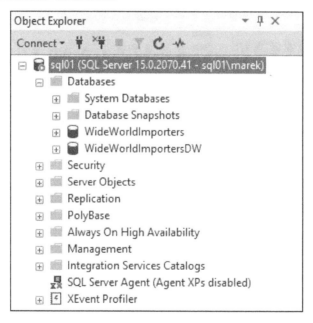

Fig. 2.1 – SQL Server Object Explorer (build version)

The build version of the currently installed SQL Server is **15.0.2070.41**. We can parse this version into the following portions:

- **15**–indicates we work with SQL Server 2019

- **2070.41**—4517790 Servicing Update (GDR1) for SQL Server 2019 **Release to Manufacturing (RTM)**

> **Note**
> You can find a nice list of updates for all SQL Server versions at
> `http://sqlserverbuilds.blogspot.com/` where you
> can identify the correct build of your SQL Server.

Based on the data available either on the *Buildlist* site or on the *Microsoft.com* site, which
publishes the latest updates for all SQL Server versions (`https://docs.microsoft.`
`com/en-us/sql/database-engine/install-windows/latest-updates-`
`for-microsoft-sql-server?view=sql-server-ver15`), we can see that the
latest update (at the time of writing this book) is *Cumulative Update 2 for SQL Server 2019*.

Historically, there were several types of updates released for SQL Server, as follows:

- **Service packs**
- **Cumulative updates**
- **Security updates**

When you work with older SQL Server installations, you can install all three types of
update for your SQL Server environment.

Service packs are usually the largest update option for your SQL Server. They frequently
include updates released by more cumulative updates and should be tested more
thoroughly regarding performance and stability of the system. It's also important to keep
your environment healthy with recent Microsoft system support service packs. Service
packs not only fix issues but often also bring new features to SQL Server. A good example
was the service pack 1 for SQL Server 2016, which enabled many features previously
available only in the Enterprise and Standard editions. This had a tremendous impact on
many smaller environments that were not utilizing the Enterprise edition, as **database
administrators (DBAs)** and developers were able to start using many new features that
were previously unavailable to them.

Cumulative updates are smaller compared to service packs and are released more
frequently. They usually fix many errors and include more updates, undergoing the same
comprehensive tests as service packs. As an example, we can see that SQL Server 2014
had only three service packs available, but for the first service pack, Microsoft had already
released 12 cumulative updates with additional fixes for errors, performance, and stability.
You can now install cumulative updates proactively with the same level of confidence as
you would service packs. Cumulative updates are incremental in nature, so cumulative
update 4 includes all the updates that were released in cumulative updates 1 to 3.

Security updates are smaller than cumulative updates and usually fix some sort of error or security vulnerability. These are usually released in a monthly cycle alongside the regular Windows updates and should be evaluated for your environment. Usually, a **Chief Security Office (CSO)** team or a security team in general may request you to install such security updates in a reasonable time frame to your SQL servers, which may be a complex task if you're managing larger environments. For patching such large environments, you most likely won't install any of these updates manually, but you'll utilize a centralized deployment tool such as **System Center Configuration Manager (SCCM)**.

> **Note**
> Since SQL Server 2017, service packs are no longer used for SQL Server updates. The servicing model has been simplified to include only cumulative updates and security updates. However, while working with older versions of SQL Server, it is still important to understand both concepts.

Installing updates

If you need to install an update to your SQL Server, you first need to download the correct bits from the Microsoft site and store them locally in your SQL Server. Some updates are downloaded as `.exe` files and some are available as `.zip` files, so you need to extract the update.

When you first start the installation, it will automatically extract to a random folder on one of your drives on the SQL server, as shown in the following screenshot:

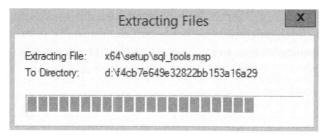

Fig. 2.2 – Service pack installation

This folder will automatically get deleted once the installation is over. This might not seem important at first glance; however, there are situations where you will need to reestablish the original hotfix structure to apply newer patches, especially with older SQL servers due to missing installation files on your system, as illustrated in the following screenshot:

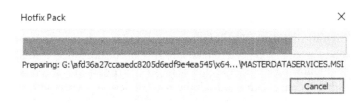

Fig. 2.3 – Hotfix extraction

When you accept the license terms for the installation, you need to select the instance from the list to which you would like to install the update. You can see the list of features installed for each instance, and the last installation option is **Shared Features**. These include **Integration Services**, **Data Quality Services**, **Client Connectivity Tools**, and, on older systems, **SQL Server Management Studio** as well. Via the update installer, you can also see the current build and whether the update was installed or only partially installed due to some error.

Once you select the instance to which you'd like to install the update, you can proceed to the installation. It's common practice to restart the server after the installation. If you're installing more updates in a sequence, they perform system checks and one of them is **Restart Pending** anyway. After the restart, you need to verify that applications can correctly connect to the SQL server and there is no impact after the update installation. The following screenshot shows the dialog from the SQL Server 2019 setup:

Fig. 2.4 – SQL Server installation dialog

> **Note**
>
> For any **high-availability** (**HA**) solution such as failover clusters and mirroring or availability groups, you need to take into special consideration installing updates and following a proper sequence between primary and secondary nodes (with respective naming for all the HA/DR options (where **DR** stands for **disaster recovery**). For more information, consider checking books online to find detailed procedures relating to this.

If you are deploying many SQL Servers at once or very frequently, you might consider customizing your installation media to include the latest updates.

In complex environments, you can integrate the installation bits of service packs and cumulative updates in your installation source and use this modified installation to install new SQL Servers directly with proper service packs or cumulative updates. This will speed up your deployment, as the installation will already include the required service packs, updates, or security updates that may be required by your security or architecture team.

Configuring SQL Server environment

Once you have installed your **SQL Server** and performed the patching to the current patch level required, you need to configure basic settings on the **SQL Server** and also on the **Windows Server** itself. There are several settings on the **Windows Server** that have an impact on your **SQL Server**'s performance and security, and these need to be updated before you put the server into production. The following are the basic options that you need to configure on the operating system:

- Configuring security rights for your SQL Server account
- Configuring power settings
- Configuring firewall rules

Configuring security rights for your SQL Server account

During the installation of the SQL Server, you're choosing an account that will be used to run all SQL Server services. There are quite a few considerations for a proper choice but, in this chapter, we'll focus more on the follow-up configuration. Such an account needs to have proper rights on the system. Since SQL Server 2016, you can add one specific system right to your SQL Server account directly during installation. The **SeManageVolumePrivilege** right can either be granted directly by the installer or you can modify system settings later to customize the assignment of rights. Two other important system rights (**Lock pages in memory**, **Generate security audits**) cannot be granted via the SQL Server installer and you must modify the system settings manually, as described in the following paragraph.

In the following screenshot, you can see a dialog from **SQL Server 2019 Setup**, where you can configure SQL Server **Service Accounts** for services that you're installing. On the same dialog, you can grant the aforementioned system rights:

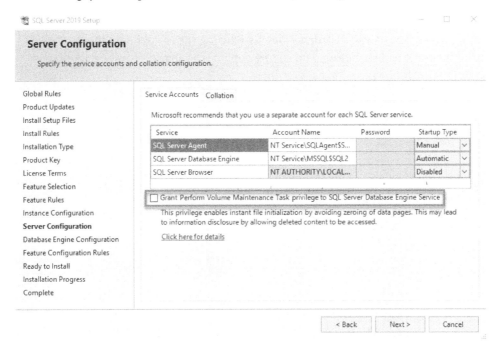

Fig. 2.5 – Server configuration during SQL Server setup

System rights can be configured via **Group Policy Editor** in the **Computer Configuration** segment of the policy. To open up the console for the rights' configuration, perform the following steps:

1. Run `gpedit.msc`.

2. Expand **Computer Configuration | Windows Settings | Security Settings | Local Policies**.

3. Double-click on the system right that you want to edit.

4. Add the account or group to which you want to grant the rights.

The first one will be **Perform volume maintenance tasks**. This right can be granted directly during installation of the SQL Server, but if you skip this, here's where and how you can add this right to your SQL Server account. The reason for granting this right is to enable **Instant File Initialization**, which can speed up disk operations to allocate new space for data files on the disk. **Instant File Initialization** does not work for log files, which in any case have to be zeroed out.

Instant File Initialization is used when the data file for the database is growing and allocating new space on the disk drive and also during the restoring of the database to create all files on the disk, before data can be copied from backup to the data files, as illustrated in the following screenshot:

Fig. 2.6 – Windows rights' configuration

Another system right that we will assign as part of the post-installation configuration will be **Generate security audits**. As you can see in the previous screenshot, this right is granted to two accounts: **LOCAL SERVICE** and **NETWORK SERVICE**. Our SQL Server is running with a different account and this account needs to be added to the list. This right will, later on, allow our SQL Server to store audit events in the **Windows Event Log** to the **Security Log**. This may come in handy once we see how SQL Server Audit is working and what the options to audit are.

The last system right that we will assign is **Lock pages in memory**. This right will allow SQL Server to lock the memory pages and prevent the Windows operating system from paging out memory in the case of memory pressure on the operating system. This one has to be taken into careful consideration, with more configuration on the SQL Server engine and proper system monitoring. We'll talk about the SQL Server settings later.

Configuring power settings

When you install a Windows Server operating system, you need to check for power settings that are configured on such systems. There are several options for how you can verify which power setting plan is currently in use. If you open Command Prompt or PowerShell, you can use the powercfg utility to see which plan is used on your server, as follows:

```
powercfg.exe -list
```

By default, you will see a **Balanced** plan selected, which is great for most servers and offers a lot of power-saving features, but this plan is not usually optimal for SQL Servers. SQL Server can put quite some load on the **central processing unit** (**CPU**), and switching between CPU speeds may cost you precious time as well as performance issues. If you open the **Task Manager** tool, you can see that your CPU is not running at the maximum speed and may be running with a much lower value.

As an example, you can see the following screenshot from one of the physical servers with a **2.40 GHz** CPU, which is running on **1.25 GHz** due to a power-saving plan:

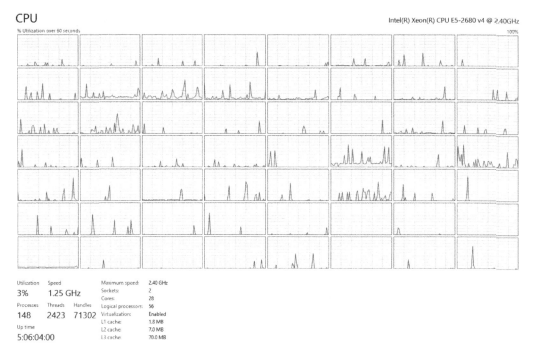

Fig. 2.7 – Task Manager load and CPU speed

You can verify this with tools such as **CPU-Z** or similar, and the best option we have here is to update the power plan to high performance, which is common for SQL Server workloads. To update the power plan setting, you can either use a control panel where you can find settings for power options or you can use a command line again. When we listed the plans on the server with the previous command, you saw in the output that they come with name and GUID. To update the plan via the command line, we need to use the GUID with the powercfg tool, as follows:

```
powercfg.exe -SETACTIVE <GUIDofThePlan>
```

The following screenshot gives an illustration of updating the plan via the command line:

```
Administrator: Windows PowerShell

PS C:\>
PS C:\>
PS C:\> powercfg -list

Existing Power Schemes (* Active)
---------------------------------
Power Scheme GUID: 381b4222-f694-41f0-9685-ff5bb260df2e  (Balanced) *
Power Scheme GUID: 8c5e7fda-e8bf-4a96-9a85-a6e23a8c635c  (High performance)
Power Scheme GUID: a1841308-3541-4fab-bc81-f71556f20b4a  (Power saver)
PS C:\> powercfg -SETACTIVE 8c5e7fda-e8bf-4a96-9a85-a6e23a8c635c
PS C:\> powercfg -list

Existing Power Schemes (* Active)
---------------------------------
Power Scheme GUID: 381b4222-f694-41f0-9685-ff5bb260df2e  (Balanced)
Power Scheme GUID: 8c5e7fda-e8bf-4a96-9a85-a6e23a8c635c  (High performance) *
Power Scheme GUID: a1841308-3541-4fab-bc81-f71556f20b4a  (Power saver)
PS C:\>
```

Fig. 2.8 – Power plan configuration via PowerShell

Once the power plan is updated, the CPU is no longer using any power-saving mode and runs at full speed, and possibly even turbo boot for extreme loads, while performing complex queries on your server.

Configuring firewall rules

Each SQL Server instance running on your server is using a different port number to listen for incoming connections, but during the installation of the SQL Server, there are no firewall rules created on your local firewall. You can even see this during installation of SQL Server, where the installer is presenting you with a warning that you have to configure your firewall to include rules for SQL Server services. So, SQL Server is perfectly accessible locally, but not from remote hosts if the local firewall is active. You can run with a built-in firewall on the Windows Servers or have some third-party software in your environment that requires additional configuration.

In the following screenshot, you can see a generated warning by **SQL Server Setup** that provides you information about the need to configure the firewall rules:

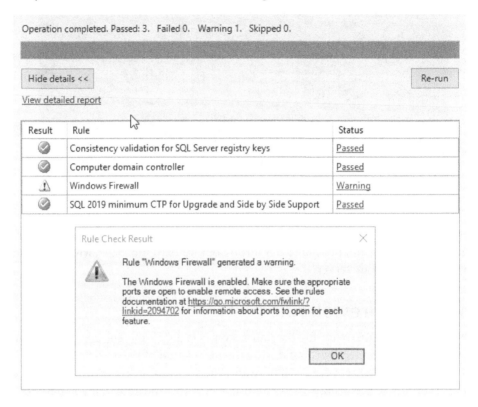

Fig. 2.9 – SQL Server Setup firewall warning

During the installation of the SQL Server, you had to make a choice between deploying SQL Server as a default instance or a named instance. The SQL Server default instance is listening on port 1433 by default, which you can verify in the **SQL Server Configuration Manager** tool. This port is set as static and will not change over time. **Named instances**, on the other hand, use a randomly selected port that may not be fixed and can change after a system reboot, because named instances use dynamic ports as a default option.

> **Tip**
> It's advised to change the dynamic port to static so that the port number does not change, and this does not have any impact for any security configuration such as the service principal name, which we'll discuss in another chapter.

The following screenshot gives a good idea of the default instances:

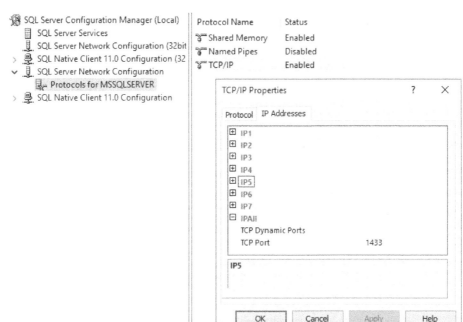

Fig. 2.10 – SQL Server Configuration Manager port configuration

Once we know which port our SQL Server instance is listening to, we need to configure the firewall to allow the traffic to our SQL Server service. Windows Server comes with a built-in firewall that can be controlled via a **Graphical User Interface (GUI)**, the command line, and PowerShell.

We will add three different rules to the firewall with the PowerShell tool, as follows:

- The first rule is for the SQL Server service with the proper port number. We have seen the port number in the configuration manager. For a default instance, this is 1433; for a named instance, the port number would be mostly random on each system.

- The second rule is used for the **dedicated admin connection (DAC)**, which is used for troubleshooting the system. Enabling just the firewall rule does not allow you to remotely connect to the DAC session; this also has to be turned on in the SQL Server configuration, and we'll cover this topic later.

- The third rule is for a service called SQL Server Browser, which is used for connection to the named instances.

All three rules can be seen in the following code snippet:

```
New-NetFirewallRule -DisplayName "SQL Server Connection" -
Protocol TCP -Direction Inbound -LocalPort 1433 -Action allow

New-NetFirewallRule -DisplayName "SQL Server DAC Connection" -
Protocol TCP -Direction Inbound -LocalPort 1434 -Action allow

New-NetFirewallRule -DisplayName "SQL Server Browser Service" -
Protocol UDP -Direction Inbound -LocalPort 1434 -Action allow
```

If you're running more instances on the server or any other services such as Analysis Services or Reporting Services, or you use any solutions for HA/DR such as mirroring or always on, then you need to carefully examine which firewall rules are needed, and the list may get much longer than the three basic rules we have seen. The complete list of ports required by each service is available on the documentation site at https://docs.microsoft.com/en-us/sql/sql-server/ install/configure-the-windows-firewall-to-allow-sql-server- access?view=sql-server-ver15.

Also, keep in mind that two specific editions of SQL Server–**Express** and **Developer**—restrict remote communication to the **SQL Server Database Engine** by default. This can be configured on SQL Server via using a sp_configure stored procedure, as illustrated in the following code snippet:

```
sp_configure 'remote access', 1
GO
RECONFIGURE
```

Also, in the **SQL Server Configuration Manager** tool, check for allowed protocols for connection to your SQL Server. For remote connectivity, you need the TCP/IP protocol enabled. Reconfiguring the available protocols requires a restart of your SQL Server service.

SQL Server post-installation configuration

So far, we have configured our Windows Server and we have made a few configurations related to SQL Server, but we haven't configured any **Structured Query Language** (**SQL**)-specific items inside SQL Server itself. For the post-installation configuration, there are plenty of settings worth exploring, some of course with careful consideration.

When the server is deployed, many configuration values are configured with defaults that may be modified for your environment. We'll start with some basic configuration for the databases. During the installation, you had to enter the paths for data, log, and backup file locations, which you can later modify if you need to update the location of the default files.

In the **Database Settings** section of the server configuration, you can again configure all three paths, as shown in the following screenshot:

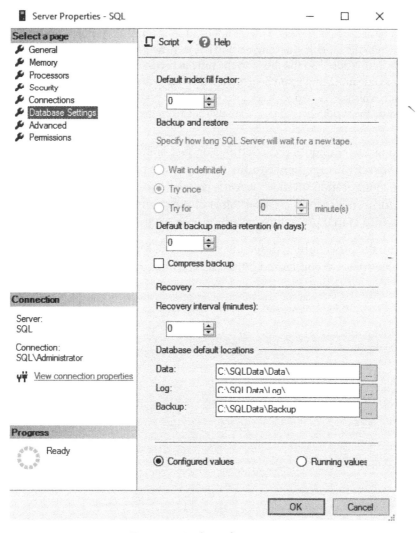

Fig. 2.11 – Path configuration

On this same settings page, you can configure two additional important parameters. The first one is the **Compress backup** option. We'll talk more about the backup settings and methods to perform backup in a different chapter, but as part of post-installation configuration, you can configure this setting on most servers.

> **Note**
>
> Bear in mind that turning on backup compression puts additional load on the CPU while performing the backup, so this may cause higher peaks in the performance monitor. Also, if the server is under heavy load, causing additional load by backup compression might not be ideal in terms of response times for users. On the other hand, compression has its benefits, combining a smaller backup size stored on the disk and the time needed to create a backup. Actually, there's one more important benefit, and this one is the time needed to restore, which is also decreased with compressed backup versus an uncompressed one, because the system gets to read a smaller file from the disk or network.

If you would like to configure these settings on just one server, you'll be fine with the GUI of our **SQL Server Management Studio**, but if you are preparing a script for a post-deployment configuration on more servers, you will most probably use an SQL script that can perform such a configuration. Most of the configuration at the server level is performed with a stored procedure called `sp_configure`.

If you just run the procedure without any parameters, it will display all basic parameters and their values that are configured on the server, as shown in the following screenshot:

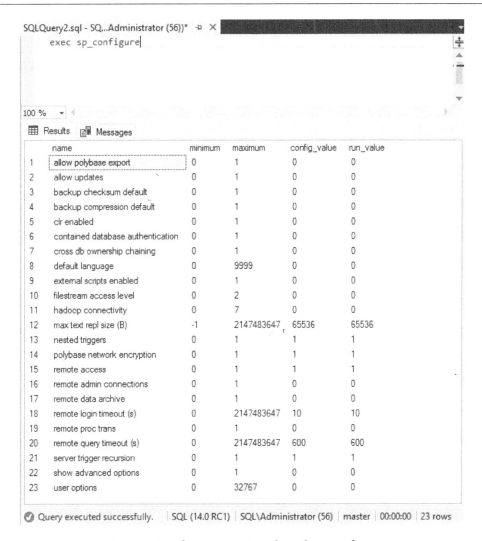

Fig. 2.12 - Configuration options through sp_configure

You don't need to memorize all the options as we won't configure all of these. It's just a basic set of the items; as you can see, second from the bottom is an option called **show advanced options**, which will display more of the items for configuration. Backup compression is listed in the basic set and can be configured with the following code:

```
USE master
GO
EXEC sp_configure 'backup compression default',1
GO
RECONFIGURE
GO
```

Some other options that we will explore are visible only when you display the advanced features. To display all the advanced features, you can simply run `sp_configure` again and you'll set the option for **show advanced options**, as in the previous example. With advanced options displayed, SQL Server will let you configure 85 (on SQL Server 2019; with other versions, this may be different) options, in contrast to 25 when you display only the basic set.

With regard to post-installation configuration, we'll configure the memory and CPU settings for our server too. By default, SQL Server is allowed to use as much memory as possible and the Windows operating system won't make any larger reserve of other applications or even for itself, so you can limit the amount of memory available to SQL Server. You should reserve memory to the operating system so that it does not get unresponsive under heavy load on SQL Server. The following screenshot shows how to configure SQL Server memory from **SQL Server Management Studio**:

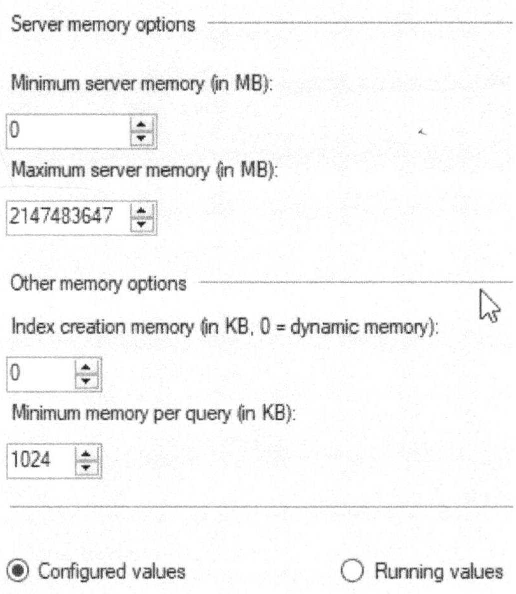

Server memory options

Minimum server memory (in MB):

0

Maximum server memory (in MB):

2147483647

Other memory options

Index creation memory (in KB, 0 = dynamic memory):

0

Minimum memory per query (in KB):

1024

◉ Configured values   ○ Running values

Fig. 2.13 – SQL memory configuration

There have been many situations when DBAs could not connect to the SQL Server operating system because all the memory was allocated to SQL Server itself. You can limit the memory available to the SQL Server with a setting called **Maximum server memory (in MB)**. This setting has to be considered carefully as you need to keep some memory for the operating system. As a general guideline, you need to keep **1 to 2 gigabytes (GB)** for the operating system and then **1 GB for each 8 to 16 GB** on the system. So, for a SQL Server with 256 GB **Random-Access Memory (RAM)**, you would configure the max server memory setting to a value between 224 and 240 GB. The code to perform the configuration is as follows (don't forget that the procedure is using **megabytes (MB)** as a unit of measure):

```
sp_configure 'max server memory',245760
```

> **Note**
>
> SQL Server editions provide different limits to use system memory on SQL Server. The **Standard edition** can use only up to 128 GB RAM for the SQL Server buffer pool, whereas the **Enterprise edition** can use all the system memory available on the server. You can find different limits for the editions available in the online documentation. The differences in the editions are not only about RAM, but also about CPU and core support for different SQL Server **stock keeping units (SKUs)**.

Another situation where configuring SQL Server memory is very important is in a **multi-instance** and **multi-service** environment. Consider that you are running multiple instances of SQL Server on the same host, where you would like to limit and control how much system memory can be used by each instance. This also applies in scenarios where you run multiple different services such as **Database Engine**, **Analysis Services**, and **Reporting Services**, where you can limit the amount of memory used by Database Engine. Not all services have the feature to limit memory usage, so you need to consider all performance impacts that can be caused by your configuration.

There is another setting that can be very useful when you're troubleshooting your SQL Server and it gets unresponsive—this is called **DAC**. By default, such a connection is not allowed remotely, and you can only connect to DAC locally while being logged on to the server. If the system faces performance issues and even the Windows Server won't allow you to connect via **Remote Desktop**, you can connect to DAC remotely if you have enabled this setting. To enable remote DAC, you need to run the following procedure:

```
sp_configure 'remote admin connections',1
GO
RECONFIGURE
```

Additional items that we will configure have an effect on the performance of SQL Server and require a deeper understanding of your workload, hardware, and requirements of your applications. These will include configuring parallelism on your server.

There are two main configuration items that we're using to control parallelism at the server level, and these are as follows:

- **Max degree of parallelism** (default is 0)
- **Cost threshold for parallelism** (default is 5)

The first one sets the maximum amount of threads to be used in a query when it's processed in parallel. This does not mean that each query will be processed with multiple threads, and, if it will be, it can be a lower amount. It's a default server setting that you can later override on different levels, but as a general option, it's a good idea to configure this value. What is the proper value depends greatly on several factors, and they are as follows:

- **Your hardware**: CPUs and cores
- **Your workload**: **Online Transaction Processing (OLTP)** versus **Online Analytical Processing (OLAP)**
- **Your environment**: Physical versus virtual

In most cases, you can examine the number of CPUs and cores on your system and assign a value that determines the number of cores on one CPU. So, for example, if you have two eight-core CPUs used for your SQL Server, you will configure the max degree of parallelism to the value of eight. Again, you can use **SQL Server Management Studio** or the sp_configure procedure. At the same time, in the GUI, you can also update the cost threshold for parallelism value, which is something such as the virtual cost of a query when the query optimizer component is generating a serial or parallel plan.

If the cost is too low there might be too many parallel plans, which can increase the load on the CPU and memory of your SQL Server. This configuration is subject to testing, but you can start with values ranging from 20 to 50 and evaluate the load on your SQL Server and your application performance. Let's look at the following screenshot from **SQL Server Management Studio**, where we can see **Server Properties – sql01**:

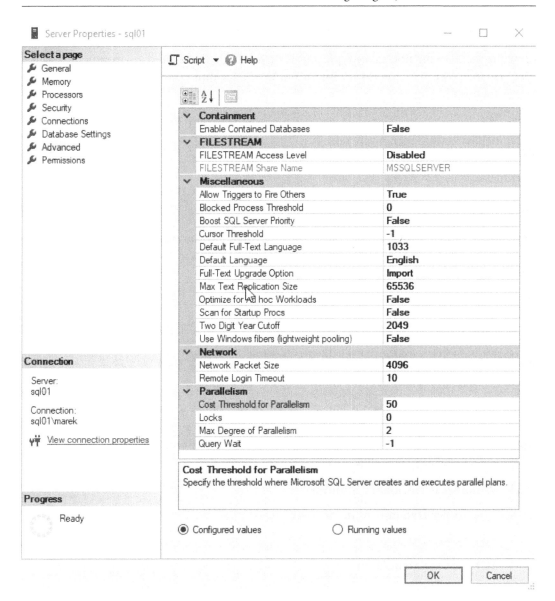

Fig. 2.14 — SQL Server Management Studio — Server Properties

Once you have deployed and configured your SQL Server, you can create a performance baseline.

Creating a performance baseline

Baseline refers to the normal or typical state of your SQL Server and environment performance. This baseline is very important to you for numerous reasons, and these are as follows:

- When you start troubleshooting the server, you need to know how your server will behave toward something odd.

- You can proactively tune the system if you find a weak spot in the baseline.

- When you plan to upgrade your server, you know how the load was increasing over time, so you can plan properly.

As a matter of fact, you won't have just one single baseline, but you can create multiple baselines depending on the variable workload. In such a case, you will have a baseline for the following:

- Business hours

- Peak usage

- End of week/month/quarter due to closures; reporting

- Weekend

Creating a performance baseline and capturing performance information for your server is, hence, a very crucial task and should be deployed to each of your servers. There are numerous sources that you can use to collect useful information about your SQL Server, and these include the following:

- **Windows Performance Monitor**

- **SQL Server Dynamic Management Views**

- **SQL Server Catalog Views**

- **SQL Server Extended Events**

With the Windows **Performance Monitor**, you can capture many different performance counters that are related not only to the SQL Server but also to the operating system counters and **hardware** (**HW**) resource counters such as CPU, disk, network, and so on. The list of counters can be quite large, but you should select only those counters that are important to you and keep yourself from overwhelming your data collection. The **Performance Monitor** can be very useful for log correlation as you can load the performance data to other tools such as the **SQL Server Profiler** or the **Performance Analysis of Logs** (**PAL**) tool.

Some interesting counters worth capturing at the operating system level would include the basic subsystems—memory, CPU, and disk, which can be correlated together to have a better overview of the system's performance. These include the following:

- **Processor**: % processor time
- **System**: Processor queue length
- **Memory**: Available MB
- **Memory**: Pages/sec
- **Physical Disk**: Disk reads/sec
- **Physical Disk**: Disk writes/sec

Although there are numerous counters available, don't get overwhelmed by choosing too many of them. One of the possible suggestions for a list of counters is Jimmy May's list, available at `https://docs.microsoft.com/en-us/archive/blogs/ jimmymay/perfmon-objects-counters-thresholds-utilities-for- sql-server`. Although this list is more than 10 years old, it still provides a good baseline target for your SQL Server.

These counters will give you a very basic overview of the system's performance and must be combined with more information to get any conclusion from the values. As a starting operating system performance baseline, these are very useful and can be tracked and stored for historical overview and troubleshooting. Of course, you need to consider many factors such as change in the system load during business hours, after business hours, and weekends. There may be some peaks in the values in the mornings, and during some maintenance, backup, and so on. So, understanding what your system is doing over time is an essential part in reading the performance baseline.

There are numerous SQL Server counters available in the **Performance Monitor** and it's not necessary to include them all, so we'll again see some basic counters worth monitoring over time to have a baseline that we can use for troubleshooting. These would include the following:

- SQL Server: Buffer manager—buffer cache hit ratio
- SQL Server: Buffer manager—page life expectancy
- SQL Server: Memory manager—total server memory (KB)
- SQL Server: Memory manager—target server memory (KB)
- SQL Server: Memory manager—memory grants pending
- SQL Server: Access methods—full scans/sec

- SQL Server: Access methods—index searches/sec

- SQL Server: Access methods—forwarded records/sec

- SQL Server: SQL statistics—SQL compilations/sec

- SQL Server: SQL statistics—batch requests/sec

- SQL Server: General statistics—user connections

- SQL Server: Locks—Lock Waits/sec

- SQL Server: Locks—Number of Deadlocks/sec

Another tool that you can use is SQL Server **Dynamic Management Views (DMVs)**, which can return the state of SQL Server and its objects and components. You can query the DMVs with the SQL language as with any other table, and, most of the time, you'll combine several of the views to have better information, as illustrated in the following code snippet:

```
SELECT * FROM sys.dm_exec_requests er
JOIN sys.dm_exec_sessions es
ON er.session_id = es.session_id
-- remove all system sessions and yourself
WHERE es.session_id > 50 and es.session_id != @@SPID
```

This simple query as an example will combine two DMV views together to display all user requests/sessions with all information stored in these two views, excluding all system sessions connected to SQL Server and your query window. For a baseline, you shouldn't use all the columns as you will store quite a lot of data, and you should limit your queries only to important parts.

Some important DMVs worth investigating and capturing for a baseline include the following:

- `sys.dm_io_virtual_file_stats`

- `sys.dm_db_index_physical_stats`

- `sys.dm_db_index_usage_stats`

- `sys.dm_db_missing_index_details`

- `sys.dm_os_wait_stats`

- `sys.dm_os_sys_memory`

- `sys.dm_os_process_memory`

> **Note**
>
> You can find many ready-to-use DMV queries online. An awesome source is a list of queries compiled by Glenn Berry, which are available on his blog, `https://www.sqlskills.com/blogs/glenn/category/dmv-queries/`. Another great tool that is available for free is WhoIsActive by Adam Machanic, available at `http://whoisactive.com/`, which queries multiple DMVs at the same time to provide a current view of system performance.

If you schedule a data collection of these values to some monitoring database with a reasonable schedule, you can see how the performance of the system changes over time; by combining all of these, you can have a comprehensive overview of your system.

Summary

In this chapter, we have seen how to build a healthy SQL Server environment and how to configure not only the SQL Server but also Windows Server for a stable and secure SQL Server workload. Keeping your server up to date, secure, and monitored is extremely crucial for the stability of applications and your ability to perform any troubleshooting at the SQL Server level.

In the next chapter, we will build on our healthy SQL Server and introduce backup and recovery procedures so that you can understand how to keep your server safe and how to recover from failures.

Section 2: Server and Database Maintenance

Every database administrator has a wide range of responsibilities. In this section, you will understand how to keep up with such responsibilities on SQL Server. The section contains recipes for database recovery scenarios, security best practices, and several performance topics.

This section contains the following chapters:

- *Chapter 3, Implementing Backup and Recovery*
- *Chapter 4, Securing Your SQL Server*
- *Chapter 5, Working with Disaster Recovery Options*
- *Chapter 6, Indexing and Performance*

3
Implementing Backup and Recovery

One of the many responsibilities of an administrator is to keep data backed up in case of any data failure. SQL Server helps administrators fulfill this responsibility via sophisticated backup and restore features. In this chapter, we will learn in detail what you need when choosing an appropriate database disaster recovery strategy in conjunction with the database's usage and configuration, as well as how to use stored backups to restore a database in case of failure.

We will cover the following topics in this chapter:

- Data structures and transaction logging
- SQL Server recovery models
- Designing a backup strategy
- Using database and log restore

Let's get started!

Data structures and transaction logging

We usually think of a database as a physical structure consisting of tables containing columns and rows of data and indexes. However, this is just a human point of view. From SQL Server's perspective, a database is a set of precisely structured files described in the form of **metadata**, also saved in the same database structures within the database. We are starting this chapter with an explanation of **storage internals** because a conceptual imagination of how every database works is very helpful when the database needs to be backed up correctly.

How data is stored

Every database on SQL Server must have at least two files:

- The **primary data file** with the usual suffix, mdf
- The **transaction log file** with the usual suffix, ldf

For most databases, this minimal set of files is enough. However, when the database contains big amounts of data or the database has big data contention, such as systems with thousands of transactions handled in seconds, it's good practice to design more data files. Another situation when a basic set of files is not enough can arise when documents or pictures are saved along with relational data. However, SQL Server can still store all our data in the basic file set, but it can lead to a performance bottleneck and management issue. That's why we need to know about all the possible storage types that are useful for different scenarios of deployment. A complete structure of files is depicted in the following diagram:

Fig. 3.1 – Database file structure

For administrators who have not focused on the database structure of SQL Server before, this tree of objects may be unclear and confusing. To make sure there's no confusion, let's explore every single node illustrated in the preceding diagram.

Database types

A **relational database** is defined as a complex data type. This complex type consists of tables with a given number of columns. Each column has a domain, which is actually a **data type** (such as an **integer** or a **date**) that's optionally complemented by some constraints.

SQL Server takes a database as a record written in metadata containing the **name** of the database, **properties** of the database, and the **names** and **locations** of all files or folders representing storage for the database. This is the same for **user databases**, as well as for **system databases**.

System databases are created automatically during SQL Server installation and they are crucial for correctly running SQL Server. We know of five system databases. Let's take a look at them now.

The master database

The master database is the basis for correctly running the SQL Server service. Logins, all databases and their files, instance configurations, linked server definitions, and lists of error messages are all examples of data stored in the master database. SQL Server finds this database at startup using two startup parameters, `-d` and `-l`, followed by the paths to master `mdf` and `ldf` files. These parameters are very important in situations where the administrator wants to move the master's files to a different location. Changing their values is possible in **SQL Server Configuration Manager** by selecting the **Startup Parameters** tab in the **Properties** dialog in the SQL Server service. When the master database is not found or it is corrupted, it prevents the SQL Server instance from starting.

The msdb database

The `msdb` database serves as the storage for **SQL Server Agent objects**, **Database Mail definitions**, **Service Broker configurations**, **Integration Services objects**, and so on. This data is used mostly for **SQL Server automation**, such as **SQL Server Agent jobs**, or for diagnostics, such as **SSIS logs** or **database mail logs**. The `msdb` database also stores logs about backups and restores the events of each database. If this database is corrupted or missing, SQL Server Agent cannot start and many other features such as **Service Broker** or **Database Mail** won't be accessible.

The database model

The **database model** can be used as a template for every new database while it is being created. During a database's creation (see the `CREATE DATABASE` statement on **MSDN**), files are created on defined paths and all the objects, data, and properties of the database model are created, copied, and set in the new database during its creation. This database must always exist on the instance because when it is corrupted, the `tempdb` database cannot be created at instance startup!

The tempdb database

Even if the `tempdb` database seems to be a regular database like many others, it plays a very special role in every SQL Server instance. This database is used by SQL Server, as well as developers, to save temporary data such as temporary tables, table variables, and static cursors (although this is not the best practice). As this database is intended for the short lifespan of all the objects stored in it (temporary data only, which can be stored during the execution of a stored procedure or until the session is disconnected), SQL Server clears this database by truncating all the data from it or by dropping and recreating this database every time it's started.

As the `tempdb` database will never contain durable data, it has some special internal behavior. This is the reason why accessing data in this database is several times faster than accessing durable data in other databases. If this database is corrupted, restart SQL Server.

The resourcedb database

The `resourcedb` database is the fifth in our enumeration and contains the definitions of all the system objects of SQL Server; for example, `sys.objects`. This database is hidden and read-only, and we do not need to care about it that much.

It is not configurable, and we do not use regular backup strategies for it. It is always placed in the installation path of SQL Server (in the `binn` directory) and it's backed up within the **filesystem** backup. In case of an accident, it is recovered as part of the filesystem as well.

We will now explore the filegroup node.

Filegroup

Filegroup is an organizational metadata object that contains one or more data files. Filegroup does not have its own representation in the filesystem – it's just a group of files (or folders). When any database is created, a filegroup called primary is always created. This **primary filegroup** always contains the primary data file.

Filegroups can be divided into the following:

- **Row storage filegroups**: These filegroups can contain data files (`mdf` or `ndf`).

- **Filestream filegroups**: This kind of filegroup does not contain files, but folders, to store binary data such as scanned documents or pictures. Using filestream filegroups for **blob** data brings better performance for manipulation because the blob's byte stream is stored in a secured folder on disk, rather than on the row storage filegroups. It facilitates better read and write operations.

- **In-memory filegroup**: Only one instance of this kind of filegroup can be created in a database. Internally, it is a special case of a filestream filegroup and it is used by SQL Server to persist data from in-memory tables.

Every filegroup has four simple properties:

- **Name:** This is the descriptive name of the filegroup. The name must fulfill the naming convention criteria.

- **Default**: In a set of filegroups of the same type, one of these filegroups has this option set to on. This means that when a new table or index is created, but not assigned a specific filegroup to store data in, the default filegroup is used. The primary filegroup is the default filegroup. The in-memory filegroup does not contain this property because we cannot have two or more in-memory filegroups in one database.

- **Read-only**: Every filegroup, except the primary filegroup and in-memory filegroup, can be set to **read-only**. Let's say that a filegroup is created for last year's historical data. When data is moved from the current period to the tables created in this historical filegroup, the filegroup could be set to **read-only**. Marking the filegroup as **read-only** prevents users from making any changes to the data placed in the read-only filegroup. For administrators, read-only filegroups can reduce the time of backing up as the read-only setting ensures that the data in the filegroup cannot be changed.

- **Autogrow All Files**: This property of row storage filegroups is new on SQL Server 2019. When more files are added to certain filegroups, SQL Server distributes data across all files using the **Proportional Fill Algorithm** (**PFA**). This means that more data is added to a bigger file within a set of files in the same filegroup. This behavior can lead to the uneven distribution of data. Hence, turning on the **Autogrow All Files** property ensures that SQL Server keeps the size of all the files within the filegroup the same when an autogrow event occurs.

> Tip
> It is a good approach to divide the database into smaller parts, known as filegroups. It helps to distribute data across more physical storage and makes the database more manageable; backups can be done part by part in shorter times, which fit better in a service window.

Data files

Every database must have at least one data file, called a **primary data file**. This file is always bound to the primary filegroup. This file stores all the metadata of the database, such as structure descriptions (these can be seen through views such as `sys.objects`, `sys.columns`, and others), users, and so on. If the database does not have other data files (in the same or other filegroups), all user data is also stored in this file, but this approach is good enough for smaller databases.

Considering how the volume of the data in the database grows over time, it is a good practice to add more data files. These files are called **secondary data files**. Secondary data files are optional and contain user data only.

Both types of data files have the same internal structure. Every file is divided into 8 KB small parts called **database pages**. SQL Server maintains several types of database pages, such as data pages, index pages, **Index Allocation Maps** (**IAMs**) to locate the data pages of tables or indexes, **Global Allocation Maps** (**GAMs**), and **Shared Global Allocation Maps** (**SGAMs**) to address objects in the database. Regardless of the type of a certain database page, SQL Server uses a database page as the smallest unit of logical I/O operations in memory. Let's describe some common properties of a database page:

- A data page never contains the data of several objects.

- Data pages do not know each other (and that's why SQL Server uses IAMs to allocate all the pages of an object).

- Data pages do not have any special physical ordering.

- A data row must always fit into a data page (this property is not completely true as SQL Server uses **row overflow data** to keep data that overflows over the 8060 B limit for records).

These properties could seem useless, but when we know about these properties, we can use this knowledge to better optimize and manage our databases.

> **Did you know that a data page is the smallest storage unit that can be restored from a backup?**
>
> As a data page is quite a small storage unit, SQL Server groups data pages into bigger, logical units called **extents**. An extent is a logical allocation unit containing eight physically coherent data pages. When SQL Server requests data from disk, extents are read into memory. This is the reason why 64 KB NTFS clusters are recommended to format disk volumes for data files. Extents can be **uniform** or **mixed**. A uniform extent is a kind of extent containing data pages belonging to one object only; on the other hand, a mixed extent contains the data pages of several objects.

Transaction log

When SQL Server processes any transaction, it works in a way called the **two-phase commit**. When a client starts a transaction by sending a single **Data Manipulation Language (DML)** request or by calling the `BEGIN TRAN` command, SQL Server requests data pages from disk to memory through a **buffer cache** and makes the requested changes in these data pages in memory. When the DML request is executed or the `COMMIT` command comes from the client, the first phase of the commit is completed, but the data pages in memory differ from their original versions in a data file on disk. The data page in memory is in a state called **dirty**.

When a transaction runs, a transaction log file is used by SQL Server for a very detailed chronological description of every single action that was done during the transaction. This description is called **write-ahead logging (WAL)**, and it is one of the oldest processes known on SQL Server.

The second phase of the commit usually does not depend on the client's request and it is an internal process called a **checkpoint**. A checkpoint is a periodical action that does the following:

- Searches for dirty pages in the buffer cache

- Saves dirty pages to their original data file location

- Marks these data pages as **clean** in the buffer cache (or drops them out of memory to free memory space)

- Marks the transaction as a checkpoint or **inactive** in the transaction log

WAL is needed for SQL Server during the **recovery process**. The recovery process is run on every database every time the SQL Server service starts. When the SQL Server service stops, some pages could remain in a dirty state and be lost from memory. This can lead to two possible situations:

- The transaction is completely described in the transaction log (from `BEGIN TRAN` to `COMMIT`), the new content of the data page is lost from memory, and the data pages are not changed in the data file.

- The transaction is not completed when SQL Server stops, so the transaction is not completely described in the transaction log. Data pages in memory are not in a stable state (because the transaction did not finish and SQL Server cannot know if `COMMIT` or `ROLLBACK` will occur), and the original versions of the data pages in the data files are intact.

SQL Server decides these two situations when it is starting. If a transaction is complete in the transaction log but was not marked as a checkpoint, SQL Server executes this transaction again with both phases of `COMMIT`. If the transaction is not complete in the transaction log when SQL Server stops, SQL Server will never know what the user's intention with the transaction was, and the incomplete transaction will be erased from the transaction log as if it had never started.

Accelerated Database Recovery

The described recovery process ensures that every database is in its last known consistent state after SQL Server's startup. The recovery process could take a long time in some cases. A common situation would be when SQL Server is stopped (sometimes unexpectedly) when some long-running transaction is being executed. The recovery process takes almost the same time as executing the transaction. It leads to unacceptable database unavailability. SQL Server 2019 brings a new database-scoped feature that bypasses this issue. The feature is called **Accelerated Database Recovery** (**ADR**). ADR basically keeps track of changes in data using **internal row versioning**. When SQL Server stops working and is restarted, SQL Server does not recover all the transactions from the transaction log, but simply recovers the proper versions of the records from the **in-database row version** store.

To turn on ADR, we can use the following **Data Definition Language** (**DDL**) statement:

```
ALTER DATABASE AdventureWorks SET ACCELERATED_DATABASE_RECOVERY
= ON
(PERSISTENT_VERSION_STORE_FILEGROUP = myPvsFG)
```

The preceding statement consists of two parts. The first part is just turning `ON` (or `OFF`, if needed) ADR. The second part of the statement, enclosed in brackets, is optional. Versions of records that have been changed during transactions are stored on a disk in a filegroup. We can set a filegroup dedicated to row versions (which is a good practice for performance). Row versions are stored in the filegroup called `myPvsFG`. When this part of the configuration is omitted, row versions are stored in the `primary` filegroup.

The ADR feature is useful for workloads with long-running transactions or when the transaction log of a certain database grows significantly.

It is important for DBAs to understand write-ahead logging when planning a backup strategy because the restore process finishes with the recovery process as well. When restoring the database, the administrator has to recognize if it's time to run the recovery process or not. Now, let's learn about the different backup options that are available in SQL Server by using a properly configured recovery model.

SQL Server recovery models

Each database hosted by SQL Server contains a property called a **recovery model**. This property basically affects which backup strategy can be designed. This short section briefly explains recovery models.

How to configure a database's recovery model property

Every database has a property called the recovery model. The recovery model determines how transactions are logged, and for what timespan the transactions will be stored in the transaction log. The recovery model is set by the ALTER DATABASE TSQL command:

```
-- setting full recovery model
ALTER DATABASE <database_name> SET RECOVERY FULL
```

The recovery model has three possible options:

- SIMPLE
- BULK_LOGGED
- FULL

We'll take a look at these now.

Using the SIMPLE recovery model

When the recovery model is set to SIMPLE, SQL Server clears transactions from the transaction log at every checkpoint. This approach leads to a relatively small transaction log file, which seems to be a good behavior. On the other hand, the transaction log does not hold transaction records, so we are not able to use more sophisticated strategies to minimize data loss.

The SIMPLE recovery model is a good option when data stored in the database is not mission-critical, or when potential data loss is not critical for users, or for databases that could be reloaded from other sources. As an example of a database where data is not crucial for business, we can imagine development databases where data is sometimes damaged intentionally.

Another example of a SIMPLE recovery model could be a database whose content is loaded repeatedly. We can imagine a data warehouse for statistical purposes being loaded periodically from an operational database such as accounting, order processing, or production tracking.

Using the FULL recovery model

When the recovery model is set to SIMPLE, SQL Server keeps transaction log records in the transaction log file up until the checkpoint only. When the recovery model is set to FULL, SQL Server keeps the transaction log records in the transaction log file until the BACKUP LOG statement is executed. It allows complex and sophisticated backup strategies. With the recovery model set to FULL, SQL Server keeps all transaction records indefinitely until the transaction log file is full; then, the database stops working and becomes inaccessible. That is why we need to back up the transaction log regularly as it clears the transaction log, keeps it to a manageable size, and defends the database against it not functioning. As an advanced point, we have to say that when the recovery model is set to FULL, we can restore the database at any point in time.

Using the BULK_LOGGED recovery model

What is the BULK_LOGGED recovery model for? This option has almost the same behavior as a full recovery model, but bulk-logged operations (for example, BULK INSERT of flat files into database tables) are described briefly in the transaction log file. The BULK_LOGGED recovery model does not allow us to restore the database at any point in time. It is used only on databases where some small data loss is allowed. One example of its usage can be as follows:

1. Before periodical data load, set the recovery model to BULK_LOGGED

2. Load flat files, images, or other LOBs

3. Set the recovery model back to FULL

4. Back up the database

Even if this section is very short, it is very important, and we will recall information from here throughout the rest of this chapter. We will work with the recovery model immediately in the following section to successfully back up our databases.

Designing a backup strategy

A backup can be understood as a copy of used data pages or a copy of transaction log records. Backups should be done regularly. Backups are needed not only to restore databases in the case of physical or logical failure but for when, for example, we want to make a copy of the database or migrate the database to another SQL Server instance. To have our backups proper and complete, we need to consider the following points:

- How to configure the database
- Which types of backups to combine
- How to use backup strategies in conjunction with database usage

Let's first look at the types of backup supported by SQL Server.

Backup types

SQL server basically supports three main types of backup:

- **Full backup**
- **Transaction log backup**
- **Differential backup**

Each of these types has several variants and we will go through each of them.

Full backup

A full backup is simply a backup of a complete database. When performing a full backup, SQL Server stores metadata of the database (its name, creation date, all options set to the database, paths to all files belonging to the database, and so on), the used data pages of every data file, and also the active part of the transaction log (which means all the transactions that are not checkpoints yet and all running transactions, even if they are not finished).

At the end of the backup process, SQL Server stores the last **Log Sequence Number** (**LSN**) for possible additional backups.

> **Note**
> A full backup never clears the transaction log file!

A full backup can be performed without following a recovery model set. However, the correct option is to have a SIMPLE recovery model if we do not intend to add additional backups to our backup strategy.

The command for a full database backup is as follows:

```
BACKUP DATABASE <database name> TO DISK = '<full path to
backup>'
```

We can write the following as an example to back up an AdventureWorks database:

```
BACKUP DATABASE AdventureWorks TO DISK = 'D:\myBackups\
AdventureWorks.bak'
```

Let's describe the preceding example in more detail. A database called AdventureWorks must exist on the server and it must be in a consistent state; in other words, we never can back up a database (with any kind of backup) that is not online or that is not working normally. The second mandatory condition is that the D:\myBackups path must exist on the filesystem. Backups are not installers; they never create folders.

The filename for the backup is arbitrary; the .bak extension is recommended. The file itself need not exist; it is created with the first backup. It is possible to store more backups in one file. When we want to have more backups in one file, we must add a new option to the backup command:

```
BACKUP DATABASE AdventureWorks TO DISK = 'D:\myBackups\
AdventureWorks.bak'
WITH NOINIT
```

When the preceding example is run for the first time and the .bak file does not exist, it will be created. When the same command is executed a second time with the same path and filename, the backup file will grow in volume because additional backups will be added to it. This scenario is not useful for big database backups because of the quickly growing size of the backup file. But since many databases are not very big, we can use the NOINIT option to store a full backup, along with the transaction log backups of the small database, in one backup file. Recursively, when we want to erase all the backups from the backup file and start a new backup cycle, we can change the NOINIT option with the INIT option. The INIT option erases all the backups from the backup file and stores only the new backup in it.

Full backups tend to have a big volume. This could lead to disk insufficiency, as well as the backup operation being time-consuming. That is why it is highly recommended to compress backups. There are two ways to do this. The first way is to set the server level to default for backup compression. The command for this server setting is as follows:

```
EXEC sp_configure 'backup compression default', 1
GO
RECONFIGURE
GO
```

The sp_configure system stored procedure is used in many cases, as seen in the preceding example. The first parameter, 'backup compression default', is the name of the configuration property. It is quite hard to remember all the configuration parameters by name, so we should remember that we can execute sp_configure just as is, without parameters. This procedure will return the result set, along with a list of parameter names and currently configured values.

The second parameter in the preceding script sample (the number 1) is a bit value indicating that we want to switch the backup compression at the instance's level on. For some configuration values, only bit is used; for example, when setting the maximum degree of parallelism, the integer value indicates how many CPUs can be used for the parallel processing of one TSQL request.

The RECONFIGURE command causes the configured property to load immediately, without the need for a service restart.

The second way of setting compression is to simply add another option directly to the BACKUP command:

```
BACKUP DATABASE AdventureWorks TO DISK = 'D:\myBackups\
AdventureWorks.bak'
WITH NOINIT, COMPRESSION
```

SQL Server compresses the backup file itself when it is written (no particular backup stored in the file), so we cannot have a part of the file uncompressed and the rest of the same file compressed. If we do not want to compress some backups, the opposite option is NO_COMPRESSION.

> **Note**
>
> To use backup compression, let's take an uncompressed backup. In this case, the `INIT` option of the `BACKUP` command is too smooth. We need to replace the `INIT` option with the stronger `FORMAT` option. The `FORMAT` option physically deletes the backup file and creates a new one. Use the `FORMAT` option carefully because it will cause all your backups in certain backup files to be lost forever.

A full backup serves as a baseline for more advanced backup strategies. It is often combined with transaction log backups, and this dependency is driven by the last LSN written to every backup. When an additional transaction log backup is executed, SQL Server remembers the last LSN from the previous backup and starts the current backup operation from the next LSN. Hence, when a full backup is executed, the last remembered LSN is replaced with a new one and the backup strategy obtains a new baseline.

In some cases, this is undesired behavior; for example, in situations where we need to create a copy of a certain database with a full backup, but without breaking out of the backup sequence. For this case, one more full backup variant exists:

```
BACKUP DATABASE AdventureWorks TO DISK = 'D:\myBackups\
tempBackupOfAdventureWorks.bak'
WITH COPY_ONLY
```

The `COPY_ONLY` option in the preceding command causes the LSN sequence that was tracked for backup consequences to not restart and the exceptional full backup to not establish a new baseline for the backup strategy.

A full backup is relatively straightforward but less efficient when we need to minimalize potential data loss. That is why we need to have a stronger mechanism, such as the transaction log backup, to keep our data safe and sheltered against physical as well as logical damage.

Transaction log backup

As mentioned in the previous section, a full backup establishes a baseline for more efficient backup strategies. In other words, one full backup must be created before we can start a backup transaction log. A **transaction log** backs up all transaction log records from the last LSN, which is contained in the previous backup.

In other words, a full backup is a backup of the state of the database, while a transaction log backup is a backup of the additional changes from the last LSN that was stored by a previous backup. Using a transaction log backup ensures that the **recovery point objective (RPO)** that the database could be restored to is very close to the moment when the database was damaged.

Another important property of transaction log backups is that this backup type erases the inactive virtual log files (logical parts in the transaction log file) of the transaction log file. It keeps the transaction log file at a reasonable size.

To be able to use a transaction log backup, the database's recovery model property must be set to the BULK_LOGGED or FULL value. Remember that unlike the FULL recovery model, the BULK_LOGGED recovery model does not allow you to restore the database at a certain point in time.

When the recovery model is set correctly and a full backup is executed, we can start a backup of the transaction log on a regular basis. The basic syntax for a transaction log backup is as follows:

```
BACKUP LOG AdventureWorks TO DISK = 'D:\myBackups\
AdventureWorksLog.bak' WITH <additional options>
```

As seen in the preceding code example, the BACKUP LOG syntax is very similar to the BACKUP DATABASE syntax. The database must already exist, and it must be in an online state; the path to the .bak file must exist in the filesystem as well. If the .bak file does not exist, it will be created when the BACKUP LOG statement is executed for the first time.

The additional options are basically almost the same as the full backup statement:

- The INIT/NOINIT pair controls whether the content of the backup file will be replaced.
- The FORMAT/NOFORMAT pair is a stronger variant for INIT/NOINIT options.
- The COMPRESSION/NO_COMPRESSION pair controls the backup's compression.

The meaning of these options is the same for all backup types.

Now that we have enough information about basic backup types, we can go through more complex examples. The following code sample shows you a set of backup statements and their sorting. The only difference in the real world is that every statement is executed separately and that, typically, the execution is planned by SQL Server Agent.

> **Note**
>
> SQL Server Agent will be described later, in *Chapter 9, Configuring Always On High-Availability Features.*

Let's take a look at this assignment. The AdventureWorks database is used as a typical operational database with lots of incoming transactions. These transactions must not be lost because the clients of the database write their data through a sales web application. The backup cycle will be restarted every day. The AdventureWorks database is relatively small, so all the backups can be stored in the same file. An important business need is that the database must be recoverable to a certain point in time. How do we prepare the AdventureWorks database for proper backups and which backup statements do we use? The following recipe shows the complete process:

1. We must ensure that the database is in FULL recovery mode:

    ```
    -- this statement will be run once only
    -- if database is in FULL recovery model already, nothing
    happens
    ALTER DATABASE AdventureWorks SET RECOVERY FULL
    GO
    ```

2. Every day at, for instance, 3 a.m., we will execute a full backup:

    ```
    -- following statement will reset content of the backup
    file
    BACKUP DATABASE AdventureWorks TO DISK = 'D:\backups\
    AdventureWorks.bak'
    WITH INIT
    GO
    ```

3. Every hour or maybe more often, if needed, we will repeat the transaction log backup:

    ```
    --     following statement will append the backup to the
    backup file and clears
    --     transaction log
    BACKUP LOG AdventureWorks TO DISK = 'D:\backups\
    AdventureWorks.bak'
    WITH NOINIT
    GO
    ```

As seen in the previous code sample, it is not very complicated to create a simple and strong backup strategy. The transaction log backup should be executed often to maintain the transaction log file's size. This will improve the runtime of the backup operation, making it fast and small, and not in conflict with regular user requests.

So far, everything has just been routine, but what if damage occurs? A very common mistake is to think that the only kind of damage is physical damage, for example, file corruption. However, we should keep in mind that another kind of damage is logical damage, for example, accidental deletion of data or some structures. When such logical damage occurs, SQL Server does not detect the problem and the database remains online. However, for the user, the database is useless and damaged.

For either type of corruption, SQL Server provides a special transaction log backup called a **tail-log backup**. The tail-log backup is a variant of the transaction log backup. It backs up transaction log records written to the transaction log file up to the moment of their corruption, hence why it is called a backup of the tail of the transaction log. The tail-log backup switches the state of the database to restoring. The restoring state of the database causes the database to be inaccessible to users. It is very important to use the tail-log backup in case of logical corruption. It is not probable that all the data in the database can be logically damaged at the same moment. However, we still need to stop a user from working on the rest of the data because we know that the database is going to be restored, and all user changes will be lost. An example syntax to execute a tail-log backup is as follows:

```
BACKUP LOG AdventureWorks TO DISK = 'D:\backups\tailLog.bak'
WITH NORECOVERY
```

The NORECOVERY keyword is the option that forms the tail-log backup.
The preceding syntax is just enough for logical accidents such as unwanted deletes of data. But for every backup operation, the database must be in a consistent and online state. What if the database is in a **suspect** state?

The suspect state of a database is set by SQL Server in situations where the database is somehow corrupted physically and not accessible to users. In this case, we have two additional options that can be added to the BACKUP LOG statement:

```
BACKUP LOG AdventureWorks TO DISK = 'D:\backups\taillog.bak'
WITH
NORECOVERY, NO_TRUNCATE, CONTINUE_AFTER_ERROR
```

Let's describe these new options in more detail.

When the database is corrupted, no backup can be executed apart from the preceding code. The CONTINUE_AFTER_ERROR option says to SQL Server that we know about the corruption, but we want to keep all possible transaction log records captured by the transaction log until the moment of damage. Even if the transactions are incomplete or some of the transaction log records are not readable, the rest of the transactions will be kept by the BACKUP LOG statement. If we do not use the CONTINUE_AFTER_ERROR option, SQL Server assumes that the database is in a consistent online state and the BACKUP LOG statement will fail.

The second NO_TRUNCATE option causes no maintenance to be done by SQL Server on completion of the backup. This is the intended behavior because we know that the database is in an unstable state and it is probable that any write operation will fail. We also know that, after the tail-log backup's completion, we will start the restore process of the database, so any additional maintenance is wasteful.

Differential backup

SQL Server maintains an internal structure called a **differential map**. This structure keeps track of all changes made upon user requests in database extents since the last full backup. This is very useful in cases where just a portion of a database is updated frequently. We can use differential backups in conjunction with frequent transaction log backups to speed up the process of restoring later when the need occurs. A differential backup has the following characteristics:

- It is a kind of full backup (backs up extents changed from the last full backup and does not maintain the transaction log).

- It is cumulative (backs up extents changed from the last full backup, which allows you to skip more transaction log backups during a restore).

- It is faster and smaller than a full backup (does not slow down the database for a long time and can be executed concurrently for common user work without decisive influence on performance).

- It does not need any additional settings at the database or server level.

The time a differential backup takes depends on how much part of the database has changed since the last full backup. We can use the sys.dm_db_file_space_usage view and execute the following query to test how many extents have changed:

```
SELECT total_pages_count, modified_extent_page_count FROM sys.
dm_db_file_space_usage
```

The preceding query returns two columns:

The first column, `total_page_count`, shows the total number of data pages in the database.

- The second column, `modified_extent_page_count`, shows how many data pages were modified since the last full backup was executed.

As the `modified_extent_page_count` value goes closer to the value of `total_pages_count`, the more extents will be backed up by the differential backup and the differential backup operation will slow down.

The syntax for a differential backup is as follows:

```
BACKUP DATABASE AdventureWorks TO DISK = 'D:\myBackups\
AdventureWorksDiff.bak'
WITH DIFFERENTIAL
```

From a syntactical point of view, a differential backup is just a database backup with one more option. Other options such as `INIT/NOINIT` are also possible. If the use of differential backups is recognized, the timeline of backups will be according to the following table. This table describes a daily-based strategy for smaller databases, with all the backup types stored in the same backup file:

Time of day	Backup type	INIT/NOINIT
3:00 a.m.	FULL	INIT
3:15 a.m.	LOG	NOINIT
3:30 a.m.	LOG	NOINIT
...		
8:45 a.m.	LOG	NOINIT
9:00 a.m.	DIFFERENTIAL	NOINIT
9:15 a.m.	LOG	NOINIT
...		
12:00 a.m.	DIFFERENTIAL	NOINIT
...and so on until the next 3 a.m.		

Figure 3.2 – Daily-based strategy for smaller databases

The preceding table summarizes the flow of the database backups within a 1-day cycle. The cycle starts every day at 3 a.m. with a full backup. The following transaction log backups make a chain of changes made to the database's data. Differential backups are executed at 9 a.m., 12 a.m., and, let's say, at 3 p.m. and 6 p.m., which allows us to speed up the process of the database restore.

So far, we have explained the backup options used to maintain the recoverability of a simple database. We will now use the same options in more complicated scenarios.

Advanced backup scenarios

Now that we have understood all three basic types of backup, we can decide how to summarize our needs and choose the right backup strategy. It is also very important to ensure that our backup is reliable and fast. We must also maintain backups for larger databases composed of more files or filegroups. SQL Server provides you with a set of features that cover all three of these needs.

Backup media

In previous chapters, we worked with backups stored on disk files. It is a very common destination for backups because a **tape**, as a backup destination, must be attached directly to the server. Due to the usual usage of backup tape devices to back up overall company infrastructures, SQL Server does not improve tape backup possibilities and relies on third-party backups. Another target of backups could be the **blob container** in **Azure**. We will describe backups to Azure, as well as other scenarios involving Azure, in *Chapter 11, Combining SQL Server 2019 with Azure*. That is why all the examples in this chapter will use just disk files as their backup devices.

> **Note**
> If SQL Server databases are going to be backed up by third-party backup devices, never mix the execution of these backups with SQL Server's native backup!

When we need to improve the speed of the backup, we can join more backup places into one set, called the **media set**. The media set is formed of one or more devices of the same type. SQL Server spreads data across all devices in the media set evenly. We can imagine the media set as a striped disk. The media set is created the first time the backup is executed. The following example creates a media set:

```
BACKUP DATABASE <database name> TO
DISK = '<path to first file>',
DISK = '<path to second file>'
```

```
WITH
MEDIANAME = '<name of the media set>'
```

Every backup saved to the same media set is then called a **backup set**. Once the media set is created, all files in the backup set must be used together. An attempt to use one of the files for additional backup without using the whole media set will fail. Using media sets makes backup operations faster, but it also increases the risk of backup loss.

Let's look at the following example:

```
BACKUP DATABASE <database name> TO
DISK = '<path to first file>'
-- second file from previous example is not used
WITH
FORMAT
```

The FORMAT option causes the media set to break, and all the backups saved there are lost! Use media sets carefully.

Backup reliability

Everything saved on disk could be somehow broken or unreadable. That is why SQL Server provides you with two features to improve backup reliability:

- The first option is to use a backup with the CHECKSUM option. This option is simple to use and causes the computation of the checksum value upon backup completion. This value is saved in the backup and when we prepare for the restore process, we can test the backup's readability using the CHECKSUM option:

```
BACKUP DATABASE <database name> TO DISK = '<path to
file>'
WITH
CHECKSUM
```

We can also turn on the checksum option at the instance's level using the sp_configure system stored procedure. The following script shows how to use it:

```
EXEC sp_configure 'backup checksum default', 1
RECONFIGURE
```

- Another option used to distribute backups across more devices is called **mirrored backup**. Mirrored backup is an enterprise feature of SQL Server, and when we use it, two identical backups are written synchronously to two backup devices. When we use backup mirroring, the syntax looks as follows:

```
BACKUP DATABASE <database name> TO
DISK = '<path to file>'
MIRROR TO DISK = '<path to file>'
WITH <additional options like CHECKSUM>
```

The preceding example adds a second path to the backup medium, followed by the `MIRROR TO` keyword.

File or filegroup backup

One of the reasons why a database should be distributed into more files or filegroups is better manageability. As the database's size grows from time to time, the backup size also increases, even if backup compression is used. In this case, SQL Server provides a very useful feature called **file backup**, or **filegroup backup**.

The following examples are being shown for filegroup backups because file backups are almost the same except that we use the `FILE` keyword instead of the `FILEGROUP` keyword. The syntax of the file/filegroup backup uses the logical filenames or filegroup names in the header of the backup. First of all, let's create a database called `BiggerSystem`. We can use the following script (remember that the paths to the physical files should be set accordingly with your existing drives and folders):

```
CREATE DATABASE BiggerSystem
ON
(name = 'BiggerSystem_Data', filename = 'D:\SqlData\
BiggerSystem.mdf')
LOG ON
(name = 'BiggerSystem_Log', filename = 'L:\SqlLogs\
BiggerSystem.ldf')

ALTER DATABASE BiggerSystem ADD FILEGROUP OPERDATA
ALTER DATABASE BiggerSystem ADD FILEGROUP ARCHIVE2016

ALTER DATABASE BiggerSystem
ADD FILE
(name = 'BiggerSystem_Data2', filename = 'D:\SqlData\
BiggerSystem2.ndf')
```

```
TO FILEGROUP OPERDATA
```

```
ALTER DATABASE BiggerSystem
ADD FILE
(name = 'BiggerSystem_Data3', filename = 'D:\SqlData\
BiggerSystem3.ndf')
TO FILEGROUP ARCHIVE2016
```

The preceding script creates the example database called `BiggerSystem`, along with the following filegroups:

- `PRIMARY` (mandatory in every database)

- `OPERDATA` (filegroup containing hot data instantly used for transactions)

- `ARCHIVE2016` (filegroup containing cold data without any DML operations on it)

The setting for the recovery model option for this database is set to `FULL`.

The filegroup backup syntax is as follows:

```
BACKUP DATABASE <database name>
FILEGROUP = <filegroup name>, FILEGROUP = <another filegroup
name>
TO DISK = '<file path>'
WITH
<additional options>
```

In the following example, we are using the `BiggerSystem` database and its filegroups:

```
-- monday 3 a. m.
BACKUP DATABASE BiggerSystem
FILEGROUP = 'PRIMARY'
TO DISK = 'L:\backups\bigsysprimary.bak'
WITH INIT, CHECKSUM, COMPRESSION
-- monday every hour
BACKUP LOG BiggerSystem TO DISK = 'L:\backups\bigsyslogs.bak'
WITH NOINIT, CHECKSUM, COMPRESSION

-- tuesday 3 a. m.
BACKUP DATABASE BiggerSystem
FILEGROUP = 'OPERDATA'
TO DISK = 'L:\backups\bigsysoper.bak'
WITH INIT, CHECKSUM, COMPRESSION
-- tuesday every hour
```

```
BACKUP LOG BiggerSystem TO DISK = 'L:\backups\bigsyslogs.bak'
WITH NOINIT, CHECKSUM, COMPRESSION

-- wednesday 3 a. m.
BACKUP DATABASE BiggerSystem
FILEGROUP = 'ARCHIVE2016'
TO DISK = 'L:\backups\bigsysarch2016.bak'
WITH INIT, CHECKSUM, COMPRESSION
-- wednesday every hour
BACKUP LOG BiggerSystem TO DISK = 'L:\backups\bigsyslogs.bak'
WITH NOINIT, CHECKSUM, COMPRESSION

-- and so on, thursday we start to backup the PRIMARY filegroup
again
```

As seen in the preceding example, we must not miss any filegroup out from a certain database.

Let's assume that the filegroup called ARCHIVE2016 is not used for DML operations and that, in such cases, its repeating backup becomes unnecessary. SQL Server provides an enterprise feature called **partial backup**. This partial backup saves the primary filegroup, all read-write filegroups, and explicitly written read-only filegroups. That is why it is very useful to set filegroups containing historical or other read-only data as read-only.

Let's go through one more example (for the sake of simplicity, the transaction log backups in the following code sample have been omitted):

```
-- run once: set the ARCHIVE2016 filegroup as read-only
ALTER DATABASE BiggerSystem MODIFY FILEGROUP ARCHIVE2016
READONLY

-- first time backup after setting the filegroup read-only
BACKUP DATABASE BiggerSystem
READ_WRITE_FILEGROUPS, FILEGROUP = 'ARCHIVE2016'
TO DISK = 'L:\backups\bigsys.bak'
WITH INIT, CHECKSUM, COMPRESSION

-- transaction backups follow for the rest of day

-- next daily backups
BACKUP DATABASE BiggerSystem
READ_WRITE_FILEGROUPS
TO DISK = 'L:\backups\bigsysadd.bak'
```

```
WITH INIT, CHECKSUM, COMPRESSION

-- transaction backups follow
```

The preceding SQL sample consists of three statements:

- The first statement sets `ARCHIVE2016 filegroup` to the `read-only` state. It ensures that there is no way to modify data placed within `ARCHIVE2016 filegroup`.

- The second statement adds `ARCHIVE2016 filegroup` to backup. It is the last backup of this filegroup.

- The third statement will back up all `read-write filegroups`; `ARCHIVE2016 filegroup` is not backed up from now on.

So far, we've discussed how to back up user databases. Now, let's focus on system databases. The following sections will explain how to back up system databases properly.

Backing up system databases

In simple words, system databases need backups like user databases do. Backup strategies for system databases are often much more straightforward than for user databases. In the following table, you can see the common backup strategies for every system database:

Database name	Recovery model	Backup description
master	SIMPLE	Full backup once a week
msdb	User settable (SIMPLE recommended)	Full backup every day
model	User settable (affects newly created user databases)	Full backup once a week
tempdb	SIMPLE	N/A

Figure 3.3 – Common backup strategies

The preceding table enumerates all visible system databases and suggests how to back up each of the system databases. As we explained in the introductory part of this chapter, each system database plays its unique role on SQL Server. The suggested frequency of backups reflects how many changes in the data are made within every database.

This section was quite big, wasn't it? So, let's briefly summarize the knowledge we've gained throughout this section.

Backup summary

Managing our backups properly is a very important task that we must perform. As we described in this chapter, we need to decide which types of backups to use, how often to use them, how reliable they are, and where to store them. This decision has a strong impact on the ability to restore data in minimal time with minimal loss. The following table describes several types of databases and example backup strategies:

Data contention	Recovery model	Backups used
Smaller (for example, up to 20 GB) OLTP database	FULL	FULL TRANSACTION LOG (optionally DIFFERENTIAL)
Big OLTP database with read-only archive filegroups	FULL	FULL or FILEGROUP (partial backup if possible) TRANSACTION LOG
OLAP database with periodical data load (data load can be repeated)	SIMPLE	FULL or FILEGROUP (partial backup highly welcome)

Figure 3.4 – Database types and backup strategies

The preceding table is a rough key for you to decide how to plan backup strategies.

In the next section, we will work with database backups and restore corrupted databases in many scenarios.

Using database and log restore

The restore feature in SQL Server is used for data recovery in case of corruption and heavily relies on how data is backed up. In this section, we will cover the following topics:

- Preparation steps before the restore process starts
- Restore scenarios, depending on backup strategies

We'll start with the preparation steps first.

Preparing for restore

Before a database is restored, we must decide on the type of corruption and which backup sets are already available for restore. If we have more backups to be restored (a full backup combined with other backup types), we need to handle the recovery process as well.

The recovery process was described in the *Transaction log* section but let's recall the recovery process one more time. SQL Server uses **write-ahead logging (WAL)** for very detailed transaction actions. These transaction log records are written before the action is actually performed against data pages in the buffer cache (transaction log records are buffered for a short time and written in batches, but from a conceptual viewpoint, this does not matter). At any moment, a certain transaction can be in these states:

- Transaction has not been committed by the user yet; **transaction is running**.

- Transaction is committed by the user, but its data pages are in a dirty state (a different version of the data page in memory and on disk); **transaction is active**.

- Transaction is committed by the user, SQL Server executed the checkpoint, and the data pages in memory are in a clean state (the memory version of the data page was persisted on disk); **transaction is inactive**.

When SQL Server runs a backup, running and active transactions are saved within the backup, even if they are not finished yet. Backups go one after the other; we must remember that incomplete transactions saved in the first backup will continue in the consequential backup. This is true mainly when transaction log backups are used in the backup strategy. Every RESTORE statement contains a RECOVERY/NORECOVERY option. As a part of the RESTORE statement, if either one of the options is not set explicitly, then SQL Server will recover the restored database when the execution of a RESTORE statement is done. It is best to prevent this from happening until the last of the RESTORE statements are executed, because premature recovery prevents the restore process from continuing.

> Tip
> The first and the most important decision to make is when to enable the recovery process. As we'll see shortly, the recovery process is commonly executed within the restore of the last backup in the timeline.

Great, but which backups do we have? Are they readable? Where were the files of my database originally placed? These questions can be answered with the simple preparation of RESTORE statements:

1. The first action is to check whether the backup files are readable. The following statement is often placed directly after the BACKUP statement to ensure that nothing accidental happened when the backup files were copied:

    ```
    RESTORE VERIFYONLY FROM DISK = 'D:\myBackups\
    AdventureWorks.bak' WITH CHECKSUM
    ```

    The preceding statement tests the readability of the backup file. The CHECKSUM option can be used only if it was also used during the backup operation. The result of this command is just saying that the backup set on file 1 is valid.

2. The second piece of information needed is the content of a certain backup file. The following command explores a valid backup file and returns the result set with a list of backups saved:

    ```
    RESTORE HEADERONLY FROM DISK = 'D:\myBackups\
    AdventureWorks.bak'
    ```

    The result set contains many columns, such as LSNs, which are needed for internal restore purposes, and database properties, such as the version of the database, collation, and others, but from an administrator's perspective, the main columns are as follows:

    a) BackupType: This column contains the enumeration (1–full backup, 2–transaction log backup, 4–filegroup backup, and so on).

    b) Position: This column contains the numeric ordering of backups; this value is used in the RESTORE statement to address the correct backup to be restored.

    c) BackupStartDate: This is the date and time when the backup was started.

    d) BackupFinishDate: This is the date and time when the backup was finished.

    As we go through various restore scenarios, we will use this statement to recognize what to restore.

3. Last, but not least, the metadata RESTORE statement is used in situations where restoring the database recovers files to different locations. In such situations, we need to know logical filenames to be able to reference them and set different places on disks:

```
RESTORE FILELISTONLY FROM DISK =    'D:\myBackups\
AdventureWorks.bak'
```

The result of this statement returns more columns for internal purposes. For the administrator, just the first three columns are interesting:

a) LogicalName: The name of the file used as a reference

b) PhysicalName: The full path of the file

c) Type: D for data files, L for logs

Voila! Now, we know how to prepare for the restore process. In the following sections, we will go through several sample scenarios and perform complete restores.

Executing restores

A backup strategy is the main criteria that determines how a database should be restored to the most up-to-date point. In the upcoming sections, we will go through several restore scenarios.

Using the full backup strategy

The restore process consists of several phases. The first phase is called a **safety check**. If we attempt to restore a database with the same name but different files, the restore process will be terminated. When the database does not exist on the instance of SQL Server but some file on disk is in conflict with some filename that is going to be restored, the restore process is terminated as well.

> **Tip**
> If restore is used for database creation, do not create an empty database beforehand. SQL Server will do this for you using information from the backup device.

The second phase tries to remove the rest of the corrupted database. After this phase, the database is recreated and recovered from the backup.

> **Note**
>
> Never try to drop corrupted databases or delete their files before RESTORE.
> Even if DROP DATABASE is the last action in the database's lifetime, SQL
> Server assumes it is in a consistent state, so there's a high probability that
> the DROP DATABASE statement will fail. The RESTORE statement is
> prepared for this case and will remove the debris of the corrupted database
> correctly.

Repeating full backups regularly is the best approach to a backup strategy when the database is small, has a small amount of transactions in it, and is not so mission critical. A crucial requirement is to have this database in the SIMPLE recovery model. We can think of databases as being used for development or testing purposes.

In this case, we can imagine an everyday full backup. When the database is corrupted, the only point that the database can be restored and recovered to is the time when the backup (often the last full backup) was created. This is also the simplest restore that can be done:

```
RESTORE DATABASE <database name> FROM DISK = '<path to backup
file>'
WITH RECOVERY
```

The preceding statement attempts to restore the database with the given name, which does not exist. All the files are placed in the original locations, but if some file with the same name exists for a different database, the restore fails. If a database with the same name exists already, it is not overwritten by this statement (when we want to overwrite an existing database, we must add the REPLACE option to the RESTORE statement). The RECOVERY option ensures that the recovery process is executed by SQL Server on restore completion and that the database is online and consistent after RESTORE.

> **Note**
>
> If the database was backed up, for example, in the read-only state, it will
> remain in this state after RESTORE.

If we want to skip the safety check, say, in situations where the database is completely lost from SQL Server, but some file remained on disk, we can add the REPLACE option to the RESTORE statement.

Let's look at a database called `DevDemo`. This database is small and is used just for development purposes, so the data within it is not very important; it is full of test values created during development and testing. A backup is executed every night. The database becomes corrupted one morning, and we need to recover it. The statement will be as follows:

```
RESTORE DATABASE DevDemo FROM DISK = 'L:\backups\devdemo.bak'
WITH RECOVERY, REPLACE
```

The preceding statement erases wreckages of the corrupted database and restores it to an available and consistent state.

Let's imagine that we have one `devdemo.bak` file that's recycled every week. In other words, we start our backup strategy every Monday morning (for example, at 3 a.m.), so seven backups are potentially contained in the file. The corruption occurs on Wednesday at 10 a.m.. We need to find the last and the freshest backup from the backup file and then use it. The complete example is as follows:

```
-- this statement will return result set with backups in the
file
-- our backup will have value 3 in column Position (Monday's
backup will be 1,
-- Tuesday's backup will be 2, our corruption occurred on
Wednesday)
RESTORE HEADERONLY FROM DISK = 'L:\backups\devdemo.bak'

-- we need to provide the value of desired backup to actual
RESTORE statement
RESTORE DATABASE DevDemo FROM DISK = 'L:\backups\devdemo.bak'
WITH
FILE = 3,
RECOVERY
```

The preceding example shows the restore process of a simple database. Pay attention to the comments contained within the preceding and following scripts as they recall where we are in time.

Let's look at another example. Let's move our `DevDemo` database to another instance of SQL Server. On the original instance, the data file of the database is placed on disk D, but on the new server, the data file disk is placed on disk E. We need to use the following sequence of statements:

```
-- this statement will return result set with backups in the
file
-- as in previous example (remember that Wednesday = 3)
```

```
RESTORE HEADERONLY FROM DISK = 'L:\backups\devdemo.bak'

-- this statement will show LogicalName and physical location
of each file
-- in the database
-- for example LogicalName of .mdf file is "devdemo_Data"
-- and LogicalName of .ldf file is "devdemo_Log"
RESTORE FILELISTONLY FROM DISK = 'L:\backups\devdemo.bak'

-- we need to provide the value of desired backup to actual
RESTORE statement
-- and also we need to say where to place files
RESTORE DATABASE DevDemo FROM DISK = 'L:\backups\devdemo.bak'
WITH
FILE = 3,
MOVE 'devdemo_Data' TO 'E:\data\devdemo.mdf',
MOVE 'devdemo_Log' TO 'L:\logs\devdemo.ldf',
RECOVERY
```

The preceding example moves database files to their new location. The MOVE .. TO pair is used just for files that should be moved; it is not necessary to write this option for every file.

In this section, usage of the simplest backup/restore strategy was shown and common options of the RESTORE statement were described. Now, let's dive deep into more sophisticated scenarios.

Using the full and transaction log backup strategy

For this and the next backup strategies, we must consider two conditions:

- The BULK_LOGGED recovery model must be set on the database
- Correct handling with the RECOVERY/NORECOVERY pair of options

Combining full and transaction log backups in the backup strategy is the best approach for **online transaction processing (OLTP)** databases with continual data contention. This strategy also allows us to restore the database to a certain point in time. It covers situations where there's been logical corruptions such as accidental delete statements, failed structure updates, and so on. To be able to recover the database to some point in time, we need to have the database's recovery model option set to FULL.

The restore process usually starts with the BACKUP statement. This action might look odd, but it is used for rescuing the latest possible transaction. Yes, this is the tail-log backup. If the database is damaged logically, the tail-log backup sets its state to **restoring**. If the database is damaged physically (and is in the **suspect** state so far), the tail-log backup saves all readable transaction log records from the active portion of the transaction log.

The following statement does a tail-log backup when logical damage occurs on the database:

```
BACKUP LOG <database name> TO DISK = '<path to tail log .bak
file>'
WITH NORECOVERY
```

The following statement is better for physical damage of the database:

```
BACKUP LOG <database name> TO DISK = '<path to tail log .bak
file>'
WITH NORECOVERY, NO_TRUNCATE, CONTINUE_AFTER_ERROR
```

The CONTINUE_AFTER_ERROR option is crucial because, if omitted, SQL Server will fail our tail-log backup due to inconsistency in the database.

With that, everything that could be saved has been and we can start to write RESTORE tatements in the correct order. Every restore starts with the RESTORE DATABASE statement, as we described in the *Using the full backup strategy* section. The only important difference is that we do not want to execute the recovery process with each RESTORE command. That is why we must use the NORECOVERY option.

Let's look at a database called Accounting. This database is fully backed up every morning at 3 a.m. and then the transaction log is backed up every hour. All backups are saved to the same file on a daily basis. The physical corruption appears at 9:30 a.m. The following code example describes the full process of the data recovery:

```
-- try to save the latest user work
BACKUP LOG Accounting to DISK = 'L:\backups\taillog.bak'
WITH NORECOVERY, NO_TRUNCATE, CONTINUE_AFTER_ERROR

-- let's check out backup ability
RESTORE VERIFYONLY FROM DISK = 'L:\backups\accounting.bak' WITH
CHECKSUM

-- It's readable, what about content?
RESTORE HEADERONLY FROM DISK = 'L:\backups\accounting.bak'
```

```
-- now we have full backup on position 1
-- and six following trans. log backups on positions 2 - 7

-- restoring initial state of database
-- note: the FILE position need not to be written because 1 is
the default
RESTORE DATABASE Accounting FROM DISK = 'L:\backups\accounting.
bak'
WITH NORECOVERY

-- restoring incremental states from backups 2 - 7
RESTORE LOG Accounting FROM DISK = 'L:\backups\accounting.bak'
WITH
FILE = 2,    -- this value changes for every additional log
backup
NORECOVERY

-- restoring the tail-log backup
RESTORE LOG Accounting FROM DISK = 'L:\backups\taillog.bak'
WITH RECOVERY   -- this option recovers the database and sets
its state ONLINE
```

As seen in the preceding example, only the last backup that was restored has the RECOVERY option. We can think about the NORECOVERY/RECOVERY pair as a TV series. NORECOVERY is the restore process that will continue by restoring the next log backup, like a cliffhanger that leads to the next episode, while RECOVERY is the happy.

As NORECOVERY is used in every RESTORE statement except the last one, it is simple to make a mistake and use NORECOVERY in the last RESTORE. Fortunately, it is very simple to correct this mistake; just repeat the restore of the last transaction log backup with the correct RECOVERY option.

The full backup and transaction log backup strategy has one big advantage as it can be used for point-in-time recovery. However, every coin has two sides and the disadvantage of this strategy is that a relatively big number of backups needs to be maintained, readable, and complete. In the next two sections, we will learn how to profit from this strategy's advantage and how to handle its disadvantage.

Point-in-time recovery

In most situations, the right point in time for a database restore is the most recent state of the database before failure. Sometimes, the database becomes incorrect in a small way; for example, when some tables or other objects are lost. When such a situation occurs, it is recommended that you know how to recover the database. SQL Server provides very useful mechanisms that can be used to restore a database to the desired, but not the last, moment. The first option is to set a date and time for data recovery, while the second is to use a transaction log mark. We will go through both options in the form of examples.

Let's look at a database called Accounting. It is the same database as in the previous section. A full backup is executed every morning at 3 a.m.; transaction log backups are executed every hour. The problem appears at 9:30 a.m. The following are the list of steps that we will perform:

1. Obtain the current time from SQL Server.

2. Create a tail-log backup.

3. Restore the database using a regular full and transaction log backup strategy.

4. Stop the recovery process, not at the end of the last transaction log backup but earlier.

In the preceding steps, we have two exceptional moments, the first one and the last one. Obtaining the current time is very simple:

```
SELECT SYSDATETIME()
--or
SELECT GETDATE()
```

We need to consider that the time that's returned is the time when we noticed the problem, so depending on the actual situation, we will subtract some time from the current time (for example, 30 seconds).

The second and third steps are a regular way of working on the restore process. This means that we will obtain the available backup files, we will explore their quality and content, and then we will start the restore process step by step.

When the restore process comes closer to the moment of failure, we need to pay attention to the correct transaction log backup that's covering the time interval with the failure. When we touch this backup (for example, the backup executed at 9:45 a.m., so the interval is from 9 a.m. to 9:45 a.m.), we will use the following syntax:

```
RESTORE LOG Accounting FROM DISK = 'L:\backups\somelog.bak'
WITH
STOPAT = '2017-08-01 9:30am', RECOVERY
```

The `STOPAT` option recovers the database exactly to this point. The `RECOVERY` option is then needed because the rest of the transaction log backups (if they exist) are useless if the time interval from 9:30 a.m. is ignored and we cannot omit part of the transactions.

If we are not sure which transaction log backup contains the desired point in time, we can write `WITH STOPAT = 'time', RECOVERY` to restore each log statement. When a certain transaction log backup ends before that time, SQL Server reports a warning and the database will stay in the restoring state. When the time is within the transaction log backup, the point-in-time restore is successful and the database is recovered to its online state. If the time set in the `RESTORE` statement is before the current transaction log backup is executed, the restore fails with an error.

This feature has one more option. If a transaction is risky (for example, ts has an unusual data update), we can mark it in the transaction log. The mark for the transaction is written as part of the `BEGIN TRAN` statement. The complete syntax is `BEGIN TRAN myRiskyTran WITH MARK`. The text, `myRiskyTran`, is our transaction name. The transaction's name could be helpful for developers as it acts as an orientation point in source code, has no impact on SQL Server, and is not saved to the transaction log. However, `WITH MARK` changes the situation completely. The name is written to the transaction log and can be read from the transaction log backup. In this case, we can use the transaction name to determine where to execute the recovery process. The syntax for this is similar to the `STOPAT` option:

```
RESTORE LOG Accounting FROM DISK = 'L:\backups\somelog.bak'
WITH
STOPATMARK = 'myRiskyTran', RECOVERY
```

When we need to exclude the transaction from the restore, we should write the following statement:

```
RESTORE LOG Accounting FROM DISK = 'L:\backups\somelog.bak'
WITH
STOPBEFOREMARK = 'myRiskyTran', RECOVERY
```

The STOPATMARK option includes the marked transaction in the recovery process, while STOPBEFOREMARK executes the recovery process exactly before the marked transaction began.

The rest of the restore process is almost the same. If we are not sure in which transaction log backup the marked transaction is, we can use the same approach as when using STOPAT. This means we could write STOPATMARK = 'my risky tran', RECOVERY (STOPBEFOREMARK = 'my risky tran', RECOVERY, respectively) to every RESTORE LOG statement. The only difference is that SQL Server cannot recognize if the desired mark is in further log backups or if the mark has been left behind. When the mark is not present in the already restored current transaction log backup, SQL Server never fails this backup but issues a warning and the database will not be recovered.

This procedure reports a very good value regarding the **Recovery Point Objective** (**RPO**). It is used to measure how much data was lost (a lesser value is better). In the next section, we will show you how to reduce the **recovery time objective** (**RTO**).

Using full, transaction log, and differential backup strategies

The only possible issue when using transaction log backups is that the number of backups becomes quite big. It has an impact on RTO. This is a measure that determines when the downtime will be noticed before the database is recovered.

In the previous sections, we went through a set of backups, beginning with full backups and continuing with transaction log backups one by one. The differential backup is added to the backup strategy for better jumps in time. As we described in the backup part (*Designing a backup strategy*) of this chapter, a differential backup contains all the extents that have been changed from the last full backup. When using this strategy, we can have a set of backups, as shown in the following list:

1. 3 a.m.: Daily full backup (backup position 1)

2. 4 a.m. to 8:30 a.m.: Transaction log backed up twice an hour (backup positions from 2 to 11)

3. 9 a.m.: Differential backup (backup position 12)

4. 10 a.m. to 1:30 p.m.: Transaction log backed up twice an hour (backup positions from 13 to 20)

5. 2 p.m.: Differential backup (backup position 21)

6. 3 p.m. to 6:30 p.m.: Transaction log backed up twice an hour (backup positions from 22 to 29)

7.   7 p.m.: Differential backup (backup position 30)

8.   8 p.m. to 2:30 a.m. next day: Transaction log backed up twice an hour (backup positions 31 and so on)

Let's imagine that our Accounting database will fail at 5 p.m. The only difference from the previous examples is that we do not need to restore every backup from our set. The restore process consists of the first, fifth, and (partially) sixth points from the preceding list. Let's describe the syntax (the following example will omit the preparation steps):

```
-- rescue last user transactions
BACKUP LOG Accounting TO DISK = 'L:\backups\taillog.bak'
WITH NORECOVERY

-- restore initial state of the database
RESTORE DATABASE Accounting FROM DISK = 'L:\backups\accounting.
bak'
WITH NORECOVERY

-- restore the most recent differential backup created before 5
p.m.
RESTORE DATABASE Accounting FROM DISK = 'L:\backups\accounting.
bak'
WITH FILE = 21, NORECOVERY

-- restore trans. log backups between the last diff. backup and
failure point
-- this statement is repeated with changing FILE option
RESTORE LOG Accounting FROM DISK = 'L:\backups\accounting.bak'
WITH FILE = 22, -- and 23, 24 and so on until 26
NORECOVERY

-- restore tail-log backup and recover the database
RESTORE LOG Accounting FROM DISK = 'L:\backups\taillog.bak'
WITH RECOVERY
```

As seen in the preceding example, the restore from a differential backup is just a kind of database restore with no extras. The only reason to use differential backups in a backup strategy is to make the restore process shorter.

In the next section, we will take a look at partial database recovery from file or filegroup backups.

Using file or filegroup backups

As the database becomes large over time, it becomes very complicated to hold a short maintenance window for its backups. This is one of the reasons why we use file or filegroup backups. In this section, we will show you how to recover a certain filegroup in the case of failure.

The task list is as follows:

1. Execute the `tail-log` backup of the database.

2. Restore every corrupted data file/filegroup from its last backup.

3. Restore transaction log backups from the oldest file/filegroup backup.

4. Restore the `tail-log` backup and recover the database.

Let's look at a database called `BiggerSystem`. The database consists of three filegroups: `PRIMARY`, `OPERDATA`, and `ARCHIVE2016`. One filegroup is backed up every day at 3 a.m. Each day, transaction log backups are created every hour. The backup process is planned as follows:

1. Monday 3 a.m.: `PRIMARY` filegroup backup

2. Monday from 4 a.m. to Tuesday 2 a.m.: Transaction log backups

3. Tuesday 3 a.m.: `OPERDATA` filegroup backup

4. Tuesday from 4 a.m. to Wednesday 2 a.m.: Transaction log backups

5. Wednesday 3 a.m.: `ARCHIVE2016` filegroup backup

The failure occurs in the `OPERDATA` filegroup on Wednesday at, 10:30 a.m. The process for the restore is as follows:

```
-- create tail-log backup
BACKUP LOG BiggerSystem TO DISK = 'L:\backups\taillog.bak'

-- restore the damaged filegroup
RESTORE DATABASE BiggerSystem
FILEGROUP = 'OPERDATA'
FROM DISK = 'L:\backups\bigsysoper.bak'
WITH NORECOVERY

-- restore all trans. log backups from Tuesday 4 a.m. until
most recent
RESTORE LOG BiggerSystem FROM DISK = 'L:\backups\bigsyslogs.
bak'
WITH
```

```
FILE = x,     -- where "x" is the position of backup in backup
file
NORECOVERY

-- recover the database
RESTORE LOG BiggerSystem FROM DISK = 'L:\backups\taillog.bak'
WITH RECOVERY
```

As seen in the preceding example, the only difference from a regular full restore is the FILEGROUP keyword, which is being used to address the filegroup that is to be restored. This restore procedure ensures the most recent, consistent state for all the databases.

So far, we've restored a whole database and its most important part. In the next section, we will turn our attention to the smallest recoverable part of the database.

Restoring data pages

SQL Server provides a feature called **page restore**. It allows us to shorten the restore time to a minimum and restore just the corrupted data pages. The process of a page restore is very similar to a file or filegroup restore. It needs a full or file/filegroup backup and transaction log backups.

The most challenging part is how to find out which data pages are corrupted. We have two options when it comes to detecting corrupted data pages:

- The first option is to monitor the msdb.dbo.suspect_pages table. SQL Server maintains a table called suspect_pages in the msdb database. This table is used by SQL Server to hold information about data page corruptions. Consider that the table has up to 1,000 rows, so if it is not monitored for a long time and 1,000 rows are returned from a query, we will never know how many corrupted data pages we have in our database.

  The most important columns in this table are as follows:

  a) database_id: The ID of the database containing suspect pages

  b) file_id: The ordinal position of the file containing suspect pages

  c) page_id: The page identifier

The `file_id` and `page_id` identifiers are used together to address the page that needs to be recovered. If, for example, page number 12345 is corrupted in the primary data file (the primary data file is always number 1) in database ID 13, we can use this statement:

```
-- list of potentially corrupted data pages
-- result will be for example AdventureWorks, 1, 12345
SELECT DB_NAME(database_id) AS databaseName
, file_id
, page_id
FROM msdb..suspect_pages
```

The preceding statement is very simple and provides all the information needed for the page restore action.

- The second option is to check the database's consistency regularly with the DBCC CHECKDB() function. This function returns errors whenever any data page corruption is detected. The following statement calls the function:

```
DBCC CHECKDB() WITH NO_INFOMSGS
```

The NO_INFOMSGS option used in the preceding example eliminates all informational messages from the output of the function. When the function detects some corrupted pages, one error message containing the complete data page identification is generated for each corrupted page.

From this moment, the restore process starts using almost the same task list as in the filegroup restore. The only exception is when identifying the part of the database that is being restored. This is shown in the following syntax:

```
RESTORE DATABASE AdventureWorks
PAGE = '1:12345'
FROM DISK = 'L:\backups\aw.bak'
WITH NORECOVERY
```

The page identifier is provided in the form of `file_id:page_id`; in our example, it is page number 12345 of the primary data file. The rest of the restore process stays unchanged.

After restoring all the data pages, we should remove all the records from the `suspect_pages` table.

So far, we've paid attention to user databases, but system databases also need some care. This final section will show how the system database restore process differs from the user database restore process.

System database restore

System databases are databases created during SQL Server installation and have special meanings. That is why special attention must be paid when restoring them.

The simplest situation is when restoring the `tempdb` database. The `tempdb` database is never backed up, so the restore operation is not possible. When some damage appears, we just need to restart the SQL Server service. SQL Server recreates the `tempdb` database at startup.

Restoring the `msdb` database is quite simple as well. It often has a (recommended) simple recovery model, so in case of failure, we will restore `msdb` in the way we restore the user database: by using the `RESTORE DATABASE .. WITH RECOVERY` statement.

Restoring a database `model` is a little more complicated. When the database `model` is corrupted, the first task is to restart SQL Server with the `-T3608` trace flag in the startup parameters. Then, the restore process is the same as a simple restore process for every user database, but with the trace flag switched on. The database model is sheltered by SQL Server against restoring.

The last and most complicated way to complete the restore process is by restoring the master database. When SQL Server cannot start, we must start the restore process by rebuilding the master database from SQL Server setup. Sometimes, SQL Server can start in **single-user** mode with minimal configuration. We can attempt to start SQL Server in this mode using the proper command switches with the `sqlserver.exe` command. We will use two Command Prompt windows.

In the first Command Prompt, we will start SQL Server in single-user mode with minimal configuration:

```
sqlservr.exe -m -f
```

When SQL Server is started, we must not close this window. Then, we will use the second Command Prompt with the `sqlcmd` utility:

```
sqlcmd.exe -E -S myServerName\instanceName
```

When the `sqlcmd` utility is started (where `-E` means Windows login and `-S` means server name), we will just execute a regular `RESTORE` statement for the master database with recovery. When the restore is successfully executed, SQL Server is stopped in the first Command Prompt. We can then restart SQL Server normally.

Summary

When working with databases, we always need to know how to recover them when damage occurs. This chapter was intended mostly as a syntactical guide for correct backup planning and performing for several types of databases, such as OLTP user databases, big databases, and system databases. A GUI alternative is also possible, but using syntax is a better approach when automating backup tasks when some corruption occurs. Syntax is never lost in dialogs of SQL Server Management Studio.

In this chapter, we learned about internal data handling. This knowledge is an advantage not only for backups and restores, but also for a better understanding when we cover optimizing databases.

We also learned about the backup capabilities of on-premises SQL Server instances. Through examples, we understood how to use backups to restore databases in many scenarios. We also learned the impact of backup procedures already being used on restore abilities that are measured by the RPO and RTO criteria.

Another big task is to secure SQL Server properly. This involves using the security best practices for the service itself, as well as for the authentication and authorization of users. We will describe this in detail in *Chapter 4, Securing Your SQL Server*.

4
Securing Your SQL Server

Securing SQL Server is a crucial task, as SQL Server usually holds very important and sensitive information in your environment. You need to apply many principles in order to properly secure your databases. Fortunately, SQL Server offers many options to help you with securing the data you store on it. Securing an SQL server is quite a complex task; you need to consider that SQL Server is a client application running on the Windows server, which is accessible via a network. In order to fully secure the environment, you need to secure the Windows **Operating System** (**OS**) too and put proper security measures on the network as well.

In this chapter, we will be covering the following topics:

- Configuring SQL Server service accounts
- Configuring authentication and authorization
- Encrypting SQL Server data
- Data Discovery and Classification
- SQL Server vulnerability assessment
- Encrypting SQL Server connections

Configuring SQL Server service accounts

An important part of the configuration of your SQL Server environment is the service accounts that are used for running your SQL Server services. Many of these can be configured immediately during the installation of your SQL Server. There are several options for you to select from while configuring an account for SQL Server services, as follows:

- **Virtual accounts**
- **Managed service accounts**
- **Group managed service accounts**
- **Built-in system accounts**
- **Domain user accounts**
- **Local Windows accounts**

Let's now get into each of the accounts in detail.

Virtual accounts

The default choice of any OS higher than Windows Server 2008 R2 is a **virtual account**. A virtual account is a managed local account for the simple administration of your services. One of the important benefits of virtual accounts is their auto management, so you don't need to worry about regular password updates on your accounts like you have to with domain and local accounts, where you're bound with your enterprise account and password policy.

A virtual account has two forms, depending on whether the account is used for named or default SQL Server instances.

If you are using a default instance, then the account is as follows:

- **NT SERVICE\MSSQLSERVER** for the **Microsoft** (**MS**) SQL database service
- **NT SERVICE\SQLSERVERAGENT** for the MS SQL Server Agent service

If you are using named instances, then the instance name is part of the account name. If your instance name is SQL1, then the accounts will be as follows:

- **NT SERVICE\MSSQL$SQL1** for the MS SQL database service
- **NT SERVICE\SQLAGENT$SQL1** for the MS SQL Server Agent Service

If you are also running SQL Server integration services under virtual account credentials, then the **NT Service\MsDtsServer140** account is used for this service.

When you are configuring the account for SQL Server, enter the virtual account name and supply a blank password during configuration in the SQL Server configuration manager, as shown in the following screenshot:

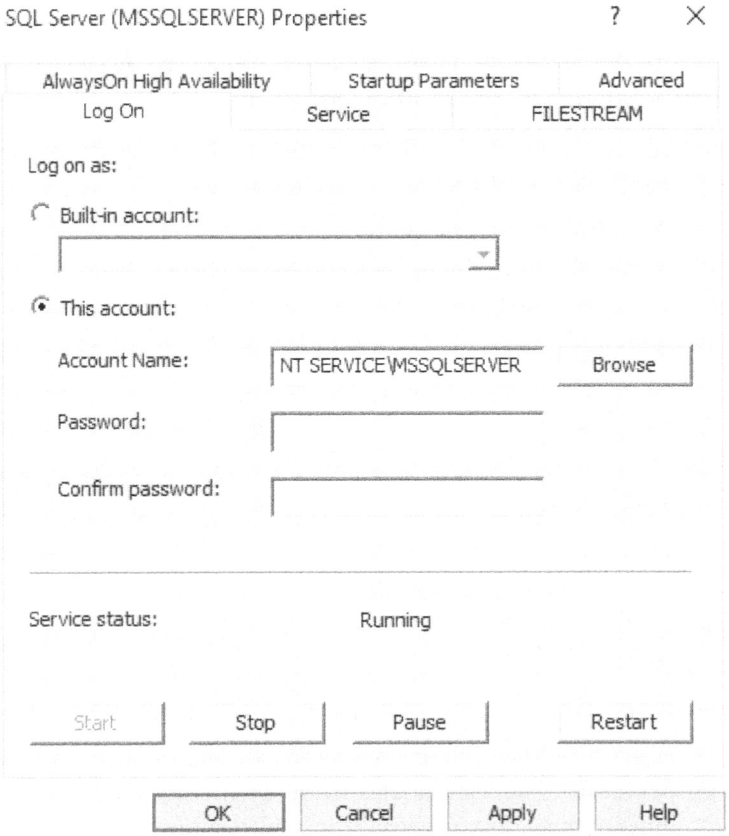

Fig. 4.1 – Configuration for SQL Server service account

Managed service accounts

Another option to run SQL Server services are **Managed Service Accounts** (**MSAs**) and **group Managed Service Accounts** (**gMSAs**).

MSAs were introduced with Windows Server 2008 R2. A new type of such an account called a gMSA was introduced with Windows Server 2012 and offers more options for deployments with SQL Server, especially for **High Availability** (**HA**) scenarios.

MSAs allow you to create an account in the `ActiveDirectory` module and tie that account to a specific computer. Such an account has its own complex password that is, like a virtual account, managed automatically. As MSAs are used only for services running on the computer, you can't use such an account for an interactive login. As this account is tied to just one computer account in the `ActiveDirectory` module, one of the big limitations of MSAs is that they can't be used together with failover cluster configuration.

To create a MSA, we need to use PowerShell with the `ActiveDirectory` module that is being loaded. The code to create a MSA will be as follows:

```
#run this on the Domain Controller
Import-Module ActiveDirectory
New-ADServiceAccount -Name SQLService -Enabled $true
Add-ADComputerServiceAccount -Identity SQL -ServiceAccount
SQLService
#SQL will be the host here, SQLService is the name of the MSA
account
```

Once you run this command, we will have one account ready and tied to a `SQL` computer account. Now, we need to add this account to the SQL Server so that we can use the account for services, as follows:

```
#run this on the SQL Server
Import-Module ActiveDirectory
Install-ADServiceAccount -Identity SQLService
```

Now, we can use the account for the SQL Server services. We will update the configuration again via the SQL Server configuration manager and we will use the name in the form of the `name\MSA$` domain name. Just as with the virtual account, you do not need to supply the password again. The following screenshot illustrates the process:

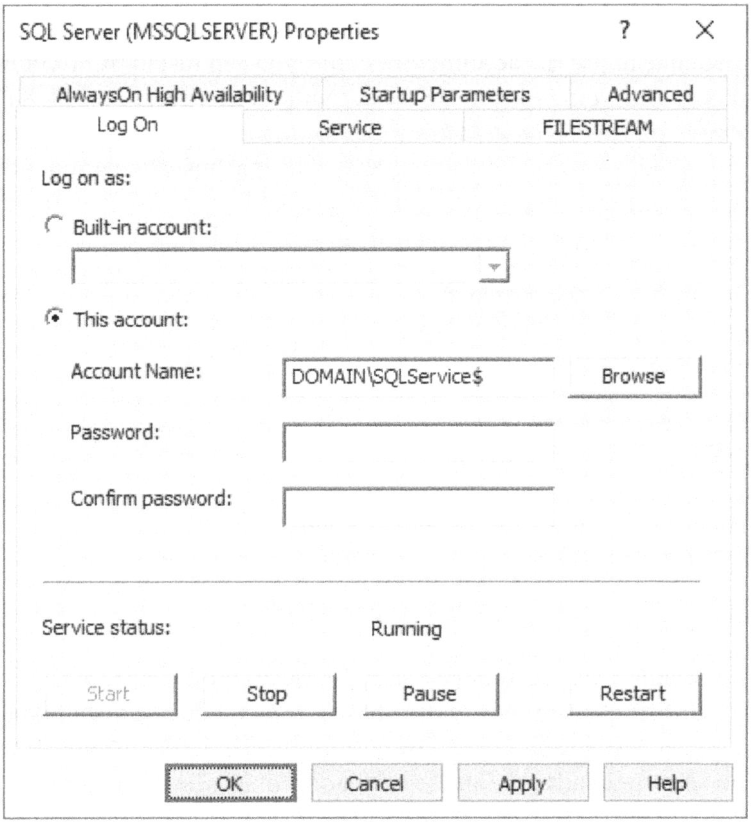

Fig. 4.2 – MSA account as SQL Server service account

gMSAs

gMSAs provide the same functionality as MSAs, but they can be used on multiple servers. gMSAs provide a single identity for services running on a farm, cluster, or behind a load balancer, so they are a perfect fit for a failover cluster scenario in which the previous type of managed service accounts couldn't be used. gMSAs have the same benefit as the older MSAs, where `ActiveDirectory` module automatically manages the account password without any service disruption.

You can create gMSAs with a similar PowerShell script, as with MSAs, as shown in the following code snippet:

```
#run this on the Domain Controller
Import-Module ActiveDirectory
New-ADServiceAccount -name SQLService -DNSHostName sql.contoso.
com -PrincipalsAllowedToRetrieveManagedPassword sql.contoso.com
```

Once you have created the gMSA, you need to install the account again on the server where you would like to use the account. This time, you can install the account on multiple servers. If you would like to use the account on more servers, you have to specify this in the `PrincipalsAllowedToRetrieveManagedPassword` parameter of the PowerShell command, where you have to specify multiple hosts or a group of hosts. These have to be created as computer objects, and if you would like to use the group, you need to add them to the `ActiveDirectory` security group, as follows:

```
#run this on the SQL Server
Import-Module ActiveDirectory
Install-ADServiceAccount -Identity SQLService

#test the account with
Test-ADServiceAccount SQLService
```

This module is available as a part of the **Remote Server Administration** tools, and you can verify the availability of the module via PowerShell, as follows:

```
Get-Module -ListAvailable ActiveDirectory
```

Once you have installed the account, you can add the account via the SQL Server service configuration manager or even specify the account directly during installation of the SQL Server. As this account has to be created by your Active Directory administrator, you can ask for such an account in advance and use the account for the installation.

Built-in system accounts

Mainly with installations of previous versions of SQL Server, you can encounter systems using built-in system accounts that are not recommended for today's deployments. These accounts are still valid and do work; however, they don't provide any isolation from other services and provide too many rights and permissions on the operating system. These built-in accounts include the following:

- **NT AUTHORITY\NETWORKSERVICE**
- **NT AUTHORITY\SYSTEM**
- **NT AUTHORITY\LOCALSERVICE**

Domain user accounts and local Windows accounts

If you would like to use a Windows account to run SQL Server services, make sure that you're using a minimally privileged local or domain account to run your SQL Server. Once you have designated your account to be used with the SQL Server services, **SQL Server Setup** will automatically configure all the required permissions and user rights to your service account so that SQL Server runs correctly.

To change the account, you can again use the configuration manager tool. One disadvantage of domain or local accounts over virtual or managed accounts is the password maintenance required. You need to supply the password to the SQL Server services in the configuration manager and your account will adhere to the Windows password policy.

> **Note**
>
> The Windows password policy is configured at the `ActiveDirectory` domain level with group policy objects, which apply to the whole `ActiveDirectory` domain, or with more detailed password setting objects, which can be linked to specific accounts. By default, passwords for domain accounts have to be updated, and if the password expires, your SQL Server environment may stop working. You need to take special consideration, especially in larger environments, if you're using domain accounts with non-expiring passwords.

Configuring authentication and authorization

SQL Server security works in layers. As a first step, SQL Server will perform authentication, whereby SQL Server determines who you are and if you can log in. If you're successfully logged on, then SQL Server will perform authorization, determining if you can do what you're trying to do. In the next part of the chapter, we will see how to configure server authentication, how to work with server objects, and how to assign server-level permissions.

Authentication

SQL Server comes with two authentication modes, as follows:

- **SQL Server and Windows Authentication mode** (frequently called **Mixed mode**)
- **Windows Authentication mode**

As the names of the modes would suggest, you can always log in with some sort of Windows credential. On top of that, SQL Server can be configured to use its own accounting and isolated accounts stored directly on SQL Server.

You can choose the authentication mode during installation and you can always change the mode afterward in the SQL Server configuration, which requires a service restart after the change. The following screenshot gives a good idea of authentication options:

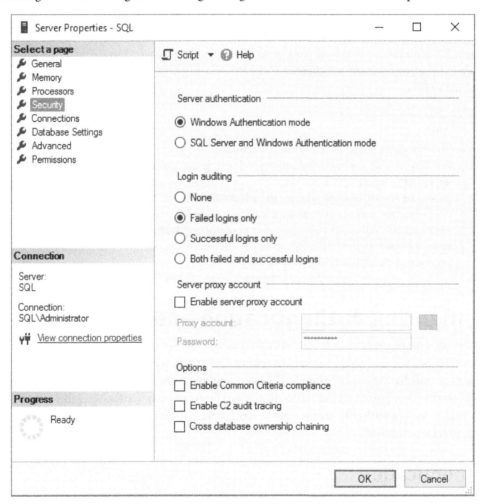

Fig. 4.3 – SQL authentication configuration

As part of the **Windows Authentication mode**, SQL Server can use several different principals to evaluate your access, as follows:

- **Local Windows account**
- **Local Windows group**
- **Domain account**
- **Domain group**

Server logins

For authentication, you need to create a login on SQL Server for one of the four Windows principals mentioned earlier, either with **SQL Server Management Studio**, **TSQL**, or with the `sqlcmd` command-line tool. Having a login on the SQL Server will allow a user to authenticate on the SQL Server if the login is enabled. Logins can be also disabled, which would prevent authentication. Let us take a look at the command script for creating a login:

```
--to add a group run the command
CREATE LOGIN [SQLSERVER\DBA Team] FROM WINDOWS
--this command expects that a group DBA Team is present on the
SQL Server

--to add a single user run the command
CREATE LOGIN [SQLSERVER\Marek] FROM WINDOWS
```

This sample code will add a group called DBA Team as a login to our SQL Server. Any member of such a Windows group will automatically have access to the SQL Server, so you need to be careful on the group membership. It's a simple start for role-based access and administration on the server. Notice that you haven't supplied any password for the Windows login, as SQL Server will utilize the Windows system to perform the authentication for you and does not need to have a password of the login stored anywhere.

This does not apply for SQL Server authentication mode, where you create the same type of object—LOGIN, but this time, it's a SQL Server type of principal that is not created anywhere in the Windows system or ActiveDirectory domain. The SQL Server login is created only on SQL Server and is stored in the master database. Syntax to create the SQL Server login is very similar; notice that we'll just skip the FROM WINDOWS part of the command to create a SQL Server login, as follows:

```
CREATE LOGIN [Marek] WITH PASSWORD = 'P@ssw0rd'
```

When creating a SQL Server type of login, you have to specify a password for the login. SQL Server can enforce several checks on such a password and it's a good idea to use these so that the passwords for SQL Server logins comply with the Windows password policy or your ActiveDirectory domain password policy. To create a login with these checks, you can use the following command:

```
CREATE LOGIN [Marek] WITH PASSWORD='P@ssw0rd',
CHECK_EXPIRATION=ON, CHECK_POLICY=ON
```

> **Note**
>
> Domain password policies are configured at the ActiveDirectory level and are outside the scope of this book. Such a policy usually controls the length of the password, maximum password age—which enforces the changes on the password—and complexity setting to force using more character types such as uppercase, lowercase, and numbers.

Managing login properties

Many logins could have been created without the policy and expiration checks, so if you would like to find them all, you can use the following query to list all SQL Server types of login, where the checks are not in place:

```
SELECT serverproperty('machinename') as 'Server Name', [name],
[is_policy_checked], [is_expiration_checked] FROM master.sys.
sql_logins
WHERE ( [is_policy_checked] = 0 OR [is_expiration_checked] = 0
) and name not like '##MS_%'
```

One more option that you can select while creating a SQL Server type of login is to force the login to change the password during the next login, which is useful when the SQL login is utilized by a developer or administrator but not particularly useful if the login is used by some application that just needs to log in to the SQL Server. By selecting the SQL Server authentication, you are actually extending the options of the authentication as you can't turn off the Windows authentication at all.

You can check many of the parameters of the login with the LOGINPROPERTY function, which can list more than a dozen attributes of your login. The following sample script will check for all SQL logins where the password has not been updated for more than 6 months:

```
SELECT name,loginproperty([name], 'PasswordLastSetTime')
FROM sys.sql_logins
WHERE loginproperty([name], 'PasswordLastSetTime') <
DATEADD(month,-6,GETDATE())
```

> **Note**
>
> For more information about the built-in function, refer to the *Microsoft Books Online* documentation at `https://docs.microsoft.com/en-us/sql/t-sql/functions/loginproperty-transact-sql`, which lists all the parameters for the function.

Taking the preceding script into a scheduled task that can check for such logins on a weekly or monthly basis and running such a script manually is not that big a help. It can turn out to be very useful to run such a script automatically on a regular basis. For such a task, you need a SQL Server Agent job with a proper schedule, and you can update the script to send out an email with results to the **database administrator** (**DBA**) team.

This regular check on your logins is not the only one you can do on your server. If you create a SQL Server login and you don't enforce any policies, you can actually create the login with any password you want, despite the complexity or the length. You'll be surprised how many logins are created with a password the same as the login name on many systems. The following script will help you find all those logins on your machine:

```
SELECT SERVERPROPERTY('machinename') AS 'Server Name', name AS
'Login With Password Same As Name'
FROM master.sys.sql_logins
WHERE PWDCOMPARE(name,password_hash) = 1
ORDER by name
```

The worst-case scenario is that the logins with blank passwords can be found as well with the same PWDCOMPARE function. The following code will reveal all SQL Server logins with a blank password:

```
SELECT name FROM sys.sql_logins
WHERE PWDCOMPARE('', password_hash) = 1 ;
```

Authorization

Once you have successfully logged in to SQL Server, SQL checks your access level with each operation—in other words, if you're authorized to perform any operation. This is controlled via the permissions that are assigned to the logins, or the server roles.

Roles are there to simplify the administration for us as they include many permissions on the server and can speed up the securing of the server. A server role is a principal that groups other principals such as logins together at the server level. There is a default set of nine server roles that are configured automatically on each SQL Server installation.

Fixed server roles

There are nine predefined fixed server roles on each server that you can use as a starting point for securing the SQL Server environment. These roles cannot be dropped; you can only update the role membership. The roles are listed in the following screenshot:

sysadmin	Members of this role can perform any activity on the server
bulkadmin	Members can run BULK INSERT and use the bcp.exe tool
diskadmin	Members can manage disk files
processadmin	Members can KILL processes running on SQL Server
public	Each login is a member of the public role; if a principal is not granted any permission on an object, it inherits the permissions from the public role
securityadmin	Members can manage logins and their properties
serveradmin	Members can change server-level configuration and shut down SQL Server
setupadmin	Members can create linked servers with TSQL commands
dbcreator	Members can create, alter, drop, and restore databases

Fig. 4.4 – Server roles

If you would like to assign a login to a role, you can update the role membership via **TSQL** or **SQL Server Management Studio**. With **SQL Server Management Studio**, you can select multiple roles at the same time via the checkboxes and then by clicking on **OK**, as shown in the following screenshot:

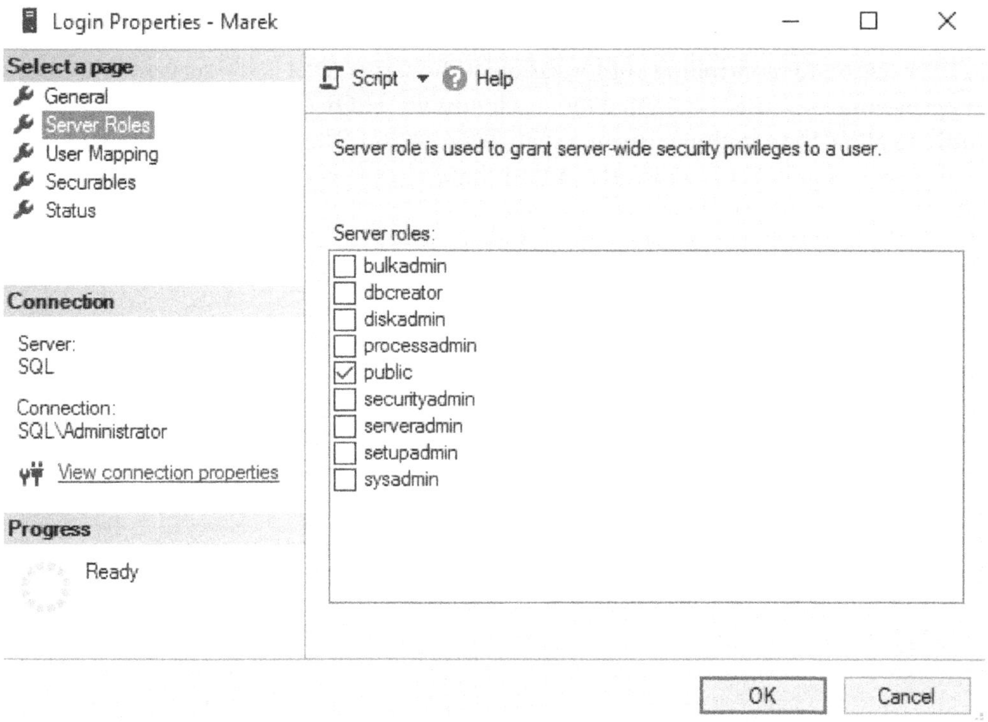

Fig. 4.5 – Server role assignment

With **TSQL**, it's quite simple; to add a login to any role, you just enter the following command:

```
ALTER SERVER ROLE [sysadmin] ADD MEMBER [Marek] --for SQL Login
type
ALTER SERVER ROLE [sysadmin] ADD MEMBER [DOMAIN\Marek] --for
Windows Login type, including the domain name
```

To remove a member from a role, you can use a similar command with just the DROP MEMBER syntax, as follows:

```
ALTER SERVER ROLE [sysadmin] DROP MEMBER [Marek] --removes
login Marek from sysadmin server role
```

Working with permissions on the server

Another option for controlling authorization at the server level is the server permissions. Server permissions can be assigned to your logins via **TSQL** or **SQL Server Management Studio** to allow the login to perform a specific operation. The list of permissions available on the server is quite long, and you can find the whole list via the following query:

```
SELECT * FROM sys.fn_builtin_permissions('') where class_desc =
'SERVER'
```

Server permissions that you can grant are as follows:

ADMINISTER BULK OPERATIONS	Allows the user to bulk insert data into the SQL Server via the bcp.exe tool, BULK INSERT statement, and OPENROWSET(BULK) statement	AUTHENTICATE SERVER	Allows the user to authenticate to this SQL Server
ALTER ANY AVAILABILITY GROUP	Right to failover any availability group, including to create one	CONNECT ANY DATABASE	Allows the user to connect to all databases on the SQL Server
ALTER ANY CONNECTION	Allows the user to terminate any connection with the KILL statement	CONNECT SQL	Allows the user to connect to the SQL Server
ALTER ANY CREDENTIAL	Allows the user to modify any credential objects	CONTROL SERVER	Allows the user to have nearly sysadmin-equivalent rights, which combine multiple permissions
ALTER ANY DATABASE	Allows the user to change database options and create new databases	CREATE ANY DATABASE	Allows the user to create new databases and restore databases
ALTER ANY ENDPOINT	Allows the user to modify endpoints, including creating new ones	CREATE AVAILABILITY GROUP	Allows the user to create new Availability groups
ALTER ANY EVENT NOTIFICATION	Allows the user to modify event notifications and create new ones	CREATE DDL EVENT NOTIFICATION	Allows the user to create a server DDL trigger
ALTER ANY EVENT SESSION	Allows the user to modify event traces and create new traces	CREATE ENDPOINT	Allows the user to create SQL Server endpoints
ALTER ANY LINKED SERVER	Allows the user to create new linked servers, but only with T-SQL commands; via GUI, it's available only to sysadmin role members	CREATE SERVER ROLE	Allows the user to create user-defined server roles
		CREATE TRACE EVENT NOTIFICATION	Allows the user to create trace event notifications
ALTER ANY LOGIN	Allows the user to modify logins on the instance, reset passwords, and create new logins	EXTERNAL ACCESS ASSEMBLY	Allows the user to create assemblies that require external access
ALTER ANY SERVER AUDIT	Allows the user to modify and create audits and server audit specifications	IMPERSONATE ANY LOGIN	Allows the user to impersonate any login on the SQL Server
ALTER ANY SERVER ROLE	Allows the user to modify user-defined server roles	SELECT ALL USER SECURABLES	Allows the user to view all data in all databases, where the user can connect to
ALTER RESOURCES	Allows the user to change system resources	SHUTDOWN	Allows the user to shut down a SQL Server instance via the TSQL command
ALTER SERVER STATE	Allows the user to change server state, including the right to view server state	UNSAFE ASSEMBLY	Allows the user to create assemblies that require unsafe access
		VIEW ANY DATABASE	Allows the user to view the definition of any database
ALTER SETTINGS	Allows the user to change server-level settings	VIEW ANY DEFINITION	Allows the user to view the definition on any object on the SQL Server instance, including the VIEW ANY DATABASE permission
ALTER TRACE	Allows the user to modify server trace sessions	VIEW SERVER STATE	Allows the user to view server state, which is used by Dynamic Management Views and functions

Fig. 4.6 – Server permissions list

As an example, let's take **Dynamic Management Views (DMVs)**, many of which are restricted only to high-privileged users (members of server roles) or users who have a VIEW SERVER STATE permission. To grant such a permission, you can run the following SQL statement:

```
GRANT VIEW SERVER STATE TO [Marek]
```

This will allow one login to query most of the DMVs to troubleshoot and diagnose SQL Server. With many of the permissions, you can use one more option, WITH GRANT OPTION, which will allow the login to not only perform specific actions but also to grant this action to another login. To remove the permission, we use the REVOKE keyword, which will remove the previously granted permission to the login, as follows:

```
REVOKE VIEW SERVER STATE TO [Marek] AS [sa]
```

Bear in mind that the permission may be part of some server-wide role permission list. Revoking the explicit permission does not necessarily prevent the user from viewing the server state. To do that, you will need to explicitly deny the permission to the user by running the following command:

```
DENY VIEW SERVER STATE TO [Marek]
```

To remove the DENY permission, you have to use the REVOKE command again in the same way as we did with the GRANT permission option. As you can see, REVOKE clears either a granted or a denied permission.

Auditing

SQL Server comes with several options that can be used for the auditing of login events and much more. One of the options is to use basic login auditing, which can be configured on the **server properties/security** page via **SQL Server Management Studio**. There, you can choose what sort of login audit is performed. By default, SQL Server comes with the **Failed logins only** option selected, which may not be enough for many environments where, due to business or security requirements, you have to capture all login attempts.

This audit stores all the information to the SQL Server log, which you can review via Management Studio or, if needed, via any text editor, as the log is a plain text file. On a highly loaded system, this log can generate an enormous amount of information, so you need to consider if this is really the best option to store information about login sessions. This log is also used as an error log, so any error that is logged is then surrounded by many noise messages about successful or failed login events.

SQL Server comes with another audit object that can be utilized. This audit object is available for several versions already (since 2008) and can be used to audit the same failed and successful logons and much more. A great benefit of this audit object is the flexibility of the configuration, as the specifications for the audit can be either server-wide or database-wide. You can choose if the audit should store the information to a text file or directly to Windows event logs. Database-level auditing was previously available only in the Enterprise Edition, but since SQL Server 2016 Service Pack 1, it's available in all editions.

Configuring a server audit

Audit configuration has several components—two of them are primary audit and audit specifications. Audit is a configuration object where you have to select how to store the captured events, how resilient the audit will be, and so on.

The specification is another object that you have to create, and there you specify which events should be captured, as illustrated in the following screenshot:

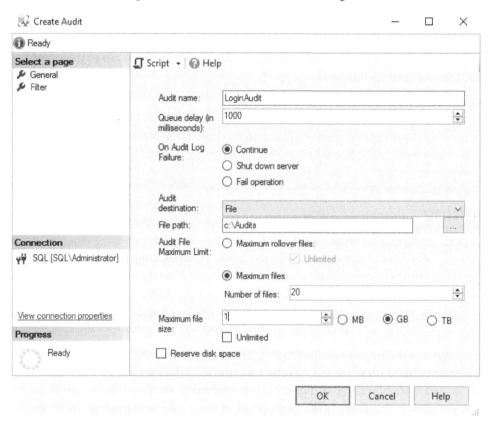

Fig. 4.7 – Audit configuration

To create the audit on the server, you can use the following **TSQL** code:

```
CREATE SERVER AUDIT [LoginAudit]
TO FILE ( FILEPATH = N'E:\Audits', MAXSIZE = 1024 MB ,MAX_FILES
= 20,RESERVE_DISK_SPACE = OFF )
WITH ( QUEUE_DELAY = 1000 ,ON_FAILURE = CONTINUE )
```

This query will create an `Audit` object that will store all the information to text files. These will be located in the `E:\Audits` folder on your server and can use up to 20 GB of space on your drive—a maximum of 20 files with a maximum size of 1 GB each. If such an audit fails to store any event, all operations will continue. Until now, we have only configured the storage for the events but we have not configured any events to capture. This is where **server audit specifications** come into the picture.

Server audit specifications

Server audit specifications define which action groups (events grouped by the scope of action) will be tracked by your audit. To configure the audit specifications, use a **TSQL** scriptor a **Graphical User Interface** (**GUI**). Let us look at the following script to create a server audit:

```
CREATE SERVER AUDIT SPECIFICATION [LogonAuditConfig]
FOR SERVER AUDIT [LogonAudit]
ADD (FAILED_LOGIN_GROUP),
ADD (SUCCESSFUL_LOGIN_GROUP)
```

With this **TSQL** script, we have configured the audit to collect information about successful and failed login events to a separate file on your SQL Server. You can, of course, add many more action groups to this audit and create more audits on your server. One of my favorite action groups for the auditing is `SERVER_ROLE_MEMBER_CHANGE_GROUP`, which tracks information about changes in your server roles. You can then see who updated any role membership and when, by either adding or dropping a member from the role.

As you can see in the following screenshot from **SQL Server Management Studio**, there are many other useful action groups worth considering for the audit on your server:

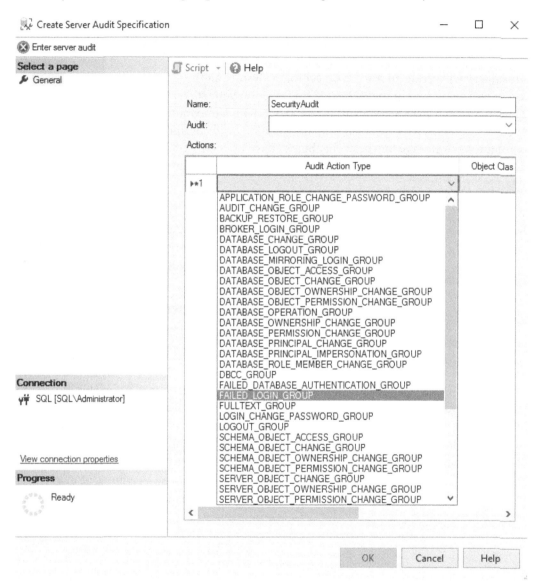

Fig. 4.8 – Audit specification configuration

Even though this audit is quite lightweight (based on **Extended Events**, to be discussed in following chapters), you should not just select everything and expect no performance hits on the server. As with everything else in SQL Server, you need to carefully consider which events you should collect. My favorite basic set for security auditing on the server includes just a few action groups and can be configured as follows:

```
CREATE SERVER AUDIT SPECIFICATION [Security audit
specifications]
FOR SERVER AUDIT [SecurityAudit]
ADD (SERVER_ROLE_MEMBER_CHANGE_GROUP),
ADD (AUDIT_CHANGE_GROUP),
ADD (SERVER_PERMISSION_CHANGE_GROUP),
ADD (SERVER_PRINCIPAL_CHANGE_GROUP),
ADD (LOGIN_CHANGE_PASSWORD_GROUP)
WITH (STATE = ON)
```

Such a basic set can be always modified, filtered, and tuned to fit your environment needs and requirements. Usually, a compliance and governance team will help you in designing the required collection in larger environments.

Configuring credentials

A credential is an object associated with authentication information required to connect to an external resource. If you need to connect to any external resource outside of SQL Server, you need a proper way of authenticating to the resource. This resource can be, for example, a file share with important **Extensible Markup Language** (**XML**) files to be processed daily on SQL Server. In such cases, a credential object can be used to connect to this file share.

Creating a credential can be done via TSQL or SSMS; in most cases, it's a Windows account with a proper password. The following code will create a new credential on the server:

```
CREATE CREDENTIAL [WindowsAcct] WITH IDENTITY = N'DOMAIN\
ServiceAcct', SECRET = N'P@ssw0rd'
--you need to specify the password for the Windows account here
as a plain text
```

You can map the credential to any amount of SQL Server logins so that the login has access to external resources. One credential can be used many times, but a SQL login can have only one credential mapped for usage. To map a credential to a SQL Server login, you can use the following **TSQL** query:

```
ALTER LOGIN [Marek] ADD CREDENTIAL [WindowsAcct]
```

Credentials and proxies in SQL Server Agent

Credentials are frequently used with SQL Server Agent jobs. When you are configuring SQL Server Agent jobs for any automated task, you have to choose a category for the job step. Several categories allow you to select the security context, which will be used to run the particular part of the scheduled task. There is usually an option visible to run the job step within the context of the SQL Server Agent account, but that is reserved to **sysadmin** role members only.

If you are not a **sysadmin**, you need to choose a job proxy, which is in the end mapped to the existing credential. This choice is active for most of the step types, except the TSQL script step, which does not utilize a proxy, as illustrated in the following screenshot:

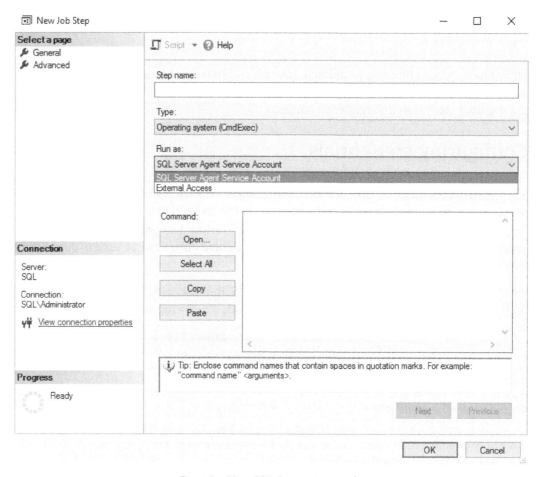

Fig. 4.9 – New SQL Server Agent job

We already know how to create a credential, so now we need to create an agent proxy that will utilize the credential. We can do this via **SQL Server Management Studio**. In this case, it's simpler compared to the **TSQL** script, where we would need to use several stored procedures with proper parameter mappings.

In the dialog for creating a new proxy, we need to select a proper subsystem that will be used by the proxy. With SQL Server 2019, the choices are smaller than with older versions, and the available subsystems are as follows:

- **Operating System (CmdExec)**

- **PowerShell**

- **SQL Server Analysis Services Query**

- **SQL Server Analysis Services Command**

- **SQL Server Integration Services Package**

The following screenshot gives us a good idea of the different subsystems in SQL Server 2019:

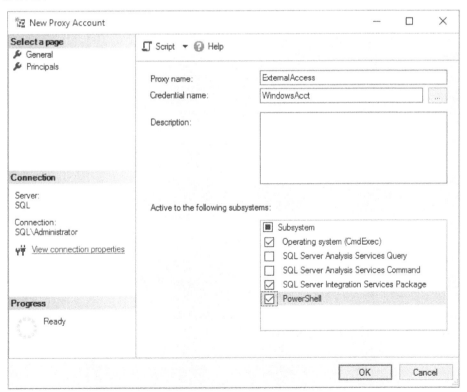

Fig. 4.10 – Configuration of a proxy account

You can configure one proxy for more subsystems, as you can see in the preceding screenshot. Once you create the proxy, you need to configure who can utilize the proxy via the **Principals** tab in the proxy configuration. Yet again, only sysadmin role members have default access to utilize the proxy for the agent jobs. You can add the following principals to the proxy security:

- **Server logins**
- **Server roles**
- **Roles from MSDB database**

To add a new proxy account, you can use the **Management Studio** and **SQL Server Agent** sections, where you can configure the proxies for various subsystems, as illustrated in the following screenshot:

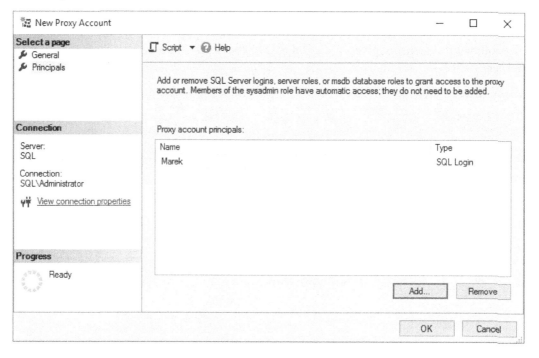

Fig. 4.11 – Security configuration of a proxy

Once we have added proper principals (**SQL Login Marek**, in this case), such a login can utilize the proxy to run the OS commands from SQL Server Agent jobs.

Encrypting SQL Server data

When you are storing sensitive data on your SQL Server, you may need to encrypt the data to protect the data from accidental misuse. Your company may have business and technical requirements to encrypt the data, or even legal requirements to encrypt any sensitive information.

SQL Server has many options on how to protect data with encryption, depending on the need to protect data at rest or in transit. The whole encryption ecosystem in SQL Server is quite complex and offers many options, as can be seen in the following diagram:

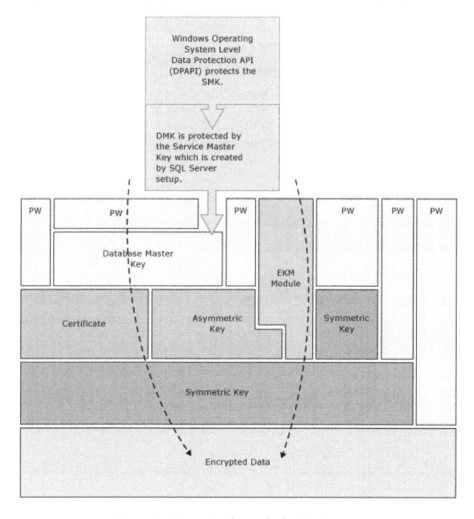

Fig. 4.12 – Encryption hierarchy for SQL Server

Transparent Data Encryption

One of the options on how to encrypt the data in the database is **Transparent Data Encryption** option. This feature has been available since SQL Server 2008 and works at the **input/output (I/O)** level. Both file types—data and log—are encrypted on the disk, and SQL Server does the encryption once the data is written to disk and the decryption once the data is retrieved from the disk into memory. This encryption works at the page level and does not have an effect on the size of the database.

Data encryption is totally transparent to the application, so you can turn on the encryption for any database and any application. This encryption is symmetric using a **Database Encryption Key (DEK)**, which is stored in the database boot record and is protected with either one of the following:

- Server certificate created in the master database

- Asymmetric key protected by the **Extensible Key Management** or **EKM Module**

The server certificate is then protected by the master key stored in the master database. To turn on the transparent database encryption, you need to do the following:

1. Create a master key in the master database.

2. Create a server certificate in the master database.

3. Create a database encryption key protected by the certificate.

4. Turn on the encryption.

You can use the following code to turn on the encryption:

```
USE master;
CREATE MASTER KEY ENCRYPTION BY PASSWORD = 'Pa$$w0rdF0rM4$t3R';
CREATE CERTIFICATE MyServerCert WITH SUBJECT = 'DEK
Certificate';


USE AdventureWorks
CREATE DATABASE ENCRYPTION KEY WITH ALGORITHM = AES_128
ENCRYPTION BY SERVER CERTIFICATE MyServerCert;
ALTER DATABASE AdventureWorks SET ENCRYPTION ON;
```

Database encryption can also be managed via the GUI, where, in the **Tasks/Manage Database Encryption** option of the database, you can choose to turn the encryption on and off and configure which certificate should be used to protect the database encryption key and which key length should be used for the database encryption key, as illustrated in the following screenshot:

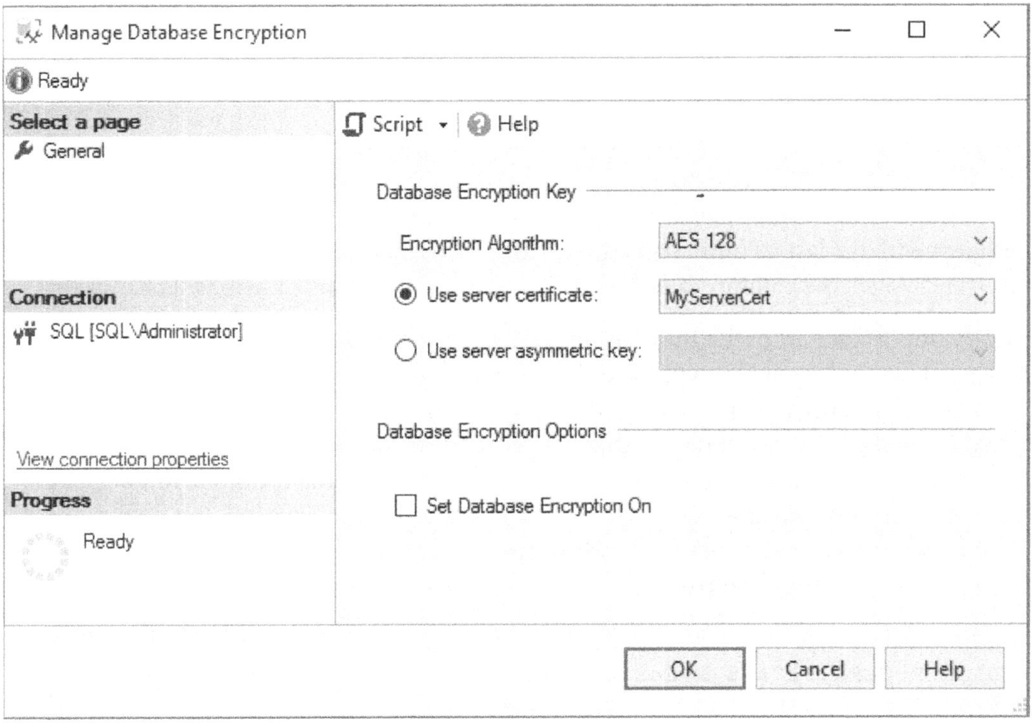

Fig. 4.13 – Database encryption management

Turning on database encryption may be a complex task that requires a lot of time. During the transition stage of your database when the database is getting encrypted, you can use the database for your application, with some limitations. You can't modify the database configuration, back up the database, work with snapshots, and so on. To monitor the progress of the encryption, you can use one of the DMVs named sys.dm_database_ encryption_keys, as illustrated in the following code snippet:

```
SELECT database_id, encryption_state, key_algorithm, key_
length, percent_complete
FROM sys.dm_database_encryption_keys
```

The result from such a query may be similar to this one on your server:

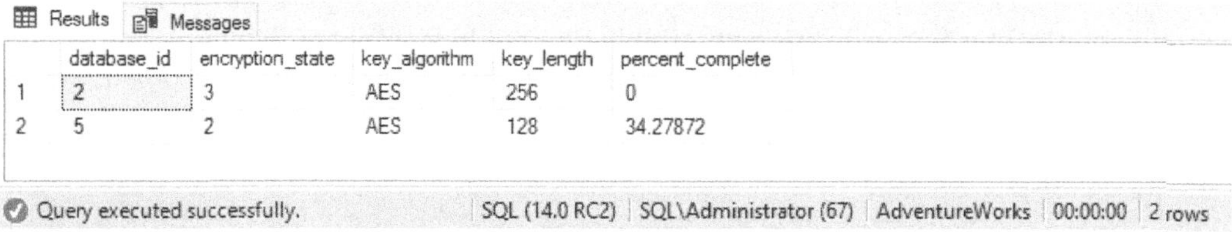

Fig. 4.14 – Encrypted databases

There are two databases with enabled encryption on this server; one of them is the AdventureWorks database for which we did turn on the encryption, and the other one is a TempDB system database that is encrypted automatically. You can monitor the progress with the last column, named percent_complete. When the database has been encrypted, the column value will be 0 and encryption_state will change to 3.

A very important part of the transparent database encryption is also the certificate management. Once you encrypt the database, you may get a warning that the certificate has not yet been backed up. This is very important for any **disaster recovery** (**DR**) situations; otherwise, you'll not be able to restore the database. Not only are the database files on the server encrypted, but backups also use the same encryption. If you need to restore the database to another server or you lose your master database and you need to rebuild your server, you won't be able to restore the encrypted database without having a certificate on the server. To back up your certificate, you can use the following code:

```
USE master
BACKUP CERTIFICATE MyServerCert TO FILE = 'C:\Certificate\
MyServerCert.cer'
WITH PRIVATE KEY (FILE = 'C:\Certificate\MyServerCert.pfx',
ENCRYPTION BY PASSWORD = 'Str0ngP@ssw0rd')
```

To create a certificate from these two files, you can use the CREATE CERTIFICATE command with proper parameters, as follows:

```
USE master
CREATE CERTIFICATE MyServerCert FROM FILE = 'C:\Certificate\
MyServerCert.cer'
WITH PRIVATE KEY (FILE = 'C:\Certificate\MyServerCert.pfx',
DECRYPTION BY PASSWORD = 'Str0ngP@ssw0rd')
```

Always Encrypted

SQL Server 2016 has introduced a new way to encrypt the data on SQL Server, which allows the application to encrypt the data and never reveal the encryption keys to the database engine. In this way, not even a sysadmin of SQL Server can read the decrypted values stored in your tables. Unlike the transparent data encryption, which works at the database level, **Always Encrypted** works at the column level. Unlike the regular column-level encryption, **Always Encrypted** allows more types of queries on the data such as equality comparisons, joins, group by queries, and so on. Its structure can be seen in the following diagram:

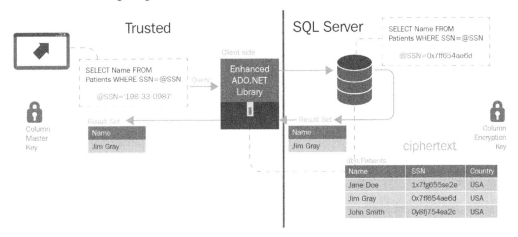

Fig. 4.15 – Always Encrypted structure

Always Encrypted comes with two flavors of encryption, as follows:

- **Randomized**
- **Deterministic**

Deterministic encryption always generates the same ciphertext for a given value, whereas **Randomized** does not and is less predictable. This has an impact on the usage of the encrypted data. With **Randomized** encryption, you can't use joins, group by, indexing, or any equality searches.

To encrypt the data with **Always Encrypted**, we go by the following steps:

1. Right-click on the database and go to **Tasks/Encrypt columns**.
2. Choose the table/column you want to encrypt.
3. Select the encryption type from **Randomized/Deterministic**.
4. Configure the **Master Key Configuration** option.

The **Master Key Configuration** option allows you to select the column master key and the key store. You can store the keys in a **Windows certificate store** or an **Azure Key Vault** service. If you're using the **Windows certificate store**, you can configure whether to use the local user or local computer store for the certificate, as illustrated in the following screenshot:

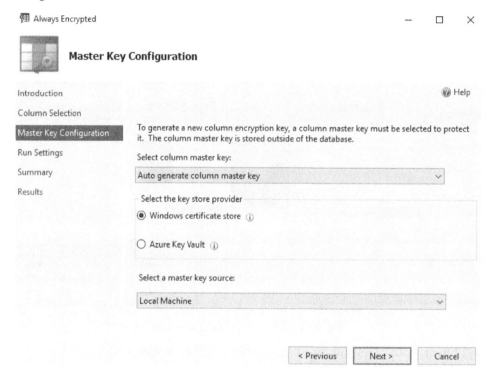

Fig. 4.16 – Master Key Configuration for Always Encrypted

Once this is turned on, it will automatically encrypt the content of the selected columns, which will be encrypted with the selected keys.

Data Discovery and Classification

Whenever you need to discover and report any sensitive data in your database, you can use a new feature called **Data Discovery and Classification** . When you are discovering the data, you must also classify and label any data found that fits your classification needs. There are several use cases for this feature, as follows:

- Meeting data privacy standards (for example, **General Data Protection Regulation (GDPR)**; **Payment Card Industry Data Security Standard (PCI DSS)**; **Sarbanes-Oxley (SOX)**; **Health Insurance Portability and Accountability Act (HIPAA)**)

- Controlling access to highly sensitive data (for example, **personally identifiable information (PII)**)

> **Note**
> This feature is available for SQL Server 2012 and newer and was introduced with **SQL Server Management Studio** 17.5; however, it's recommended to use the latest version of **SQL Server Management Studio**.

While you are connected to the SQL Server, you can run classification on your database with the following steps:

1. Right-click the database on which you would like to classify data.
2. Choose **Tasks**.
3. Select **Data Discovery and Classification**.
4. Click on **Classify data**.

In the following screenshot, you can see the classification task on the WideWorldImporters database:

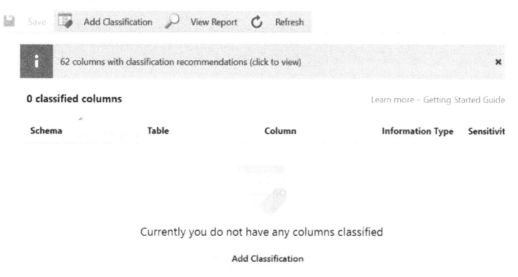

Fig. 4.17 – Classifying data in the database

The data classification task automatically detects columns possibly containing sensitive data. This is based on the column names, so if your database is using cryptic column names or non-English column names, the automatic suggestion won't find much.

You can, however, add your own classifications via the **Add Classification** button. In the following screenshot, you can see how to configure a data classification manually for a selected column:

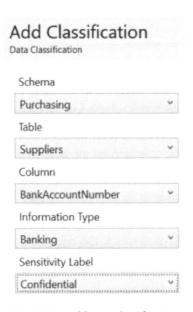

Fig. 4.18 – Adding a classification

There are several information types and sensitivity labels to choose from. As an available **Information Type**, you can use the following:

- **Networking**
- **Contact Info**
- **Credentials**
- **Credit Card**
- **Banking**

- **Financial**
- **Other**
- **Name**
- **National ID**
- **SSN**
- **Health**
- **Date of Birth**

And you can add the following labels to such info:

- **Public**
- **General**
- **Confidential**
- **Confidential – GDPR**
- **Highly Confidential**
- **Highly Confidential – GDPR**
- **N/A**

Once you have classified your data (and saved your choice with the **Save** button), you can generate a report of your data in the database based on their labels and information types by following these steps:

1. Right-click the database on which you would like to generate a report.
2. Choose **Tasks**.
3. Select **Data Discovery and Classification**.
4. Click on **Generate Report**.

In the following screenshot, you can see a sample of a generated report for the `WideWorldImporters` sample database:

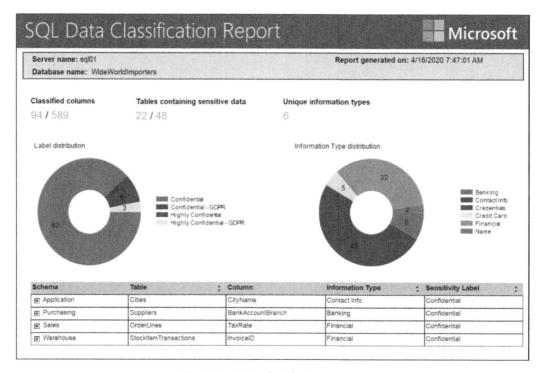

Fig. 4.19 – Data classification report

Not only you can use the Management Studio GUI for data classification—you can also use TSQL code to add sensitivity labels to your data.

The following is a sample of code that will add a `Highly Confidential` label and information type of `Financial`:

```
ADD SENSITIVITY CLASSIFICATION TO
    Purchasing.Suppliers.BankAccountNumber
    WITH (LABEL = 'Highly Confidential', INFORMATION_TYPE ='
Financial')
```

Not only can you use built-in classification, which is included in **SQL Server Management Studio,** but you can also customize the information policy and import this policy to your system. This policy is stored outside of SQL Server and is used by Management Studio. The format of the policy is a `.json` file, which includes labels, information types, and keywords that enable SSMS to detect the possible candidates for information protection.

SQL Server vulnerability assessment

SQL Server Management Studio 17.4 was released with a very handy feature—scanning for vulnerabilities on your databases. It's always better to run with the latest version of **SQL Server Management Studio** (screenshots in this book are based on the *18.4* and *18.5* versions). This vulnerability assessment is supported on any SQL Server with version 2012 and higher and checks for a predefined set of vulnerabilities.

To create a new scan, you have to do the following:

1. Right-click your database.
2. Choose **Tasks**.
3. Select **Vulnerability Assessment**.
4. Click on **Scan for Vulnerabilities**.

Once the scan is complete, you will be presented with a result view in your SSMS application, with a summary about failed and passed checks.

In the following screenshot, you can see a sample scan with several categories of findings—high, medium, and low risk:

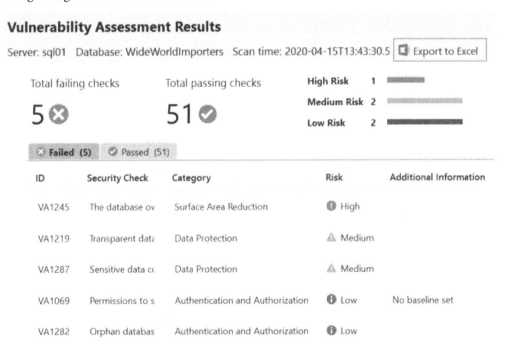

Fig. 4.20 – Vulnerability assessment report

For the failed checks, you are presented with detailed description, impact, and remediation steps. In some environments, the checks can generate false positives, so you have an option to **Approve as Baseline** setting for any checks that you're failing due to the enterprise policies of your environment.

For larger environments, it's rather impractical to use **SQL Server Management Studio** to run these vulnerability assessments. If you need to scan more servers, you can utilize the `SqlServer` PowerShell module for this task with the `Invoke-SqlVulnerabilityAssessmentScan` command.

In the following screenshot, you can see the output of the scan in PowerShell:

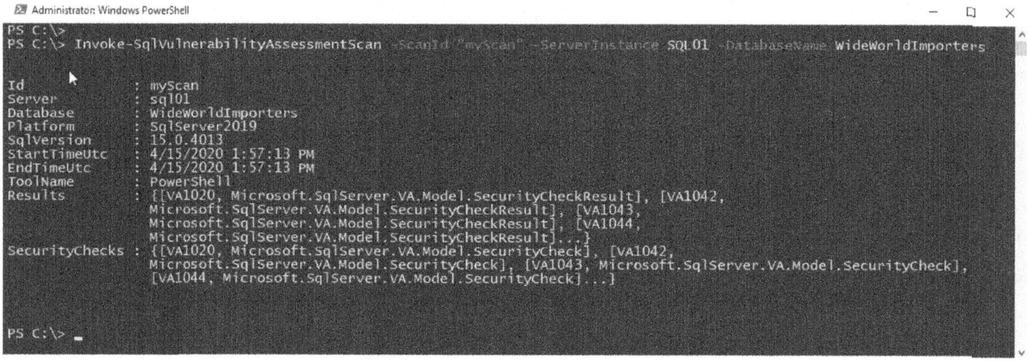

Fig. 4.21 – PowerShell vulnerability assessment scan

Let's now see how to encrypt SQL Server connections.

Encrypting SQL Server connections

Connection to the SQL Server is by default not encrypted, until you configure your server and client otherwise. When you're connecting to the SQL Server with **SQL Server Management Studio**, you can choose to encrypt your connection to the server. In the following screenshot, we can see how the server connection is configured and how Management Studio responds to such a connection attempt:

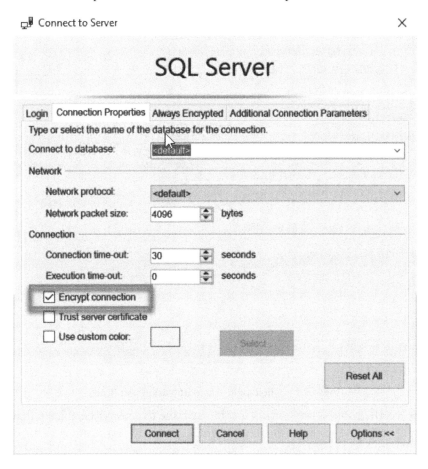

Fig. 4.22 – Encrypted connection to SQL Server

Let's see how SQL Server responds to such a connection request in the following screenshot:

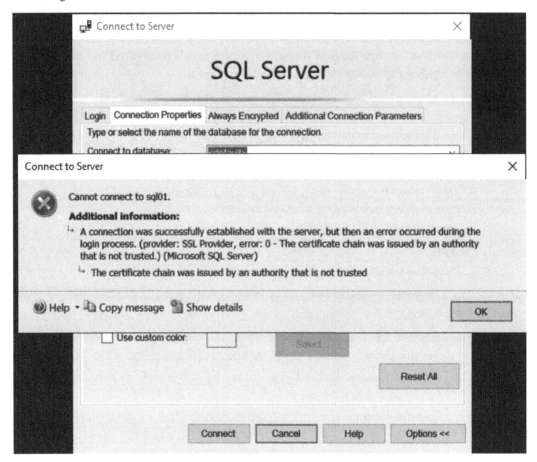

Fig. 4.23 – Failed login due to untrusted certificate

As you can see, the connection was not established due to a server certificate that is not trusted. If the SQL Server is not configured to use any certificate, it will automatically generate a self-signed one during the instance startup, as illustrated in the following screenshot:

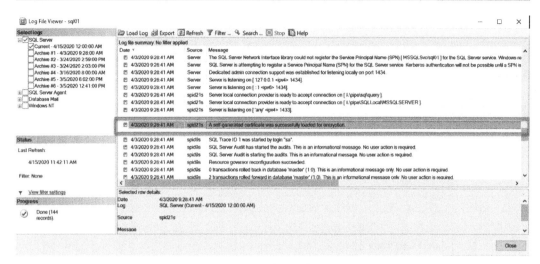

Fig. 4.24 – Log snippet with certificate creation event

What you would actually like to do is to utilize a certificate created by a **Certification Authority (CA)** for your SQL Server.

> **Note**
>
> Obtaining a certificate is a complex task that is heavily dependent on your infrastructure and business needs. You can use either an internal or external CA to get the proper certificate for your server. With HA deployments, certificate management gets more complex since you have to consider either a **SQL Server Virtual Network Name (SQL VNN)** for **AlwaysOn Failover Cluster Instances** or a **Availability Group Listener** name for **AlwaysOn Availability Groups** deployment.

Providing you have obtained your certificate for SQL Server, you can use SQL Server **Configuration Manager** to select or import (which is new for SQL Server 2019) the certificate for **Transport Layer Security (TLS)** connection encryption. The following are the steps required to install a certificate for a SQL Server instance:

1. Open SQL Server **Configuration Manager**.

2. Navigate to SQL Server **Network Configuration**.

3. Right-click **Protocols for MSSQLSERVER** (or your instance name).

4. Choose the **Certificate** tab and either locate the certificate via the drop-down menu if the certificate is already installed or choose **Import** to install a new certificate.

5. Select **Next** and **Next** again to finish the import task.

In the following screenshot, you can see the import of the certificate:

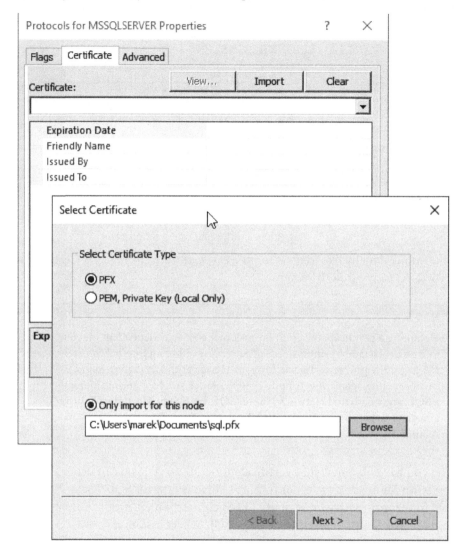

Fig. 4.25 – Importing a certificate for SQL Server

Once the certificate is imported, you need to restart your SQL Server service for the changes to take effect. In today's networks, you would like to utilize encryption based on the TLS1.2 protocol; however, if you check your operation system's registry, you may be quite surprised about default installations. In the following screenshot, you can see the registry setting from the default installation of Windows Server 2019:

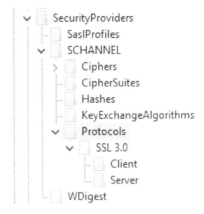

Fig. 4.26 – Encryption protocol configuration

To configure your server to use modern TLS1.2 protocol encryption, you have to do the following:

1. Open **Registry Editor**.

2. Navigate to HKLM\SYSTEM\CurrentControlSet\Control\
    SecurityProviders\SCHANNEL\Protocols hive.

3. Create appropriate TLS1.2 entries.

The required TLS1.2 entries are as follows:

```
[HKEY_LOCAL_MACHINE\SYSTEM\CurrentControlSet\Control\
SecurityProviders\SCHANNEL\Protocols\TLS 1.2]
```

```
[HKEY_LOCAL_MACHINE\SYSTEM\CurrentControlSet\Control\
SecurityProviders\SCHANNEL\Protocols\TLS 1.2\Client]
"DisabledByDefault"=dword:00000000 "Enabled"=dword:00000001
```

```
[HKEY_LOCAL_MACHINE\SYSTEM\CurrentControlSet\Control\
SecurityProviders\SCHANNEL\Protocols\TLS 1.2\Server]
"DisabledByDefault"=dword:00000000 "Enabled"=dword:00000001
```

Once all components of the configuration are in place, you can connect to your SQL Server with encrypted communication and verify that your connection is encrypted. You will need the following to check that your connection is encrpted:

*   Proper SQL Server build

*   Installed and trusted certificate

*   Configured OS registry

In the following screenshot, you can see **SQL Server Management Studio** working with encrypted connection (little padlock icon):

¥⌐ Connected. (1/1)   🔒 sql01 (15.0 RTM)   sql01\marek (74)   master   00:00:00   0 rows

Fig. 4.27 – Encrypted connection to SQL Server

Using encryption for the SQL Server connections adds another security layer to your configuration and provides protection from several possible network attacks.

Summary

Security is a very important part of your SQL Server deployment, and in this chapter, we have seen many options that you can use to secure your SQL Server environment. You are making important choices already during the setup of your environment, whereby you configure the service accounts and authentication. Once you have SQL Server up and running, you have to configure SQL Server logins for your groups and accounts, which provide them proper access to the SQL Server.

It's important to understand the difference between authentication and authorization. Just because you can log in to the SQL Server does not give you the rights to change configuration, access data, or perform any data changes. There are many configuration items that require sysadmin role membership and there's a frequent push from application teams and application DBAs to be part of this restricted server role, but you should limit the members of the sysadmin role as much as possible. The same can be said for the security admin role, which has very high privileges on the system.

In the next chapter, we will look into the backup and restore operations for SQL Server, which are an important part of the whole DR strategy.

5
Working with Disaster Recovery Options

High availability (**HA**) and **disaster recovery** (**DR**) are important solutions for an enterprise strategy concerned with data availability. SQL Server has several different features available for implementing HA and DR scenarios. These will help you increase the availability metric of your SQL Server environment and the applications that are using the data stored on SQL Server.

High availability and disaster recovery are frequently mixed up as many people think they are the same; however, they are not. HA helps you eliminate a single point of failure and provides features and services to keep your environment online, even in case of an incident. DR, on the other hand, is a process you would use to recover from larger accidents. Even if you have a solution for HA in place, this does not mean that you can recover from a disaster or that you have a DR plan.

In this chapter, we'll explore the disaster recovery basics to understand the common terms in relation to HA and DR, and we will also discuss what SQL Server has to offer regarding HA/DR options.

The following topics will be covered in this chapter:

- Understanding the basics of disaster recovery
- SQL Server options for high availability and disaster recovery
- Configuring replication on SQL Server
- Configuring database mirroring
- Configuring log shipping

Let's get started!

Understanding the basics of disaster recovery

Disaster recovery is a set of tools, policies, and procedures that help us while recovering our systems after a disastrous event. DR is just a subset of a more complex discipline called **business continuity planning**, where more variables come into place and you expect more sophisticated plans on how to recover the business operations. With careful planning, you can minimize the effects of the disaster – however, you must keep in mind that it's nearly impossible to completely avoid disasters. Such a set of tools, policies, and procedures would be used, for example, during natural disasters when your data center or site of operations is compromised. Another great example that's very relevant today is all kinds of cyberattack, where your infrastructure may be compromised.

The main goal of a DR plan is to minimize the downtime of our service and to minimize data loss. To measure these objectives, we use special metrics: **Recovery Point** and **Time Objectives**.

The **Recovery Time Objective** (**RTO**) is the maximum time that you can use to recover the system. This time includes your efforts to fix the problem without starting the DR procedures, the recovery itself, proper testing after DR, and communicating with the stakeholders. Once a disaster strikes, clocks are started to measure the DR actions, and the **Recovery Time Actual** (**RTA**) metric is calculated. If you manage to recover the system within the RTO, which means that $RTA < RTO$, then you have met the metrics with a proper combination of the plan and your ability to restore the system. If the policy requires you to bring your SQL Server back to operation after disaster within 8 hours (that's your RTO) and you manage to do this in 6 hours, (that's your RTA) then you have met your **Service-Level Agreements** (**SLAs**) for DR.

The **Recovery Point Objective (RPO)** is the maximum tolerable period for acceptable data loss. This defines how much data can be lost due to disaster. This closely relates to our backups, which were discussed in *Chapter 3, Implementing Backup and Recovery*. The RPO has an impact on your implementation of backups because you plan for a recovery strategy that has specific requirements for your backups. If you can avoid losing 1 day of work, you can properly plan your backup types and the frequency of the backups that you need to take.

The following diagram shows the very concepts that we discussed in the preceding paragraph:

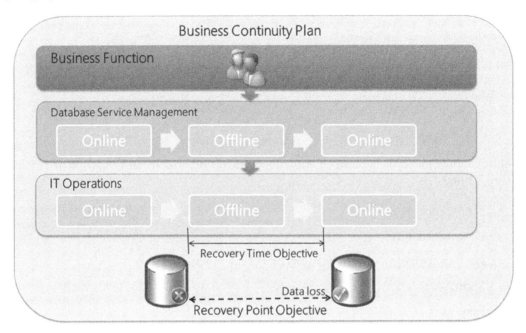

Fig. 5.1 – Business continuity planning

When we talk about system availability, we usually use a percentage of the availability time. This availability is the calculated uptime in a given year or month (any date metric that you need) and is usually compared to the *table of 9s* shown in the following figure.

Availability also expresses a tolerable downtime in a given time frame so that the system still meets the availability metric. The following table shows some basic availability options, along with tolerable downtime per year and downtime per day:

Availability %	Downtime per year	Downtime per day
90%	36.5 days	2.4 hours
98%	7.3 days	28.8 minutes
99%	3.65 days	14.4 minutes
99.9%	8.76 hours	1.44 minutes
99.99%	52.56 minutes	8.64 seconds
99.999%	5.26 minutes	less than 1 second

Fig. 5.2 – High availability "niners"

This tolerable downtime consists of unplanned downtime, which can be caused by many factors:

- Natural disasters
- Hardware failures
- Human errors (accidental deletes, code breakdowns, and so on)
- Security breaches
- Malware

For these, we can put a mitigation plan in place that will help us reduce the downtime to a tolerable range. We usually deploy a combination of HA solutions and DR solutions so that we can quickly restore the operations. On the other hand, there's a reasonable set of events that require downtime on your service due to maintenance and regular operations, but these do not affect the availability on your system. These can include the following:

- New releases of the software
- Operating system patching
- SQL Server patching
- Database maintenance and upgrades

Our goal is to have the database online as much as possible, but there will be times when the database will be offline. From the perspective of management and operations, we're talking about several keywords such as **uptime**, **downtime**, **time to repair**, and **time between failure**, as shown in the following diagram:

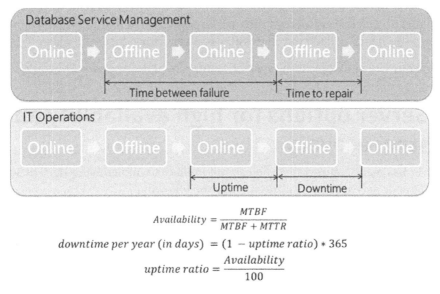

$$Availability = \frac{MTBF}{MTBF + MTTR}$$

$$downtime\ per\ year\ (in\ days) = (1 - uptime\ ratio) * 365$$

$$uptime\ ratio = \frac{Availability}{100}$$

Fig. 5.3 – DR metrics

Disaster recovery exercises

It's critical not only to have a plan for DR, but also to practice for DR itself. Many companies follow the procedure of a proper DR plan by testing with different types of exercises, where each and every aspect of the DR is carefully evaluated by teams who are familiar with the tools and procedures for a real disaster event. These exercises may have different scopes and frequencies, as listed here:

- **Tabletop exercises** usually involve only a small number of people and focus on a specific aspect of the DR plan. This would be a DBA team drill to recover a single SQL Server or a small set of servers with simulated outage.

- **Medium-sized exercises** will involve several teams to practice team communication and interaction.

- **Complex exercises** usually simulate larger events such as data center loss, where a new virtual data center is built and all the new servers and services are provisioned by the involved teams.

Such exercises should be run on a periodic basis so that all the teams and team personnel are up to speed with the DR plans. On top of verifying the procedures, you'll also discover whether the backups you have available are consistent and can be used for the recovery process. This should, however, be part of the backup routine, to verify the backups. You need to realize that RPO and RTO are restoration procedure metrics; however, someone needs to make a quick decision regarding what procedures to follow. Proper training will help your team better understand all possible recovery procedures and plans.

Now, we'll move on and look at the specific features of SQL Server for DR configuration.

SQL Server options for high availability and disaster recovery

SQL Server has many features that you can put in place to implement a HA/DR solution that will fit your needs. These features include the following:

- **Always On Failover Cluster (FCI)**
- **Always On Availability Groups**
- **Database mirroring**
- **Log shipping**
- **Replication**

In many cases, you will combine one or more of these features together since your HA and DR needs will overlap. HA/DR does not have to be limited to just one single feature. In complex scenarios, you'll plan for a primary HA solution and secondary HA solution that will work as your DR solution at the same time.

Always On Failover Cluster

An **Always On Failover Cluster (FCI)** is an instance-level protection mechanism that is based on the **Windows Server Failover Cluster (WSFC)** feature. A SQL Server instance will be installed across multiple WSFC nodes, where it will appear in the network as a single computer.

All the resources that belong to one SQL Server instance (disk, network, names, and so on) can be owned by one **node** of the cluster. During any planned or unplanned event, such as the failure of any server component, these can be moved to another node in the cluster to preserve operations and minimize downtime, as shown in the following diagram:

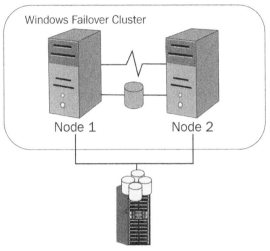

Fig. 5.4 – Failover cluster

In the next section, we'll dive into **Availability Groups**, which use WSFC too, but usually with different storage deployment options.

Always On Availability Groups

Always On Availability Groups were introduced with SQL Server 2012 to bring database-level protection to SQL Server. As with the FCI, **Availability Groups** utilize the Windows Failover Cluster feature, but in this case, a single SQL Server is not installed as a clustered instance but runs independently on several nodes. These nodes can be configured as **Always On Availability Group** nodes to host a database, which will be synchronized among the hosts. The replica can be either **synchronous** or **asynchronous**, so **Always On Availability Groups** are a good fit either as a solution for one data center or even distant data centers to keep your data safe. With new SQL Server versions, **Always On Availability Groups** were enhanced and provide many features for database HA and DR scenarios.

New features of SQL Server 2019 for **Always On Availability Groups** include the following:

- Up to five **synchronous** replicas, where the previous version of SQL Server 2017 was able to utilize only three

- **Secondary** to **Primary** replica connection redirection

- Software assurance HA/DR benefits

You can refer to the following diagram for a better understanding of the architecture:

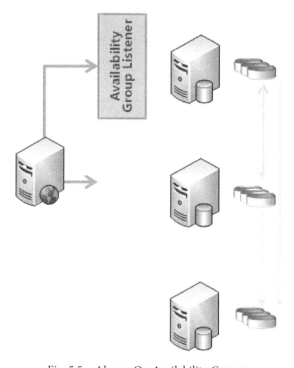

Fig. 5.5 – Always On Availability Groups

Next, we'll look at technologies such as **database mirroring**, log shipping, and **replication**, which do not require the WSFC feature.

Database mirroring

Database mirroring is an older HA/DR feature available in SQL Server that provides database-level protection. **Mirroring** allows us to synchronize our databases between two servers, where you can include one more servers as witness servers for failover quorum.

Unlike the previous two features, **database mirroring** does not require any special setup such as **failover clustering**, and the configuration can be achieved via SSMS using a wizard available via **database properties**. Once a transaction occurs on the primary node, it's copied to the secondary node of the mirrored database. With proper configuration, **database mirroring** can provide failover options for HA with automatic client redirection.

Database mirroring is not a preferred solution for HA/DR since it's marked as a deprecated feature from SQL Server 2012 and has been replaced by **Basic Availability Groups** on current versions. More details on **Always On Availability Groups**, including **Basic Availability Groups**, will be provided in *Chapter 9, Configuring Always On High-Availability Features*.

Log shipping

Log shipping configuration, as the name suggests, is a mechanism used to keep a database in sync by copying the available logs to the remote server. Log shipping, unlike **mirroring**, does not copy each single transaction, but copies the transactions in batches via a **transaction log backup** on the primary node and a **log restore** on the secondary node. Unlike all the previously mentioned features, log shipping does not provide an automatic failover option, so it's considered more of a DR option than a HA one.

Log shipping operates on regular intervals where the following three jobs run independently or may run on the same or different frequency (if required):

* A backup job to back up the **transaction log** on the primary system
* A copy job to copy the backups to the secondary system
* A restore job to restore the **transaction log** backup on the secondary system

Log shipping supports multiple standby databases, which is quite an advantage compared to **database mirroring**. One more advantage is the standby configuration for log shipping, which allows **read-only** access to the secondary database. This is mainly used for many reporting scenarios, where the reporting applications use **read-only** access and such configuration allows performance offload to the secondary system.

Replication

Replication is a feature used for moving data from one server to another and allows for many different scenarios and topologies.

> **Note:**
> **Replication** uses a **Publisher/Subscriber** model, where the **Publisher** is the server offering the content via a **replication** article and the **Subscribers** are getting the data.

The configuration is more complex compared to **mirroring** and log shipping but allows much more variety in terms of configuring security, performance, and topology.

Replication has many benefits, and a few of them are as follows:

- Works at the object level (whereas other features work at the database or instance level)
- Allows **merger replication**, where more servers synchronize data between each other
- Allows **bi-directional synchronization** of data
- Allows more than one SQL Server partner (Oracle, for example)

There's several different **replication** types that can be used with SQL Server. You can choose them based on your needs for HA/DR and the data availability requirements on the secondary servers. These options include the following:

- **Snapshot replication**
- **Transactional replication**
- **Peer-to-peer replication**
- **Merge replication**

In the next section, we will look at **SQL Server replication** in detail.

Configuring replication on SQL Server

In this section, we will focus on **SQL Server replication** in detail and we'll learn how to configure **replication** for a database between different servers. Like with many other features, the configuration can be done with **SQL Server Management Studio (SSMS)** or with **Transaction-SQL (T-SQL)** code, which sometimes provides greater flexibility. Be aware that **replication** is one of the features that you can configure immediately during installation so that it's available on your system. If you haven't installed the feature, you can always add **replication** to your existing SQL Server instance, as follows:

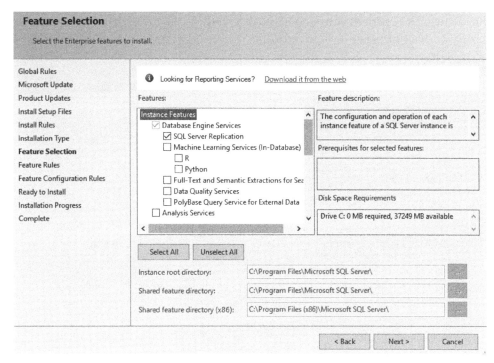

Fig. 5.6 – SQL Server Replication setup

The **replication** topology includes several roles for servers and offers various scenarios. The primary roles we will be working with are as follows:

- The **Publisher**: The **Publisher** is the primary server in the **replication** topology and hosts the source data. On the **Publisher** server, we need to create a replication publication, which is a unit for **replication** containing one or more articles that are distributed to the **Subscriber** servers.

- The **Subscriber**: The **Subscriber** is the server that stores the replica and receives updates from the original data. Between the **Subscriber** and **Publisher**, there's one more role called the **Distributor**.

- The **Distributor**: The **Distributor** server is usually collocated with the **Publisher**, but in more complex scenarios, this can be a standalone server for performance and scalability reasons. The **Distributor** utilizes a database that appears among the system databases in the SSMS, which is usually called the **Distribution**, but this can be altered during the configuration. We can start with the **Distributor** configuration and then choose if SQL Server will do one of the following:

a) Act as its own **Distributor**.

b) Utilize another SQL Server as a **Distributor**.

In the following screenshot, you can see the distributor configuration, which can either be collocated with a **Publisher** or be standalone, where the **Distributor** role is dedicated to a separate SQL server:

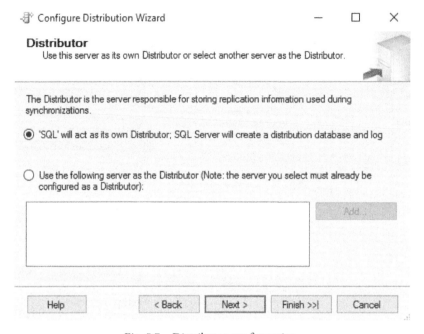

Fig. 5.7 – Distributor configuration

Once you've finished the configuration, you will have configured the following:

- The **Distributor database**
- Replication snapshot folder
- Distribution profile
- Assigned a distributor for your **Publisher**

You can then check the **Distributor** properties for your SQL Server by right-clicking on **Replication** and choosing **Distributor Properties**, as shown in the following screenshot:

Name ▲	Transaction Retention	History Retention	Transaction Delete Batch S...	Command Delete Batch Size
distribution	0 - 72 hours	48 hours	5000	2000

Distribution databases

Databases:

Fig. 5.8 – Distribution databases configuration

Now that we have configured our Distribution databases, we will learn how to create a Publication, configure the Subscription, and replicate agents in the following sections.

Creating a Publication

A **Publication** is a unit for data replication. You can create a **Publication** via SSMS if you go to the replication/local **Publications** menu item and right-click on **Local Publication**. Here, you can select a **New Publication** item, which will start a wizard for you. This wizard will guide you through the whole **Publication** configuration. The first choice that you have to make is what sort of replication publication you want to create. You can choose from the following:

- **Snapshot**

- **Transactional**

- **Peer-to-peer**

- **Merge**

In the following screenshot, you can actually see the type of publications you can create with SQL Server:

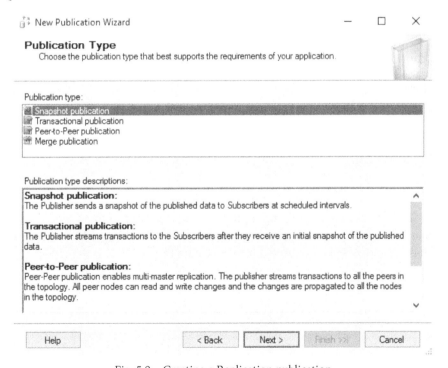

Fig. 5.9 – Creating a Replication publication

Let's read a little about each type of publication:

- A **Snapshot publication** will create a snapshot of your data, which will be periodically transferred to the subscribing servers. The snapshot will include the data that's present on the **Publisher** at the time of the snapshot's creation. Until you create a new snapshot and distribute the snapshot to the subscribing servers again, they will not receive any updates by default.

- **Transactional replication** is based on the **Snapshot publication** (it can be also based on the backup in more complex types of setup), and after the snapshot is applied to the subscribing servers, each transaction will be copied to keep the subscribing servers in sync.

- **Peer-to-peer replication** allows multi-master data synchronization, where all the nodes in the **Replication** can update the data and distribute the changes. This type of replication is available only in the Enterprise Edition and is more complex to maintain due to there being a higher chance of conflict regarding the data updates.

- **Merge replication** is based on the snapshot publication, which is distributed to the subscribing servers, and after the snapshot is applied, the **Subscriber** and **Publisher** can both update the data and merge the changes between each other.

Once you choose the type of **Publication** you wish to use, you need to configure the **Articles**.

Articles consist of the replicated objects, which can be any of the following:

- **Tables**
- **Views**
- **Indexed views**
- **Stored procedures**
- **User-defined functions**

What you might be missing here is the option to replicate user-defined types, which can be replicated either via pre-snapshot scripts or by the **Article Properties** where user-defined data types would be converted into base data types.

When you are configuring **Articles**, you can use both horizontal and vertical filtering, which means that you can choose which columns on a table to view and which rows should be replicated.

As shown in the following screenshot, if you don't use any filters, all the table columns and rows will be added to the **Publication** for **Replication** by default:

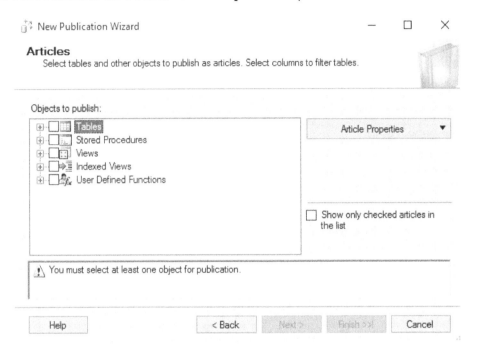

Fig. 5.10 – Configuring Replication Articles

Once you have selected the objects that you would like to publish, you have to configure the schedule for the snapshot's creation. You have two options:

- Create the snapshot immediately
- Schedule the snapshot's creation

If you are working with a small database or a small number of objects to publish, you can create the snapshot immediately because if it's small, it won't put much load on your server. However, if you're planning to create a snapshot for a large database with a large amount of objects, you may need to postpone the snapshot's creation until after business hours or in a time window when your server is less loaded. This is recommended due to the load on the I/O subsystem caused by generating the snapshot.

In the following screenshot, you can see the configuration settings for **Snapshot Agent**, which are used either to run the agent immediately or schedule the snapshot's creation. Scheduling will be used to optimize the server load and postpone the snapshot's creation until after business hours:

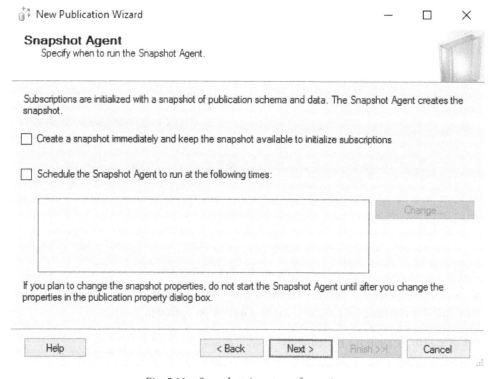

Fig. 5.11 – Snapshot Agent configuration

After you've configured the schedule, you have to configure **Snapshot Agent Security**, where you need to set up credentials for **Snapshot Agent** and configure how the agent will connect to the **Publisher** to get the data for the snapshot. You can either use the SQL Server Agent account or configure your own account for the connection and agent credentials:

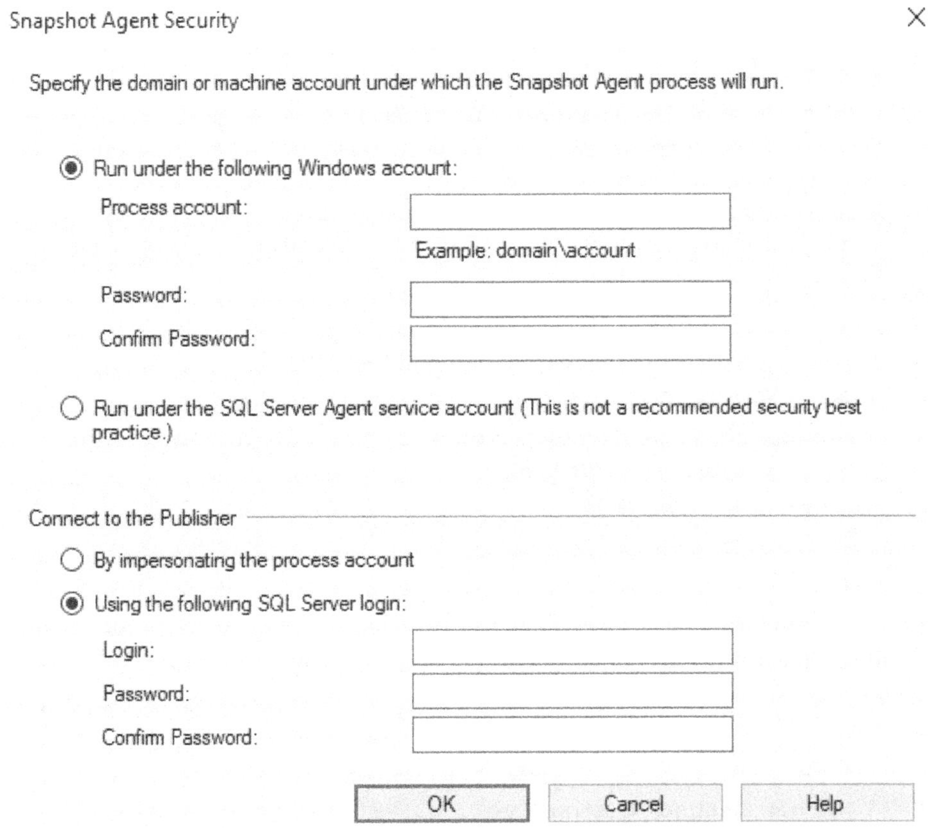

Snapshot Agent Security   ✕

Specify the domain or machine account under which the Snapshot Agent process will run.

◉ Run under the following Windows account:

Process account: [   ]

Example: domain\account

Password: [   ]

Confirm Password: [   ]

○ Run under the SQL Server Agent service account (This is not a recommended security best practice.)

Connect to the Publisher

○ By impersonating the process account

◉ Using the following SQL Server login:

Login: [   ]

Password: [   ]

Confirm Password: [   ]

[OK]   [Cancel]   [Help]

Fig. 5.12 – Replication Agent Security configuration

If you would like to use the T-SQL scripts to create the publication for snapshot **Replication**, you can use the following code, assuming that you have the AdventureWorks database available on your SQL Server:

> **Note:**
>
> You can download sample databases for the MS SQL Server at https://
> github.com/Microsoft/sql-server-samples/
> tree/master/samples/databases/adventure-
> works, where you can find the AdventureWorks database,
> the WideWorldImporters database, and samples for analysis, reporting,
> and integration services. There are also specific databases for data warehouse
> scenarios, which may be helpful for your learning purposes. Such databases
> should be deployed only to test/dev servers and it's a good practice never to put
> those on production systems.

1. The following code can be used to enable **Replication**:

```
use [AdventureWorks]
exec sp_replicationdboption @dbname = N'AdventureWorks',
    @optname = N'publish',
    @value = N'true'
GO
```

2. Once **Replication** has been enabled for the database, you can create the publication and add the snapshot:

```
exec sp_addpublication @publication = N'AWorks - Test',
  @description = N'Snapshot publication of database
  ''AdventureWorks'' from Publisher ''SQL''.',
  @sync_method = N'native',
  @snapshot_in_defaultfolder = N'true',
  @repl_freq = N'snapshot',
  @status = N'active',
  @independent_agent = N'true'
GO

exec sp_addpublication_snapshot @publication = N'AWorks -
Employee', @frequency_type = 1
```

Finally, you have to add some articles to the publication – in this case, one table from the HumanResources schema called Employee:

```
use [AdventureWorks]
exec sp_addarticle @publication = N'AWorks - Employee',
    @article = N'Employee',
    @source_owner = N'HumanResources',
    @source_object = N'Employee',
    @destination_table = N'Employee',
    @destination_owner = N'HumanResources',
    @schema_option = 0x000000000803509D
GO
```

In this way, we have created a snapshot for one single table from the AdventureWorks database named HumanResources.Employee, which is now available as a publication. Once we have the publication in place, we can configure the subscription.

Configuring the subscription

We can subscribe to existing publications again via the GUI or T-SQL scripts. You need to know the server name where you're hosting your publications so that you can connect to the proper **Publisher**. Once you are connected to the **Publisher**, you can select the **Publication** that you want to subscribe to, as shown in the following screenshot:

Fig. 5.13 – Subscription configuration

Subscriptions can be configured in two ways:

- **Push subscription**
- **Pull subscription**

The difference between these two is where the **Distributor** agent will run. With push subscription, the **Distributor** agent will run on the **Distributor** server (usually collocated with the **Publisher**), whereas the pull subscription configuration uses **Subscribers** to run the agents. This has a performance impact for larger environments, but for simple configurations, it's fine to run the distribution agents on the **Distributor** server. For higher loads, I would recommend having isolated distributor or agents running on the **Subscriber** with pull subscriptions. Once you have selected the **Publication**, you need to configure the **Subscribers**, mainly the server names and the subscription databases. Subscription databases may already exist and the **Publication** will add data to the existing database, or the dialog will let you create a new database for your subscription:

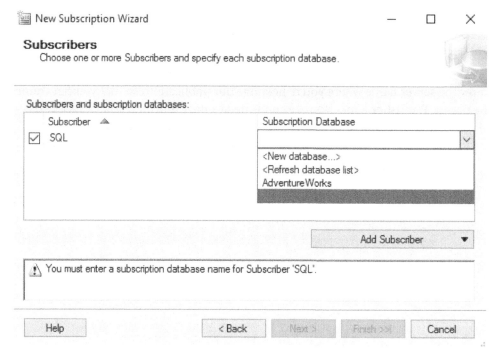

Fig. 5.14 – Subscriber database configuration

Last but not least, you have to configure the security profiles for your **Distribution Agent security** and, as with **Snapshot Agent**, you can use a separate account or impersonate the account used by the SQL Server Agent service:

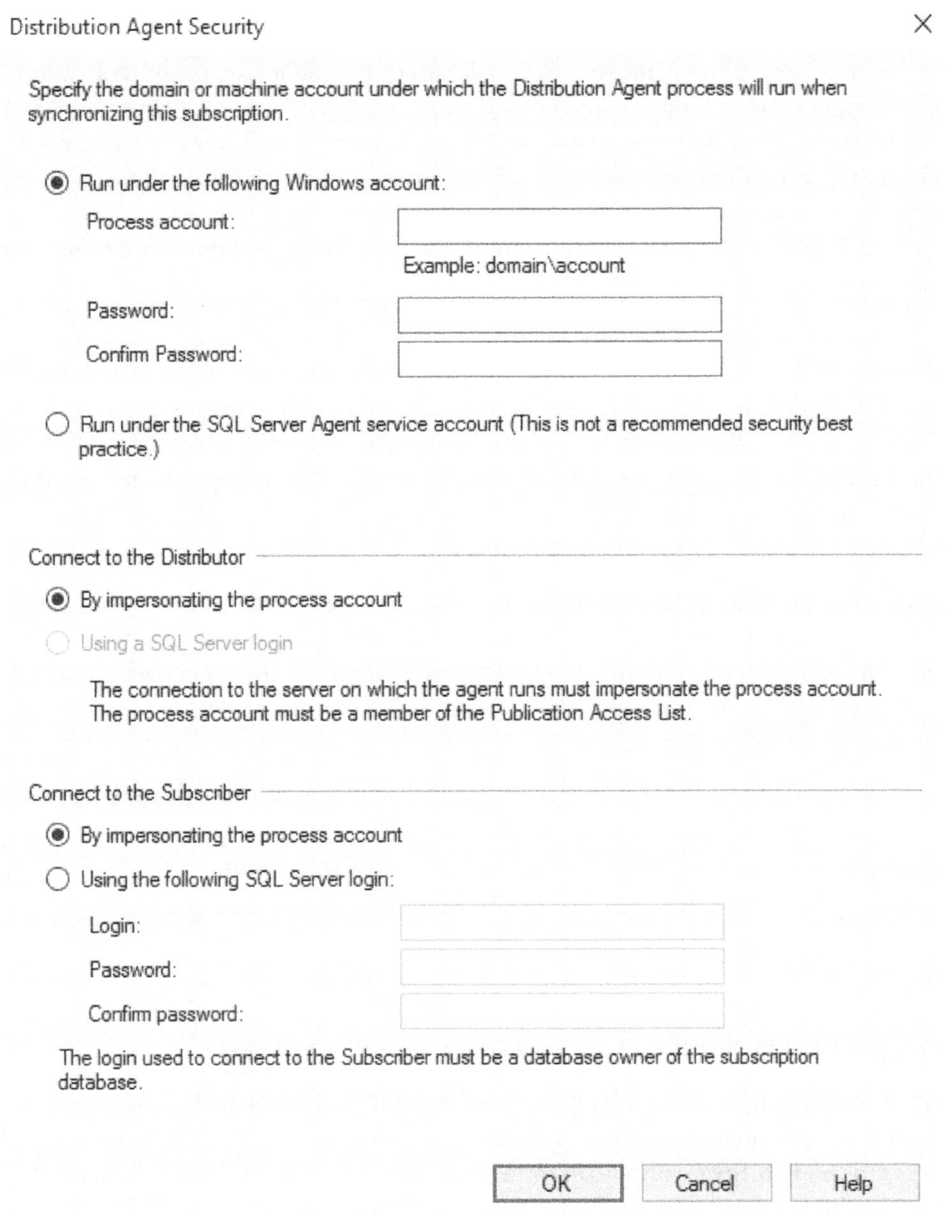

Distribution Agent Security   ✕

Specify the domain or machine account under which the Distribution Agent process will run when
synchronizing this subscription.

◉ Run under the following Windows account:

  Process account: [_____]

                                 Example: domain\account

  Password: [_____]

  Confirm Password: [_____]

○ Run under the SQL Server Agent service account (This is not a recommended security best
  practice.)

Connect to the Distributor ──

  ◉ By impersonating the process account

  ○ Using a SQL Server login

    The connection to the server on which the agent runs must impersonate the process account.
    The process account must be a member of the Publication Access List.

Connect to the Subscriber ──

  ◉ By impersonating the process account

  ○ Using the following SQL Server login:

    Login: [_____]

    Password: [_____]

    Confirm password: [_____]

  The login used to connect to the Subscriber must be a database owner of the subscription
  database.

                          [OK   ]   [Cancel]   [Help]

Fig. 5.15 – Distribution Agent Security configuration

Once you've finished the configuration dialog, you will have an active subscription for
your publication with snapshot replication.

Replication agents

So far, we have seen a **Snapshot Agent**, which we configured for snapshot replication. The **Snapshot Agent** runs a binary named `snapshot.exe`, which usually runs on the **Distributor** server. In many cases, the **Distributor** and **Publisher** are the same. This agent is not only used for snapshot replication, but also for any other replication types as they rely on snapshot in the beginning. The **Snapshot Agent** stores the data in the configured snapshot folder and captures important information about synchronization in the distribution database.

Another important agent is the **Log Reader Agent**, which is used to configure the **Replication** as transactional. The **Log Reader Agent** runs a binary named `logread.exe`, which is used to check all the databases that are configured for transactional replication. The **Log Reader Agent** scans the transaction log of a published database for any new transactions. Once new transactions are found, they are put into the distribution database and marked for replication. The distribution agent is then responsible for distributing the transactions to the subscribers.

Both snapshot and transactional replications also use a distribution agent. This agent runs a binary named `distrib.exe`, which is responsible for moving snapshots and transactions from the distribution database to **Subscribers**. If the replication is configured as a push replication, then the agent will run on the **Distributor** server; in the case of pull, it will run on the **Subscribers**.

More complex scenarios for transactional replication utilize a **Queue Reader** agent, which is used in situations where transactions are not applied immediately to the **Subscribers**. **Merge replication** uses its own type of agent, called a **Merge agent**.

With that, we have finished the replication configuration and we're ready to move on to another HA/DR technology.

Understanding database mirroring

Database mirroring is a technology used for both HA and DR, which allows for rich configuration. **Mirroring** is largely replaced by other features of MS SQL Server, mainly **Always On Availability Groups**. Mirroring should not be considered a primary HA/DR option for new deployments; however, it's still important to understand mirroring, especially because of migrations from older SQL Server installations, which may still use mirroring for HA/DR.

Mirroring uses up to three server roles:

- Principal
- Mirror
- Witness

The principal server holds the database that is mirrored. This database has to be configured with the **Full Recovery model** in order to participate in the mirroring configuration. The mirror server holds a mirrored copy of the database, but unlike **replication** or **log shipping**, this database is not available for user access. The witness server can be configured in case you would like to utilize automatic failover of the mirrored database between the principal and mirror server due to unavailability of the principal.

Database mirroring operates in three modes. Each mode has its advantages and disadvantages, and it's important to understand these in order to choose the right mode for your setup. These modes are as follows:

- **High performance**
- **High safety without automatic failover**
- **High safety with automatic failover**

High performance mode requires the Enterprise Edition of SQL Server, whereas the other two modes can work with the Standard Edition as well. **High performance** mode uses asynchronous processing, which means that a transaction is committed on the principal server first and then on the mirror without any delays. The other two modes use synchronous processing, so the transaction has to be committed on the mirror and the principal in order for the application to continue. Due to the two commits – one on the principal server and one on the mirror server – high safety modes are not used on slower networks because they can cause slower application performance.

Automatic failover can only occur with **witness server** configuration. The **witness server** is connected to both partners – the principal and mirror servers – and can operate with minimum resources and lower editions, such as Express.

To prepare for **mirroring**, you need to have the database on both servers. To do this, you need to take a database backup and a log backup and restore both to the mirror server. You can use GUI or T-SQL scripts to perform the backups and restore the database to its operational state using the recovery option.

Configuring database mirroring

To configure **mirroring**, you need to perform several steps. A lot of important information about mirroring your database can be found in the mirroring item in the database properties.

First, you need to configure your security options, where you will define your principal, witness, and mirror servers, including their port numbers. These port numbers will be used for creating endpoints on each SQL Server, which will be used for mirroring sessions, as shown in the following screenshot:

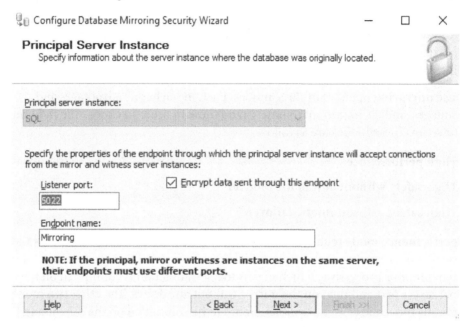

Fig. 5.16 – Principal Server Instance configuration for mirroring

Once you have configured the security aspects, you can start the **mirroring** process for the selected database via the **Start Mirroring** button in the dialog:

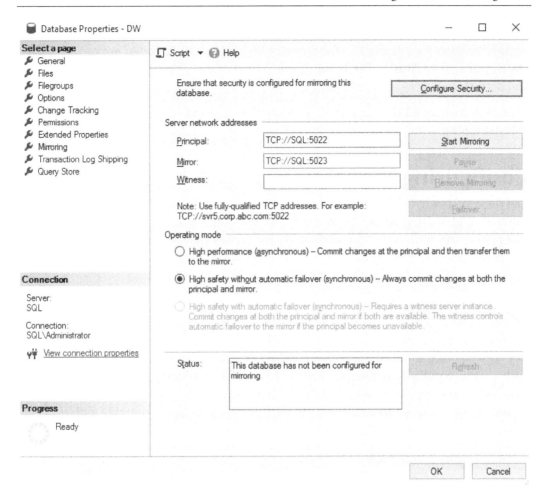

Fig. 5.17 – Mirroring settings in the Database Properties window

As you can see, the **High safety with automatic failover (synchronous)** option is not available as the configuration for the witness server was skipped. Once mirroring is operational, you can use the **Failover** button to switch the roles of the mirror and principal servers.

Mirroring is usually not used on new deployments and runs mostly on legacy environments as it's a deprecated feature since SQL Server 2012. Today, **mirroring** is largely replaced by **Availability Groups**, which offer more flexibility, monitoring options, and performance.

With that, we have finished this section about mirroring and we're ready to start looking at **log shipping**, which is a pure DR technology.

Configuring log shipping

Log shipping is a DR technology as there is no automatic failover available with this solution. With a database configured for log shipping, there are several automated jobs that periodically back up the transaction log and restore the log to a different server. This server can be used for many scenarios, such as the following:

- **Warm standby for Disaster Recovery**
- **Reporting offloads**

DR configuration is mainly used for a warm standby server. This server has data in near sync – which is not 100% the same as the primary server. One of the advantages of such a warm standby is that you have the option to bring up the server quickly during a disaster. Log shipping has quite a simple architecture, where you have only two main server roles – primary and secondary. With log shipping, you can configure more secondary servers that will host the database for DR scenarios for warm standby or reporting. The same configuration can be achieved with replication, where you can have multiple **Subscribers** for the published database.

To start with the log shipping configuration, you have to open **Database Properties** and go to the menu item for **Transaction Log Shipping**, as shown in the following screenshot:

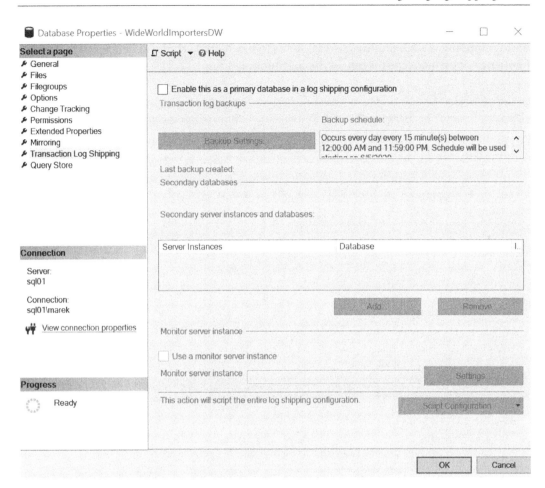

Fig. 5.18 – Transaction Log Shipping configuration page

You need to enable the primary database in the **Transaction Log Shipping** configuration and configure the backup job. This backup job requires configuration for the following:

- Network path where the backups will be stored
- Job schedule – frequency of the backups
- Backup file retention – how long to keep the backups
- Compression settings
- Alert threshold to notify the DBA if backups don't run

In the following screenshot, you can see that you can use the backup setting configuration for log shipping, which requires several items to be entered. This also defines the frequency of the backups for one of the log shipping jobs:

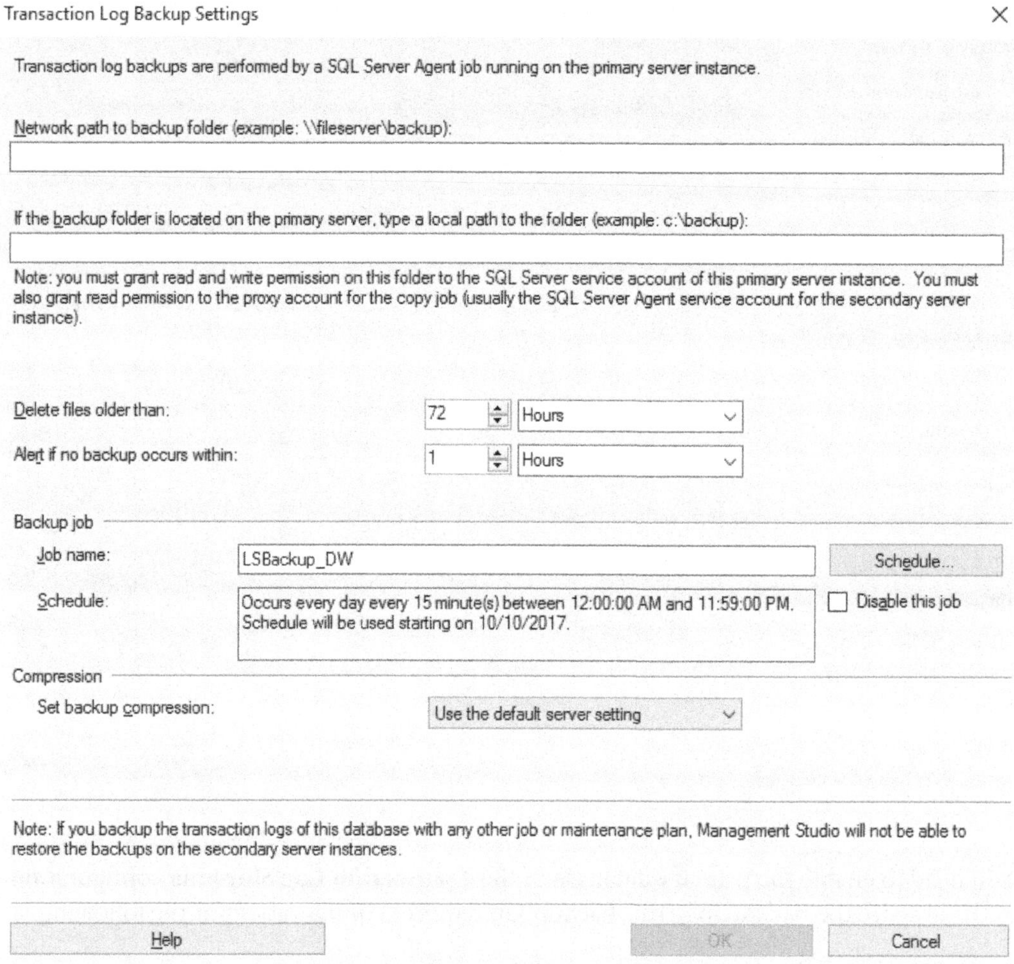

Transaction Log Backup Settings   ✕

Transaction log backups are performed by a SQL Server Agent job running on the primary server instance.

Network path to backup folder (example: \\fileserver\backup):

If the backup folder is located on the primary server, type a local path to the folder (example: c:\backup):

Note: you must grant read and write permission on this folder to the SQL Server service account of this primary server instance. You must also grant read permission to the proxy account for the copy job (usually the SQL Server Agent service account for the secondary server instance).

| Delete files older than: | 72 | Hours | |
| Alert if no backup occurs within: | 1 | Hours | |

Backup job

Job name: LSBackup_DW   Schedule...

Schedule: Occurs every day every 15 minute(s) between 12:00:00 AM and 11:59:00 PM.   ☐ Disable this job
              Schedule will be used starting on 10/10/2017.

Compression

Set backup compression: Use the default server setting ∨

Note: If you backup the transaction logs of this database with any other job or maintenance plan, Management Studio will not be able to restore the backups on the secondary server instances.

Help   OK   Cancel

Fig. 5.19 – Configuring log shipping backups

Once you have configured the job, you can add the instances that will be used as secondary servers to the log shipping configuration. You can configure the initial database load option, which will take a fresh backup of the database and restore the database to the secondary server.

If you have done all the initialization steps manually, you can skip this option using the **Initialize Secondary Database** setting. On the **Copy Files** tab, you have to configure the copy job settings, mainly how often the copy job copies the backups from the primary server to the secondary server. The third tab will allow you to choose the restore options for the database. There are two restoring options that you can choose from:

- **No recovery mode**
- **Standby mode**

No recovery mode will keep your database in restoring mode and will not be accessible to your users. The database will only be used by the log shipping feature on the secondary server to restore the logs periodically. If you would like to work with the database on the secondary server, then you need to use **Standby mode**, which allows **read-only** access to the databases. This is particularly useful for any offloading for reporting applications, which mostly use **read-only** access to data.

The following screenshot shows the option for choosing between these choices:

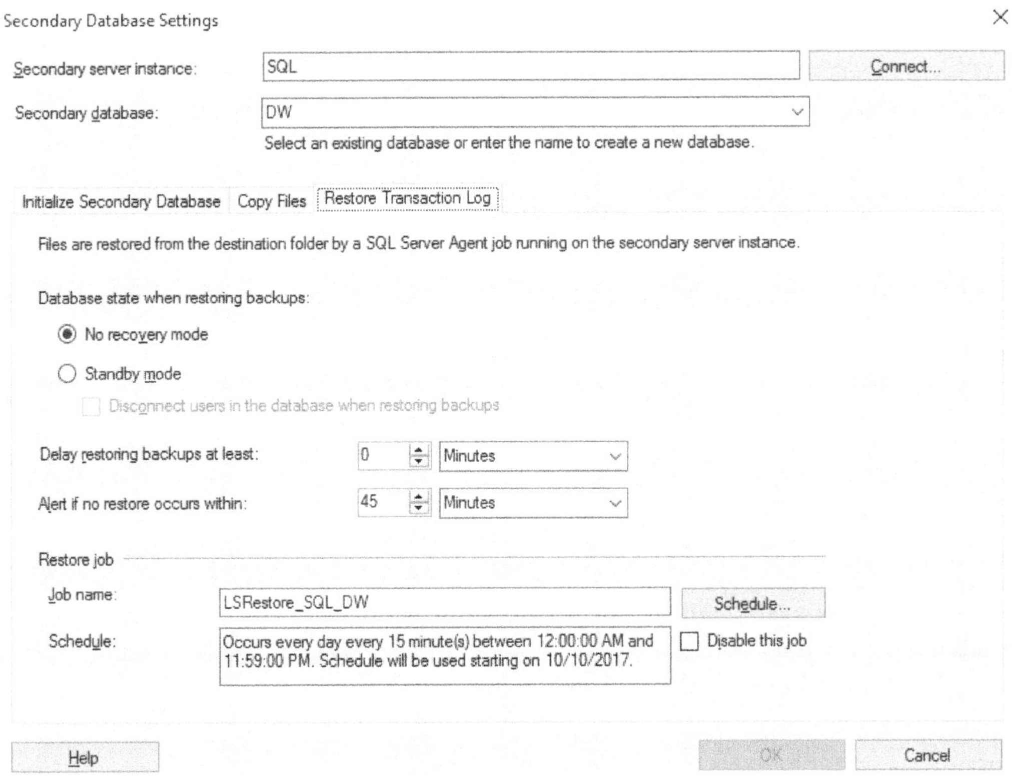

Fig. 5.20 – Log shipping configuration – restore options

Once the configuration has been completed, the database will be placed into the proper mode on the secondary server based on the configuration, as shown in the following screenshot:

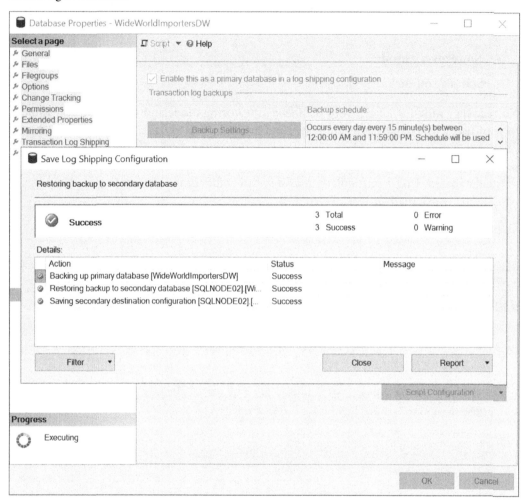

Fig. 5.21 – Log shipping configuration

In the following screenshot, you can see two databases, where one is set to no recovery mode the other is set to standby mode. When set to standby mode, the database allows **read-only** access to the data, which can be very useful for reporting purposes and offloading the **read-only** workload from the primary server:

☐ 🖥 SQLNODE02 (SQL Server 15.0.4033.1 - sqlnode02\marek)
   ☐ 📁 Databases
      ⊞ 📁 System Databases
      ⊞ 📁 Database Snapshots
      ⊞ 🗗 WideWorldImporters (Restoring...)
      ⊞ 🖳 WideWorldImportersDW (Standby / Read-Only)
   ⊞ 📁 Security
   ⊞ 📁 Server Objects
   ⊞ 📁 Replication
   ⊞ 📁 PolyBase
   ⊞ 📁 Always On High Availability
   ⊞ 📁 Management
   ⊞ 📁 Integration Services Catalogs
   ☐ 🔧 SQL Server Agent

Fig. 5.22 – Databases on the secondary server

You can also use T-SQL for configuring log shipping. For such a task, there's a bunch of stored procedures you can use. The steps for configuring log shipping via T-SQL would be as follows:

1. Initiate the database on the secondary server using backups.

2. On the primary server, use `sp_add_log_shipping_primary_database`.

3. On the primary server, use `sp_add_jobschedule` to add a schedule for the log shipping backup job.

4. Enable the backup job since the job is automatically disabled.

5. On the secondary server, use the `sp_add_logshipping_secondary_primary` procedure to supply details about the primary server.

6. On the secondary server, use `sp_add_jobschedule` to add a schedule to the copy and restore jobs.

7. On the primary server, use the `sp_add_logshipping_primary_secondary` procedure to update the primary server with information about the secondary instance.

Switching log shipping roles

Servers in the log shipping configuration can be utilized for DR, but this process is mostly manual. Let's begin!

1. To switch the primary and secondary servers, you need to copy all the available backups to the secondary server. If this is a planned role switch, then you need to take a `tail-log` backup on the primary database, as follows:

    ```
    USE master
    GO
    BACKUP LOG DW TO DISK = 'c:\backups\DW.trn' WITH
    NORECOVERY
    ```

2. Once you have finished the `tail-log` backup, you have to copy the backup to the secondary server and restore the backup using the following script:

    ```
    RESTORE LOG DW FROM DISK = 'c:\backups\DW.trn' WITH
    RECOVERY
    ```

    As you have taken a `tail-log` backup on the primary server, this has left the database in restoring mode, which allows you to quickly configure the log shipping again and make the primary server the secondary server.

3. If the primary server is not accessible and you can't take the `tail-log` backup anymore, you need to make sure that all the copied transaction log backups have already been restored, and then just make the database available with the following command:

    ```
    RESTORE DATABASE DW WITH RECOVERY
    ```

    This command will bring the database online, but due to the unavailability of the `tail-log` backup, you'll be introducing some data loss to the environment, depending on the schedule for your backups and the volume of the data changes on the primary server.

In the following table, you can see a matrix comparing the solutions in terms of automatic failover and RPO/RTO:

HA/DR Solution	Potential Data Loss	Automatic Failover	Recovery Time
Backup, Restore	Minutes	No	Varies
Log Shipping	Minutes	No	Minutes to hours
Replication	Seconds	No	Varies
Mirroring	Seconds/possibly zero	Yes, with high safety	Seconds

Fig. 5.23 – HADR feature comparison

Summary

In this chapter, we introduced you to the DR discipline and the big picture of business continuity on SQL Server. DR is not only about having backups, but about the ability to bring the service back so that it can perform operations after severe failures.

We have looked at several options that can be used to implement part of DR on SQL Server, such as log shipping, replication, and mirroring. An HA/DR configuration is an essential step in most SQL Server deployments. All three features we discussed in this chapter are still in use today, although mirroring has been retired in many environments and is being replaced with the more flexible Availability Groups, which will be discussed in *Chapter 9, Configuring Always On High Availability Features*. Throughout this chapter, you have seen the configuration options for all three features, which can help you deploy them in to your environments.

In the next chapter, we'll focus on indexing strategies and introduce various index types that you can use to optimize the performance of your SQL Server environment.

6
Indexing and Performance

Maintaining and troubleshooting Microsoft SQL Server's performance entails a very wide set of tasks that depend on several factors, all of which are handled by administrators and developers, sometimes independently and sometimes in conjunction. There's a strong need for the cooperation of these two roles when working with SQL Server, which is why even if this book is taking SQL Server topics from an administrator's point of view, we will go through some development tips and tricks briefly to show some cases of performance lag.

In this chapter, we will understand what performance is and enumerate the prerequisites required for successful monitoring and tuning. We will also provide a top-level overview of monitoring procedures. We will learn how use the tools required, as well as how to read and interpret results measured by the tools. For developers, we will look at the usage of different kinds of indexes and how they work. From an administrator's perspective, we will find out how to diagnose the usefulness and health of indexes. Finally, with the help of examples, we will see how typical issues with performance occur, how to identify them, and how to resolve such issues.

All this will be covered under the following topics:

- Explaining SQL Server internals

- SQL Server protocols

- Performance monitoring overview

- Tools for monitoring performance

- Indexes and maintenance

- Common performance issue patterns

Let's get started!

Explaining SQL Server internals

Your SQL Server workload and environment may not run with the performance you expect or require, and you'll need to troubleshoot SQL Server. For a good troubleshooting approach, you need to have a basic understanding of the SQL Server architecture and internals since SQL Server is a very complex software. There are four main components of the SQL Server architecture:

- SQLOS

- Storage engine

- Query processor

- Protocol layer

In the following image, you can see all these components and their relationship:

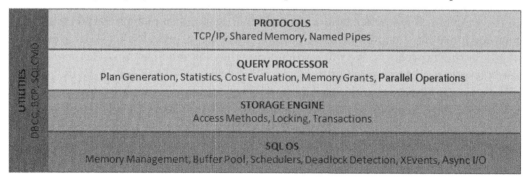

Fig. 6.1 – SQL Server architecture components and relationships

We'll look at the protocols first.

SQL Server protocols

Any application that requires a connection to our SQL Server needs to communicate either over a network or locally on the same server via a protocol layer. SQL Server communication is based on tabular data stream packets, which are encapsulated into a common communication protocol. There are several options available for you, which you can configure in the **SQL Server Configuration Manager** tool. If you expand **SQL Server Network Configuration**, you'll see the network configuration for your instance:

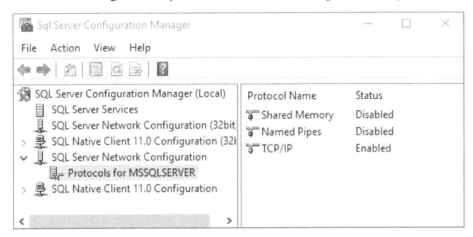

Fig. 6.2 – SQL Server Network Configuration for your instance

The available protocols are as follows:

- **TCP/IP**: This is the most common choice for SQL Server deployments.

- **Shared Memory**: This is the simplest protocol and can only be used locally, and not for remote connections.

- **Named Pipes**: This is a protocol developed for LAN connections. It can work remotely.

For most deployments, we need to properly configure the instance **TCP/IP** settings with regards to the available port numbers, which, on the default instance, are set to TCP/1433. However, on named instances, these are selected randomly. These random port numbers can cause issues with the **Service Principal Name** (**SPN**) registration. The SPN is a unique identifier of a SQL Server instance used by Kerberos authentication. To check the registered SPNs, you can use the following command. Here, <account> is the service account used to run your SQL Server services:

```
setspn -l <account>
```

There can be two types of SPNs registered for your SQL Server, which are `MSSQLSvc` for your SQL Server database engine and `MSOLAPDisco.3` for the analysis services. To register the SPN for a named instance, you'll need to know the name of the instance and the port on which the instance is running. Considering that our SQL Server will run with the `CONTOSO\sqlService` account, we can use the following code to register the SPNs:

```
setspn -S MSSQLSvc/sql.contoso.com sqlService
setspn -S MSSQLSvc/sql.contoso.com:1433 sqlService
```

There will be two SPN records registered in Active Directory – one for the default instance name and one for the default port number, `1433`. With a named instance, you'll also need to enter the instance name on the first record.

Through **SQL Server Configuration Manager**, you can also configure additional properties for the network configuration. You can configure the certificate for your SQL Server, force the encryption, and hide the instance so that the instance is not visible in the local or remote servers in SQL Server Management Studio.

To start using SSL/TLS – that is, `TLS1.2` – for your SQL Server, you will have to provide a proper certificate via the configuration manager, as shown in the following screenshot:

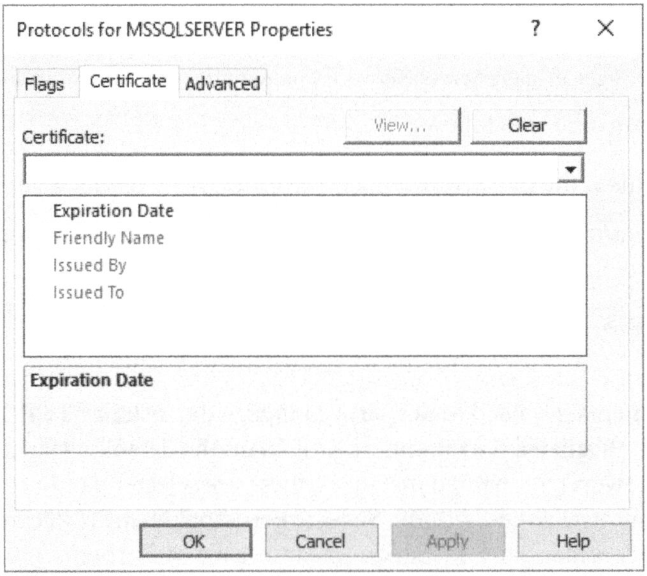

Fig. 6.3 – Certificate

Once you've selected the certificate, you must modify the Windows OS registry to enable the `TLS1.2` transport protocol encryption. To turn on `TLS1.2` support on the Windows OS, you'll have to modify the following registry entries:

```
[HKEY_LOCAL_MACHINE\SYSTEM\CurrentControlSet\Control\
SecurityProviders\SCHANNEL\Protocols\TLS 1.2]
```

```
[HKEY_LOCAL_MACHINE\SYSTEM\CurrentControlSet\Control\
SecurityProviders\SCHANNEL\Protocols\TLS 1.2\Client]
"DisabledByDefault"=dword:00000000 "Enabled"=dword:00000001
```

```
[HKEY_LOCAL_MACHINE\SYSTEM\CurrentControlSet\Control\
SecurityProviders\SCHANNEL\Protocols\TLS 1.2\Server]
"DisabledByDefault"=dword:00000000 "Enabled"=dword:00000001
```

SQL Server 2017 and newer versions do support `TLS1.2` without any problems, but versions older than 2017 require specific updates to be installed. If you enforce `TLS1.2` via the OS registry before you have a proper update in place, your SQL Server may stop working and won't start.

> **Important**
>
> You may find many errors in the error log of your SQL Server, which will lead you to the required `TLS1.2` hotfix installation. The common errors that you may find look as follows:
>
> a) The server was unable to initialize encryption because of a problem with a security library.
>
> b) The security library may be missing. Verify that `security.dll` exists on the system.
>
> c) `TDSSNIClient` initialization failed with error **0x139f**, status code **0x80**. Reason: Unable to initialize SSL support.
>
> d) The group or resource is not in the correct state to perform the requested operation.

Query processor

The query processor is a crucial part of the architecture and includes more internal components. We can split them between query optimization and query execution. Query processor works with the query tree (which is basically an internal representation of a query written in T-SQL) and determines the possible ways of optimization. Many of the complex commands can be optimized with more approaches, and the optimizer can find those, especially for typical DML commands: `SELECT`, `INSERT`, `UPDATE`, `DELETE`, and `MERGE`.

The query optimizer is based on the following two main inputs:

- **Cost**: This indicates the cost of the plan. The cost is an internally calculated value containing the estimated CPU time and I/O effort needed to process the query.

- **Cardinality**: This indicates the number of rows being processed. The cardinality estimation is mostly based on predicates seen in the query (the WHERE clause), and SQL Server tries to estimate how many records will be processed by the query. Index and column statistics are used for this estimation.

The cardinality metric is used as an input to the cost metric, so the better the cardinality estimation is, the better the whole cost of the plan is. The cardinality, if it can be determined, is based on histograms of the statistics and index information. Since SQL Server 2014, a new cardinality estimator is available, which can be controlled via the following:

- Database compatibility level

- Trace flags

- Database-scoped configuration

- Hints

With the latest SQL Server versions, we can use **Database Scoped Configuration**, which is available for each individual database. When you click on any database and select **Properties/Options**, you will find a scoped configuration like this one:

Database Scoped Configurations	
Legacy Cardinality Estimation	OFF
Legacy Cardinality Estimation For Secondary	PRIMARY
Max DOP	0
Max DOP For Secondary	
Parameter Sniffing	ON
Parameter Sniffing For Secondary	PRIMARY
Query Optimizer Fixes	OFF
Query Optimizer Fixes For Secondary	PRIMARY

Fig. 6.4 – Database scoped configuration

In this configuration, you can control interesting behavior for your database, where the first two options are related to the cardinality estimator. As you can see, by default, the legacy estimator is off, and secondary replicas from the availability groups use the same setting as the primary replica.

The same settings are also available for three other very important configurations, which previously had to be configured on the server level, instead of the database level. These are as follows:

- **Max DOP**: Maximum degree of parallelism. This property limits the number of CPUs that can be utilized during one query. Generally, the more the database serves as a data warehouse (OLAP database), the more CPUs will be allowed to be used for one query. This is because data warehouses are intended to process queries with big scan operations and batch data loads. Also, OLTP databases typically process many seek operations and small transactions from multiple user connections, so every connection needs at least one CPU for its requests.

- **Parameter Sniffing**: Parameter sniffing can occur when the execution plan is compiled for a certain value of some parameter. Say the value is used in the WHERE clause and limits the number of records that are processed by the query to several tens of records. But then, the same plan is used with a different parameter value, which does not limit the number of records so strongly. In other words, the cardinality of the query significantly changes, but the plan remains the same and performs poorly because it is cached. As per the **Parameter Sniffing** property, the plan should be reviewed each time it is executed.

- **Query Optimizer Fixes**: This property allows SQL Server to automatically apply all query optimizer fixes that are delivered as a part of any **cumulative updates** (**CUs**) that are installed on it.

The query optimizer is constantly being improved by new updates on SQL Server 2019, called cumulative updates. Any time a new update is installed, by default, you won't see any fixes for the query optimizer being used by your SQL Server, unless you turn this on for individual databases or globally by using the T4199 trace flag. Trace flags can be configured via **SQL Server Configuration Manager** on the properties of your instance. If you go to the **Startup Parameters** tab, you can add your trace flags to the list.

The other major part of the query processor is the query execution engine. This engine uses the plans generated by the query optimizer and runs them. Running the plan or executing the query can involve many operations on the storage engine and in memory to return the entire required dataset. To see the query plan, you can use the **SQL Server Management Studio** (**SSMS**) and use one of the following options:

- Include the actual execution plan (*Ctrl + M*)
- Include live query statistics
- Display the estimated execution plan (*Ctrl + L*)

There's a considerable difference between the estimated and actual execution plans. The estimated plan is created without executing the query, whereas the actual plan is, in fact, the workflow that's used to perform the query operations. These two plans can differ either in the structure and operators that are used or in the estimates on the row counts and the size of data being pulled through the plan. Let's look at some common plan operators that you can see in the plans.

When we need to pull the data from the tables, we can see several common operators:

- **Table scan**: This retrieves all the rows from a table that does not have a clustered index (heap structure).

- **Clustered index scan**: This retrieves all the rows from a table that has a clustered index.

- **Columnstore index scan**: This retrieves all the rows from a columnstore index.

- **Clustered index seek**: This retrieves only the rows based on a seek predicate from a clustered index.

- **Non-clustered index seek**: This retrieves only the rows based on a seek predicate from a non-clustered index.

The following are the typical plan operator icons, in the same order that we just listed them:

Fig. 6.5 – Operator icons

When you capture a query plan, you will see such an operator being used, as shown in the following screenshot:

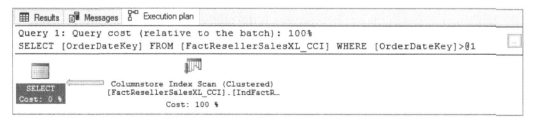

Fig. 6.6 – Operator usage in a query plan

With such a query, you can see that the columnstore index was used to retrieve all the data required by the query. When looking at the execution plan, you can move your mouse over any operator to display details about the operator – the cost of the I/O and CPU, the number of rows, and other information. The important attributes for us to watch during any troubleshooting action are as follows:

- The actual number of rows versus the estimated number of rows

- The number of executions

- Whether parallelism is used

- Whether any warnings are displayed

The following screenshot shows **Columnstore Index Scan (Clustered)**:

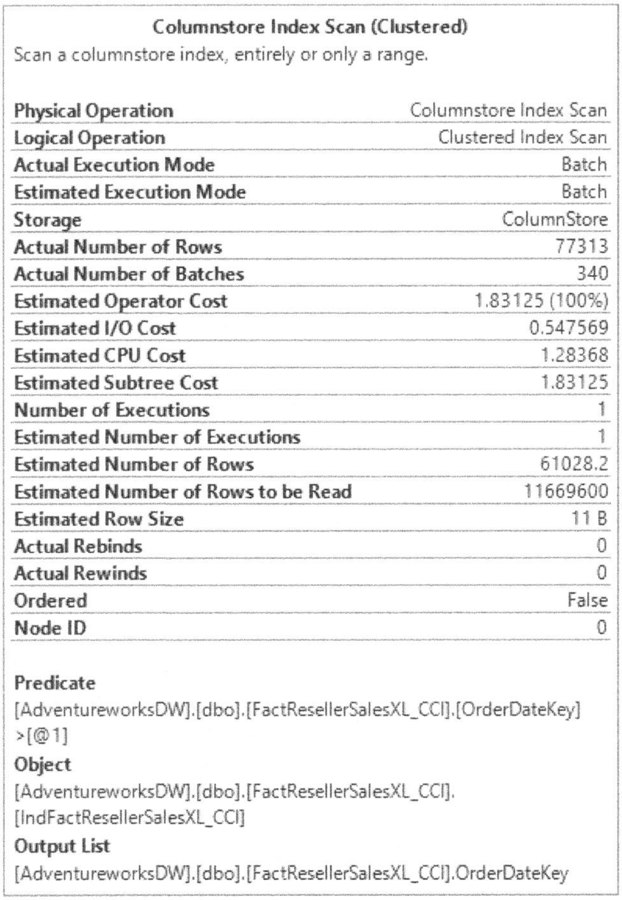

Columnstore Index Scan (Clustered)	
Scan a columnstore index, entirely or only a range.	
Physical Operation	Columnstore Index Scan
Logical Operation	Clustered Index Scan
Actual Execution Mode	Batch
Estimated Execution Mode	Batch
Storage	ColumnStore
Actual Number of Rows	77313
Actual Number of Batches	340
Estimated Operator Cost	1.83125 (100%)
Estimated I/O Cost	0.547569
Estimated CPU Cost	1.28368
Estimated Subtree Cost	1.83125
Number of Executions	1
Estimated Number of Executions	1
Estimated Number of Rows	61028.2
Estimated Number of Rows to be Read	11669600
Estimated Row Size	11 B
Actual Rebinds	0
Actual Rewinds	0
Ordered	False
Node ID	0

Predicate
[AdventureworksDW].[dbo].[FactResellerSalesXL_CCI].[OrderDateKey]
>[@1]
Object
[AdventureworksDW].[dbo].[FactResellerSalesXL_CCI].
[IndFactResellerSalesXL_CCI]
Output List
[AdventureworksDW].[dbo].[FactResellerSalesXL_CCI].OrderDateKey

Fig. 6.7 – Columnstore Index Scan (Clustered)

The displayed plans can be much more complex, and an object by object revision of the whole plan is important to spot any issues and warnings. If any warning is automatically detected by the SQL Server engine, it is displayed on the operator with a small yellow warning sign, as shown in the following image. If you then hover your mouse over the operator, you can find the entire warning:

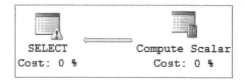

Fig. 6.8 – Warning sign displayed on the operator

Let's move on to the other category of operators, which are usually displayed with a nested lookup join:

- **Key lookup**: This is a lookup on a table with a clustered index.

- **RID lookup**: This is a lookup on a heap.

For join operators, SQL Server uses three types of physical operators:

- **Nested loop**: This join is used for many join operations, where for a row in the outer table the SQL looks for rows in the inner table and returns them. This operator is used mostly when the outer input contains many rows while the lookup table is small.

- **Merge join**: This algorithm is the most efficient way of joining two very large sets of data, which are both sorted on the join key.

- **Hash match**: This type of operator is used when the scenario doesn't fit any of the other join types. Hash match is often used when the tables are not properly sorted or if there are no indexes.

In this section, we saw that the graphical representation of the execution plan is comfortable to read and analyze. Since the internal format of the execution plan is also available in the XML file format, we can right-click anywhere on the graphical plan and save it as an XML file. This feature allows us to send and share the plan with colleagues so that we can analyze it together.

> **Note**
>
> The full operator reference can be found at `https://docs.microsoft.com/en-us/sql/relational-databases/showplan-logical-and-physical-operators-reference`. It lists all the logical and physical operators alphabetically.

The storage engine layer

The storage engine layer is responsible for accessing the data stored in the database and has two major components:

- Access methods
- Transaction and locking

Access methods are used to get the data out of the data and index pages. This is delivered as a resultant set of your SQL Server operation. The access methods then split deeper between operations on rows and indexes, which are responsible for maintaining the data in the row and index pages. There are several types of pages available within SQL Server. The user data is stored in the data pages, row-overflow pages, or LOB pages (used for large objects). If any indexes have been used, the index rows are stored on the index pages (and on the row-overflow and LOB pages too). Then, SQL Server uses several allocation maps to keep track of the used/free space in the data files. These pages are as follows:

- **Page Free Space** (**PFS**): This page keeps a bitmap of the usage of the pages in the data file.
- **Global Allocation Map** (**GAM**): The GAM page keeps track of the extents that have been allocated for uniform extents.
- **Shared Global Allocation Map** (**SGAM**): The SGAM keeps track of the extents that are used as mixed extents.

A space in the database is managed by objects called **extents**, which are made up of eight contiguous pages. Uniform extents are used by a single object, so all eight pages that form the extent are used for the same object. Here, the mixed extents can be shared by several different objects.

Performance monitoring overview

How can we define performance? We could say that it is the response time of a request. This means that we recognize which query, database, or whole instance of SQL Server is performing poorly while the response time (from the moment the request was sent by the session until the response information was received by the session) becomes unacceptable by the client. It can be caused by many factors, such as poor query syntax, missing indexes, or even network misconfiguration.

While monitoring and tuning the performance, we must not just measure the response times but also many factors affecting the performance. What's more, we need to find out the root cause for why the system slows down. Based on previous experience, it is good to consider the following points:

- **Number of requests**: Just a benchmark value that affects the level of concurrency on data and CPUs used by requests.

- **Space affected by the request**: How much data is moved between hard disk and memory? Is this amount of data necessary for request fulfillment or can it be reduced?

- **Request types**: Is the instance of SQL Server being asked for a lot of smaller random I/O operations, or is it being asked for long scanning operations such as aggregation queries?

- **Request difficulty**: Are certain requests simple (just reading data from one table) or are they complex (many JOIN operators, complicated conditions, and so on)?

As an extra consideration, we should know whether other concurrent services, such as reporting services or antivirus programs, share the server's resources with a monitored SQL Server instance.

When monitoring and troubleshooting performance, we have two perspectives on how to do it. The first and mostly recommended approach is to know the normal behavior of the OS and SQL Server. Having such knowledge, we can detect anomalies and address the reason behind them. By doing this, we could find a proper solution for the issue. The first approach to monitoring is to establish a **performance baseline**.

> **Note**
>
> The performance baseline is a set of measures showing the normal performance behavior of the system in certain areas, such as CPU or memory utilization, as well as changes to this behavior over time. When any sudden issue occurs, the performance baseline helps us address the problem quickly and accurately. Using a performance baseline is a proactive approach to performance monitoring because we can prevent serious performance issues before they occur.

We can establish the performance baseline on our own using tools, such as **Performance Monitor** or **Extended Events**, but a very good and effective tool is **Data Collection**. All these tools will be described in the following sections.

The second perspective is to react to situations where SQL Server stops responding in meaningful ways. This approach is reactive; the OS and SQL Server are not monitored on a regular basis, and the administrator just reacts to sudden failures or unacceptable delays in response to issues reported by users. This way of working seems to be ineffective, but we need to know how to start performance troubleshooting in such sudden situations.

We will also consider which role the person who monitors performance plays. In our book, we're paying attention to the administrator's point of view, but developers also have to tune their physical data structures and query performance. From a developer's perspective, we could talk about the bottom-up way of monitoring. As a developer, you start to create physical database schema consisting of tables, constraints, and indexes (we will discuss more about indexes in the *Indexes and maintenance* section). You then continue to write procedural objects such as views or stored procedures. All those procedural objects and ad hoc queries should be tuned before they are published to production.

Now, from an administrator's perspective, we could talk about top-down monitoring and performance tuning, because, as we described in *Chapter 1, Setting Up SQL Server*, and *Chapter 2, Keeping Your SQL Server Environment Healthy*, efficient working with SQL Server starts with proper OS preparation for SQL Server's installation and continues with correct installation and configuration on a SQL Server instance. Instance provisioning is not the last action taken by administrators, but this is the point where DBA starts to maintain SQL Server, as well as monitor and troubleshoot SQL Server's performance.

In the next section, we will go through the tools that are used for monitoring SQL Server's performance mostly by taking the up-to-bottom approach.

Tools for monitoring performance

SQL Server's toolset is very rich and when monitoring, we need to know which tool or tools we must use to address performance issues and how to interpret the results measured by any certain tool. In this section, we will go through all native SQL Server tools that help us monitor the performance of SQL Server.

Activity Monitor

Activity Monitor is a fast and relatively simple tool incorporated within SQL Server Management Studio. It could be used for a fast overview of current activities running on the instance. As shown in the following screenshot, **Activity Monitor** is accessible from the pop-up menu that can be called by right-clicking in **Object Explorer** at the instance level:

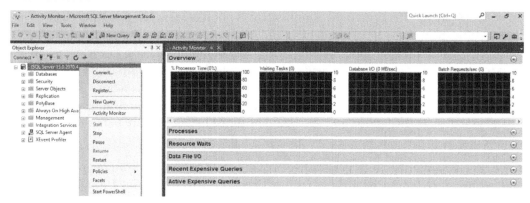

Fig. 6.9 – The Activity Monitor window

In the preceding screenshot, **Activity Monitor** is already open and has been divided into six sections:

- **Overview**
- **Processes**
- **Resource Waits**
- **Data File I/O**
- **Recent Expensive Queries**
- **Active Expensive Queries**

Let's take a look at these six sections in more detail.

Overview

The **Overview** section provides quick information about the current CPU effort that's being consumed by the instance of SQL Server, the current numbers of tasks waiting for any resource, the total amount of current physical data movement between the physical disk and buffer cache, and, as shown in the preceding screenshot, the current number of new requests coming to the instance. These diagrams are refreshed every 10 seconds by default, but it is possible to right-click on any diagram and change the refresh interval. Information provided by the **Overview** section of **Activity Monitor** is just about the current state of the instance; it does not provide comprehensive and detailed monitoring data.

Processes

Let 's take a look at the next section, called **Processes**. As shown in the following screenshot, this section provides a grid containing all the sessions that have currently been established against the instance of SQL Server, as well as their current state:

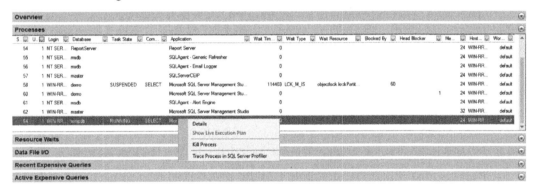

Fig. 6.10 – Process window

Let's describe the columns in the preceding grid. When opening the **Processes** section, the columns are shrunk but we can spread them.

For better orientation, the positions of these columns are also added:

- **Session ID**: This is the unique identifier of the session, also known as **SPID**. We can use the SPID when using the `kill` statement to interrupt the session when needed.

- **User process flag**: In **Activity Monitor**, it is prefiltered to **1** – only user sessions are shown. By clicking on the column name, filters can be added or changed on every column. It is very similar to filters, for example, in Microsoft Excel.

- **Login name**: This is the login context of a given session.

- **Database**: This is the database context of the session.

- **Task state**: The task state could be any of the following:

  a) **Empty**: The session exists but has no actual request to the instance.

  b) **RUNNING**: The session's request is currently processed by SQL Server (in the preceding screenshot, the only running request is for SPID **64**, which is **Activity Monitor** itself).

  c) **SUSPENDED**: Task is waiting for some resources blocked by another session; for example, we can see session **58** suspended.

- **Current type of command**: This is not a command text itself but just the type of the command, such as SELECT, ROLLBACK, and so on.

- **Application**: The application name is optionally written in connection strings. SQL Server and its services and applications always provide the application name, but in many third-party applications, the application name is not provided.

- **Wait time**: This is the time in milliseconds spent by the blocked session when waiting for the blocked resource. It is anything other than zero in rows with blocked sessions (SPID **58**, in our case).

- **Wait type**: SQL Server needs to protect its resources as it needs to control concurrency between sessions. When a resource is protected by a certain type of protection, a wait occurs. In our example, the **LCK_M_IS** wait is set on the SPID **58**. This is the wait for an incompatible lock that's held by another session.

- **Wait resource**: This is the description of the object on which the incompatible lock is set by another session.

- **Blocked by**: This is probably one of the most important columns. It says which session is the blocker of the current session. As shown in the preceding screenshot, we can see that SPID **58** is blocked by SPID **60**.

- **Head blocker**: This column contains bit flag 1 when the session holds resources while it is not waiting for another blockers. In the preceding screenshot, we can see that the blocking SPID **60** is not blocked by any other session, hence it is the head blocker. When the blocking time becomes unacceptable for the user, we can resolve the blocking conflict by killing the head blocker process.

- **Memory usage**: This shows how much memory, in KB, is currently being consumed by the session.

- **Host name**: This is the name of the SQL Server instance.

- **Workload group**: SQL Server supports a fair usage policy feature called **Resource Governor**. Resource Governor sets **workload groups** – named resource pools. Every session is assigned to the workload group and the name can be seen in the **Processes** section. (Resource Governor is beyond the scope of this book.)

> **Tip**
>
> When the user moves their mouse pointer over a column header in every section of **Activity Monitor**, a tooltip appears that provides information about the source DMV for the column.

With this section, we can do more than just look at what is working now. When you right-click on a certain session, a pop-up menu appears with these options:

- **Details**: This shows a dialog with command text (last executed or currently running).

- **Show Live Execution Plan**: This shows the execution plan of the query currently running (more about execution plans later in this chapter).

- **Kill Process**: When some process is being the head blocker, it can be disconnected by this option (or the `kill` statement can be executed; for example, `kill 60`).

- **Trace Process in SQL Server Profiler**: The **SQL Server Profiler** tool is opened and traces every activity of the session (there's more about **SQL Server Profiler** later in this chapter).

> **Tip**
>
> SQL Server does not resolve unacceptable blocking waits between sessions: the `kill` statement is the only hand-made way to resolve the conflict by an administrator. Always take a look at the process details before you kill the process. You do not want to be a murderer of some mission-critical business task.

Resource Waits

As noticed in the previous section, SQL Server needs to handle concurrency on resources between sessions. In this section, we will look at the statistics for the most frequent waits in time. This session does not provide any additional actions but shows what kind of resources sessions wait for:

Overview					
Processes					
Resource Waits					
Wait Category	Wait Time (ms/sec)	Recent Wait Time (ms/sec)	Average Waiter Count	Cumulative Wait Time (sec)	
Buffer I/O	0	0	0.0	7	
Buffer Latch	0	0	0.0	0	
Compilation	0	0	0.0	0	
Latch	0	0	0.0	0	
Lock	0	0	0.0	3193	
Logging	0	0	0.0	10	
Memory	0	0	0.0	15	
Network I/O	0	0	0.0	0	
Other	0	0	0.0	0	
Data File I/O					
Recent Expensive Queries					
Active Expensive Queries					

Fig. 6.11 – Resource waits statistics

In the preceding screenshot, a list of the most often recorded wait types issued by SQL Server instance is being displayed. The numbers in the columns are self-descriptive, but the first column, called **Wait Category**, needs some explanation. SQL Server recognizes several hundreds of wait types, and not all of them are well documented. We should know of several base categories that are common for routine operations of SQL Server.

> **Note**
>
> The wait itself is never good or bad. It is just waiting for some resource that's been blocked by another session. But when a wait starts to cause performance issues, we need to address the subsystem or the scenario where too many waits occur.

The following table describes the most common wait type categories and probable reasons of these waits:

Wait type category	Short description	Probable cause
Page Latch	Short-time lightweight protection of data pages in buffer cache. SQL Server issues this protection on data pages during operations such as read or write.	For example, non-leaf index pages are defended by latch to avoid concurrent movement of index pages during operations on indexed data. When page latch contention grows, the reason could be too many indexes on tables or neglected index maintenance.
Page IO Latch	Short-time lightweight protection of a data page when it is being read or written from or to disk.	When too many waits of this type occur, too many I/O operations are executed due to small memory or too many different queries and so on. Also a slow disk subsystem can cause this wait.
Latch	Short-time lightweight protection of other resources.	Many types of latches are covered within this wait category. When too many waits are encountered, deeper diagnostics is needed.
Lock	Protection of some part of the table (row, data page, extent, and so on) during transactions or SELECT statements.	Too many lock waits are caused by big concurrency of users or incorrectly controlled transaction. This can also be caused by fragmented data, too many indexes, or out-of-date statistics.
CXPACKET	Wait for dispatcher thread in parallel task.	CXPACKET should be a serious problem mainly in OLTP systems. For instance, it could mean that a parallel task (for example, partition scan) is executed on unevenly distributed data.
LOGBUFFER	Wait for writing to buffer for transaction log records.	Too many small transactions are executed at the same time.

Fig. 6.12 – Common wait type categories

Not every wait automatically causes performance problems. It is very usual that unacceptable waits are a symptom of another problem, which should be found and resolved.

Data File I/O

The **Data File I/O** section shows the current flow of data back and forth from every file of every database. The section is depicted in the following screenshot:

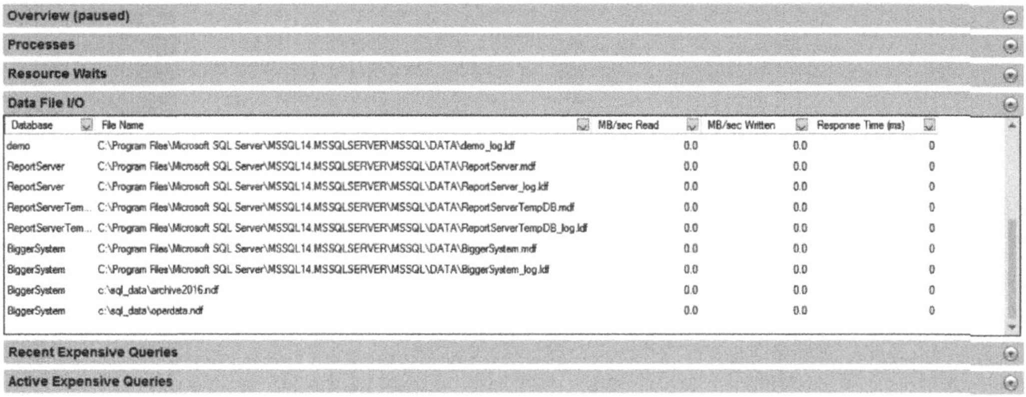
Overview (paused)
Processes
Resource Waits
Data File I/O
Database
File Name
MB/sec Read
MB/sec Written
Response Time (ms)
demo C:\Program Files\Microsoft SQL Server\MSSQL14.MSSQLSERVER\MSSQL\DATA\demo_log.ldf 0.0 0.0 0
ReportServer C:\Program Files\Microsoft SQL Server\MSSQL14.MSSQLSERVER\MSSQL\DATA\ReportServer.mdf 0.0 0.0 0
ReportServer C:\Program Files\Microsoft SQL Server\MSSQL14.MSSQLSERVER\MSSQL\DATA\ReportServer_log.ldf 0.0 0.0 0
ReportServerTem... C:\Program Files\Microsoft SQL Server\MSSQL14.MSSQLSERVER\MSSQL\DATA\ReportServerTempDB.mdf 0.0 0.0 0
ReportServerTem... C:\Program Files\Microsoft SQL Server\MSSQL14.MSSQLSERVER\MSSQL\DATA\ReportServerTempDB_log.ldf 0.0 0.0 0
BiggerSystem C:\Program Files\Microsoft SQL Server\MSSQL14.MSSQLSERVER\MSSQL\DATA\BiggerSystem.mdf 0.0 0.0 0
BiggerSystem C:\Program Files\Microsoft SQL Server\MSSQL14.MSSQLSERVER\MSSQL\DATA\BiggerSystem_log.ldf 0.0 0.0 0
BiggerSystem c:\sql_data\archive2016.ndf 0.0 0.0 0
BiggerSystem c:\sql_data\operdata.ndf 0.0 0.0 0
Recent Expensive Queries
Active Expensive Queries

Fig. 6.13 – Flow of data

We can check the amount of data and discover how big the data contention of every database is, as well as the amount of time spent by SQL Server waiting for data movement completion. We can also compare the amount of data that's moved from and to files of a certain database. This helps us see if the contention is distributed evenly across more files when they are added to the database.

Recent Expensive Queries and Active Expensive Queries

The last two sections of **Activity Monitor** are very similar to each other and both show a list of the most expensive queries, along with statistical information. The **Recent Expensive Queries** section shows statistics about finished queries, while the **Active Expensive Queries** section shows queries actually running.

Both sections are depicted in the following screenshot:

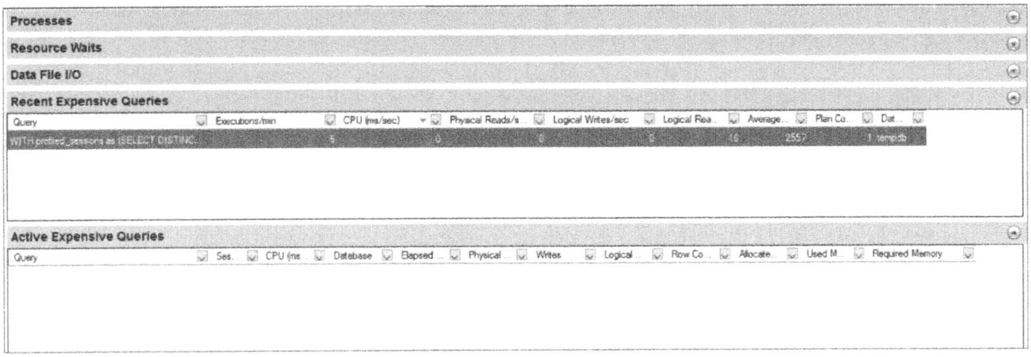

Fig. 6.14 – Recent Expensive Queries and Active Expensive Queries

The **Recent Expensive Queries** section shows the following:

- **Number of executions per minute**: How many times the query was executed during a minute.

- **Number of milliseconds spent by the query on CPUs per second**: Ratio of time spent on the CPU every minute.

- **Physical reads per second**: Amount of data page reads from a physical disk.

- **Logical reads per second**: Amount of logical read operations, which means that the data page is placed into the buffer cache and is used by the CPU.

- **Logical writes per seconds**: Similar to logical reads, logical writes are operations that make modifications to a data page in the buffer cache.

- **Average duration of the query**: Average amount of time needed for the number of executions.

- **Plan count**: Number of plan versions cached into the procedure cache.

- **Database name**: Database context of the query.

Data shown by the **Active Expensive Queries** section is similar to the **Recent Expensive Queries** section, which shows the most expensive queries in last 30 seconds, but some extra values are provided:

- **Session ID**: The SPID of the requester of the query. This could give context to the **Processes** section.

- **Elapsed time**: Total time needed for all completed executions of the query.

- **Row count**: Number of rows processed by the query execution.

- **Allocated memory**: Granted memory for the query execution.

- **Requested memory**: Memory requested by the query; if this value is less than the allocated memory, it could mean memory insufficiency.

- **Used memory**: Memory actually used by the query.

In both sections, it is possible to right-click a certain query and, from the pop-up menu, obtain query text, as well as the execution plan of the query.

Even though **Activity Monitor** serves as a quick and brief diagnostic tool, it provides a very useful set of information about SQL Server's current state and data contention. The only consideration that we must keep in mind is that all sections, except **Overview** and **Processes**, show statistical data that's erased with every restart of the data engine.

In the next section, we will explore some useful performance counters.

Performance monitor

Performance monitor is a commonly known tool that's delivered with Windows OS. It can show performance metrics from almost every part of the OS and from services running on it. We can see live data in the form of a chart, or we can grab the data by using so-called **data collection sets**. Data collection sets save values of counters selected by an administrator to a file. The file is then used for offline analysis or for correlation with trace data.

SQL Server and its services install their own performance counters. These counters can be correlated with common OS counters. These describe the current performance of subsystems, such as physical disks or memory.

> **Tip**
>
> The SQL Server service has many counters installed. A complete list of SQL Server's performance counters can be obtained by using the
> ```
> select distinct object_name, counter_name from
> sys.dm_os_performance_counters query.
> ```

A detailed list of common performance counters was mentioned in *Chapter 2, Keeping Your SQL Server Environment Healthy*.

When data is collected by the data collection set, it can be analyzed together with SQL Trace events. This extremely useful feature will be described in the next section.

SQL Server Profiler and SQL Trace

SQL Server Profiler is a GUI tool used to create and execute SQL Traces – SQL Server's proprietary server-side event providing feature. In this section, we will show you how to use **SQL Server Profiler**, **SQL Trace,** and data collection sets together.

SQL Server Profiler

SQL Server Profiler is a client tool used to create and execute **traces**. Trace is a set of events of certain types that the DBA, developer, and any other role is interested in. Through **SQL Server Profiler**, traces could be seen in the form of live data or saved to files or database tables.

> **Note**
>
> Even though **SQL Server Profiler** was announced as a deprecated tool (XE should be a successor to SQL Server Profiler), there is no replacement to open, view, and correlate traced events with performance monitor data.

SQL Profiler can be opened from SQL Server Management Studio by going to the **Tools** menu and clicking on the **SQL Server Profiler** option. When **SQL Server Profiler** is opened from SQL Server Management Studio, the **login** dialog will appear.

The second way you can access **SQL Server Profiler** is from the Start menu of Windows. Using this method causes **SQL Server Profiler** to open empty, and the user must use the **New Trace** button to start configuring the trace.

After DBA has been logged into a running instance of SQL Server, the following configuration dialog will appear:

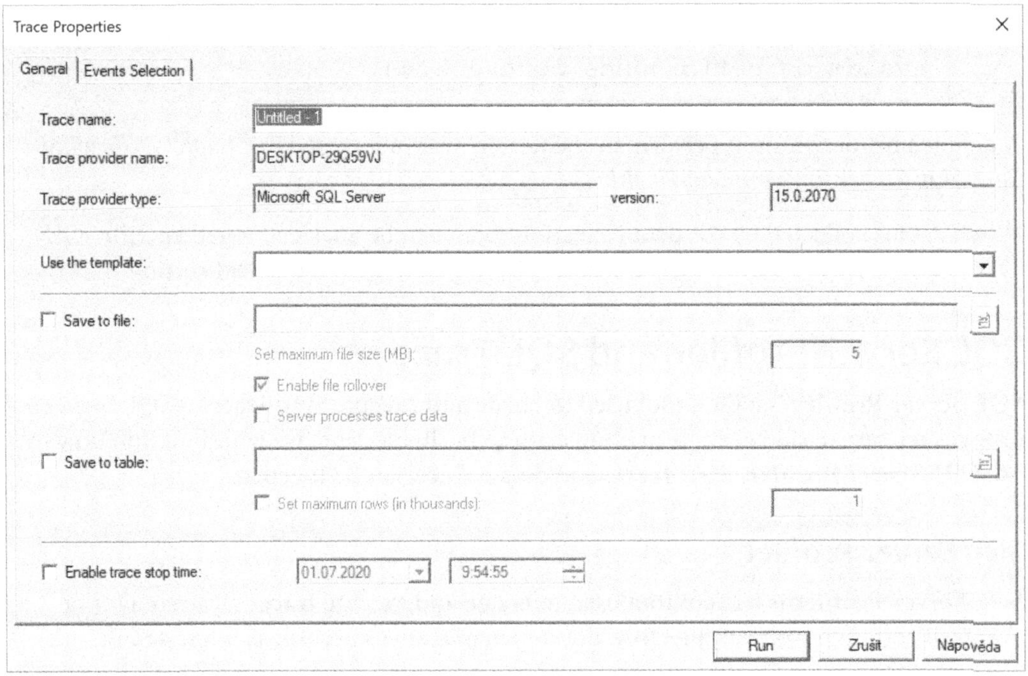

Fig. 6.15 – Trace properties configuration dialog

In one instance of **SQL Server Profiler**, more traces can be defined, which means that the trace can be named in the **Trace name** textbox for better orientation. **Trace provider name** is the name of the SQL Server instance on which the trace will be defined, while **Trace provider type** is the version description and version number of the connected instance.

SQL Server Profiler has several predefined templates that offer a simpler choice of events. We can also create custom templates or save a defined trace as a custom template for simple reuse. The drop-down control labeled **Use the template** shows all templates (predefined and custom together) and we can select one of them. We can also select the **Blank** template and then define our own set of events from scratch.

The **Save to file** and **Save to table** checkboxes are both optional. If we only need short-time monitoring, we will see live data and when we stop the monitoring process, data will be lost. We can switch on both channels together.

When saving to files, more files are often created. This is thanks to the **Enable file rollover** checkbox, which causes new file creation every time the actual file reaches the size limit set in the **Set maximum file size (MB)** textbox.

When the **Save to table** option enabled, a new login dialog appears, asking us to log into the instance of SQL Server where the data will be saved. An advantage of saving data to a table is in the ability to query the table by using regular SQL queries.

> **Tip**
>
> When saving trace data to a database table, use a SQL Server instance other than the monitored one to avoid circular contention. Files can also be queried through a function called `sys.fn_trace_gettable('c:\myTraces\', 3)`, where the first parameter is a folder containing `trc` files and the second is the number of files for reading.

The last but very useful setting on the **General** tab for trace configuration is the option to stop trace automatically. **SQL Server Profiler** is a very resource-consuming tool, and it is a very common mistake to start tracing by using **SQL Server Profiler** and then leaving the session unattended for a long time.

SQL Server Profiler will consume all available memory and, in extreme cases, could cause server crash. That's why it is a very good practice to enable the **Enable trace stop time** checkbox and set up a time for the trace to stop.

> **Note**
>
> Even though the stop time is set, never use **SQL Server Profiler** for long-term monitoring. The threshold time is a couple of hours.

Once the **General** tab has been configured, we need to get a step ahead and configure any events that we are interested in. This can be done on the second tab, called **Events Selection**:

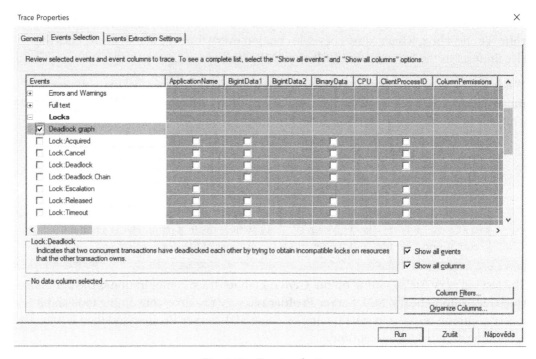

Fig. 6.16 – Events selection

As shown in the preceding screenshot, events are divided into categories for better orientation. Common examples of event categories are as follows:

- **Databases**: Contains events to monitor; for example, file growth operations

- **Errors and Warnings**: Contains events about many kinds of warnings or errors

- **Locks**: Events about different locking situations, such as deadlocks or lock escalations

- **Performance**: Events providing, for example, execution plans in several formats, including XML format used for graphical execution plan rendering in Management Studio

- **Stored Procedures**: Events showing stored procedures execution

- **TSQL**: Events showing the execution of ad hoc queries

When a certain event category is collapsed, events appear, and we can select the ones we are interested in by clicking the checkbox on the left-hand side of the event. In the preceding screenshot, the **Deadlock Graph** event has been selected as an example. The grid of events on the **Event Selection** tab shows all the possible columns for all possible events listed in alphabetical order. However, not every event provides the same data.

As shown in our **Deadlock Graph** example, almost none of the columns can be selected because this event type provides quite a small set of information. The most important column, in this case, is `TextData`; it contains the graph of SPIDs attending the deadlock, SPID rolled back by SQL Server as a deadlock victim, and resources cross-locked by the attending SPIDs.

Let's take a look at another event type, called `SQL:StmtCompleted`. This event type belongs to the category called **TSQL** and shows useful performance data, besides the ad hoc query text that was captured by the event. The most interesting columns are as follows:

- `TextData`: The text of the query.
- `Duration`: The overall response time.
- `CPU time`: The time spent on CPUs. This time could be bigger than the duration due to parallelism.
- `Reads`: The number of logical data page reads.
- `Writes`: The number of physical data page writes. When the query is `SELECT`, this indicates that the `SELECT` statement is too difficult to be processed and that SQL Server needs to save any intermediate results in the `tempdb` database. Such a query is a candidate for optimization.

Every event contains many columns, but it is a good thing to select only those columns that are needed for diagnostics. In many cases, for example, the user context or database name could be useless, especially when only one user's events are filtered in a certain database. Selecting only the required columns helps maintain saved event data.

In the bottom-right corner, there's two checkboxes called **Show all events** and **Show all columns**. Both are used to filter the event grid to show selected events and columns only. When events and cells are selected, it is very important to filter events just for the needed ones.

The **Column Filters** button opens a new dialog window where filters are configured:

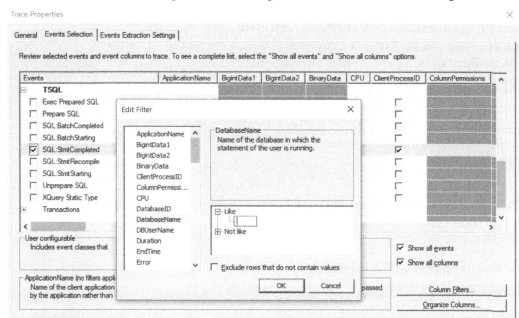

Fig. 6.17 – Configuring filters in Trace Properties

The preceding screenshot shows the filter dialog open. The column that must be filtered is selected in the left list, and any possible comparisons appear in the tree on the right0hand side of the dialog. The preceding screenshot shows that `DatabaseName` has to contain the `demo` value that was added by the user.

When everything has been configured correctly and precisely, the **Run** button closes the configuration dialog and **SQL Server Profiler** performs several actions behind the scenes. Typically, it generates a SQL Trace definition script and executes the script on the monitored instance of SQL Server. SQL Trace on the server side starts event capturing and sends the captured data back to **SQL Server Profiler**. **SQL Server Profiler** then opens a trace window to show live data and shows the events that had been obtained from SQL Trace. When an awaited event is raised, it is shown in the trace window, and it is also saved to the configured storage:

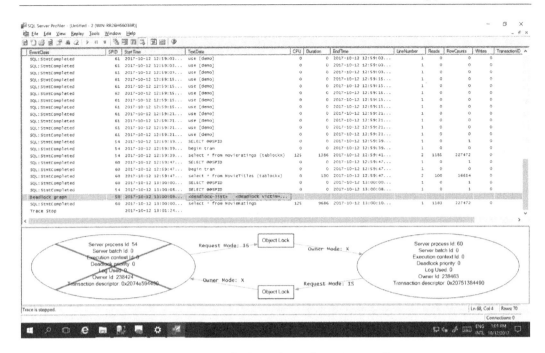

Fig. 6.18 – Deadlock graph caught in SQL Profiler

As shown in the preceding screenshot, the trace window is divided into two parts. The upper part is a grid showing captured events, along with the columns that were selected during configuration. The bottom part shows details of a selected event from the grid. For text events such as TSQL:StmtCompleted, the text of the query is shown; our example shows an event called Deadlock graph. This event type describes sessions that have been in conflict, resources that have been locked by incompatible locks, and finally the session that was selected by SQL Server as a deadlock victim, whose transaction was rolled back with Error 1205 and sent back to the client.

Data captured by SQL Profiler can be synchronized with data that's been collected by the performance monitor. This is possible when both data sources – performance monitor counters and SQL Trace data – are saved into files. If the data was captured by SQL Profiler and the trace was stopped, close and reopen the file. When you do this, a new menu option, called **Import Performance Data**, is enabled. This menu option is depicted in the following screenshot:

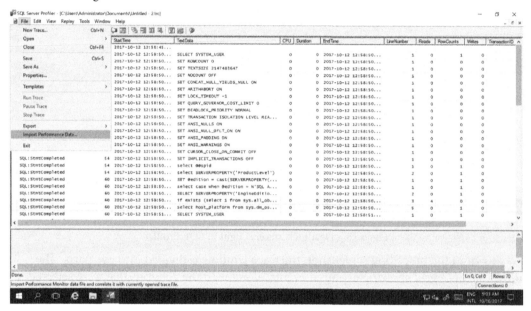

Fig. 6.19 – Import performance data

This menu option opens the **Open File** dialog. Here, you need to find the file that has a `.blg` extension. This is the file that's used by performance monitor to capture performance data.

Both data sources – that is, trace data and performance data – are synchronized by SQL Profiler. Once again, the trace window is divided to show a grid and detailed information from the trace in the top part, and then performance monitor diagrams in the bottom part, as shown in the following screenshot:

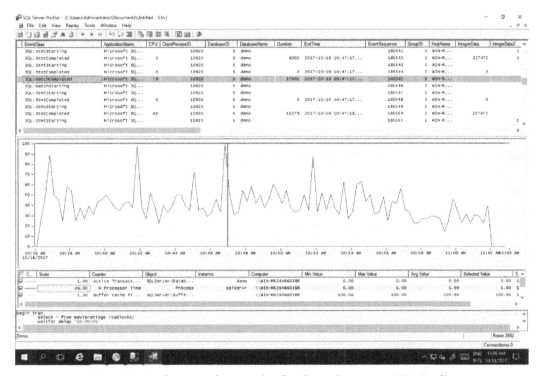

Fig. 6.20 – Performance data correlated with caught events in SQL Profile

Both SQL Trace data and Performance Monitor data are drawn together, and both parts are time-synchronized. When clicking on a certain event in the grid, the vertical red line in the chart part moves back and forth synchronously to show the moment in time with the current values from performance monitor.

The same synchronous movement occurs when you click on some place in the chart; the cursor in the grid moves onto the row that is close to the selected moment. This helps identify poorly performing queries in correlation with data captured by performance monitor.

SQL Profiler is a well-known tool that has two disadvantages. The first concerns huge resource consumption. The second problem is that SQL Profiler has been marked by Microsoft as deprecated since SQL Server 2012; hence, new events for newer features of SQL Server won't be added to SQL Profiler/SQL Trace.

When you need to monitor incoming events, you do not need to run SQL Profiler every time, but SQL Profiler does help you generate a script for more efficient server-side traditional monitoring through **SQL Trace**. In the next section, we will explore SQL Trace in more detail.

SQL Trace

SQL Trace is a non-visual server-side tracing feature of SQL Server. SQL Profiler, described in the previous section, serves as a client-side viewer of data that's been captured and provided by SQL Trace. A SQL Trace session is defined by a set of system-stored procedures. Writing a new trace from scratch is very difficult or almost impossible, which is why SQL Profiler provides a script option. When a new trace is defined in SQL Profiler, it can be scripted from the **File** menu. The exact procedure is as follows:

1. Define and run a new trace in SQL Profiler.

2. From the **File** menu, choose the **Export | Script trace definition** option, and then **For SQL Server 2005 - 2017.**

3. The **Save as** dialog will appear, where you you can give a name to your script and save the file.

The trace definition script looks like this (this example has been shortened for the sake of simplicity):

```
-- Create a Queue
declare @rc int
declare @TraceID int
declare @maxfilesize bigint
set @maxfilesize = 5

-- Please replace the text InsertFileNameHere, with an
appropriate
-- ... the description continues

exec @rc = sp_trace_create @TraceID output, 0, N'C:\myTraces\
myTrace.trc', @maxfilesize, NULL
if (@rc != 0) goto error

-- Client side File and Table cannot be scripted

-- Set the events
declare @on bit
set @on = 1
exec sp_trace_setevent @TraceID, 24, 1, @on
exec sp_trace_setevent @TraceID, 24, 9, @on
exec sp_trace_setevent @TraceID, 24, 2, @on

-- ... many sp_trace_setevent procedure calls were erased here
```

```
exec sp_trace_setevent @TraceID, 40, 61, @on
exec sp_trace_setevent @TraceID, 40, 64, @on
exec sp_trace_setevent @TraceID, 40, 66, @on

-- Set the Filters
declare @intfilter int
declare @bigintfilter bigint

exec sp_trace_setfilter @TraceID, 35, 0, 6, N'demo'
-- Set the trace status to start
exec sp_trace_setstatus @TraceID, 1

-- display trace id for future references
select TraceID=@TraceID
goto finish

error:
select ErrorCode=@rc

finish:
go
```

When the trace definition script is saved, it can be used anytime and on every instance of SQL Server. As shown at the end of the script, the script selects a new `TraceID` number. This is an integer that identifies the running trace. When the trace is no longer needed, simply call `EXEC sp_trace_setstatus <the trace id is placed here>`, `0`, which stops the trace. If `TraceID` is missed, it can be obtained from the `sys.traces` system view. The command for this is as follows:

```
select * from sys.traces
```

SQL Trace saves the server's resources because the only data provider available when it is running is the so-called **file provider**. On the other hand, when using SQL Profiler, trace's memory data provider is used to push data back to SQL Profiler, which is a much more memory-consuming approach.

In the next section, we will pay attention to the successor of SQL Trace and **SQL Server Profiler**, called Extended Events (also called **xEvents** or simply **XE**).

Extended Events

Extended Events, intended for event monitoring, is a feature developed as a successor of SQL Profiler. It works similar to how SQL Server Profiler works, but XE is a modern tool that uses the native events provided by SQL Server's features. The difference between the two is that far fewer resources than SQL Server Profiler, which inevitably makes it the preferred way to work. The other reason XE is now preferred is because SQL Profiler is marked for deprecation.

Frugality is not the only advantage of XE. Unlike **SQL Server Profiler**, XE can capture events provided by new features such as columnstore indexes, In-Memory OLTP, Machine Learning Services, and so on.

The third big advantage of XE is that the session definitions are saved in SQL Server's metadata, so the configuration of an XE session made by a DBA is not done repeatedly. Once the XE session has been created, the session can be started and stopped on demand from SQL Server Management Studio. Take look at the following screenshot:

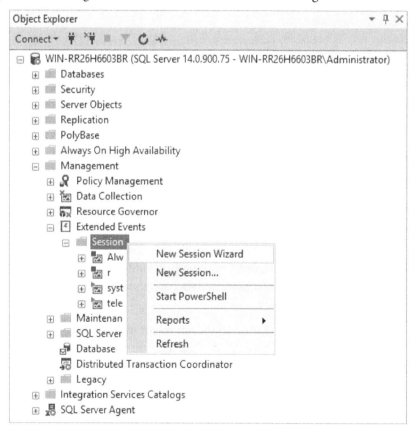

Fig. 6.21 – New Session Wizard in Object Explorer

Extended Events definitions are placed in Management Studio, under **Management node** in **Object Explorer**. Some system sessions are created during SQL Server installation and can be started and stopped when needed.

When we want to create our own XE session definition, we can do so via the wizard, but for better control over preciseness and granularity, it's better to use the second option, **New Session…**, in the pop-up menu. When the **New Session…** menu option is selected, a dialog window for the session's creation will appear, as shown in the following screenshot:

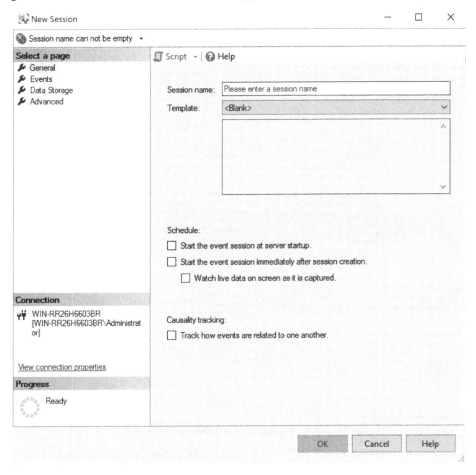

Fig. 6.22 – New session creation window

The first tab of the window is the **General** tab. The session must be named in the **Session name** text field, and a template can also be selected from the **Template** dropdown. Unlike **SQL Server Profiler**, XE provides more templates. Other controls can be edited later. A session can start every time the SQL Server instance is started if needed. This option is useful for server-level monitoring for later analysis.

When **Start the event session immediately after session creation** is selected, the session is saved and started. When the same option is left off, the session is just saved but does not start to monitor selected events. When the session is started, live data can be displayed. This option causes the window to open within Management Studio so that DBA can view how the events are coming in. The session can run in unattended mode, even if the live data window is closed.

The second, and probably the most important, tab in the session creation window is **Events**. It is shown in the following screenshot:

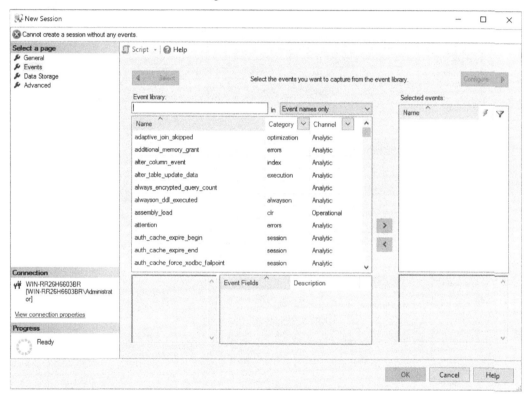

Fig. 6.23 – Event selection in the Extended Events window

The left list in the preceding screenshot contains every event that can be monitored. It provides a huge set of possibilities, so the empty text field above the list is extremely useful – we can type part of the event name in here (for example, sql) and the list will be filtered. Another option is to filter events by **Category** or by **Channel**. Once the event has been found, it can be moved to the right list by either double-clicking on it or by using the arrow buttons placed between both lists.

It is very important to refine the configuration of every selected event. An event is selected in the right list and the **Configure** button is enabled and should be used. The appearance of the **Events** tab changes and the new view is provided, as shown in the following screenshot:

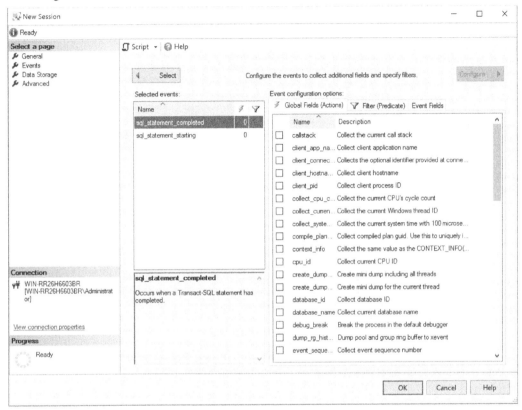

Fig. 6.24 – Events tab new look

A big difference, when comparing XE to **SQL Server Profiler**, is that the event fields are not selected by default. However, these fields should be selected by an administrator. Fields are divided into common **Global fields** or **Actions** (the first tab in the preceding screenshot), while proprietary fields hidden in the **Event fields** tab. It is typical for these event fields to intersect global fields, so decide what fields you wish to capture carefully.

The middle tab, called **Filter (Predicate)**, is intended for filter definitions. Unlike **SQL Server Profiler**, every selected event type is filtered separately. This may seem confusing, but it gives DBA more control over what to filter. The **Filters** tab is shown in the following screenshot:

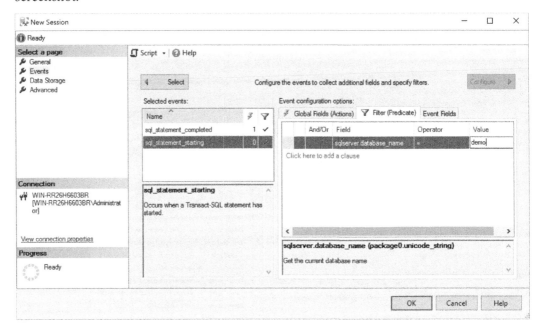

Fig. 6.25 – Filters tab

Filter configuration is quite simple – filter rows are added when the **Click here to add a clause** text box is clicked. Then, a filter attribute is selected from the dropdown when the **Field** textbox is clicked. We continue to fill in the rest of textboxes; that is, **Operator** and **Value**.

As events are configured, they can be viewed in the form of live data, but they can also be saved. The following screenshot shows the **Data Storage** tab, which is used for storage configuration:

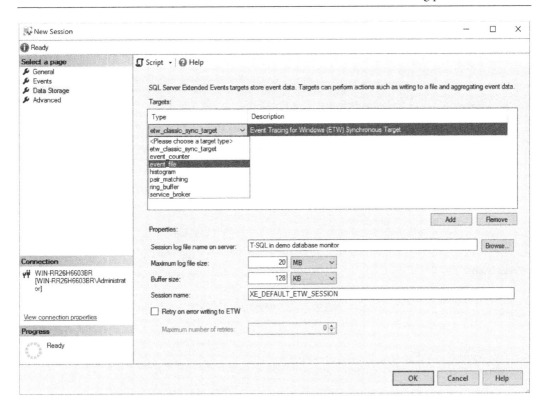

Fig. 6.26 – Data storage tab

Session data can be stored in more providers. The expanded dropdown shows all the available options, but the most typical storage targets are as follows:

- `event_file`: A standalone file for event capture.

- `pair_matching`: This storage type allows you to define the starting and ending event that establishes the pair of events. The starting event is shown when it occurs and when the matching end event is shown, both events are paired and erased.

- `ring_buffer`: Live data shown to DBA.

The following screenshot shows the **Advanced** tab:

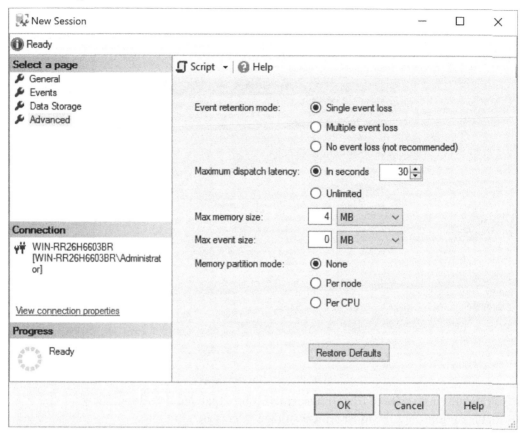

Fig. 6.27 – Advanced tab

The **Advanced** tab is used to set a limit on how many events can be lost without a session failure; how many seconds XE can hold data before it's sent to the target, such as live data or event file; and whether we can divide memory into partitions according to **NUMA** nodes for event capturing. In the preceding screenshot, the settings have been left as their default values.

When everything has been configured, the session is saved, and it's shown in the **Sessions** folder, under the **Extended Events** node in **Object Explorer**. By right-clicking (see *Fig. 6.21* in this section), the session can be started or stopped, exported, or live data can be opened and explored. The live data window is shown in the following screenshot:

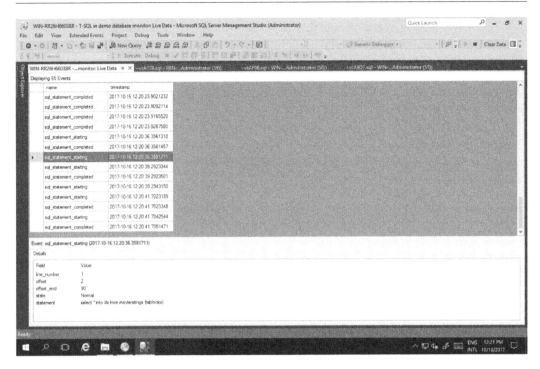

Fig. 6.28 – Live data window

XE is a very efficient tool for monitoring a wide range of events repeatedly. Sometimes, it looks confusing, but with some practice, it becomes a very good helper when monitoring SQL Server's performance.

So far, we have worked mostly with visual monitoring tools. In the next section, we will explore some source objects that provide data to these tools, as well as our needs.

Dynamic management

Dynamic management consists of a set of system views and table-valued functions intended for the querying. Many dynamic management objects are used by other tools, such as Management Studio reports or **Activity Monitor**, but we can use them to explore SQL Server ourselves. Let's take a look at some very simple naming conventions:

- Every dynamic management object is placed in the sys schema.

- Every dynamic management object starts with the dm_ prefix.

- Every dynamic management object also has a second (or sometimes a third) prefix defining subsystem monitored by this object; for example, sys.dm_db_ or sys.dm_exec_.

- Dynamic management objects that have the `_stats` suffix show data that's been captured from SQL Server's last startup. This is erased every time SQL Server is restarted.

The only property that can't be seen in the object's name is the type of the object – is it a view or a function? In this way, we can profit from Management Studio **IntelliSense**. IntelliSense is basically a dropdown that provides naming suggestions that appear when we start typing a query into Management Studio. When a dynamic management object's name is written and the object is a function, IntelliSense suggests brackets with parameters.

One more advantage is that dynamic management objects have quite long, but self-descriptive, names. When we start typing, for example, `select * from sys.coun`, which means nothing itself, IntelliSense will advise that we use the `sys.dm_os_performance_counters` view.

> **Tip**
> Do not try to remember all the names of dynamic management objects. Be guided by IntelliSense; it is more comfortable and the risk of typos is reduced.

Dynamic management objects are divided by subsystems. We've summarize some of them in the following table:

Dynamic management object prefix	Description	Example
sys.dm_db_*	Database statistics such as index state or database file usage	sys.dm_db_index_usage_stats sys.dm_db_file_space_usage
sys.dm_exec_*	Operational information such as sessions, plan cache, and many others	sys.dm_exec_sessions sys.dm_exec_requests sys.dm_exec_cached_plans
sys.dm_os_*	Information bound to the operating system, wait statistics, memory state, and so on	sys.dm_os_performance_counters sys.dm_os_buffer_descriptors sys.dm_os_virtual_file_stats
sys.dm_tran_*	Transaction state descriptions	sys.dm_tran_locks
sys.dm_sql_*	Describes object dependencies (tables used by views and so on)	sys.dm_sql_referenced_entities sys.dm_sql_referencing_entities

Fig. 6.29 – Dynamic management objects

There are many other dynamic management objects that have been defined. The full list can be found on MSDN (`https://docs.microsoft.com/en-us/sql/relational-databases/system-dynamic-management-views/system-dynamic-management-views?view=sql-server-ver15`), but it's not possible to create a list of all of them in this book. For detailed insights, we can use **Object Browser** to explore all these objects. Views are kept in every database, under the <**database name**> | **Views** | **System Views** node, while functions are placed in the `master` database. You can find these by going to **master** | **Programmability** | **Functions** | **System Functions** | **Table-Valued Functions** in **Object Explorer**.

Dynamic management provides very detailed information about any subsystem on SQL Server. Often, we need to join more objects to add readability to the results of DMV query. The next section will show an example of how to combine more system objects so that we can see what happens on the SQL Server.

How to use dynamic management

Sometimes, it is hard to combine system objects, especially dynamic management, together. No simple and unified instructions exist for it, but the following example shows a way to think about system queries.

One of the most common performance issues is frequent recompilations of execution plans. We want to have an overview of plan cache content. We want to know which plans are cached and how they are reused. The simplest information is provided by the `sys.dm_exec_cached_plans` view. Let's execute the following script:

```
select * from sys.dm_exec_cached_plans
```

We will see the following result:

	bucketid	refcounts	usecounts	size_in_bytes	memory_object_address	cacheobjtype	objtype	plan_handle	pool_id	parent_plan_handle
1	18419	2	1	81920	0x0000018F90B2E060	Compiled Plan	Proc	0x050000608D5ED731303E1F8C8F0100000100000000000000...	2	NULL
2	21020	2	1	204800	0x0000018F89658060	Compiled Plan	Proc	0x050006002DC94956D0361F8C8F0100000100000000000000...	2	NULL
3	2269	2	1	57344	0x0000018F89668060	Compiled Plan	Proc	0x05000600F4A45555702F1F8C8F0100000100000000000000...	2	NULL
4	3471	2	1	49152	0x0000018F89630060	Compiled Plan	Proc	0x050000604BC4A36310281F8C8F0100000100000000000000...	2	NULL
5	38287	2	1	57344	0x0000018F8962E060	Compiled Plan	Proc	0x05000600D9B4DF5550FFA0988F0100000100000000000000...	2	NULL
6	13396	2	1	188416	0x0000018F8508A060	Compiled Plan	Proc	0x05000600A329877A90F1A0988F0100000100000000000000...	2	NULL
7	17208	2	1	98304	0x0000018F8FC02060	Compiled Plan	Proc	0x0500060068796868F0F7A0988F0100000100000000000000...	2	NULL
8	28554	2	1	573440	0x0000018F8FE0C060	Compiled Plan	Proc	0x050004009BA4491230EAA0988F0100000100000000000000...	2	NULL
9	11989	2	1	49152	0x0000018F8BAA0060	Compiled Plan	Adhoc	0x060005006F63993560C14E838F0100000100000000000000...	2	NULL
10	17452	2	1	49152	0x0000018F835BC060	Compiled Plan	Adhoc	0x0600060046C9161E5019A1988F0100000100000000000000...	2	NULL
11	35630	2	1	40960	0x0000018F8A322060	Compiled Plan	Adhoc	0x060005008E790D27D011A1988F0100000100000000000000...	2	NULL
12	38417	2	2	253952	0x0000018F8AC84060	Compiled Plan	Adhoc	0x06000600AACD810E500AA1988F0100000100000000000000...	2	NULL
13	32141	2	2	163840	0x0000018F88718D60	Compiled Plan	Adhoc	0x060006001BA31F37D002A1988F0100000100000000000000...	2	NULL
14	1977	1	2	65536	0x0000018F8A644060	Parse Tree	View	0x0500FF7FEC5CE6D85041648A8F0100000100000000000000...	2	NULL
15	281	1	12	49152	0x0000018F844F4060	Parse Tree	View	0x050004007B1DC57350414F848F0100000100000000000000...	2	NULL
16	576	1	7	40960	0x0000018F84118D60	Parse Tree	View	0x0500FF7F8053E1F5508111848F0100000100000000000000...	2	NULL

Fig. 6.30 – Overview of plan cache content

Such a result is full of almost unreadable and hence useless numbers. Some columns make sense to us, namely the following:

- `usecounts`: How many times the plan was reused.
- `size_in_bytes`: This is the size of the plan in memory (bigger plans are scratched later than smaller plans).
- `objtype`: Describes the origin of the plan, such as stored procedures (**Proc**) or ad hoc query call (**AdHoc**).

The most important column is `plan_handle`. It is the unique identifier of the plan that's kept in the plan cache. To uncover the actual query that's hidden under this terrible number, we should use the `sys.dm_exec_sql_text` function. This function consumes `plan_handle` as a parameter and returns the SQL definition of the query.

Let's execute the following query:

```
select
  cp.usecounts
  , cp.size_in_bytes
  , cp.objtype
  , sqltext.dbid
  , sqltext.objectid
  , sqltext.text
from sys.dm_exec_cached_plans as cp
  cross apply sys.dm_exec_sql_text(cp.plan_handle) as sqltext
```

The `cross apply` operator substitutes a `JOIN` operator when classical `JOIN` can't be used due to the missing join criteria on the function's result set. This join is done through the parameter of the function. The result of the preceding query is much more readable now:

	usecounts	size_in_bytes	objtype	dbid	objectid	text
2	6	57344	Proc	6	1431676148	CREATE PROCEDURE [dbo].[GetAnnouncedKey] @Install...
3	6	49152	Proc	6	1671677003	CREATE PROCEDURE [dbo].[GetAllConfigurationInfo] AS ...
4	6	57344	Proc	6	1440724185	CREATE PROCEDURE [dbo].[GetCurrentProductInfo] AS ...
5	3	573440	Proc	4	306816155	CREATE PROCEDURE sp_sqlagent_get_perf_counters ...
6	1	81920	Proc	6	836198029	CREATE PROCEDURE [dbo].[GetMyRunningJobs] @Com...
7	1	49152	Adhoc	5	NULL	select cp.usecounts , cp.size_in_bytes , cp.objtype , sql...
8	1	188416	Adhoc	1	NULL	SELECT dtb.name AS [Name], dtb.database_id AS [ID], CAS...
9	1	65536	Prepared	1	NULL	(@_msparam_0 nvarchar(4000))SELECT CAST(COLLATION...
10	1	368640	Prepared	1	NULL	(@_msparam_0 nvarchar(4000))SELECT dtb.collation_name ...
11	1	57344	Adhoc	5	NULL	select * from sys.dm_exec_cached_plans as cp cross apply...
12	2	49152	Adhoc	6	NULL	select top 1 NtSecDescState from SecData where NtSecDe...
13	1	40960	Adhoc	5	NULL	select * from movieratings (tablockx)
14	7	253952	Adhoc	6	NULL	declare @BatchID uniqueidentifier ...
15	7	163840	Adhoc	6	NULL	declare @BatchID uniqueidenti...
16	2	24576	View	32767	-852794453	create function sys.fn_helpcollations ( ) returns table as ...
17	4	1236992	View	32767	-213	CREATE VIEW sys.databases AS SELECT d.name, d.id ...
18	3	24576	View	32767	-242583247	CREATE VIEW sys.fulltext_languages AS SELECT lcid, na...
19	3	114688	View	32767	-194	CREATE VIEW sys.syslanguages AS SELECT langid, datef...
20	4	32768	View	32767	-245973352	CREATE FUNCTION sys.dm_exec_sql_text(@handle varbin...
21	4	65536	View	32767	-655991572	create view sys.dm_exec_cached_plans as SELECT b...
22	12	49152	View	4	1942297979	CREATE VIEW sysalerts_performance_counters_view AS ...
23	7	40960	View	32767	-169782400	CREATE VIEW sys.dm_os_performance_counters AS SEL...

Fig. 6.31 – plan_handle query results

As shown in the preceding screenshot, the column set was reduced in the SELECT clause to provide more readability, which means it is now much more useful. The new columns that came from the sys.dm_exec_sql_text function are as follows:

- dbid: ID of the database in which the query was executed (pay attention to ID 32767 – it is the resource database).

- objectid: ID of the object saving the query definition (for example, stored procedure). Ad hoc queries do not have objectid.

- text: The text of the cached plan itself.

We want the information to be a little easier to read. We want to filter the database context through the monitored one, and we also want to see the database name, as well as object name. Let's adjust the query one more time:

```
select
  cp.usecounts
  , cp.size_in_bytes
  , cp.objtype
  , db_name(sqltext.dbid) as dbname
  , sqltext.objectid
  , s.name as schemaname
```

```
    , o.name as objname
    , sqltext.text
from sys.dm_exec_cached_plans as cp
    cross apply sys.dm_exec_sql_text(cp.plan_handle) as sqltext
    left join sys.objects as o on o.object_id = sqltext.objectid
    left join sys.schemas as s on s.schema_id = o.schema_id
where sqltext.dbid = db_id('demo')
```

Some new functions and joins were added to the query. Let's describe them:

- db_name(): The metadata function used in the SELECT clause. It translates the database ID into a name.

- Joining the sys.objects view: We can use the object_name() function. It translates the object ID into its name but without the schema name. That's why the sys.objects view (not the dynamic view, just the catalog view) is added to the SELECT statement.

- Joining the sys.schemas view: Its purpose is the same as when joining sys.objects – we want to know the full object's identifier within the database in the form of <schema>.<object>.

- Instead of joining the sys.objects and sys.schemas catalogs, we can use OBJECT_NAME() and OBJECT_SCHEMA_NAME() functions. The OBJECT_SCHEMA_NAME() function accepts the object_id parameter and returns the name of the object's schema in the database.

Ad hoc queries are not saved objects. That's why LEFT JOIN operators are used to see ad hoc query plans and object plans together.

Do we want more? We always want more, and the preceding information is extremely useful when it comes to analyzing query performance and adding a query plan. A query plan is a tree containing a set of operators that are needed by SQL Server to fulfill the user's request. A query plan is very desirable for developers who work on query optimization; for now, let's just capture it. The last dynamic management object we used in our example was a function called sys.dm_exec_query_plan. This function returns the plan in XML format. A situation can arise where the query plan can be NULL. This is typically caused when the batch or stored procedure contains a statement that has not been compiled by SQL Server (that is, OPTION RECOMPILE is used in one or more statements in the batch).

This query is shown in the following example:

```
select
  cp.usecounts
  , cp.size_in_bytes
  , cp.objtype
  , db_name(sqltext.dbid) as dbname
  , sqltext.objectid
  , s.name as schemaname
  , o.name as objname
  , sqltext.text
  , qplan.query_plan
from sys.dm_exec_cached_plans as cp
  cross apply sys.dm_exec_sql_text(cp.plan_handle) as sqltext
  cross apply sys.dm_exec_query_plan(cp.plan_handle) as qplan
  left join sys.objects as o on o.object_id = sqltext.objectid
  left join sys.schemas as s on s.schema_id = o.schema_id
where sqltext.dbid = db_id('demo')
```

One more `cross apply` operator is added to join the new function to the query, and a column called `query_plan` is added to the `SELECT` clause. The result is depicted in the following screenshot:

	usecounts	size_in_bytes	objtype	dbname	objectid	schemaname	objname	text	query_plan
1	1	49152	Proc	demo	1845581613	NULL	NULL	create proc dbo.procSelectMovieByRating @rating ..	<ShowPlanXML xmlns="http://schemas.microsoft.com...
2	1	16384	Adhoc	demo	NULL	NULL	NULL	SET SHOWPLAN_XML OFF	<ShowPlanXML xmlns="http://schemas.microsoft.com...
3	1	16384	Adhoc	demo	NULL	NULL	NULL	SET SHOWPLAN_ALL OFF	<ShowPlanXML xmlns="http://schemas.microsoft.com...
4	1	16384	Adhoc	demo	NULL	NULL	NULL	SET SHOWPLAN_TEXT OFF	<ShowPlanXML xmlns="http://schemas.microsoft.com...
5	5	368640	Adhoc	demo	NULL	NULL	NULL	SELECT dtb.name AS [Name], dtb.state AS [State] F...	<ShowPlanXML xmlns="http://schemas.microsoft.com...
6	2	106496	Adhoc	demo	NULL	NULL	NULL	select cp.usecounts , cp.size_in_bytes , cp.objty...	<ShowPlanXML xmlns="http://schemas.microsoft.com...
7	1	98304	Adhoc	demo	NULL	NULL	NULL	select cp.usecounts , cp.size_in_bytes , cp.objty .	<ShowPlanXML xmlns="http://schemas.microsoft.com...
8	1	98304	Adhoc	demo	NULL	NULL	NULL	select cp.usecounts , cp.size_in_bytes , cp.objty .	<ShowPlanXML xmlns="http://schemas.microsoft.com...
9	2	40960	Adhoc	demo	NULL	NULL	NULL	select * from movieratings (tablockx)	<ShowPlanXML xmlns="http://schemas.microsoft.com...

Fig. 6.32 – query_plan column

The right-most column contains links to the XML representation of the query plan. When clicked, the graphical query plan is opened in a separate window in Management Studio. This plan is shown in the following screenshot:

Fig. 6.33 – Graphical query plan

The query plan in the preceding screenshot is very simple. It shows a full scan of the table (recall that the table is heap). From the scan result, the result of the query is formatted and sent back to the client.

So far, we have been working with several complicated tools to monitor and analyze SQL Server's performance from different viewpoints. It is really difficult to join and correlate monitoring results with such wide monitoring tools. However, it is very good to know these techniques as they are the base for the next monitoring approach we'll be looking at, called data collection.

Data collection

Detailed observations of SQL Server's performance are needed when the given instance gets into trouble. It is not possible to monitor more than a few instances in this way. That is why Microsoft offers a tool for centralized monitoring of more SQL Servers. This tool is also very useful for proactive monitoring and performance baselining. This section is dedicated to **data collection**. Data collection consists of the following objects:

- A relational database called **Management Data Warehouse** (**MDW**) hosted on a SQL Server instance

- Jobs reading data from XE and dynamic management objects

- SSIS packages pushing captured data into the MDW

- Reports showing information about several aspects of contention and performance over time

The MDW database can be centralized. In big environments, it is a good practice to place the MDW database on a dedicated SQL Server instance. When working with data collection, we need to do three tasks:

- Set up the MDW

- Set up data collection jobs and packages

- Read reports regularly

The first two tasks are done by short wizards in Management Studio; the reports are placed within Management Studio as well. Let's go through these tasks.

Setting up the MDW

Working with **Data Collection** is quite easy. The following screenshot shows where to find configuration tools for **Data Collection**:

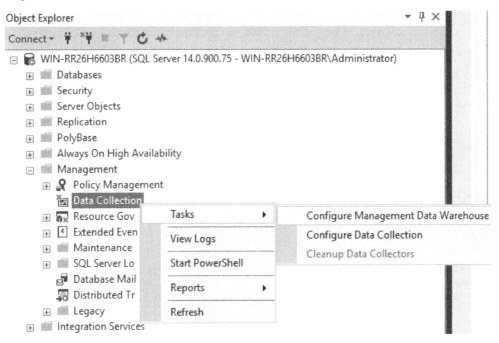

Fig. 6.34 – Data Collection configuration tools

Data Collection can be found in **Object Explorer**, under the **Management** node. Right-clicking this opens a popup menu showing the **Tasks** option. The first option under **Tasks** is **Configure Management Data Warehouse**. This option should be selected when the MDW database is going to be created. Using this option opens a wizard, and the first step (the **Welcome** step is omitted) has two settings:

- **Server name**: The name of the server that the MDW database will be hosted on.

- **Database name**: When a new MDW is going to be created, the **New** button (on the right-hand side of the drop-down) is clicked to open the database creation window.

The wizard is shown in the following screenshot:

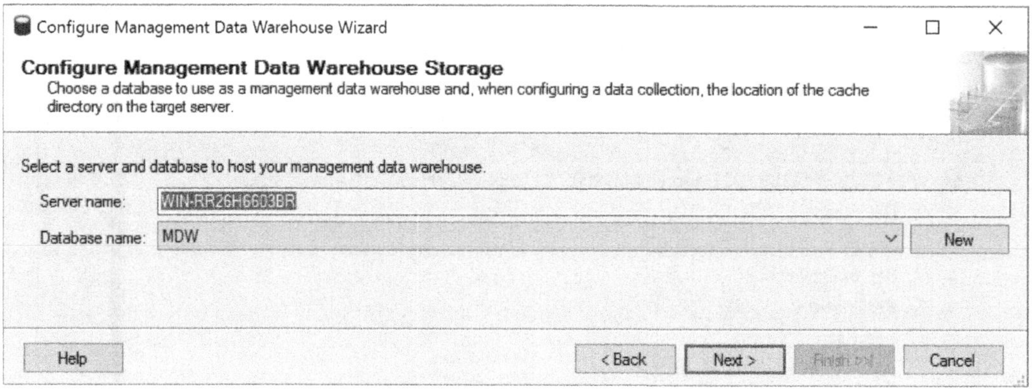

Fig. 6.35 – Configure Management Data Warehouse Wizard

The next step of the wizard is about security. Logins are mapped to the MDW database roles. This enables users without administrative privileges to write data to the MDW database or read it:

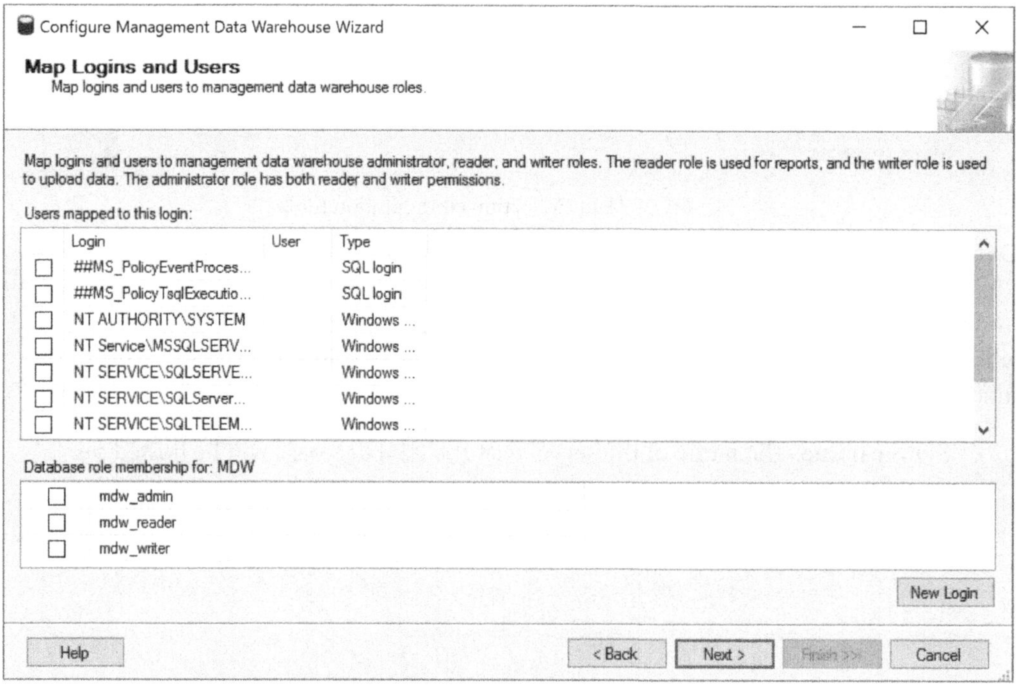

Fig. 6.36 – Mapping logins and users

When the wizard is finished, the MDW database is created and logins are mapped to users and database roles.

This task establishes a centralized point for data collection. In the next section, we will enable monitoring for the same instance of SQL Server.

Collecting performance data

Setting up data collection from a certain instance of SQL Server is done via the **Configure Data Collection Wizard** option, which can be called from the **Tasks** popup. When this option is used, the wizard is opened and in the first step, the wizard asks for **Server name** (the instance hosting MDW) and **Database name** (actual name of MDW). It also asks for a temporary **Cache directory**. Data is saved to files and then pushed to the MDW database. The first step is shown in the following screenshot:

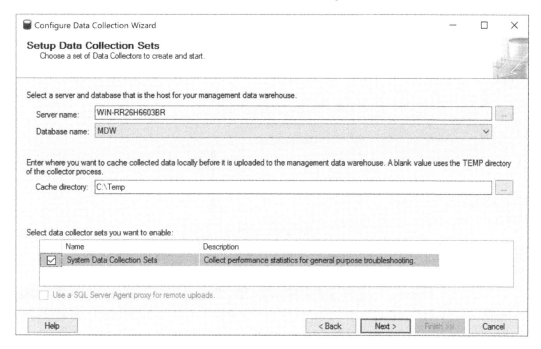

Fig. 6.37 – Data collection – first step

When all these questions have been answered, the wizard finishes and creates SQL Agent jobs that perform data capturing.

When this task is finished, you will have to wait at least an hour before you get to see the first results in the reports. However, if you want to find out more about SQL Server's behavior, you should wait at least 2 to 3 days.

Viewing Data Collection reports

The main purpose of Data Collection is to show overall resource consumption, as well as long-term query statistics. This information is shown in a very readable graphical form. Reports can be invoked from **Object Explorer** by right-clicking on the MDW database in the **Databases** node. The complete path to **Reports** is shown in the following screenshot:

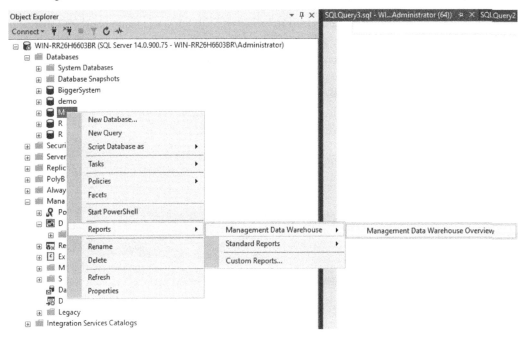

Fig. 6.38 -- Reports

This option opens a report showing a list of all the instances of SQL Server being monitored by MDW:

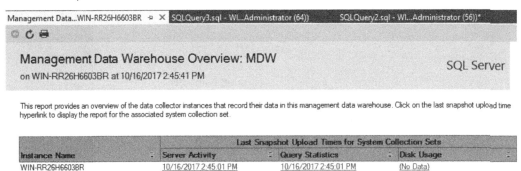

Fig. 6.39 – List of MDW monitored instances

As shown in the preceding screenshot, the overview enables you to click through three sections:

- **Server Activity**: Shows detailed information about disk, memory, CPU, and network usage
- **Query Statistics**: Operational statistics about queries
- **Disk Usage**: Amount of space consumed by every database file for every database

All three detailed reports offer time play control – the ability to set a time range for monitoring. All three reports are very self-descriptive and intuitive, so the best practice is to set up Data Collection and review these reports on your own.

Data Collection has one big advantage over tools such as Dynamic Management. Data in `MDW` is stored for up to 2 years and not cleared when SQL Server restarts. This allows DBAs to establish the performance baseline over a long time. This baseline then allows us to detect anomalies or metric changes over time. As a benefit of this, the monitoring outputs are very readable. They do not force the DBA to grab metrics manually using DMVs or XE. However, data collection mainly provides server metrics. A similar tool on the database scope is called **Query Store**. In the next section, we will set it up.

Query Store

Query Store was introduced with SQL Server 2016 because many DBAs and developers missed long-term monitoring for certain database performance. All tools, except for data collection, that have been mentioned in this chapter were able to provide data until the SQL Server instance was restarted. Query Store provides durable storage that's created by requests in the database where such monitoring is desired. Query Store captures and saves data asynchronously so that the query's performance, from the user's perspective, is not affected.

When configuring Query Store, navigate to **Database Properties** (right-click on a certain database in **Object Explorer** and choose **Properties** from the pop-up menu), as shown in the following screenshot:

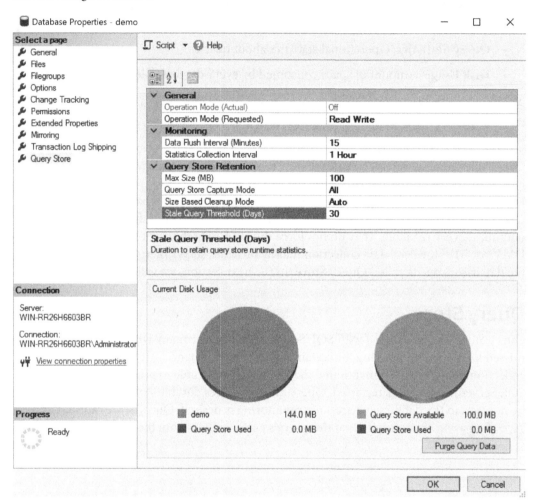

Fig. 6.40 – Configuring Query Store | Properties

The preceding screenshot shows all the settings already filled in with the defaults. When switching **Query Store** on, we must change the **Operation Mode (Requested)** property to **Read Write**. Other options include **Off** (data is not captured and cannot be explored) and **Read Only** (data is not captured but can still be explored). The **Monitoring** section of the properties shows how often data will be saved from the cache into the database (the default value is **15** minutes) and how often data will be aggregated for analysis (the default is **1** hour).

The last section, labeled **Query Store Retention**, allows us to set how big **Query Store** will be and for what amount of time data will be kept before it will be erased in a first-in-first-out manner. Once set up, **Query Store** starts to collect data about queries, including costs, statistics, execution plan, and connection settings.

From DBA's perspective, a new node, called **Query Store**, will appear under the database node in **Object Explorer**. The **Query Store** node offers several windows showing query statistics and enables the DBA to analyze performance issues at the query level. One of its features is called **Force Plan**. This button can be found in the **Regressed Queries** window, under the **Query Store** node. If, under certain circumstances, something goes wrong and a query's performance becomes poor, the **Force Plan** option serves as a workaround until the root cause of the performance issue is addressed and corrected.

Query Store helps DBAs, as well as developers, easily find the most resource-consuming queries and correct their performance. Similar to data collection, as explained in previous sections, Query Store collects and stores information about queries, their execution plans, and statistics such as CPU times or I/O operations to the database where it is configured. This collected information is very easy to read because it is mostly graphical.

As versions of SQL Server change, query optimization metrics and algorithms are enhanced by Microsoft. Sometimes, this causes the queries that were tuned well in the previous version of SQL Server to become slow. **Query Store** can help address such queries very efficiently because it compares different execution plans for the same query.

This section has provided an overview of performance monitoring tools and some performance monitoring techniques. The next section will talk about how physical data structures affect performance.

Indexes and maintenance

Indexes are sometimes seen as some magic objects that resolve all performance problems in the world of relational databases. Nothing could be further from the truth. In this section, we will look at the index types offered by SQL Server, and then discuss how indexes work. Finally, we will summarize some guidelines for using indexes.

Types of indexes

Sorting in relational databases makes no sense. Even though this statement sounds strange, it comes from the set theory, which forms a theoretical base of relational databases. However, sorting is still needed when the database engine must find proper records from a table efficiently. When no sorting structure is present, the engine needs to scan all the records to recognize which of them are candidates for the result of a certain query. An index is a type of object that brings sorting and seeking possibilities over unsorted relational data.

SQL Server provides several types of indexes. The most traditional are B-tree indexes, while columnstore indexes were introduced in SQL Server 2012 and enhanced with every new version of SQL Server. Besides relational indexes, indexes for several not-really-relational data types are present on SQL Server. Their usage is often straightforward, so we will pay the most attention to B-trees.

Heap

A heap is an unsorted table that has no clustered index. Keep in mind that primary key or unique constraints are implemented by B-tree indexes internally, so a pure heap is a very rare form of relational data table.

Data pages in the heap do not have any particular order; they are not connected by offsets to each other and records can be placed anywhere in the heap. When SQL Server executes tasks over the heap, it always scans all the data pages to retrieve the desired ones and work with them.

When SQL Server inserts a new record into the heap, it finds the first data page with sufficient space for the new record and places the inserted record there.

When SQL Server updates an existing record, two situations can occur:

- The record fits the size of the original data pages and nothing special happens.

- The record grows after the update and it does not fit into the original page, so the record is deleted from the previous data page and is moved to any data page with sufficient space. The original record version is marked as a ghost record; SQL Server does not actually erase records.

When a record is deleted from the heap, it is marked as a ghost record. Fragmentation of data occurs rarely, and it depends on several ghost records.

The heap is not a complicated structure, but it is useless for tables bigger than several rows. As an additional disadvantage, we must say that a table with no constraints is not actually a relational table. That's why at least one index is often present.

Non-clustered B-tree index

The B-tree is sometimes interpreted as a binary tree, which is not correct. The letter **B** means **balanced tree**. A balanced tree is a tree consisting of root (this is the virtual root page in B-tree indexes) and intermediate nodes (if needed) that help us to navigate down to leaf nodes that contain sorted copies of indexed column(s). **Balanced** means that the leaf information is accessed with the same level of depth in every section of the tree.

SQL Server enables the creation of up to 499 non-clustered indexes on one table, but this is a theoretical limit in most cases. Each index can have up to 16 columns with sum of byte lengths of up to 900 bytes. A record that's saved in the index structure is called an **index key**.

B-tree indexes can be unique (values or combination of values in the index key must never repeat) or duplicated. Unique indexes are often created behind the scenes of unique constraint creation.

Data pages on the same level in an index tree are interconnected by an offset as double-linked lists. In other words, every index page knows its predecessor and successor. This helps SQL Server skip to the next index page quickly and efficiently according to the sorting rule defined by the index.

When a non-clustered index is built on top of a heap, leaf records are created as copies of values from indexed column(s). These point to data pages in the heap to address the record that they come from. SQL Server uses internal 8-byte row identifiers for addressing.

Let's describe the operations that are performed by SQL Server when a non-clustered index is built on a heap. When a read operation is executed, SQL Server resolves if the index is useful for the query. There are two general conditions of index usefulness:

- The first column in the index is used in the WHERE clause of the query; this causes SQL Server to not scan all over the heap but to invoke the index seek operation. This decision is made upon statistics and cardinality estimation. The index seek operation is a road from virtual root navigating to proper intermediate index pages (often, it's about the index's depth) and from intermediate pages to the leaf page containing the key value mentioned in the query.

- The WHERE clause is selective, which means that the ratio of records fulfilling the filter versus amount of records in the table is small. This selectivity is recognized by cardinality estimation, which is a formula that computes the estimated number of rows returned by the query. The base of query estimation is index statistics.

When executing a `SELECT` query containing only columns present in a non-clustered index, SQL Server uses just the leaf level of the index, even if no `WHERE` clause is contained within the query. When no additional columns are needed for the query result, SQL Server scans (or seeks) just the leaf level of the index.

The index scan operation is usually very efficient because less data I/O operations must be performed. We're mentioning these indexes because they completely cover query needs. Covering indexes are preferred because they save many I/O operations.

SQL Server follows pointers from leaf pages of found index. These pointers point to the locations in the heap where records are stored. the rest of the records (columns not included in the index key) which will form the result of the query.

On the other hand, SQL Server seeks proper index keys. So, SQL Server follows pointers from leaf pages of found index. These pointers point to the locations in the heap where records are stored. This operation is needed to retrieve the rest of records (columns not included in the index key) which will form the result of the query. When we want to enhance the covering ability of a non-clustered index, we can add **included columns**. Included columns are not indexed; their values are just added with an index key, though the index key itself is still small.

A new record that's inserted into the heap with a non-clustered column is placed anywhere in the heap, but the index key of the new record has to be placed in the correct index page. This can lead to some internal non-clustered index maintenance, mainly **page split**. Page split is an operation that causes the index page to break into two new ones. This frees up space for a new index record when the original index page is too full.

When a record is updated, almost the same two situations can occur:

- The new version of the updated record fits back in the original data page, so nothing special happens.
- The new version of the updated record is bigger and does not fit into the original data page, so the record is moved to a data page with more free space. However, a little navigation object, called a forwarding pointer, is created for the original page because it's cheaper for SQL Server than to update the index key.

When a record is deleted, it is marked as a ghost record and the pointer from the index key is invalidated.

When many forwarding pointers and ghost records are created over time, the table becomes fragmented and must be defragmented. The same occurs on indexes as index pages are split and reduced. That's why regular maintenance is needed to keep these structures less fragmented.

Clustered B-tree index

The clustered B-tree index seems to be very similar to non-clustered indexes, but there's one big difference. The index key is not copied to its separate storage, but the table itself forms the leaf level of the index. It's obvious that only one clustered index can be created by a table. When a clustered index is created, the records in the table are sorted according to the index definition, and the data pages are ordered in a double-linked list. This sorting operation becomes very complex and expensive when a large composite clustered index is being created.

When SQL Server performs a read on a clustered index, it can use these operations:

- **Clustered index scan**: This is executed when the SELECT statement is issued. The entire table is retrieved.
- **Clustered index seek**: The WHERE condition of the query contains a predicate for the clustered index key.

When SQL Server performs an insert operation on the clustered index, the new record must be placed in the correct position within the index. This can cause more index splitting operations.

When SQL Server updates a record in a clustered index, the following situations might occur:

- The column that is not a clustered index key is updated and the record is not grown beyond the data page free space. Nothing special occurs.
- The column that is not a clustered index key is updated but the record is grown beyond the data page free space. The record must still be placed in the same place, a new data page is needed, and an index split occurs.
- The column that is a clustered index key is updated. The whole record must be moved to the new position to continue sorting; an index split may occur.

When SQL Server deletes a record from a clustered index, the record is marked as a ghost record.

Non-clustered and clustered index cooperation

It's typical for a table to have more than just one index, and often, a combination of indexes are used. When a clustered index exists, leaf pages of non-clustered indexes do not point to data pages addressing their records, but every non-clustered index key keeps association with a proper clustered index key.

In other words, when a non-clustered index is used in a query that needs, for example, all the columns of selected records, non-clustered index key values are found. Then, SQL Server iterates through those values and searches the rest of the records over the clustered index.

This operation is known as **key lookup** and it works as a loop. Any keys that are found in a non-clustered index are searched one by one in a clustered index. When several records are retrieved, this operation is correct and should not be a performance issue, but when SQL Server reuses the same execution plan with other parameter values in the WHERE clause of the query, this may lead to poor performance. This situation is sometimes called **parameter sniffing**. We can help reduce occurrences of key lookup in several ways, but usually, it's recommended to cooperate with the developer.

Columnstore indexes

Columnstore indexes were introduced in SQL Server 2012 with many limitations. Most of them are gone now, which is why columnstore indexes became very popular in data warehouse applications. Columnstore indexes use segments as a store unit rather than data pages. Columnstore indexes can be both clustered and non-clustered.

When a columnstore index is created, a table is divided into **row groups** – sections containing approximately a million records. Every row group is divided into **segments**. A segment is a storage unit containing the data of one column in one row group. Data in segments is strongly compressed. This is a very good approach when many aggregation queries are issued; for example, for reporting purposes or data cube processing.

When creating a non-clustered columnstore index, we create just one. The index cannot contain columns of big data types such as nvarchar (max) or special data types such as XML or geography. When a non-clustered columnstore is created, it does not affect data contention flow, because SQL Server executes columnstore index maintenance asynchronously, so no locks are requested.

The clustered columnstore index has the same limitation for data types. Since all columns are obligatory in columnstore, the presence of these data types can be a roadblock.

The clustered columnstore index can cooperate with non-clustered B-tree indexes, and this cooperation is usually very efficient.

Other index types

B-tree, as well as columnstore, indexes are heavily used in conjunction with classical relational data. However, modern databases often handle bigger and more complicated data types. For some of them, SQL Server offers special indexes:

- **XML indexes for XML data type**: XML indexes are divided into the following:

    a) **Primary XML** index: This forms the internal structure of all nodes from the XML column. These nodes are associated with a unique clustered index value in the same table.

    b) **Secondary XML** indexes: These are index structures that sort the paths, values, or attributes of the XML nodes that are stored in the primary XML index. Secondary XML indexes are always built on top of the primary XML index.

- **Spatial indexes for geometry and geography data types**: Spatial index structures zoom-in on the spatial value three times in the form of grids. This approach helps to simplify resolving queries such as do spatial objects intersect with one another? However, spatial indexes cannot completely cover all the task types that are executed on spatial data.

Indexing considerations

No exact recipe exists for indexing, but some considerations and best practices have been created:

- A poorly normalized database design cannot be saved by indexes. This is a big mistake that many developers make.

- The best candidate column for a clustered B-tree index is the one that contains a simple value, such as an integer. The value grows with every new record.

- When a primary key constraint is created with defaults, a clustered unique index is created behind the scenes. This is a good approach when integers (especially with the IDENTITY property set) are used. However, this is a very bad approach when uniqueidentifier is used as a data type for the primary key because it is an expensive operation.

- It's better not to have a clustered index than to have a bad one.

- In OLTP databases, non-clustered indexes with fewer columns are often better.

- As the database resolves, more data warehouse tasks such as aggregated queries and more composed B-tree indexes or columnstore indexes are useful.

- Use `sys.dm_db_index_usage_stats` to check whether your indexes are useful.

- Use `sys.dm_db_index_physical_stats` to check the level of fragmentation.

- Check the accuracy of statistics using the `DBCC SHOW_STATISTICS` function.

Indexing is a big discipline in terms of SQL Server optimization. To design efficient indexes, you need to know about data contention; you also need to monitor databases regularly and often consult the design with a supplier of the database, if possible. It is also good to keep in mind that indexing is just a small part of optimization; not every performance issue can be resolved using indexes. If indexing is used in excess, it causes over-indexing. Over-indexing arises when too many indexes are created on one table. The result is that with every DML request, not just a data in the table, but also related data in all indexes must be changed. This leads to many waits and data fragmentation. This means we still need to consider the trade-off between index efficiency in reads against its expenses during writes. In the next section, we will look at some of the most common performance issues and how to detect them.

Common performance issue patterns

So far, we've seen how SQL Server works internally and which tools we can use for monitoring. We will find many areas that can be optimized on SQL Server. We can work with memory, physical disks, or CPUs, but we should always start our performance tuning work with the most basic thing – query response times. This section provides a real-life example that shows us how to explore response issues, as well as how to save system resources with just a couple of simple steps.

No real-time scenario has just one potential cause. Hence, there is not just one way to resolve an issue. In many cases, administrators try to resolve every issue with more system resources, but this approach is very expensive, and we do not have a bottomless pool of system resources (and, by the way, most performance bottlenecks are NOT caused by insufficient resources). That is why we should find the root cause of the performance issue and try to resolve it using resource savings, along with proper configuration or appropriate indexing strategies. Sometimes, performance issues are caused by poorly written client applications. Even if the DBA tries their best to resolve poorly performing queries, the DBA usually does not have control over poorly written queries. When this situation occurs, it is time to call for support from the developer's site.

In the following sections, we will combine various tools and techniques to identify performance bottlenecks and explain how to resolve them.

Unacceptable slow response from SQL Server to a query

Almost every administrator has experienced the following situation: the overall performance of the instance of SQL Server is good, but some queries are constantly slow, or they have unpredictable response times. How can we identify such queries? We can use an on-demand solution, which means that we will react to emails or tickets that are sent by disappointed users or we can monitor poorly performing queries proactively.

Which monitoring tools can we use for proactive monitoring? The following list shows the available tools:

- **Activity Monitor in SQL Server Management Studio**: This window, and especially its Recent Expensive Queries and Active Expensive Queries sections, is good for provided a quick overview when a query goes wrong suddenly. But this tool cannot serve for constant monitoring as it just shows the current situation on the SQL Server instance.

- **Reports in Management Studio**: SQL Server Management Studio contains a set of reports. We can consider using instance-level reports such as Performance Dashboard or reports whose names begin with "Performance". Reports take data from dynamic management objects, which gives us valuable insight into a behavior of SQL Server (and we can also use dynamic management objects directly). A common property of dynamic management objects is that they are cleansed with every restart of the SQL Server instance.

- **Data Collection**: Data Collection allows us to monitor SQL Server behavior at the instance level. Data Collection also contains a section called Server Activity, which stores and shows the operational statistics of the most expensive queries.

- **Query Store**: Another very useful feature, but unlike Data Collection, which is configured at the database level, is Query Store. It is intended for query monitoring so that we can explore poorly running queries and have all our operational statistics (that is, the number of reads or writes, CPU time, and so on), as well as a query plan, in XML format at our disposal. Query Store also allows us to compare all the execution plan alternatives that are generated by SQL Server for the same query.

I found the poor query; what's next?

When a slow query is identified, we should explore why the query is executed so poorly. We should concentrate on the following options in the graphical plan:

- **Plan warnings**: We can see small exclamation marks in operators shown in the graphical plan.

- **Number of reads and writes made by query**: We can compare the amount of data pages that have been processed with an operator with the amount of data pages used by one table or index.

- **Parallel operators within the execution plan**: When a stamp with two arrows is placed on an operator in the query plan, such an operator is executed in parallel. This is not good or bad by itself, but in connection with extensive CXPACKET waits (see *Resource Waits* in the *Activity Monitor* section), this could be an index for overutilized CPUs.

- **Situations when the query waits for some resource**: Wait times are not typically seen in execution plans, so we will use **Extended Events** for it.

Typically, we will take a graphical execution plan and explore it. Let's explain how to read the execution plan accordingly while taking the preceding bulleted points into account.

This example requires that we perform some preparation tasks. We will use data from the AdventureWorks database, which you can access for free at https://docs.microsoft.com/en-us/sql/samples/adventureworks-install-configure?view=sql-server-ver15.

We can use the AdventureWorks2016.bak or AdventureWorks2017.bak backup files for our purposes. When the database backup is restored (you can learn how to restore a database by rereading *Chapter 3, Implementing Backup and Recovery*), we will create a new table as a copy of the existing table called Sales.SalesOrderHeader. The reason we're doing this is so that we start with a table with no indexes on it:

```
use AdventureWorks
go


select * into Sales.SalesOrderHeaderCopy
from Sales.SalesOrderHeader
go


alter table Sales.SalesOrderHeaderCopy
add constraint pk_SalesOrderHeaderCopy primary key clustered
```

```
(SalesOrderId)
go
```

The preceding script creates a copy of the `Sales.SalesOrderHeader` table to a new table called `Sales.SalesOrderHeaderCopy` and adds a clustered primary key (which is the only index in the new table) to it.

The following statement turns on so-called statistics – textual messages that are returned besides a query result as additional information about how many I/O operations were done during the query's execution:

```
set statistics io on
```

Now, we can start to identify the reasons why the query is being executed so slowly. The following query was executed by a business user to show how big the subtotal of orders was. These were received by the Adventure Works company in 2012 and 2013. Before executing this query in Management Studio, remember to use the *Ctrl + M* keyboard shortcut. This turns on the actual execution plan. The execution plan will be received alongside any necessary I/O statistics and the query result itself:

```
select
year(OrderDate) as OrderYear
, sum(SubTotal) as YearlySubtotal
from Sales.SalesOrderHeaderCopy
where SubTotal > 100 and YEAR(OrderDate) in (2012, 2013)

group by year(OrderDate)
```

Now that we've executed this query, we'll explore the result itself, as well as the I/O statistics and the execution plan. When you look at the **Messages** tab of the results pane in the query window, you will see a message very similar to the following:

```
(2 rows affected)
Table 'Worktable'. Scan count 0, logical reads 0, physical
reads 0, read-ahead reads 0, lob logical reads 0, lob physical
reads 0, lob read-ahead reads 0.
Table 'Workfile'. Scan count 0, logical reads 0, physical reads
0, read-ahead reads 0, lob logical reads 0, lob physical reads
0, lob read-ahead reads 0.
Table 'SalesOrderHeaderCopy'. Scan count 1, logical reads 784,
physical reads 0, read-ahead reads 0, lob logical reads 0, lob
physical reads 0, lob read-ahead reads 0.
```

```
(1 row affected)
```

The most important row in the preceding message is the one that begins with `Table` `'SalesOrderHeaderCopy'`. There are several numbers there, but here, we are concerned with the number of logical reads and the number of physical reads. The logical reads metric shows how many data pages were accessed in the buffer cache by SQL Server during query processing. The physical reads metric, on the other hand, shows how many data pages were moved from physical disk to the buffer cache.

In our case, all the data pages were placed in the buffer cache, which is a good thing for us (this is because the table is freshly created and if your environment doesn't have low memory, the data pages have not been saved to a physical disk yet). But the number of logical reads shows that all the data pages were accessed during the query's execution, even if we have a `WHERE` predicate in the query (and we guess that records should be filtered). That is why we need to do some more investigation using the graphical query plan. The graphical query plan looks as follows:

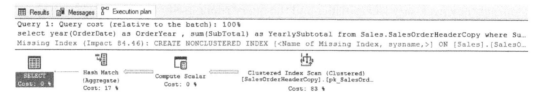

Fig. 6.41 – Graphical query plan

Here, we can see that the query scanned the whole table using the `Clustered Index` `Scan` operator (because our table contains clustered primary key) and that it was also the most expensive operator during the query's execution (see its relative cost, which is approximately `83%`). We can also see that the graphical plan contains a green line in its header. This green line marks that some index is missing, and it also suggests how to design the missing index.

> **Tip**
> If you want to explore all the missing indexes in a certain database, you can do so by querying the `sys.dm_db_missing_index_details` DMV. We should use this DMV carefully because the final decision about the new index is up to the DBA.

If we right-click on the green line, a pop-up menu will appear with an option called **Missing Index Details**. When this option is used, Management Studio opens the script template of the suggested index in a new query window. The result is shown in the following script:

```
/*
USE [AdventureWorks]
GO
CREATE NONCLUSTERED INDEX [<Name of Missing Index, sysname,>]
ON [Sales].[SalesOrderHeaderCopy] ([SubTotal])
INCLUDE ([OrderDate])
GO
*/
```

The script template is commented out because it needs two revisions. The first thing we need to do is review the index definition, because missing index detail never suggests modifications to existing indexes. A very similar index may already exist on the table, in which case we should redesign the existing index instead of creating the suggested index. Our example also has one potentially strange thing: the query filters the record using the `OrderDate` column, but the column is not the index key, while it should be. Hence, we need to go back to the query definition and analyze why the column is not a candidate for the index key. Let's recall the WHERE clause of the query:

```
where SubTotal > 100 and YEAR(OrderDate) in (2012, 2013)
```

The preceding script is not executable; however, it shows that a whole condition has been placed on the WHERE clause. This condition is composed from two predicates. The first predicate filters out orders with a small subtotal value makes it easy to take and can be read by SQL Server. However, the second predicate is called **Non-SARGable predicate** (**SARG** is a shortcut for the term **Search ARGument**), which means that SQL Server's cardinality estimator cannot use values from the `OrderDate` columns. This is because the column is not added to the predicate on its own and is instead covered by the YEAR() function.

The cardinality estimator does not evaluate results during the optimization of the query, so the cardinality estimator does not know the raw values of the YEAR(OrderDate) expression. That is why the OrderDate column is added just as an included column to the index suggestion, not as the key column of the index. To make the query more efficient, we should avoid Non-SARGable predicates wherever possible. As we can see, the optimal execution of queries begins at the query design phase. Let's review the rewritten query:

```
select
year(OrderDate) as OrderYear
, sum(SubTotal) as YearlySubtotal
from Sales.SalesOrderHeaderCopy
where SubTotal > 100 and OrderDate between '20120101' and
'20131231'
group by year(OrderDate)
```

In the preceding query, we changed the definition of the Non-SARGable predicate to a SARGable predicate with the same meaning. Now, we can review the missing index suggestion, as shown in following script:

```
/*
USE [AdventureWorks]
GO
CREATE NONCLUSTERED INDEX [<Name of Missing Index, sysname,>]
ON [Sales].[SalesOrderHeaderCopy] ([OrderDate],[SubTotal])

GO
*/
```

Now, the index design is much more meaningful as it uses both columns from the WHERE clause of the analyzed query as the index key columns. Let's create the index using the following command:

```
CREATE NONCLUSTERED INDEX ix_SalesOrderHeaderCopy_Agg
ON [Sales].[SalesOrderHeaderCopy] ([OrderDate],[SubTotal])
```

When the index is created using the preceding script, we can review changes in the amount of I/O operations, as well as the resulting execution plan. The new look of the execution plan is shown in the following screenshot:

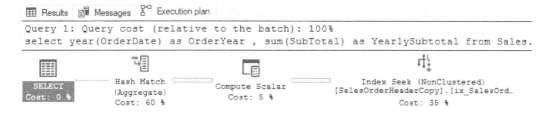

Fig. 6.42 – I/O operation execution plan

The preceding screenshot of the actual plan shows that two things were changed: the missing index line disappeared, and the `Clustered Index Scan` operator was replaced with the `Index Seek` operator. The `Index Seek` operator is much cheaper than `Clustered Index Scan`. We can also observe messages and see that the number of logical reads was reduced from approximately 780 reads to roughly 60 reads. Even if the sample table is very small, we made an approximate 90% saving in one simple query with two simple steps.

Can I want more from indexes?

The simple answer to this is: Sure! We must want more! For instance, business analysts explore the sales order data to get good insights. They will use different grouping columns or more columns within their queries because they need to see different categories in their query results.

Let's say that the `TerritoryID` column will be used as a categorical column in the same query, and that the issue we've resolved so far is repeated because the `TerritoryID` column is not indexed at all. We can continue with other columns in the table as well since this is a very typical scenario. We could resolve the repeating issue with more and more indexes, similar to what we have with the already created index. However, this would be counterproductive because every index will cause more waits for locks and latches during transactions, and we're assuming that sales orders come into the table constantly. Fortunately, we have columnstore indexes for such cases. Unlike suffering with many B-tree indexes, which are used to cover analytical query needs, the design of the columnstore index is very straightforward and SQL Server uses it very efficiently.

Let's see how it works. We will drop the unnecessary B-tree index we've created so far and then create a new, non-clustered columnstore index containing all the columns that will be used by our analytical queries. The following commands will do this for us:

```
DROP INDEX ix_SalesOrderHeaderCopy_Agg ON Sales.
SalesOrderHeaderCopy

CREATE COLUMNSTORE INDEX ncs_SalesOrderHeaderCopy_Agg ON Sales.
SalesOrderHeaderCopy
(
[RevisionNumber]
, [OrderDate]
, [DueDate]
, [ShipDate]
, [Status]
, [OnlineOrderFlag]
, [SalesOrderNumber]
, [PurchaseOrderNumber]
, [AccountNumber]
, [CustomerID]
, [SalesPersonID]
, [TerritoryID]
, [BillToAddressID]
, [ShipToAddressID]
, [ShipMethodID]
, [CreditCardID]
, [CreditCardApprovalCode]
, [CurrencyRateID]
, [SubTotal]
, [TaxAmt]
, [Freight]
, [TotalDue]
)
```

The preceding script drops the index we created previously to help the aggregate query. With this, the new columnstore index is created. Now, let's test the result. We will use two queries. The first query is the original query we analyzed throughout this example, while the second query is very similar, but uses the `TerritoryID` column as a grouping criterion. We will execute the following queries and then explore their I/O statistics and execution plans:

```
select
year(OrderDate) as OrderYear
, sum(SubTotal) as YearlySubtotal
from Sales.SalesOrderHeaderCopy
where SubTotal > 100
    and OrderDate between '20120101' and '20131231'


group by year(OrderDate)
```

```
select
TerritoryID
, sum(SubTotal) as YearlySubtotal
from Sales.SalesOrderHeaderCopy
where SubTotal > 100
    and OrderDate between '20120101' and '20131231'


group by TerritoryID
```

The I/O statistics for the preceding queries look like this:

```
Table 'SalesOrderHeaderCopy'. Scan count 2, logical reads 0,
physical reads 0, read-ahead reads 0, lob logical reads 73, lob
physical reads 1, lob read-ahead reads 98.
Table 'SalesOrderHeaderCopy'. Segment reads 1, segment skipped
0.
```

```
(1 row affected)
```

```
(10 rows affected)
```

```
Table 'SalesOrderHeaderCopy'. Scan count 2, logical reads 0,
physical reads 0, read-ahead reads 0, lob logical reads 39, lob
physical reads 0, lob read-ahead reads 0.
```

```
Table 'SalesOrderHeaderCopy'. Segment reads 1, segment skipped
0.
```

```
(1 row affected)
```

As we can see, the I/O metrics do not show how many data pages were processed, but how many segments were used by the query. Unlike data pages, segments do not have a strictly defined size. A segment is a storage unit that contains a portion of the data from one column only. This means that the data in the columnstore index is divided into groups of rows (the ideal size is 1,048,576 rows in one row group), and then the row group is divided into columns. The one part that contains the data values in one column is the segment. Finally, the segment is compressed so that every scan operation is very efficient. SQL Server only uses segments for certain queries, so SQL Server does not need to work with whole records when it uses B-trees or heap.

> **Note**
>
> That is why we describe heaps and B-trees as row storage (SQL Server needs to use a whole row, even if just one column's value is needed for query purposes), while the previously explained storage is described as a column store (SQL Server works just with columns needed by a certain query).

The preceding queries have the following execution plans:

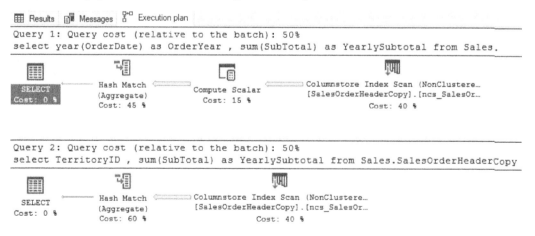

Fig. 6.43 – Execution plans

Since the queries were executed together, the preceding screenshot shows both execution plans, which makes it easy to compare them. Both execution plans are almost the same. The important operator is `Columnstore Index Scan`. It says that the index will be used, even if there is no B-tree index on the `OrderDate` or `TerritoryID` columns. The `Columnstore Index Scan` operator is very efficient because it redirects big read requests to separate storage structure, but it also works in BATCH processing mode. This means that unlike in B-trees or heaps, values are used in batches; up to 900 values are processed together. This example uses a very small amount of data, but on huge tables, the processing time of analytical queries is reduced approximately to 1% of the time needed by SQL Server when the B-tree approach is used.

Finally, you should know about the `Compute Scalar` operator, which is the only operator present in the first execution plan. This is because the first query uses not just raw values from the `OrderDate` column, but the `YEAR(OrderDate)` expression, which must be calculated during query execution. Also, the calculation is executed by the `Compute Scalar` operator.

The last but very important benefit when using non-clustered columnstore indexes is that they hugely reduce waits when data is updated in the original table. This reduction is due to the following:

- SQL Server uses optimistic row versioning transaction isolation for data modifications in columnstore. This is a lock-free approach to data modification, so the columnstore does not increase the number of locks requested during transactions.

- B-tree indexes that are created to cover analytical query needs can be dropped so that the original table has less storage space. This also reduces locking.

This example showed that making small changes to the query and indexes can bring about big I/O savings. In other words, before we rush to the shop for a new server with a bunch of memory, we should play around with our data structures. This will save system resources, as well as our money. In this example, we also combined the role of DBAs (how to design and create indexes and how to measure their efficiency) with the role of SQL developers (non-SARGable predicates). Also, it is good to know that even if the developer and DBA roles differ, both roles should cooperate to make SQL Server perform well and satisfy users.

Summary

Monitoring performance and resolving performance issues could take up a book on their own, but any information is useful information.

First, we described several approaches that are typically used in performance monitoring; that is, the top-down approach and proactive monitoring.

A lot of information was covered in the *Tools for monitoring performance* section. Microsoft provides a wide set of tools and techniques we can use to monitor and troubleshoot SQL Server. Most of them are graphical, but it is also recommended to have a brief knowledge of non-visual objects such as DMV and functions.

The *Indexing and maintenance* section demystified typical index types, their usage by SQL Server in common situations, and provided some guidance regarding indexing.

In the last part of this chapter, we look at some real-life use cases for performance troubleshooting on SQL Server.

In the next chapter, we will show you what to do when things go wrong. We will use some similar techniques to what we covered in this chapter to detect the causes of problems and find solutions to them.

Section 3: High Availability and the Cloud with SQL Server 2019

In this section, you will be introduced to several advanced topics, such as hybrid or cloud deployments of SQL Server, including migration to the cloud and the automation of a database administrator's work. You will also find several more topics on improving the reliability and performance of the deployed SQL Server.

This section contains the following chapters:

- *Chapter 7, Planning Migration and Upgrade*
- *Chapter 8, Automation – Using Tools to Manage and Monitor SQL Server 2019*
- *Chapter 9, Configuring Always On High Availability Features*
- *Chapter 10, In-Memory OLTP – Why and How to Use It*
- *Chapter 11, Combining SQL Server 2019 with Azure*
- *Chapter 12, Taming Big Data with SQL Server*

7

Planning Migration and Upgrade

Although this book is about SQL Server 2019, you will not always be working with the latest versions and editions of SQL Server. You may be surprised how many diverse versions of SQL Server are still in production. Quite frequently, you'll face a task of upgrading and migrating the server configuration and content to the new server running the latest version of SQL Server. Each new version of SQL Server brings out many new features that are not available in older versions, and those features may be very useful for your environment to bring better performance, stability, and many other factors to your application. In this chapter, we'll explore the upgrade options for SQL Server and what you have to actually think about during the planning phase of the upgrade. This information will help you in upgrading your SQL Server systems to the latest version in a real environment.

> **Note**
> Migration of SQL Server is also usually bound to new hardware for the server or a **virtual machine** (**VM**) with the latest operating system using new features, so you can actually upgrade the whole platform and not just SQL Server.

We will be covering the following topics in the chapter:

- The importance of keeping up with latest version
- Planning the upgrade
- Performing the upgrade
- Migrating from other platforms

The importance of keeping up with latest version

An important reason to upgrade is to continue to obtain the latest support for SQL Server. Once the mainstream support for SQL Server ends, there will be no more service packs or cumulative updates bringing fixes and updates to your current version of SQL Server.

As you can see from the following table, just three SQL Server versions are supported as of now (summer 2020) and those are SQL Server 2016, SQL Server 2017, and the current SQL Server 2019:

SQL Server version	Release date	End of mainstream support
SQL Server 2000	Nov 2000	4/8/2008
SQL Server 2005	Jan 2006	4/12/2011
SQL Server 2008	Nov 2008	1/14/2014
SQL Server 2008 R2	Jul 2010	1/14/2014
SQL Server 2012	May 2012	7/11/2017
SQL Server 2014	June 2014	7/9/2019
SQL Server 2016	June 2016	10/12/2021
SQL Server 2017	Sept 2017	10/11/2022
SQL Server 2019	Nov 2019	1/7/2025

Fig. 7.1 – SQL version support end dates

Although many of the older versions are not supported anymore, this does not mean they are not used in production environments. The preceding table does not list all the SQL Server versions. There are even older systems that can be used today, but those fell out of support a long time ago. Also, note that SQL Server 2008 and SQL Server 2008 R2 share an end date for mainstream support, although those two are separate products released in different years.

In the following table, you can find support dates for the operating system, where the common Windows Server 2012 and Windows Server 2012 R2 have already reached the end of the mainstream support provided, with Windows Server 2016's end date coming up in 2022:

Windows Server version	End of mainstream support
Windows Server 2003 R2	7/13/2010
Windows Server 2008 with SP2	1/13/2015
Windows Server 2008 R2 with SP1	1/13/2015
Windows Server 2012	1/9/2018
Windows Server 2012 R2	1/9/2018
Windows Server 2016	1/11/2022

Fig. 7.2 – Windows Server support end dates

Upgrading your SQL Server version and the operating system can bring you many new features that can work together to achieve better performance and availability for your environment.

Planning the upgrade

Upgrading a complex infrastructure is not an easy task and should not be executed without any preparation. Careful planning of the required steps will help you eliminate possible issues to the minimum, and the upgrade will run smoothly. Throughout the versions of SQL Server there have been many changes, so it's worth exploring your options when planning the new installation, also from the perspective of the available edition.

While upgrading SQL Server from older versions, you also have to understand changes in the licensing for SQL Server, whereby SQL Server versions 2008 R2 and older used the per-processor licensing model or used a **client access license** (**CAL**) licensing model. Starting with SQL Server 2012, Microsoft has moved to core-based licensing, where you need to have a license for each **central processing unit** (**CPU**) core used on your operating system.

> **Note**
>
> SQL Server licensing is a very complex topic that goes beyond the scope of the book. There are many minor details that have an influence on SQL Server licensing, starting with the platform—be it a physical server or a virtual one—and much more. For more information about licensing, you can visit the Microsoft website at `https://www.microsoft.com/en-us/sql-server/sql-server-2019-pricing` where you can find the SQL Server licensing datasheet, which will be a great start for you.

From the edition perspective, there are two very important aspects you need to consider during upgrade—**hardware limits** and **feature limits**. SQL Server is usually deployed with two major editions—**Standard** and **Enterprise**. Enterprise has more features and offers more scalability, **high availability** (**HA**), security, and so on. With SQL Server 2016 **Service Pack 1** (**SP1**), many Enterprise features were made available also for the Standard Edition, which may allow you to upgrade to a lower edition while keeping the application working with all the required features. For the choice of edition, you also have to consider the hardware limits of the CPU/cores and memory, which have a huge impact on the overall server performance. You always have to consider upgrade rules that will force you to use a specific edition during the upgrade. You can visit `https://docs.microsoft.com/en-us/sql/database-engine/install-windows/supported-version-and-edition-upgrades-version-15?view=sql-server-ver15` for more information.

SQL Server Standard Edition supports up to 128 GB **random-access memory** (**RAM**) (for SQL Server 2016, 2017, and 2019; older versions had lower limits) and can use up to four CPU slots and 24 cores. This is mainly important with current servers, which can have many more CPU cores than the Standard Edition limit, and those can't be used for the SQL Server workload.

> **Note:**
> All the differences between editions are outlined in the online documentation available at `https://docs.microsoft.com/en-us/sql/sql-server/editions-and-components-of-sql-server-version-15?view=sql-server-ver15#Cross-BoxScaleLimits`.

The following is a list of features that are now available in the Standard Edition:

- Change data capture
- Database snapshot
- Columnstore index
- Partitioning
- Data compression
- In-Memory OLTP
- Always encrypted
- PolyBase
- Fine-grained auditing

A standard practice is to have a production and development server for an application, and we must aim to have those two so that we're not surprised in production after deploying the new code. Since SQL Server 2014 we can use the SQL Server Developer Edition for free, which is an ideal candidate for development/test servers.

> **Note**
> The only limitation of the Developer Edition is that it can't be used in production. You have to keep in mind that the Developer Edition is similar to the Enterprise Edition. So, if your production environment is based on the SQL Server Standard Edition, you need to watch closely which features to use so that they can be used in the Standard Edition.

Exploring upgrade scenarios

As a part of the planning phase, you have to carefully consider the upgrade path for your environment. The following are the three main types of upgrades you can choose from:

- SQL Server in-place upgrade
- Side-by-side migration
- Rolling upgrade

SQL Server in-place upgrade

In this scenario, the SQL Server setup upgrades your existing SQL Server installation. If you have more SQL Server instances on the same server, you have to choose a specific instance to upgrade. There are advantages and disadvantages to this upgrade path.

The main advantages are these:

- It's easy and fast.
- It does not require new hardware or a new VM.
- It does not require extra storage.
- The operating system is not upgraded.

The disadvantages are these:

- It requires a longer downtime compared to a side-by-side type of upgrade.
- It may require a complex rollback.
- It does not support all scenarios of deployed SQL Server services.

An in-place upgrade is mostly used for non-production systems, where some downtime is acceptable. During the upgrade there will be a limited time when the SQL Server services will be stopped and upgraded to a newer version, during which they are unavailable to end users.

You can use the in-place upgrade for SQL Server 2012 to 2017 to directly upgrade to SQL Server 2019. To upgrade, simply choose **Upgrade from a previous version of SQL Server**, as you can see in the following screenshot:

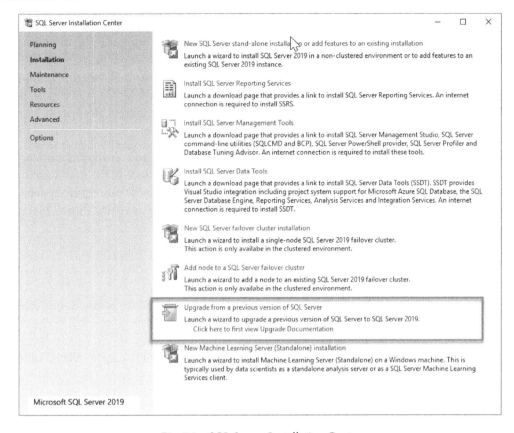

Fig. 7.3 – SQL Server Installation Center

If the in-place upgrade is not a feasible option, you still can perform side-by-side migration of your SQL Server environment.

Side-by-side migration

The side-by-side upgrade path is more complex compared to the in-place upgrade type, but it offers you more control over the overall process. In this type of upgrade, you will have two SQL Servers running and you will move the objects from one server to another. This will allow you a lot of space for testing, where two SQL Servers—the original and the new/upgraded one—can be evaluated from the application teams to resolve any possible issues. The original server will be intact, and you will need to install a fresh new SQL Server with many choices, such as the following:

- New hardware
- New VM
- New SQL Server instance (least recommended option)

With new hardware or a new VM, you have the benefit of installing the SQL Server on the latest operating system, which is not covered by the in-place upgrade. The in-place upgrade is only to upgrade the SQL Server version, so the Windows operating system has to be handled usually by the Windows admin team of your company. Having the option of using the latest Windows operating system and new hardware or VM can give you many performance benefits with newer and faster CPUs, more RAM, different storage options, and much more.

When you are using the side-by-side migration option, you have to consider that many objects won't be part of the databases that you will eventually restore to the new system. There are many system objects stored in master or MSDB databases that require special attention; otherwise, your new SQL Server won't work as you may expect. Those objects include the following:

- SQL Server logins

- SQL Server certificates

- SQL Server principals

- Linked servers

- SQL Server jobs and other **Structured Query Language** (**SQL**) agent-related objects (proxies, operators, alerts)

- SQL Server server-level triggers

- **SQL Server Integration Services** (**SSIS**) packages stored in MSDB

Login information is essential so that your **database administrator** (**DBA**) team, application team, and the application itself can log in to the SQL Server. These logins are stored in the `master` database and can be copied to the new version of SQL Server in several ways. One of them would be the use of the `sp_help_revlogin` stored procedure.

Tip

The `sp_help_revlogin` stored procedure is an old procedure available from Microsoft, which is not installed to the SQL Server by default. The source code is available at `http://bit.ly/2m5pwUY`. You can grab the code from the site, run the code on your SQL Server version, and then use the procedure to generate the required **Transact-SQL** (**T-SQL**) code for recreating logins from scratch on the new system.

To export the logins via this stored procedure, simply run the following T-SQL code after you have successfully created all the required objects:

```
EXEC sp_help_revlogin
```

This stored procedure will generate the T-SQL code needed to recreate all the logins that exist on the current SQL Server. The output also includes specific system logins and certificates, service accounts, and much more, which you may skip in order to focus only on the logins required for the application team. The output may look like this:

```
-- Login: SQL\SQLAdmins
CREATE LOGIN [SQL\SQLAdmins] FROM WINDOWS WITH DEFAULT_DATABASE
= [master]

-- Login: WebAppAcct
CREATE LOGIN [WebAppAcct] WITH PASSWORD =
0x0200FB0844C8CE6803535BB339EC378F40AF5AD003D64EF3748D3568AE49
CA2D3436C102B5F7EA44729F6ED16D3CF16DF1F4BA74C6D47D0789AEF
2915C6773B677E7FB0AC6DC HASHED,
    SID = 0x968A6D6212D4634D9CF7C3E10FFAEC84,
    DEFAULT_DATABASE = [master],
    CHECK_POLICY = ON,
    CHECK_EXPIRATION = ON
```

In the preceding example output, you can see two types of logins—**Windows login** and **SQL login**. SQL logins use passwords that are not provided in cleartext but with hash values; they also come with a **security identifier** (**SID**), which is important for the server login to database user mapping in your databases. In this way, database users will be correctly mapped to the SQL Server login once you bring the databases from the old server to the new one.

> **Tip**
> Another option would be the use of PowerShell, where you can find a module named dbatools at https://dbatools.io/download/.
> This PowerShell module is not a default module in SQL Server but offers various interesting commands to use with your SQL Server environment not only for migration but also for common operations. The Export-DbaLogin command will generate a similar output to the sp_help_revlogin stored procedure, but with a little bit more information and code control blocks.

For more complex projects, you can use **SQL Server Data Tools for Visual Studio**, or **SSDT** for short. SSDT provides you with a development platform for your database and **business intelligence (BI)** development. The most important projects for SSDT are listed as follows:

- Integration Services package project
- Analysis Services project
- Reporting Services report project

To transfer logins from one server to another, you can use the Integration Services package and use one of the tasks named **Transfer Login Task Editor**. You need to enter the following configuration items for the task:

- Source server
- Destination server
- Login list to migrate
- Whether to copy SIDs

Once you define the task parameters you can run the package, and it will copy the required logins from the old server to the new server, as the following screenshot shows:

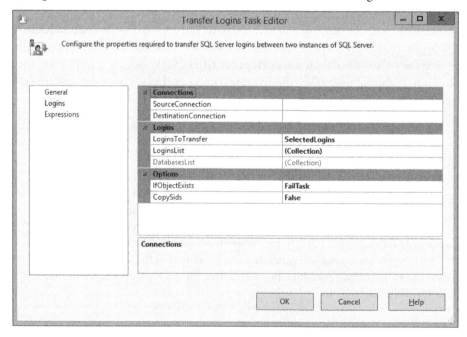

Fig. 7.4 – SSIS transfer login task

Using SSIS can be very useful for larger scenarios, because there are more types of objects that can be transferred with the side-by-side upgrade path. As we mentioned earlier, there are more system-specific objects that you will need to copy from the old server to the new one and many of these can be handled by SSIS, as can be seen from the following screenshot:

Fig. 7.5 – SSIS migration tasks

As you can see in the preceding screenshot, you can transfer many objects from the MSDB database, such as jobs and error messages, master stored procedures, or even whole databases. Using SSIS is one possible method to transfer databases from an old server to a new one.

Other possible ways include the following:

- Restoring the database from the backup

- Using attach/detach methods

- Using any **disaster recovery** (**DR**) option—replication, mirroring, log shipping, availability groups

The option chosen to bring the database to the new server will be dependent on many factors and those are mainly the size of the database, the requirement to keep the new and old server in sync, and the availability of the storage.

Rolling upgrade

The rolling upgrade method is used on the SQL Server environment, whereby you need to keep the upgrade between multiple servers and instances in the correct order. This approach is used mainly with HA or DR solutions, such as the following:

- Always-On availability failover cluster

- Always-On availability groups

- Mirroring

- Log shipping
- Replication

The rolling upgrade method is also used with several services such as **SQL Server Reporting Services** (**SSRS**) if scale-out deployment for HA and load balancing is used.

Upgrading the SQL Server version if more servers are used for HA and DR usually starts with the passive node of the installed solution. Depending on the solution, you will have to perform manual failover and then continue with the *not yet upgraded* node of the solution. The only part where SQL Server automatically determines if the failover should occur is the upgrade of the failover cluster. If more than half of the nodes were upgraded to the new version, SQL Server will automatically fail over the SQL services to an upgraded node.

> **Note**
>
> The full upgrade scenario for HA/DR solutions is out of the scope of this book, but you can find more information on availability groups at `https://docs.microsoft.com/en-us/sql/database-engine/availability-groups/windows/upgrading-always-on-availability-group-replica-instances`.

Pre-upgrade checks

Regardless of the chosen upgrade path, in-place or side-by-side, you need to check if your database can be upgraded to a new version. SQL Server 2019 comes with a **Data Migration Assistant** tool that can be used to verify if there are any blockers to your upgrade and verify whether any of the databases include features that would prevent migration to the new SQL Server 2019 version.

Data Migration Assistant

Let's see what the **Data Migration Assistant** tool looks like. The welcome page is shown in the following screenshot:

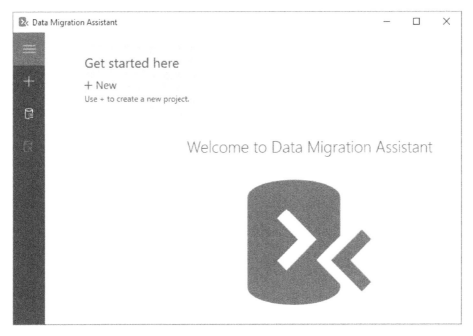

Fig. 7.6 – Data Migration Assistant

The **Data Migration Assistant** tool has to be configured to connect to your SQL Server instance, and you'll need to select the databases for evaluation. This evaluation will examine the objects in the databases, their compatibility levels, and other parameters for SQL Server 2019 and will produce a report for you.

Data Migration Assistant can be used to evaluate migration toward the following:

- A new SQL Server
- An Azure SQL database
- Azure SQL Server on a VM

The discovered issues are split into the following categories, based on the impact of your application during the upgrade:

- **Breaking changes**
- **Behavior changes**
- **Deprecated features**

You can also use the **Discover New Features** option, which will evaluate the existing database and recommend new features based on the difference between the source SQL Server version and SQL Server 2019. These recommendations will be split into the following categories:

- Performance—In-Memory OLTP and Columnstore Index

- Security—Always encrypted, transparent data encryption, dynamic data masking, and so on

- Storage

We can see in the following screenshot what **Discover New Features** looks like:

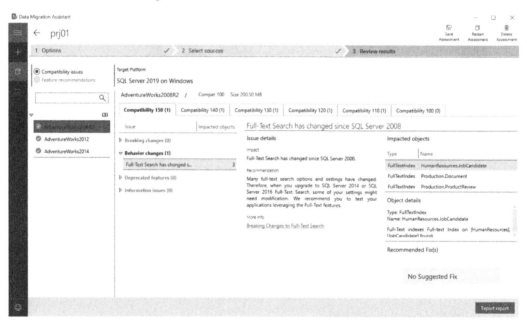

Fig. 7.7 – Data Migration Assistant assessment view

As you can see in the preceding screenshot, the evaluation of the existing databases was okay, but the **Data Migration Assistant** tool was able to detect several deprecated features and behavior changes that you should carefully examine before you proceed with the upgrade. These can have performance, security, and stability impacts on your environment.

The **Data Migration Assistant** tool can be used not only to perform assessment but also for the migration itself. In that case, you would have to create a different type of project and configure which databases and logins you would like to migrate to the new environment, as seen in the following screenshot:

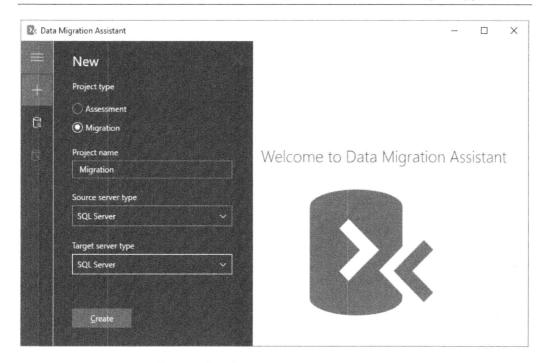

Fig. 7.8 – Data Migration Assistant new project

Data Migration Assistant can also be used from the command line, but currently, only **Assessment mode** is available. To run the assessment against the local SQL Server, use the following command:

```
DmaCmd.exe /AssessmentName="MigrationAssessment" /
AssessmentDatabases="Server=SQL;Initial
Catalog=AdventureWorks2016;Integrated Security=true"
/AssessmentEvaluateCompatibilityIssues /
AssessmentOverwriteResult /AssessmentResultJson="C:\
MigrationAssessments\AWReport.json"
```

This command will run the assessment named SQL with SQL Server for a database called AdventureWorks2016 and store the output in a local file.

SQL Server System Configuration Checker

The SQL Server setup uses the **System Configuration Checker** (**SCC**) to perform basic checks if there are any blockers for your upgrade. You can either run the SCC as a standalone task from the installation media or it will run automatically as part of the SQL Server installation, once you install a new instance or upgrade an existing one.

The SQL server setup looks like this:

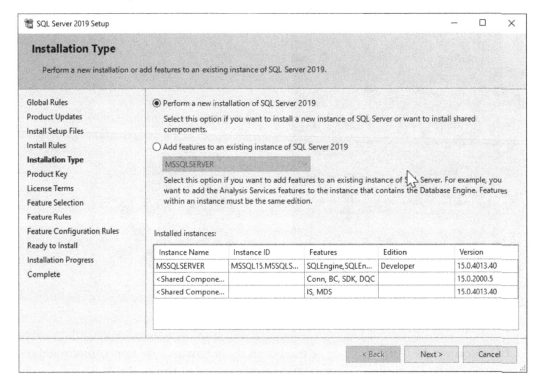

Fig. 7.9 – SQL Server setup

We just went through the options for an upgrade and all the considerations you have to make for such a task. Let's see how to perform the upgrade.

Performing the upgrade

Once you have finished the planning phase and all the preparations are done, it's time to perform the upgrade/migration of your SQL Server environment. For the scenario used in this chapter, we'll upgrade an existing SQL Server 2016 version to the latest version. One thing you also need to carefully consider is the edition upgrade path that you need to follow.

> **Note**
>
> We will be upgrading to the Enterprise Edition, and the edition will stay the same after the upgrade. You can, however, upgrade between editions. You can find the whole edition and version upgrade matrix on Microsoft's website at `https://docs.microsoft.com/en-us/sql/database-engine/install-windows/supported-version-and-edition-upgrades` where you can see which versions and editions can be upgraded.

In the next steps, we will consider the in-place upgrade of the SQL Server environment first. Once we have started the SQL Server setup, the setup program has to check the system and prerequisites so that we can continue with upgrading the SQL Server environment. If you have more instances, you will be presented with a choice of which instance to upgrade. One of the choices is to upgrade just the shared features, and those include the following:

- SSIS

- Master Data Services

- **SQL Server Management Studio** (**SSMS**). Although SSMS is a separate download, it's still listed as a shared feature.

- In the following screenshot, you can see the choice of existing instances to upgrade:

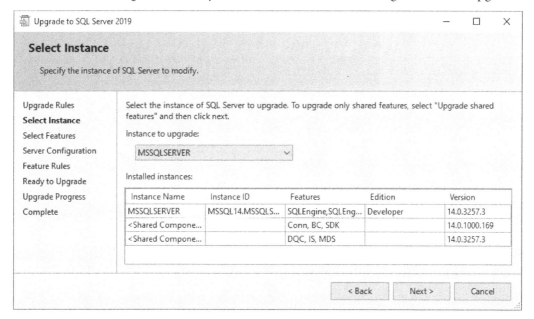

Fig. 7.10 – SQL Server upgrade

One of the services that was formerly included in the SQL Server installation—SSRS—is now a separate download, and during the upgrade it will be uninstalled. What you need to do is outlined in the setup window, as follows:

- Back up your report server databases.

- Back up your report server encryption key.

- Install new reporting services.

- Migrate the reports.

Once you go through all the remaining pages of the setup dialog, then the setup program will start the upgrade of your SQL Server environment. It's then just a measure of time, depending on the performance of your system and how long it will take to finish the upgrade. After the upgrade, you need to verify the services and connectivity to your SQL Server. If all the services are running correctly and you can connect to the SQL Server, you need to also check all the applications using your SQL Server environment to verify that the upgrade went fine.

You can also check the `log` file that is generated during the upgrade for any possible issues if any of the services do not upgrade correctly.

In the following screenshot, you can see a finished setup with a link to the setup log file:

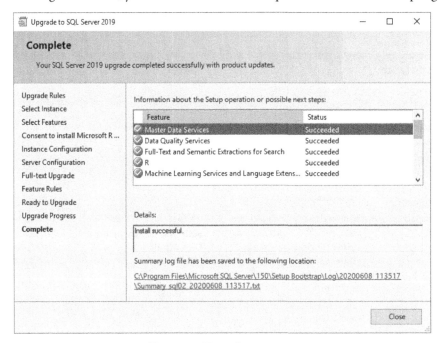

Fig. 7.11 – Upgrade summary

Once you start SSMS on the upgraded SQL Server environment, it will check for the upgrade and let you install the latest version of SSMS, which is now a separate tool, from the SQL Server installation.

To finish the upgrade, you will need to perform several additional steps, as follows:

1. You need to check your maintenance plans and take backups of your databases.

2. You should check the integrity of the databases with the DBCC command.

3. Evaluate the compatibility level of the databases and raise to the highest level with performance checks in mind.

4. Install the latest updates that were not included in the installation media (cumulative updates).

5. Rebuild indexes and update statistics.

6. Repopulate full-text catalogs.

Let's dig deeper into the upgrade process for SSRS. This service is commonly deployed for numerous Microsoft products or third-party applications. Since SQL Server 2017, this service is a separate download and is no longer included in the installation media of SQL Server.

Upgrading Reporting Services 2019

During the upgrade (following *Fig. 7.8*), we have seen that the Reporting Services service will be uninstalled, and we need to install a brand-new instance of SSRS, which is now a separate install and download. Before we can start with that, you need to back up your databases and the key to be able to migrate your reports.

Databases are on your SQL Server environment and if you're not sure about the names, in the case of multiple Reporting Services instances, you can check the database server name and database names from the **Reporting Services Configuration Manager** tool, where you can click on the **Database** configuration page, as can be seen in the following screenshot:

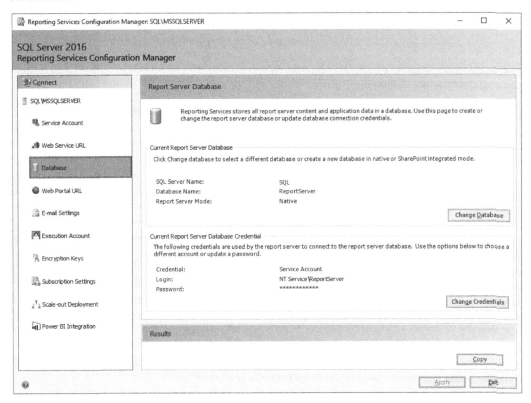

Fig. 7.12 – SSRS database configuration

To back up the key, you need to switch to the **Encryption Keys** page of the configuration to find several buttons available to you. The most important one for us in this step is the **Backup** button, which is used to back up the key. This Reporting Services key is used to encrypt sensitive data in your datasets, connections, and subscriptions.

If this key is lost, you can wipe out all sensitive information by clicking the **Delete** button, and all connections will need to be reconfigured. In the following screenshot, you can see the configuration page for SSRS encryption keys:

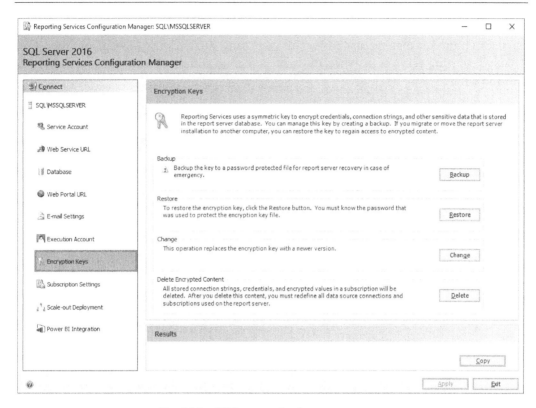

Fig. 7.13 – SSRS encryption key management

While you're performing the backup of the key, you need to provide the location to store the key on the filesystem, and also the password to protect the key.

You need to keep this password safe and available to be able to restore the key in the future. In the following screenshot, you can see the dialog box for encryption key backup, including the password for the key:

Fig. 7.14 – SSRS backup encryption key dialog

You can also use the command line to back up the key to have a scheduled task that can back up the key on a regular basis. This command will back up the key from the default Reporting Services instance and protect the key with the `P@ssw0rd` value, as illustrated here:

```
rskeymgmt -e -f c:\backup\ssrskey.snk -p P@ssw0rd
```

When you have the full backup of the databases and your keys, you can click **Install SQL Server Reporting Services**. The installation files are not present directly on the SQL Server 2017 installation but there's a link provided in the setup tool, which opens a web page where you can download the binaries needed to install the new reporting services. The following screenshot illustrates this:

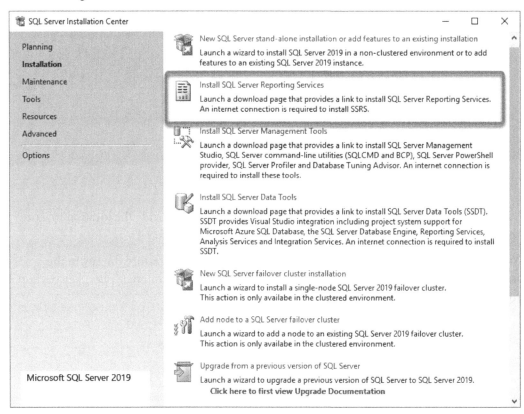

Fig. 7.15 – SQL Server Installation Center

Once you start the installation, you'll be presented with several dialog choices. The first one is **Install Server Reporting Services**. In the next one, you need to select the edition that you're about to install. Developer, Express, and Evaluation do not require any serial number, but the remaining editions do. Once you select the location to install the SSRS, you can just hit the **Install Reporting Services** button, as shown in the following screenshot, and the installation will start:

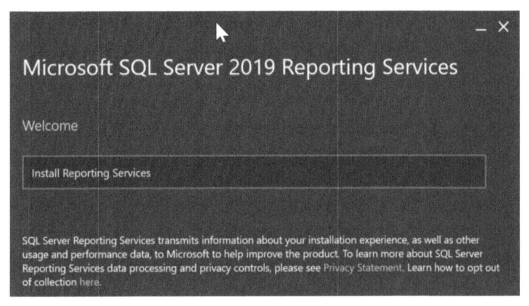

Fig. 7.16 – SSRS installation

When installing SSRS, you need to choose the proper edition that matches the SQL Server edition you purchased.

In the following screenshot, you can see how to choose the edition:

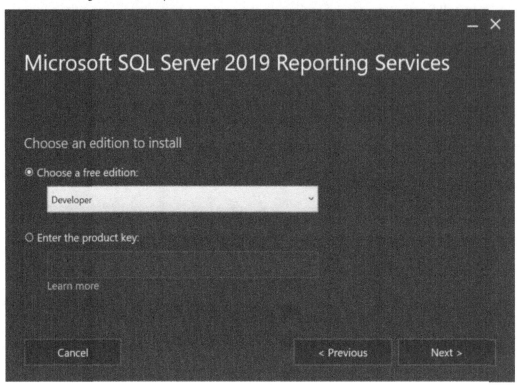

Fig. 7.17 – SSRS edition choices

Once SSRS is installed, you need to perform the configuration of the server. Just hit the **Configure report server** button and the **Reporting Services Configuration Manager** tool will open, similar to the one where we performed the key backup. This time, it's for the SQL Server 2017 version.

For the configuration, we will focus only on key aspects needed for a successful upgrade, and not the full SSRS configuration. This is illustrated in the following screenshot:

Fig. 7.18 – SSRS finished setup: configuration

You need to configure the following items in SSRS:

- **Web Service URL**
- **Web Portal URL**
- **Database**
- **Encryption Keys**

We have backed up the databases on the old system, so you need to restore the backups to your new SQL Server. When you configure the databases, you will use the **Change Database** button to open a dialog to attach the existing databases from your SQL Server.

You need to select the correct database name to attach, as you can see in the following screenshot:

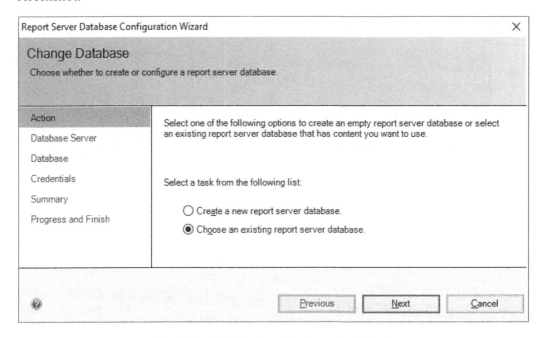

Fig. 7.19 – SSRS Database Configuration Wizard

Once you have the database available, you need to configure two **Uniform Resource Locators** (**URLs**) used for the web service and the web portal. If you don't want to make any customization to the configuration, you can navigate to the correct pages in the **Reporting Services Configuration Manager** tool and just hit the **Apply** button on those two configuration pages—**Web Service URL** and **Web Portal URL**—as seen in the following screenshot:

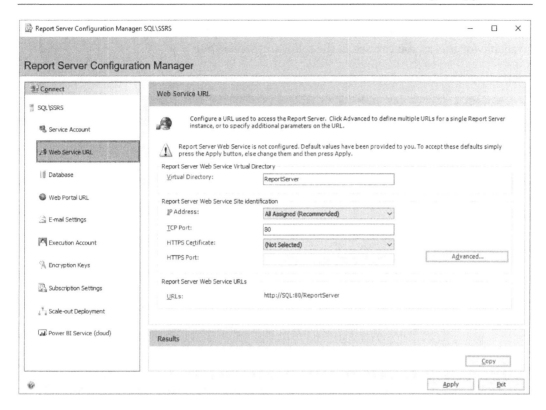

Fig. 7.20 – SSRS web service configuration

If both URLs have been configured, the last item remaining is to restore the key from the backup. I hope you have the password available, since you'll need to provide the password used during the backup of the key. On the **Encryption Keys** page, you can use the **Restore** button and provide the file with the key and password. If all these items are configured, you can navigate to the URL of the web portal, which you will find on the **Web Portal URL** page.

The new web page will be opened in your browser and you will see the new SSRS portal available for use, as you can see in the following screenshot:

Fig. 7.21 – SSRS report browser

We have seen how to plan and execute the upgrade of SQL Server from older versions to the current one. Let's explore the options for migration from other database systems to SQL Server.

Migrating from other platforms

SQL Server migration projects don't necessarily only include SQL Server as a primary data source, but there are many other platforms where you may choose to upgrade to SQL Server. You can use **SQL Server Migration Assistant** (**SSMA**), which is available for several Database Management System (DBMS) systems, as follows:

- SSMA for Access
- SSMA for DB2
- SSMA for Oracle
- SSMA for **SAP Adaptive Server Enterprise** (**SAP ASE**)
- SSMA for MySQL

SSMA is able to create a project for a number of target versions of SQL Server, where SQL Server 2017 is included with both platforms—Linux and Windows operating systems. The other targets available are listed as follows:

- SQL Server 2008/2008 R2

- SQL Server 2012

- SQL Server 2014

- SQL Server 2016

- SQL Server 2017 Windows/Linux

- Azure SQL Database

- Azure SQL Data Warehouse

If you would like to use the migration tool, you need to have drivers for correct DBMS systems in place. For Access migration, you need Microsoft Access Runtime, which you can download from Microsoft's website. The tool can open the download link for you. The migration wizard can be seen in the following screenshot:

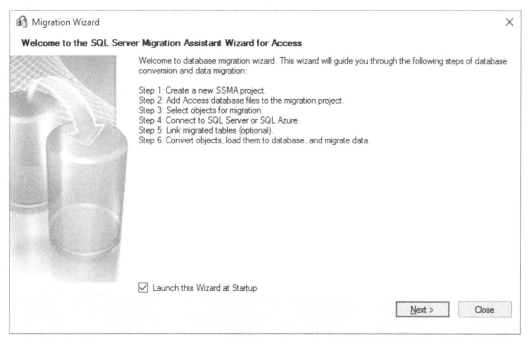

Fig. 7.22 – Database Migration Assistant

There's a lot of planning and testing required for platform migration due to type conversions, query differences, performance objects, and many other possible issues. SSMA can be a useful start for such analysis, where you can evaluate possible migration blockers and start resolving them one by one.

Migration example from Microsoft Access

We can use SSMA for Microsoft Access to convert data stored in the `Access` database to the SQL Server, and there are several possible options for us. With SSMA, you can evaluate all existing objects in the `Access` database, configure the type mapping between SQL Server and Microsoft Access, and migrate the content of `Access` to a new SQL Server database, as illustrated in the following screenshot:

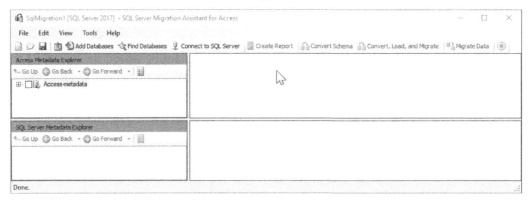

Fig. 7.23 – SSMA for Microsoft Access

You can use the **Add Database** button to open the `Access` database file and explore existing objects—tables, views, queries, and so on. To connect to your SQL Server, use the **Connect to SQL Server** button and enter your instance and database name at the location where you want to import the data. **Access Metadata Explorer** is shown in the following screenshot:

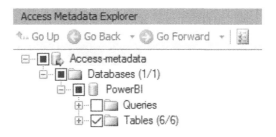

Fig. 7.24 – Access Metadata Explorer

Once you have connected to all the systems, you can evaluate the data and use any of the possible tasks, as follows:

- Convert, load, and migrate
- Create report
- Convert schema
- Migrate data

With `Access`, you have an option to use linked tables, which will allow your application to connect to `Access`, and the data will already be stored in SQL Server when you finish all the migration steps, including the configuration of the application connection information.

Summary

Upgrade and migration are important phases in the SQL Server operation life cycle. Each path has its own advantages and disadvantages. As we went through the chapter, you saw that careful planning of such a task is crucial, since there are numerous considerations for the new platform.

In-place upgrades offer you the option to utilize the current hardware of the virtual environment, allowing you to quickly upgrade your SQL Server to new versions. However, this option has more complex rollback if your upgrade fails. With side-by-side migration, you can really use the benefits of the new hardware platform, modern CPUs, and the latest operating system, which will allow you to build the SQL Server again, and then you just need to migrate the data between the old and new SQL Server. There are again numerous options for you, the most common being backup and attach/detach methods. There are many tools that can be used to plan the upgrade—especially SQL Server **Data Migration Assistant** and SSMA.

SSMA is used to migrate not only to the latest SQL Server 2019 version but also to older SQL Server platforms and Azure SQL Database, since this tool is used for migration from other supported DBMS systems.

In the following chapter, we will explore SQL Server automation capabilities. Automation is very important today since the size of the environments we manage is growing, and you may want to eliminate the manual steps in repeated tasks. These components for automation can also be used for SQL Server monitoring, so we'll explore the alerting system and other monitoring capabilities of SQL Server.

8
Automation – Using Tools to Manage and Monitor SQL Server 2019

A lot of administrator tasks are executed regularly and it's inconceivable to run these tasks manually. SQL Server offers a dedicated service called **SQL Server Agent**, helping us to automate many common tasks. Along with this service, a very helpful tool called the **maintenance plan** was developed to support regular tasks that should be run against each database.

In this chapter, we will learn what **SQL Server Agent** is and how to set up this service from reliability and security perspectives. We will also set up **Database Mail** to keep a tab on things if they go wrong. We will also look at **Maintenance Plans**. A maintenance plan is a powerful tool that helps administrators decide on the tasks that are required to maintain healthy databases and protect databases from data loss and performance degradation. It has a relatively simple wizard that covers very complicated tasks.

SQL Server Agent holds definitions for jobs, operators, and alerts; we will see the benefits of their usage and how to create them. We will also learn how to work with **SQL Server Agent**'s security objects.

In this chapter, we will cover the following topics:

- Using SQL Server Agent
- Creating and editing maintenance plans
- Creating SQL Server Agent objects
- SQL Server Agent security

Using SQL Server Agent

SQL Server Agent is a **Windows service** that serves mainly as a provider for the **automation of regular tasks**. Tasks that can be automated are not only administrative ones but also other tasks supporting the operation of information systems – for example, data movements such as **ETL processes**, **migration tasks**, and **integration package runs**. Having **SQL Server Agent** running full time is also a prerequisite for some features offered by other SQL Server services – for example, **data collection** or **reporting services**, unattended report execution or subscriptions.

The **SQL Server Agent** service is installed within the SQL Server setup without an option to skip its installation. Every edition except the Express Edition of SQL Server has **SQL Server Agent** installed.

In order to start using **SQL Server Agent**, there are a couple of simple tasks that need to be performed. These will be described in the following sections.

Setting up the SQL Server Agent service

The first setup task is to check the service startup mode of **SQL Server Agent** after installation. The check is done in **SQL Server Configuration Manager**. The procedure is very easy and it is described in a step-by-step manner with screenshots showing what to find and where to find it:

1. Start **Sql Server Configuration Manager** and in the left pane, click on **SQL Server Services**.

2. In the right pane, a list of installed services will appear, as shown in the following screenshot:

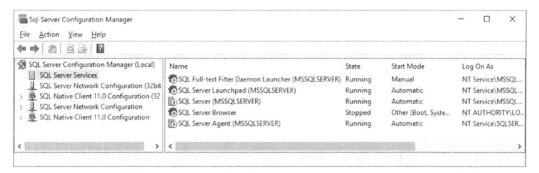

Figure 8.1 – List of installed services

3. In the right pane, right-click on the **SQL Server Agent** row (the instance name is **SQL Server (MSSQLSERVER)** in our screenshot) and select **Properties**. A modal dialog (depicted in the following screenshot) will open for us to go through:

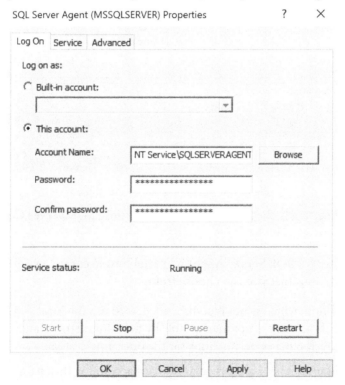

Figure 8.2 – Log On tab

4. In the **Log On** tab, we can change the service login and password. The choice of the right login depends on several factors and will be described immediately after these steps.

5. The most important tab is the **Service** tab. In this tab, we must ensure that **SQL Server Agent** has **Automatic** set as the start mode:

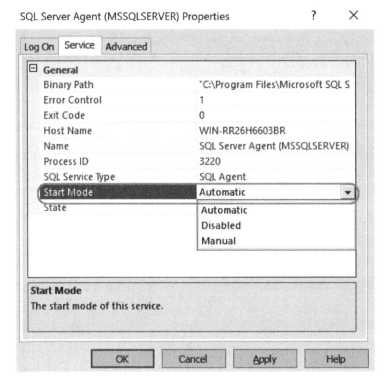

Figure 8.3 – Selecting mode - Automatic

6. When this setting is checked, click on **OK** and close **SQL Server Configuration Manager**.

The security context of **SQL Server Agent** is crucial for the correct execution of all jobs. There are three options that you can choose from:

- The first option, which is not recommended, is to use the local system built-in account. This account is not manageable by the administrator and this account also contains too many permissions for the operating system.

- The second option is to use a regular domain account with start-as-a-service permission, but we must consider the **group policy object** and the possible need to regularly change the password.

- The third option, recommended by Microsoft as the best practice, is to use **Managed Service Accounts**. This option is available on Windows Server 2012 until the latest 2019 version. Managed Service Accounts behave the same way as any other common user account, but Windows Server ensures an internal regular password change. It has two consequences:

a) Users, even DBAs, do not know the password for SQL Server Agent.

b) The password does not compromise password policies.

The account that is used should not have any elevated permissions. When set up during installation, SQL Server setup sets necessary permissions on it; otherwise, we could suffer problems while running **SQL Server Agent**. More information about security is provided in *Chapter 4, Securing Your SQL Server.*

Setting up SQL Server Agent Properties

Next, setup tasks are done in Management Studio in the **Properties** window of the **SQL Server Agent** service:

1. Open Management Studio and connect to the SQL Server instance.

2. In **Object Explorer** is a node called **SQL Server Agent**. Right-click on it and choose **Properties**:

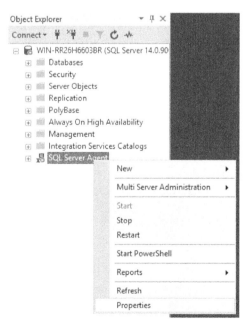

Figure 8.4 – Object Explorer - Properties

3. When the **Properties** window is open, we have to go through six pages. On the first page, called **General**, we should tick off the checkboxes as shown in the following screenshot:

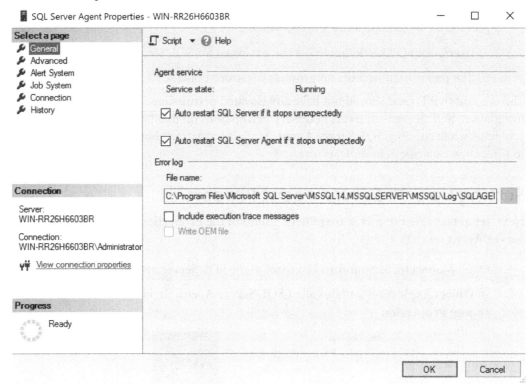

Figure 8.5 – The General page

4. Switching on these two options ensures that **SQL Server Agent** will attempt to start when it is stopped. It was very rarely noticed, but previously, **SQL Server Agent** resolved job conflicts by restarting itself.

5. The **Advanced** page has two independent parts. The upper part is sometimes used for the centralized management of SQL servers. It is called **SQL Server event forwarding**.

> **Note**
>
> Event forwarding is a feature that provides the ability to forward error messages from certain SQL Server instances to another server to establish a central point of diagnostics. A positive aspect of this feature is the ability to make one clear and comfortable place for SQL Server management, but we must consider moments when the central server collecting error log data is inaccessible. However, jobs and other tasks will not be affected by the inaccessibility.

6. The lower part of the **Advanced** settings is used to determine what it means when SQL Server's CPU is idle. As seen in the following screenshot, by default, the CPU is idle when it gets below 10 percent of utilization for at least 10 minutes. However, we can adjust these settings as needed – for example, when some concurrent service runs on the same server and we know that the CPU's effort never goes under 20 percent. The **Define idle CPU condition** checkbox needs to be ticked first, and then we can adjust the rest of the settings. Without ticking the checkbox, the **On CPU Idle** schedule will never be executed. The **Advanced** page is shown in the following screenshot:

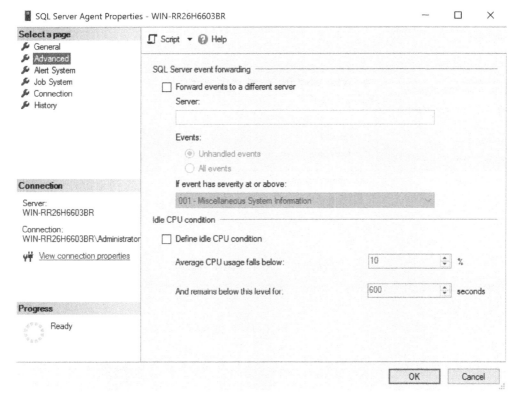

Figure 8.6 – The Advanced page

7. The **Alert System** page in the **SQL Server Agent Properties** window is seen in the next screenshot. It has more parts, but for common administration purposes, just the two parts marked in red are important. The big part in the middle of the window is obsolete as pagers are used less and less:

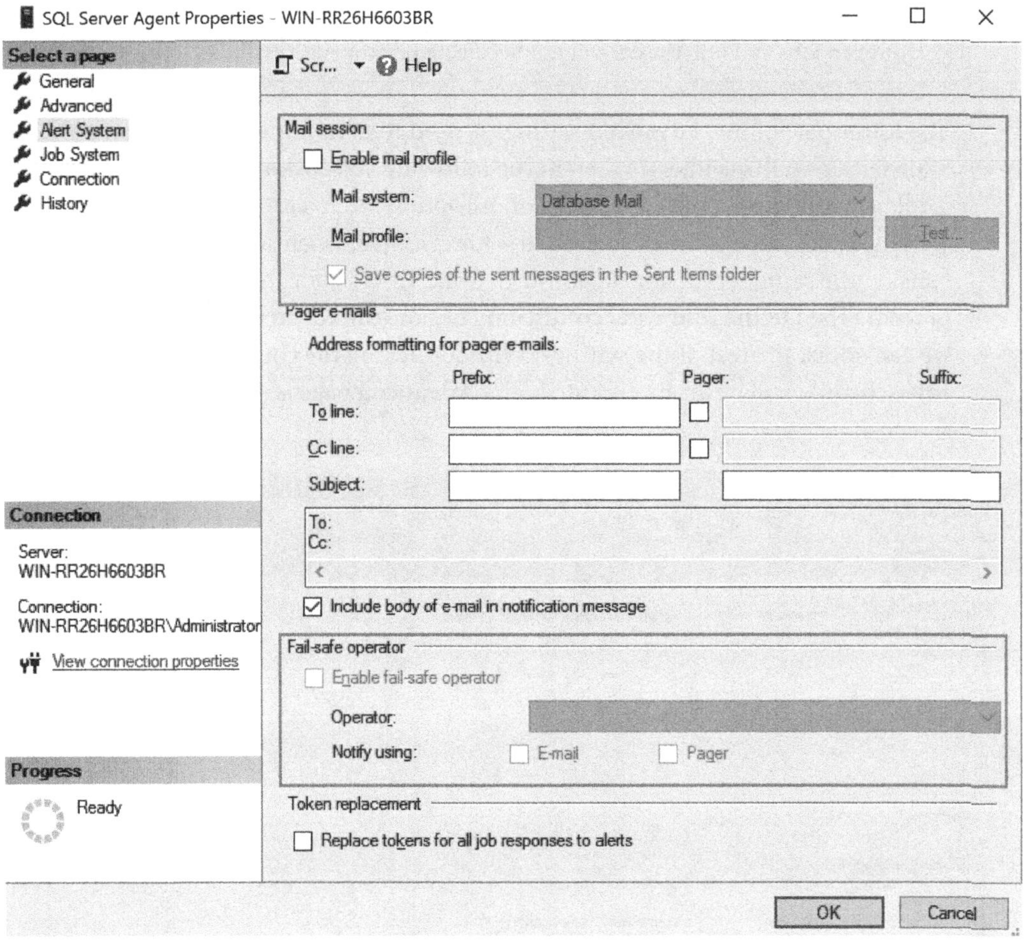

Figure 8.7 – Alert system page

It is very useful and also recommended to use an alerting system. It greatly helps administrators to stay informed about everything that might happen on SQL Server (for example, more serious errors, failed jobs, and so on). For the correct settings of **Alert System**, we need to configure the **Database Mail** profile for **SQL Server Agent** first, which will be described in the next section. When the **Database Mail** profile has been created, it should be used in the first setting of the preceding screen. The **Enable mail profile** checkbox is enabled, the **Mail system** drop down is filled with the **Database Mail** value (it's now the only possible value; the second value called **SQL Mail** was marked as deprecated several versions of SQL Server ago and now it's gone), and if some **Mail profile** were already configured, their names appear in the dropdown called **Mail profile**.

8. The second red box is **Fail-safe operator**. The fail-safe operator is a regular operator defined in **SQL Server Agent** (see the *Operators* section), but it has one extra behavior. When **SQL Server Agent** is started, the **Fail-safe operator** definition is cached to be ready in case the regular operator is not accessible, for example, due to some serious problem with the msdb database. To set the fail-safe operator, the first step is to create a regular operator. Then, when the **Enable fail-safe operator** checkbox is switched on, operator names are seen in the **Operator** dropdown.

9. The last interesting tab in the **SQL Server Agent Properties** window is the tab to set job history retention. Every step of every job writes its result in the msdb database. The history table has, by default, a maximum of 1000 records in total and a maximum of 100 records per job. When the 1000 limit is reached, the maximum records per job is reduced.

This default setting can be changed, as shown in the following screenshot (the screenshot shows default values):

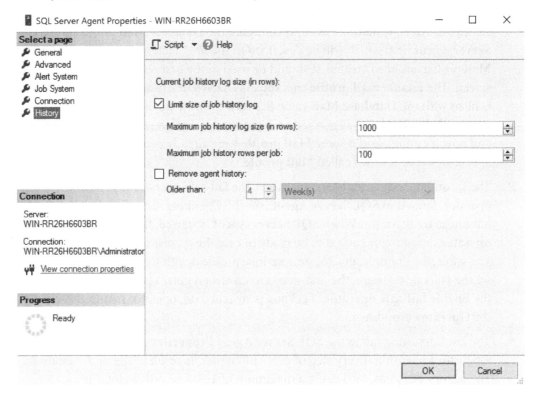

Figure 8.8 – The History page

If both checkboxes are turned off, the history will last in the `msdb` database up to its limit. We can also keep the history measured by the number of rows. A relatively new but very useful option is to turn off the **Limit size of job history log** checkbox but switch on **Remove agent history** and set up the time limit. By default, the retention period is 4 weeks. It is quite enough because it covers job histories for a month of regular automation.

The job history serves as a source of diagnostic information, typically error messages. When some job step, that is, a T-SQL job step containing a `BACKUP DATABASE` statement, fails, it is guided with an error message, which is written to the history. But reviewing the history also helps to give an insight into the additional workload added by **SQL Server Agent** jobs to the resource utilization of the SQL Server instance, because all records written to the history contain execution times as well as start and finish times.

Setting up Database Mail

Database Mail is a component of SQL Server that provides email features for any desired task. The main purpose is to be informed by SQL Server or **SQL Server Agent** when anything happens that needs the administrator's attention. When **Database Mail** is set up, administrators could be notified in the form of an email when jobs fail, alerts occur, and so on:

1. To set up as well as make changes to the **Database Mail** configuration, a wizard incorporated into Management Studio is used. This section is a walkthrough of this wizard. It is accessible from Management Studio, specifically the **Management** node, as shown in the following screenshot:

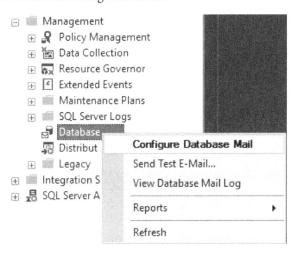

Figure 8.9 – Selecting Configure Database Mail

2. When the **Configure Database Mail** option is chosen, the wizard starts and guides us through the configuration process.

3. The first step after the welcome page is a signpost for what to do next. When the wizard is running for the first time, the first option is selected as follows:

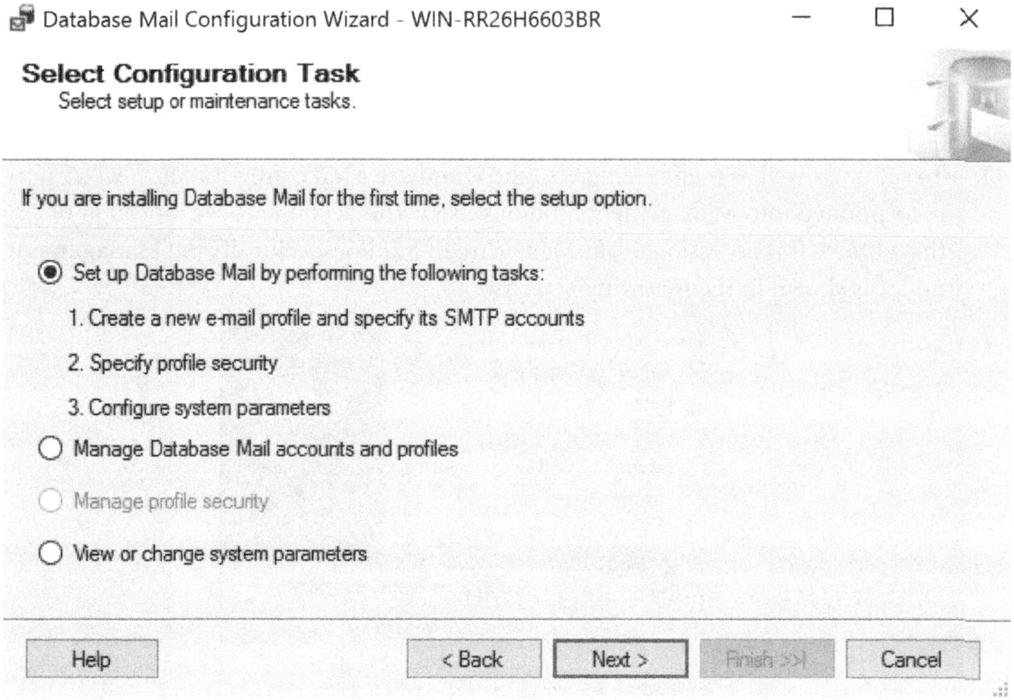

Figure 8.10 – Configuring Database Mail

When the wizard is started, additional options on the first step are enabled to skip directly to the step with the desired configuration. When passing through the wizard, we will visit all of them.

4. When the **Next** button is clicked during the first pass through the wizard, **The Database Mail feature is not available. Would you like to enable this feature?** will appear. This is because **Database Mail** is one of the features disabled at the instance level by default, and by answering **Yes** to this question, the email configuration can continue. If the feature was enabled previously by calling `exec sp_configure 'Database Mail XPs', 1` for some reason, then the question in the wizard will not be shown.

> **Note**
>
> **Database Mail** uses profiles. A profile is a secure container for one or more **SMTP accounts**. When **Database Mail** is used for more purposes than for **SQL Server Agent** emailing, it's good practice to create separate **Database Mail** profiles for such tasks due to security isolation. More email accounts assigned to one profile provide an enhanced level of reliability.

5.   When the first email account in a certain profile does not work for any reason, the second email account is used for repeated attempts to send emails and so on. In the wizard's step in the following screenshot, the profile is named and some **SMTP accounts** are created:

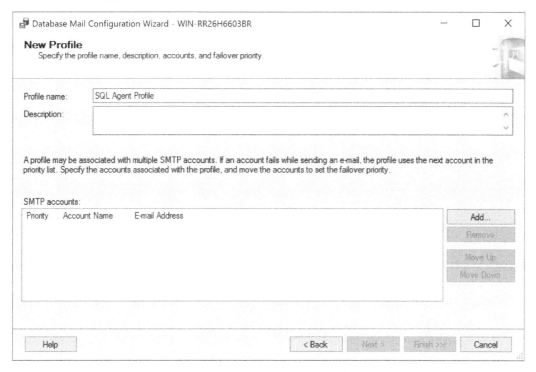

Figure 8.11 – Setting a new profile

6. **Profile name** should be filled with any descriptive name (**SQL Agent Profile** is given as an example, it's not a default). Then, click on the **Add** button and a dialog window appears for SMTP configuration:

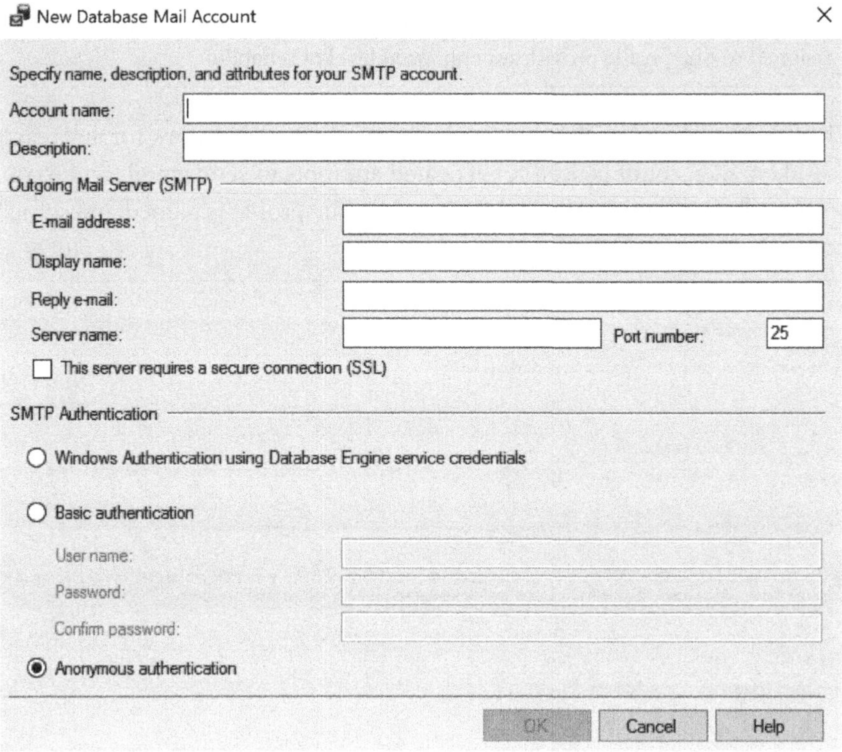

Figure 8.12 – SMTP configuration

As seen in the preceding screenshot, the SMTP account settings are quite simple. They're very similar to the email settings in any other email client. Which fields will be filled with values depends on the actual email server used. Let's go through the mandatory fields and options:

*   **Account name**: Any descriptive name of an account (for example, mydomain.com agent email).

*   **E-mail address**: The email address used within this profile as a sender's address (for example, agent@mydomain.com).

*   **Server name**: A valid name of an SMTP server (for example, smtp.mydomain.com).

*   **This server requires a secure connection (SSL)**: If needed, communication could be secured.

*   **Port number**: Often TCP port 25 or, if SSL is used, 995.

- **SMTP Authentication** options:

  a) **Windows Authentication using Database Engine service credentials**

  b) **Basic authentication** (user and password checked by the email server itself)

  c) **Anonymous authentication**

7. After adding all the required information to the email account settings dialog, click on **OK**. If needed, additional accounts could be added in the same way. When more accounts are defined, they can be prioritized by clicking on the **Move up** and **Move down** buttons in the wizard. When an email profile is defined and its account's definition is done, we can continue to the next step, which is used to define **profile security**.

8. Every profile can either be a **public** or **private** profile. When a profile is private, it is set for the SQL Server principal that the profile serves. When the profile is public, every user who has sufficient permissions can send an email by the sp_send_ dbmail procedure stored in the msdb database. When a profile is signed as a default profile, it is used when no explicit profile name is defined as a parameter of the sp_send_dbmail procedure.

The wizard step for the profile settings is shown in the following screenshot:

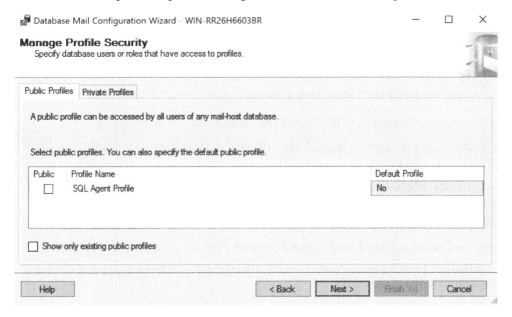

Figure 8.13 – Configuring Databse Mail profile

9. The next and last step in **Database Mail Configuration Wizard** is used to configure the system parameters. System parameters are common parameters of **Database Mail** and consist of these options:

- **Account Retry Attempts**: The number of times SQL Server tries to send an email when the sending fails. The default value is **1**.

- **Account Retry Delay (seconds)**: The period of time that SQL Server waits before it tries to send an email again (only more than one retry attempt is set). The default value is **60** seconds.

- **Maximum File Size (Bytes)**: It is not so usual when using **Database Mail** for **SQL Server Agent**, but in some user mailing scenarios, an attachment can be a part of the sent email. This setting restricts the maximum attachment size. The default value is **1,000,000** bytes.

- **Prohibited Attachment File Extensions**: This setting restricts file extensions for attachments. The default values are .exe, .vbs, .dll, and .js, but they could be enhanced by other potentially dangerous extensions, such as .com, .bat, and .ps1.

- **Database Mail Executable Minimum Lifetime (seconds)**: When the first email is sent to the queue, the service is started. This setting says how long it will be running (potentially in an idle state) before it sleeps. The default value is **600** seconds.

- **Logging Level**: This setting says how many messages will be written to the msdb database. The default value is **Extended** (errors and warnings are captured), but it can be changed to **Normal** (errors only) or **Verbose** (errors, warnings, and information messages).

A very common practice is to have the listed settings stay unchanged.

When the wizard is finished, the first email profile is created. We can run the wizard more times to add profiles or reconfigure existing ones, as well as to reconfigure all other settings. When the profile, which is intended to send an email from **SQL Server Agent**, is created, we can go back to the **SQL Server Agent Properties** window and set the **Database Mail** profile as described in *Chapter 4, Securing Your SQL Server*.

Now, when **Database Mail** is configured correctly, we can start to set up the automation of our regular tasks. In the next section, we will find a very good starting point for automated administration.

Sending emails from SQL Server

To test our **Database Mail** definition or for any user purposes, we can send emails directly from SQL Server using a stored procedure, `sp_send_dbmail`. This procedure is defined in the `msdb` database. The procedure has many parameters, but for basic needs, we can list these:

- `@profile_name`: If not set, the default public profile is used to send an email.

- `@recipients`: A list of email addresses (separated by a semicolon (`;`)).

- `@subject`: Some text, as in a regular email.

- `@body`: Some text; it's the same as when writing any email. It can be formatted as plain text or an HTML document.

- `@query`: Any query returning a result set (for example, a `SELECT` statement). The result of the query will be sent to recipients.

An important question is this: who is authorized to call the procedure? Administrators are authorized for this, but when we need to authorize regular users without administrator privileges, SQL Server prepares a special database role called `DatabaseMailUserRole` for the `msdb` database. Users added to this role have permission to call the procedure.

Let's explore how to execute the stored procedure itself:

```
exec msdb..sp_send_dbmail
  @recipients = 'administrator@example.com'
  , @subject = 'Test'
  , @body = 'Hello world'
```

The first thing that we have to consider is that even if the procedure has the `sp_` prefix, it is not defined in the master database but in the `msdb` database; hence, we need to add a database prefix, as seen in the preceding script. Our call used the default public mail profile so the `@profile_name` parameter is not needed. The rest of the script is obvious and self-descriptive. The only parameter value that needs to be changed in the preceding example is the `@recipients` parameter.

What is the result of the execution? It is an informational message, that is, `Mail (Id: 2) queued`. It says that the send operation itself is executed asynchronously and does not affect the user's waiting for the actual result of the send attempt. If we want to see the result of the sending itself, we can go to the `sysmail_sentitems` and `sysmail_faileditems` tables, respectively:

```
select * from msdb..sysmail_sentitems
select * from msdb..sysmail_faileditems
```

The two simple `select` statements show all items queued on user requests and also errors that occurred during email delivery. Both tables have the same column, called `mailitem_id`, as a joining key. There are more tables with the `sysmail_` prefix in the `msdb` database but, for testing purposes, the two listed here are sufficient.

The last thing that we have to consider is a **mail retention policy**. Just as common email clients such as Outlook do not remove emails automatically, so it is with **Database Mail**. We can find a stored procedure called `sysmail_delete_mailitems_sp` in the `msdb` database with the `@sent_before` parameter and an optional parameter, `@sent_status`.

We can plan a job that runs, for example, once a week to delete old messages. An example script for this action looks like this:

```
declare @newestDate date = dateadd(week, -4, getdate())
exec msdb..[sysmail_delete_mailitems_sp] @sent_before = @newestDate
```

The preceding script computes the date 4 weeks before, saves the result into a variable called `@newestDate`, and then the variable is used as a parameter for the stored procedure. If needed, this code could be copied and pasted as a job definition and used as-is.

Creating and editing maintenance plans

For DBAs who are not so familiar with SQL Server, the best starting point is a tool called a maintenance plan. We can think of the tool as a set of typical regular tasks that should be executed on every database hosted on our SQL Server instance. The maintenance plan itself can be created manually using the **Maintenance Plan Design Surface** or the **Maintenance Plan Wizard**, which is very good for ensuring that all the basic tasks needed to keep our database healthy are not missed.

The **Maintenance plans** node allows you to create one big sequence of many tasks scheduled together, but that is not desirable for most scenarios. For example, planning full backups and transaction log backups to be executed at the same time makes no sense. That is why a more common approach is to create one maintenance plan divided into **subplans** – units of work containing fewer tasks grouped together by their meaning. Subplans also have separate schedules.

The focus of the next two sections will be as follows:

- Creating a maintenance plan prototype using the **Maintenance Plan Wizard**
- Editing the prototype using the Maintenance Plan Design Surface

The Maintenance Plan Wizard

The creation and maintenance of **Maintenance Plans** is fully covered in Management Studio. **Object Explorer** in Management Studio contains a **Management** node, and under this node is a sub-node called **Maintenance Plans**. This is the point where all previously created maintenance plans are saved and can be edited or executed. For diagnostic purposes also, maintenance plan histories are enabled here:

1. To create a new plan, the **Maintenance Plan Wizard** is opened from the **Object Explorer** window in Management Studio, as shown in the following screenshot:

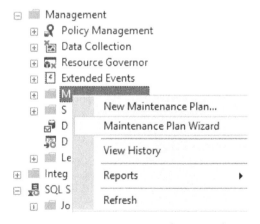

Figure 8.14 – Maintenance Plan Wizard

2. When the wizard is started and the welcome screen is skipped, the first meaningful step appears. In this step, we need to decide the following:

- **Name**: Some meaningful name, for example, **BiggerSystem maintenance**.

- **Run as**: The user context under which the plan will run.

- **Schedule distribution**: This option leads to resolution if every task has its own schedule or the entire plan will be executed at once:

  a) **Separate schedules for each task**

  b) **Single schedule for the entire plan or no schedule**

- **Schedule settings**: When separate schedules are chosen in the previous option, this setting is disabled because a schedule will be set within every task chosen later during the wizard

The first step is seen in the following screenshot:

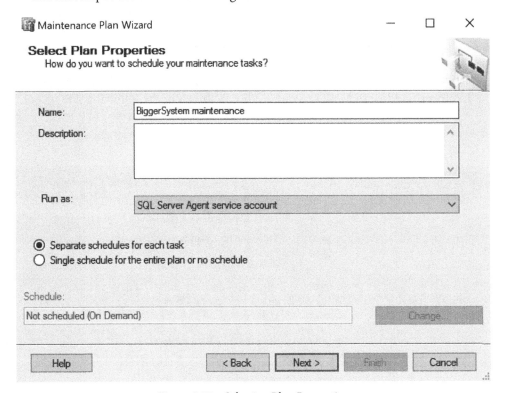

Figure 8.15 – Selecting Plan Properties

3. The second step of the wizard contains a list of all typical tasks that need to be executed regularly against every database. This is probably the most important step because this is the point where the DBA will become aware of everything important. The wizard step is shown in the following screenshot and we will explain every task type briefly:

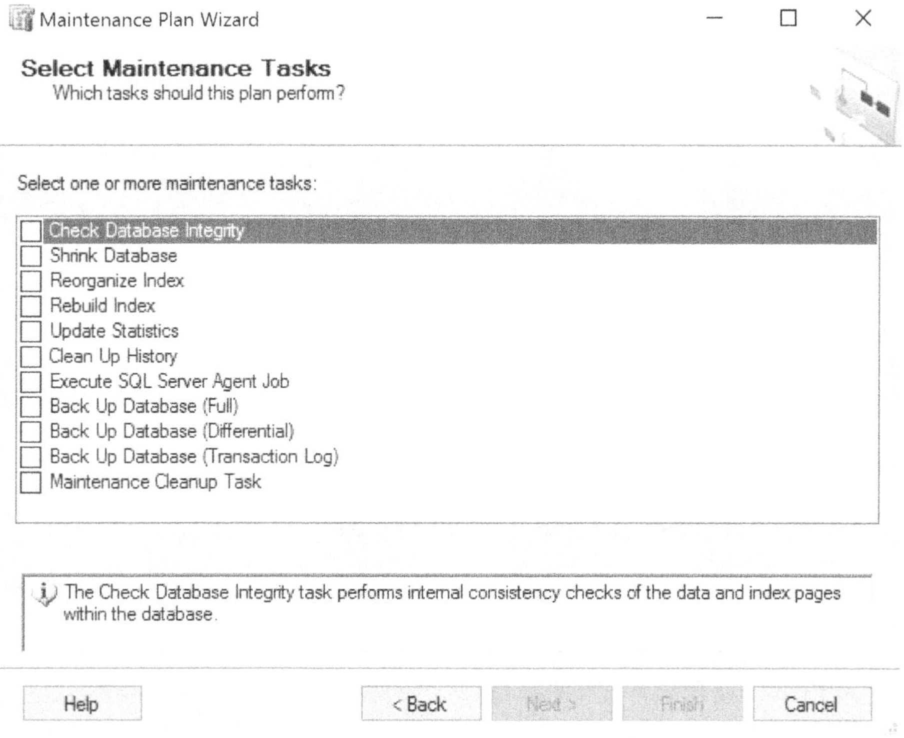

Figure 8.16 – Selecting Maintenance Tasks

Let's now go through each task briefly.

Check Database Integrity

This task uses the DBCC CHECKDB() function. There are more **Database Consistency Checker (DBCC)** functions on SQL Server – for example, DBCC SHOW_STATISTICS() to explore index or column statistics, DBCC SHRINKFILE() to return free space from database file back to the operating system, and so on. The DBCC CHECKDB() function checks the consistency and readability of the database from three perspectives, calling three other DBCCs:

- DBCC CHECKTABLE(): This function tests the readability of table data pages.
- DBCC CHECKCATALOG(): This function tests the readability of metadata objects.
- DBCC CHECKALLOC(): This function tests the logical consistency of allocation units.

The DBCC CHECKDB() function can find inconsistent places in the database. When such a situation occurs, an error is raised, and the task is failed due to the error. The error could then be seen in the **maintenance plan history**. When DBCC CHECKDB() fails, the DBA needs to immediately resolve the problem from backup. If no suitable backup is available, there is only one action possible, but data loss is highly probable. DBCC CHECKDB() has two options to resolve inconsistencies. The first is shown in the following script:

```
DBCC CHECKDB(<database_name>, REPAIR_REBUILD)
```

This option tries to repair inconsistent data pages, but if they are seriously broken, SQL Server cannot repair the lost data.

The second option is to call a more aggressive variant:

```
DBCC CHECKDB(<database_name>, REPAIR_ALLOW_DATA_LOSS)
```

When using this option, corrupted data pages are removed from the database forever. Hence, the robust backup strategy is strongly preferred.

The Shrink Database task

This task serves to return free space in data files back to the filesystem. Internally, this task is executed as the DBCC SHRINKDATABASE() function. In production, this task is almost useless because when the database has some free space, it is better for performance and fewer growth operations occur.

> **Note**
>
> The only situation to use the **Shrink Database** task is when some bigger data is loaded once to some staging tables to the database, then the data is processed to final structures, and staging tables are dropped. Maybe then the shrink would be executed. However, we can say that daily shrinking is useless and is a disk-intensive operation that should be used rarely.

The Reorganize Index task

Data stored in the database tables changes when inserting new records or updating or deleting existing ones. It leads to a situation where data pages are not full and also not in a logical order within extents. We can talk about internal (data pages not full) and external (data pages in extents not in logical order) fragmentation. This state of data leads to decreased performance over time.

An IO controller has its throughput. In a given amount of time, some finite number of data pages can be transferred through the controller. In an optimized case, every data page will be almost full of records, but when internally fragmented, the same amount of data pages will bring much fewer records.

In an ideal situation, index pages containing table or index data are ordered as a double-linked list. When SQL Server scans those data pages, it can be brought into a logical order and adjusted according to the physical order on disk. When external fragmentation occurs, SQL Server is forced to skip back and forth between data pages to follow pointers from one data page to another, because the logical order differs from the physical order of data pages.

As the examples described so far show, it is very important, for performance reasons, to maintain indexes as well as heaps in a somewhat defragmented state.

The index reorganization compacts just leaf-level of indexes. It is not a long-running process and issues fewer locks; that's why it's more suitable for day-to-day maintenance. The reorganize index task calls the following statement for every chosen index or table:

```
ALTER INDEX index_name ON table_name WITH REORGANIZE
```

The Rebuild Index task

As described in the previous section, fragmentation causes more data handling and it can lead to the degradation of performance. When fragmentation occurs heavily (typically for more indexed tables with big data contention), we need to rebuild entire indexes on such tables. When comparing REBUILD with REORGANIZE, we have to consider that more effort is needed for an index rebuild. If the SQL Server instance is not an Enterprise edition, exclusive table locks are issued when rebuilding an index.

The statement executed internally by the rebuild index task is as follows:

```
ALTER INDEX index_name ON table_name WITH REBUILD
```

Rebuilding is also possible for heaps. The statement then looks like this:

```
ALTER TABLE some_table_without_clustered_index WITH REBUILD
```

The Update Statistics task

For every index and for some columns, statistics are created automatically or manually. Statistics provide a very important description of data density and distribution for SQL Server's **cardinality estimation** when optimizing and compiling queries. A statistic, when it is created within an index creation, contains a histogram of values from the leading column in the created index only. SQL Server can create additional column statistics automatically during query time. Additional statistics contain histograms of the second, third, and up to fourth columns in the same index. Every statistic's histogram contains up to 200 buckets. Statistics, unlike indexes, are not refreshed with every query-modified data. That is why statistics get out of date, even if SQL Server has an auto-update statistics feature.

Maintaining up-to-date statistics is the DBA's responsibility. The simplest way to achieve it is to use the **Update Statistics** task in the **Maintenance Plans**. This task calls two different statements depending on its setting. When update all statistics is set, the system sp_updatestats stored procedure is executed. If statistics (or objects) are selected during task configuration, the following statement is called for every selected object:

```
UPDATE STATISTICS statistics_name
```

> **Note**
> When rebuilding an index, SQL Server drops and recreates the index entirely. Also, statistics are recreated, and updating them makes no sense in this case.

The Clean Up History task

This is quite a straightforward task. It just deletes records from historical tables in the msdb database. The previous histories, such as backup and restore history, maintenance plan history, and so on, are cleaned.

Execute SQL Server Agent job

This is an empty task prepared to execute manually prepared jobs that cannot be known by SQL Server as a regular administrative task. For example, some ETL processes or the refreshing of some test database from a production database backup can be used here.

Backup tasks

Backup tasks in **Maintenance Plans** cover **Full**, **Differential**, and **Transaction Log** backup types. All these tasks are described in detail in *Chapter 3, Implementing Backup and Recovery*. Let's remember that various scenarios combining different types of backup operations can be established. These backup tasks in **Maintenance Plans** are a typical example of the need for several subplans in one plan.

The Maintenance Cleanup Task

This task clears all files created during the execution of a maintenance plan.

All right, now we know which tasks we have to execute regularly; but what about their combination?

As an example, for an OLTP database, we can create combinations given in the following table:

Subplan	Frequency	Task
subplan_1	Weekly, off hours (for example, Sunday)	Check database integrity Back up database (full) Clean up history
subplan_2	Weekly, off hours (for example, Wednesday)	Reorganize index Update statistics
subplan_3	Hourly	Back up database (log)

Figure 8.17 – OLTP database task combination

As mentioned at the start of this section, the wizard is a very good starting point for working with maintenance plans. When executed, a maintenance plan is saved and can be edited later by the designer. The manual work will be described in the next section.

The Maintenance Plan Design Surface

The **Maintenance Plan Wizard** hides one very interesting thing: a maintenance plan is actually a kind of **Integration Services** package. The creation of a new plan, as well as an edit feature for existing plans, is available.

The main surface is depicted in the following screenshot, and we will go over almost every control to describe how to work with it:

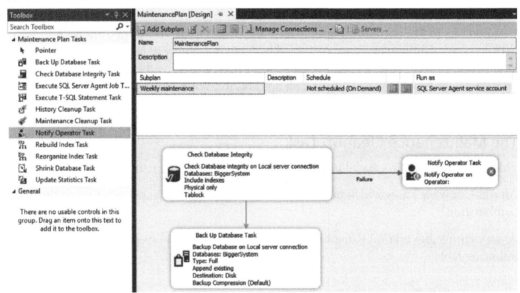

Figure 8.18 – The Maintenance Plan Design Surface

As seen in the preceding screenshot, we can divide the design surface into three main components:

- **Toolbox**: The left dockable window with tasks, which can be moved into the design surface

- **Designer header**: The upper part of the designer, for subplans and their schedule definition

- **Surface**: The graphical part containing icons of certain tasks joined by arrows

Every maintenance plan has at least one subplan. Every subplan contains a set of tasks that can be executed sequentially or in parallel.

An administrator's first task in the design surface is to create proper subplans and define their schedules. A new subplan is created by clicking on the **Add subplan** button. A new subplan is added to the list of subplans. The sorting of the subplans in the list does not matter because every subplan has its own schedule. A subplan can be empty, but that is not so useful. So, we need to add some tasks.

The administrator's second task is to define the subplan's content. It is necessary to select the subplan that we want to edit in the list of subplans. Certain tasks are then painted onto the surface from the toolbox. If the toolbox is not visible, we can call the **Toolbox** option from the **View** menu in Management Studio (*Ctrl + Alt + X* also exists, but do we remember that?). When the task is dropped onto the surface, it needs some configuration according to its purpose. If the task is not properly configured, a big red sign (an X mark) is visible on it (in the preceding screenshot, we can see it in the notify operator task). Task properties are available by double-clicking on a task.

Tasks need to be executed in some logical order. The logical order of tasks is controlled with arrows pointing from the preceding task to its successor. That is why we can see a green arrow hanging from every task. The arrow is called a **precedence constraint**. We have to connect tasks using the arrows by clicking an arrow and pulling it to the next task. The colors of the arrows matters. A **green arrow** says that the next task will be executed only when the preceding task ends successfully. **Red** means that the consequent task will be executed when its predecessor fails, and **black** means that the next task will be executed no matter how its predecessor finishes. To change the precedence constraint's behavior, we have to right-click a certain arrow and, in the pop-up menu, select the **Success**, **Failure**, or **Completion** option.

The last task is to create the subplan's schedules. It can be reached by clicking on the **Calendar** button in the **Schedule** column of the subplan list. A very intuitive dialog appears, and we can select the most appropriate time interval to execute the subplan.

When using **Maintenance Plans**, a big advantage is that all the basic regular maintenance operations are encapsulated in one big and very well-arranged object. We don't need to explore hundreds of jobs and schedules created one by one. Let's consider that a maintenance plan is just a base, not an advanced technique for full database administration. To refine our maintenance needs, we need to handle smaller objects, such as operators, jobs, and alerts. In the next chapter, we will describe features covered under these three object types.

Creating SQL Server Agent objects

In the previous sections, we described how to configure an environment for automation. Maintenance plans were also discussed in detail in the previous section. However, what is working behind the scenes? How do we automate some specific tasks? In this section, we will take a look at three types of objects that actually participate in automation:

- **Operators**
- **Jobs**
- **Alerts**

Operators

One of the first tasks when setting up an automation environment is the enabling of **Database Mail** and mail profile creation. Although mail profiles can be used for regular emailing, their main purpose is to use emails for administrators' notifications about job results or when some alert is raised. **SQL Server Agent** does not notify directly to an email address; it uses a special object called an **operator**. The operator is a named address defining where to send notifications mainly about job results.

The address of the operator may be as follows:

- **Email address**: A person, some people, or a distribution group can be set as an email.

- **Pager email**: Pagers were signed as deprecated on SQL Server 2014, but when needed, they are still possible to use. This chapter will not pay attention to pagers.

Many administrators ask for SMS notifications, but SQL Server does not support cellular phone text messages. If a mobile provider supports some SMS gateway for its customers, the user is usually informed by SMS when a new email comes. This mobile operator's email can be a way to get notified by SMS, because SQL Server just needs any valid email address, no matter what email provider and domain is used. Just add the email address bound to some mobile phone number to the operator's definition and enable SMS notification in your phone provider's email profile.

Operator definition

Defining a new operator or editing an existing one is quite simple. Management Studio keeps all definitions operators in **Object Explorer** in a folder called **Operators** under the **SQL Server Agent** node. By right-clicking on this folder, a pop-up menu appears, and the first option is **New operator....** A dialog will open as seen in the following screenshot:

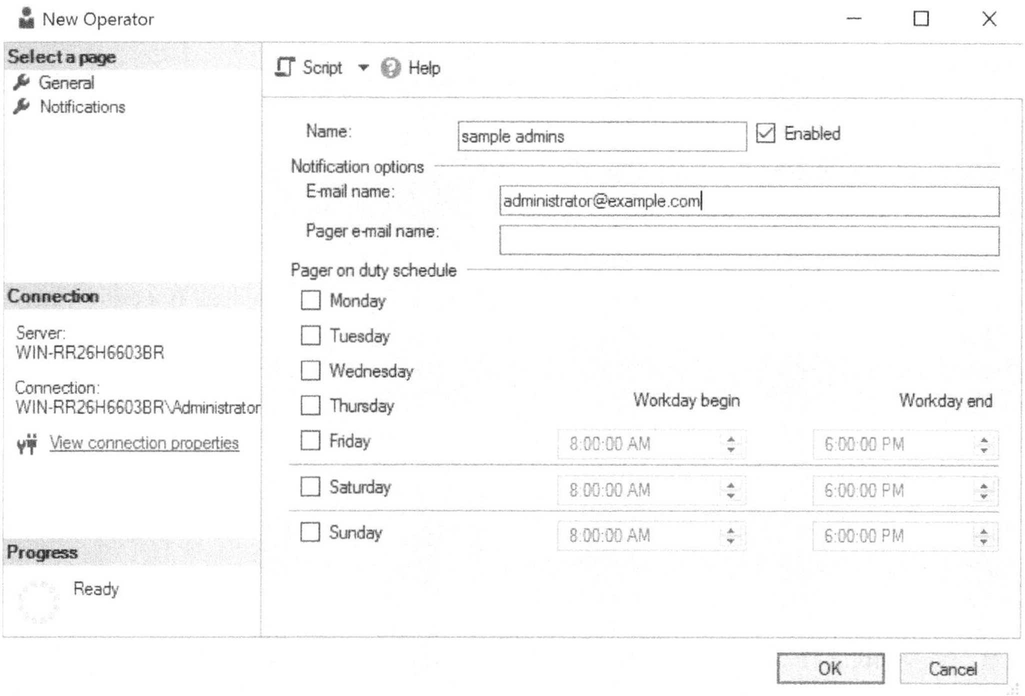

Figure 8.19 – New Operator

An operator's definition consists of three fields:

- **Name**: Any descriptive name (for example, *sample admins*).

- **Email name**: Any valid email address or address list. When more email addresses are used, they are separated by a semicolon (;) as in a regular email client.

- **Enabled**: This checkbox is turned on by default but if needed, the operator could disable it without erasing it completely.

The second tab, not seen in the screenshot, is called **Notifications**. It is a read-only list of jobs and alerts about which the operator is notified. The list is maintained automatically when the operator is assigned to some job or alert.

Jobs

A job is an executive object maintained by **SQL Server Agent**. A job itself is a definition covering one or more **job steps** and usually one or more schedules. The operator can be notified about the whole job result optionally. Let's go through parts of a job's definition in detail.

Job definition

Starting to create a new job is very similar to creating a new operator. In **Object Explorer** under the **SQL Server Agent** node is a folder called **Jobs**. A pop-up menu appears when you right-click on it, and four interesting options are presented to us:

- **New Job…**: This option will open a window to create a new job.

- **Manage Schedules**: Schedules can be defined within a job definition, but they can also be managed separately as shared schedules. If some shared schedules are created from this option, they are just assigned to job definitions.

- **Manage Job Categories**: Jobs can be categorized for better orientation (but job categories are not seen anywhere in Management Studio). If used, the category must be defined before it is used in the job definition.

- **View History**: This option opens the **Job History** window to monitor and troubleshoot jobs.

The **Job History** window will be described later in this chapter. Schedules and job categories are obvious and straightforward, so let's skip directly to a new job definition. The window used to create a new job is depicted here:

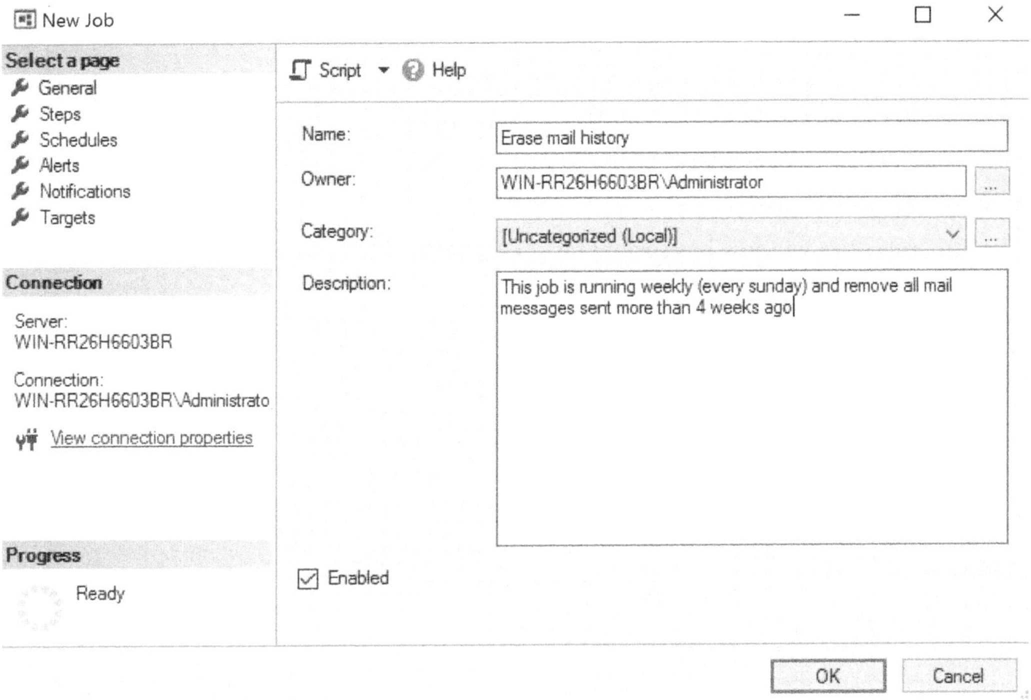

Figure 8.20 – New job

The job definition itself is quite simple. A job has to have a name (for example, `Erase mail history`), it may be categorized, it has an optional description (the description was usually omitted in previous examples but experience says that in this case, a description is highly welcome), and it can be enabled or disabled. The only tricky field in the dialog is **Owner**. The **Owner** value determines the user context of the job when it is running. There is an internal rule setting to the context:

- When the owner is a member of the **sysadmin** server role, the job is executed in the user context of the **SQL Server Agent** service.

- When the owner is not a member of the **sysadmin** server role, the job is executed within the actual user context.

Even if many jobs are used for administrative purposes, we can also see jobs created by other technologies, such as **SQL Server Reporting Services**. Sometimes, some need for application jobs (for example, data load called by end users directly from business applications) will also appear. Then, it's a good practice to think about the actual user context of the job.

A job needs to have at least one step defined because, without it, it is something doing nothing. In the next section, we will define some steps.

Job steps definition

The job properties window has several tabs. Let's reveal the first one:

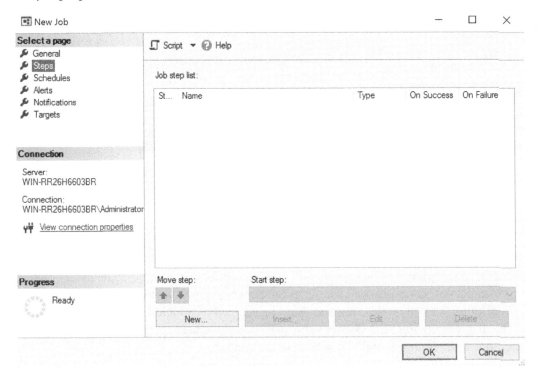

Figure 8.21 – Steps tab

Defining a new job step starts with clicking the **New...** button. A new dialog appears, and the job step definition is done in the new dialog. This original one then shows a list of steps created within the job. Job steps can be edited, deleted, and sorted by clicking other buttons in this tab.

The job step definition window is seen in the following screenshot:

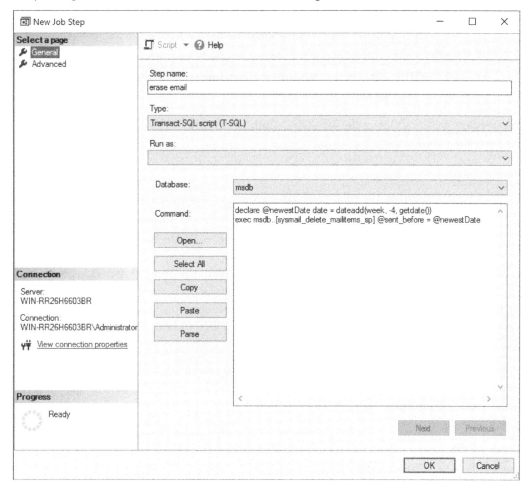

Figure 8.22 – Job step definition window

Every job step must have a unique name within the job definition. The second value to be set is **Type**. It is a dropdown containing these values:

- **Operating system**: Used for command-line calls (such as bcp.exe or any third-party command line)

- **PowerShell**: Used for PowerShell scripts, if needed. PowerShell 5.0 or higher is supported.

- **SQL Server Analysis Services command**: Used for **data cube maintenance** (for example, **XMLA** calls processing partitions in a cube).

- **SQL Server Analysis Services query**: Used for **Multidimensional Expressions (MDX)** queries.

- **SQL Server Integration Services package**: Used to schedule `SSIS` package execution.

- **Transact-SQL script**: Used in most cases to define tasks such as backing up the database or other tasks.

In our example, the script in the job step definition window is used to maintain the **Database Mail** retention period.

> **Note**
>
> As discussed in the *Creating and editing maintenance plans* section, subplans are `SSIS` packages. When subplans are created, take a look at the job steps; they are of the **SQL Server Integration Services** package type.

The **Run as** field may be used for all job step types except the T-SQL type. This property sets the execution context for certain steps more granularly. To set the context, **SQL Agent Proxy** must be defined before it can be used. SQL Agent Proxy is a pointer to some defined credential objects (credentials are described in *Chapter 4, Securing Your SQL Server*).

Depending on the job step type, the rest of the dialog changes. For our T-SQL type, the database context has to be set in the **Database** dropdown, and the SQL script has to be written to the **Command** field.

> **Note**
>
> If you are writing a command for the job step, write it in a proper tool such as **Management Studio**, and then copy and paste it into the **Command** field because the field does not completely test the accuracy of your script.

Alright, the job step has been created and we can continue creating additional steps when needed. When more steps are added, **SQL Server Agent** executes them one by one in the order that they were sorted while being created. By default, when some job fails, the whole job fails as well. We can add some very trivial logic to this behavior by resorting to the job steps or setting success and failure actions in the **Advanced** tab of the job step definition window.

When job steps are defined, we can start scheduling job execution. However, it's an optional part of the job definition.

Schedule definition

One job definition can contain anything from zero to many schedules. Creating a schedule is a very simple task. Let's take a look at the dialog to create a new schedule definition.

When the **Schedules** tab is selected in the job definition window, a list of schedules is shown, and we have two buttons:

- **New...**: This button is used to open the window for the new schedule defined within the job.

- **Pick...**: This button is used to open the window with shared schedules already defined.

When a new schedule is created, the following dialog window is opened (and it is the same everywhere when a schedule is created, for example, in **Maintenance Plans**):

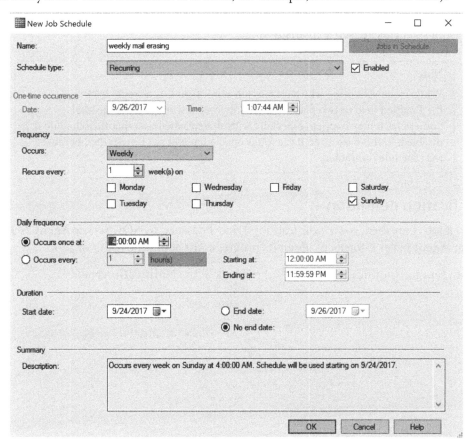

Figure 8.23 – New job schedule window

As usual, every schedule has its name and can be enabled or disabled in the **Schedule type** tab. The schedule type can be the following:

- **Recurring**
- **Start automatically when SQL Server Agent starts**
- **Start whenever the CPUs become idle**
- **One time**

In our example, the **Recurring** option is selected. Then, we can set **Frequency**. The schedule can be set to start as follows:

- **Weekly**
- **Daily**
- **Monthly**

The rest of the fields are self-explanatory.

> **Note**
> While troubleshooting why a certain job is not running, always check the **Enabled** field in two places--at the job level and at the schedule level. Sometimes it may happen, especially with shared schedules, that the schedule is disabled. In this case, even if the job is enabled, it will not be executed because the schedule is disabled.

Notification definition

When a job is finished, some notification(s) may be issued by **SQL Server Agent**. **SQL Server Agent** never informs us about its progress, just about the result of a job.

We can set more notification channels. Let's look at the **Notifications** tab:

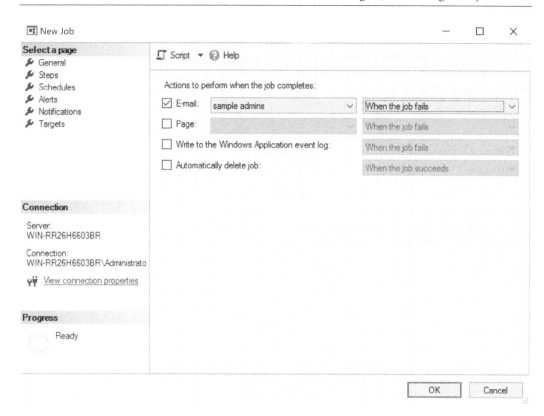

Figure 8.24 – The Notifications tab

An administrator can choose which channel of notification will be used
– **E-mail** or **Page** operators and Windows application log can be set. One extra option
is also possible – the **Automatically delete job** option – which is quite dangerous
because when a job is deleted, its history is also deleted, and diagnostics are not possible
in this case.

For every selected notification channel, one more decision has to be taken. It is the
condition when the notification is issued by **SQL Server Agent**'s alert system. It is selected
by the rightmost drop down beside each notification channel. Options are as follows:

- **When the job fails**
- **When the job succeeds**
- **When the job completes**

Now the job is defined completely and should start doing its task. In a real instance
of SQL Server, many jobs are created and executed, so a tool to monitor and troubleshoot
is needed. In the next section, we will describe how to diagnose job execution.

Monitoring and troubleshooting jobs

We need to check the correctness of our job's execution and troubleshoot it when things are going wrong. The first approach when jobs are failing is to be informed by email. However, we need to have an overview of all the jobs because it is hard to remember the schedule expiration of every single job.

A good entry point for automation monitoring is the window called **Job Activity Monitor**. This window is accessible from a shortcut placed directly under the **SQL Server Agent** node in Management Studio's **Object Explorer**. When used, a window with a list of all jobs is opened, as follows:

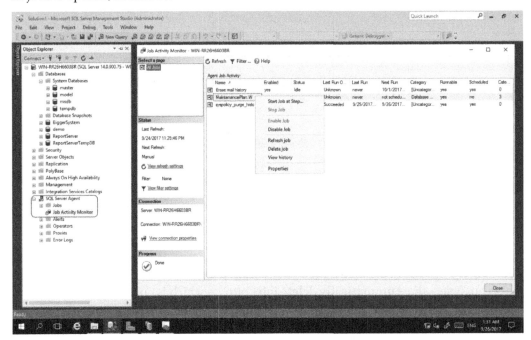

Figure 8.25 – Job Activity Monitor

The red rectangle in **Object Explorer** shows from where to open **Job Activity Monitor.** The biggest area is **Job Activity Monitor** itself. All jobs defined in a certain **SQL Server Agent** instance are seen as a list. Every record in the list provides the following information:

- **Name of the job**
- **Current status (running, idle)**
- **Last run date and time**

- **Next run date and time**

- **If the job is enabled and if it's scheduled**

- **Last run result (success, failed)**

Job Activity Monitor is not just a report. We can refresh its content manually or automatically. A manual refresh can be done by clicking the **Refresh** button in the toolbox; automatic refreshes must be set from the **View Refresh Settings** link in the left side of the window. Another feature is the ability to work with a certain job. When a DBA right-clicks on the record in **Job Activity Monitor**, a popup appears. It enables them to start the job, enable or disable it, refresh its status, and edit the job through the **Properties** option.

An important diagnostic option is **View History**. Although the history of jobs can be accessed from several places (from the **Jobs** folder in **Object Explorer** or from a certain job directly), it will always open in the same **Log File Viewer** window:

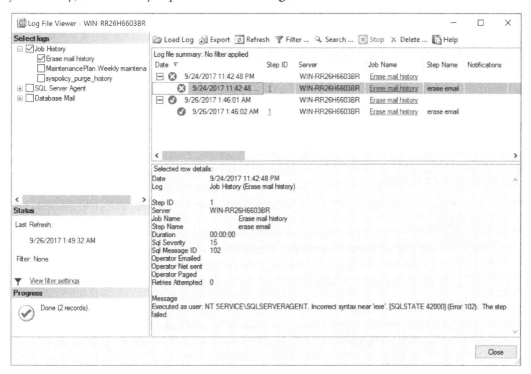

Figure 8.26 – Log File Viewer window

The **Log File Viewer** window shows every run of the job with its results. Every run consists of the overall result and when expanded (runs are collapsed by default), detailed job step results are shown. In the preceding screenshot, two executions were executed – the first was successful but the second failed (job executions are sorted by the time of execution in descending order).

To recognize the error, we need to expand the wanted record and click on the failed record for details. The actual error message is shown in the bottom part of the window. In our example, a syntactic error was raised when executing the job step, erasing the email history. Now, we have to go back to the step definition and correct the problem (it was a typo, in this case – the .exe keyword was used instead of exec).

Until this moment, we automated regular administrative tasks, usually in a timely fashion. We also need to react to situations that are not raised every night or every week. A helpful type of object maintained by SQL Server is **Alerts**. In our last section, we will explore what **Alerts** are for.

Alerts

Alerts is an object that is defined to react to a certain event. The event can be, for example, some error that is raised in SQL Server. When such a situation occurs, the alert itself just remembers the occurrence in the form of a counter (how many times the error was noticed) and the last time of the occurrence. The benefit of using **Alerts** lies in the ability to set some **response action**. A response action could be an operator notification, a job execution, or both.

We have three alert types:

- **SQL Server event alert**: This type of alert looks for SQL Server errors logged to the error log.

- **SQL Server performance condition alert**: These alerts can check the value change of a certain performance condition counter provided by SQL Server (performance counters installed with the operating system are not included in the selection of counters).

- **WMI event alert**: This type of alert is defined by a **Windows Management Instrumentation** (**WMI**) query and alerts of this type are raised by non-empty results for a query.

When we want to create an alert, we start by right-clicking on the **Alerts** folder under the **SQL Server Agent** node in **Object Explorer**. The alert definition window is depicted in the following screenshot:

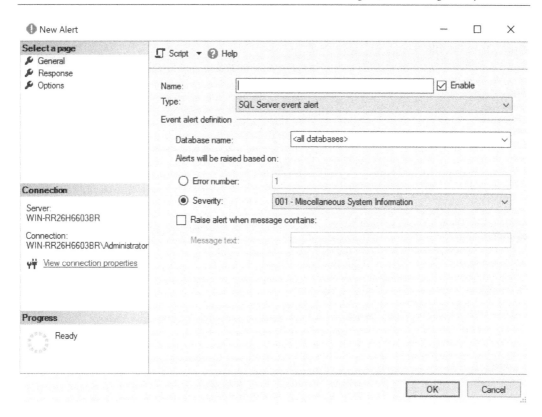

Figure 8.27 – The alert definition window

Every alert must have a name and can be enabled or disabled. The critical setting is the **Type** option. It determines the type of the alert. In the preceding screenshot, the **SQL Server event** alert type is selected. It means that the correct error number must be written in the **Error number** field or the severity level of the error has to be selected.

SQL Server has more than 13,000 error messages (for a complete set of them, the `sys.messages` view is present on SQL Server). These messages are divided into categories by their gravity, called severity levels. SQL Server has severity levels from 0 to 25. The bigger the number, the more serious the error. Errors contained in severity level 17 and higher are automatically logged into the SQL Server error log. These errors can be monitored by alerts. Sometimes, it is a better approach to monitor the whole severity level than a single error number because of the huge amount of errors in severity levels.

When defining an alert responding to an error message, we work using the reactive approach to SQL Server monitoring. Sometimes, it is quite easy to be reactive, preventing errors before they occur. For such situations, it is very useful to create SQL Server performance condition alerts.

The following screenshot shows an example of how to monitor the usage of the transaction log file:

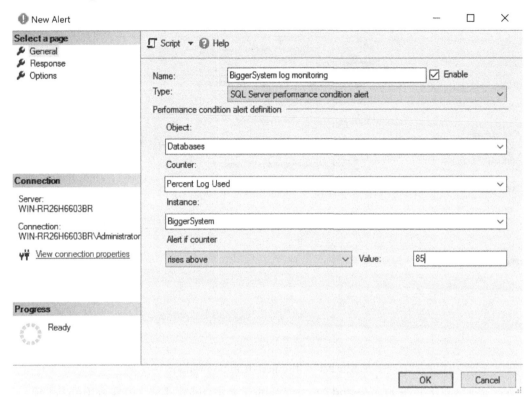

Figure 8.28 – Monitoring transaction log file usage

When the **Type** dropdown is switched to the **SQL Server performance condition alert** option, the screen changes its look. Now we need to find the correct **Object** (**Databases**, in our example), **Counter** (**Percent log used**: this counter measures the ratio of log space used/log file space allocated), and the **Instance** of the counter if needed (and it's needed in our example because _**Total** says nothing about actual log usage). Now, we must set **Alert if counter** according to the value requirement. The counter can be set to **rises above**, **be equal**, or **fall below** some value.

The value is written in the **Value** field. In our example, in the preceding screenshot, when 85% of the transaction log file of the **BiggerSystem** database (created in *Chapter 3, Implementing Backup and Recovery*) is used up, the alert is executed. It is not proactive yet; we have to set up some response action.

The **Response** tab of the alert creation window is the place where responses to alerts are set. As seen in the following screenshot, we can switch on the job execution (and also select a job from the list of already existing ones, or create a new one) and switch on the ability to notify some operator:

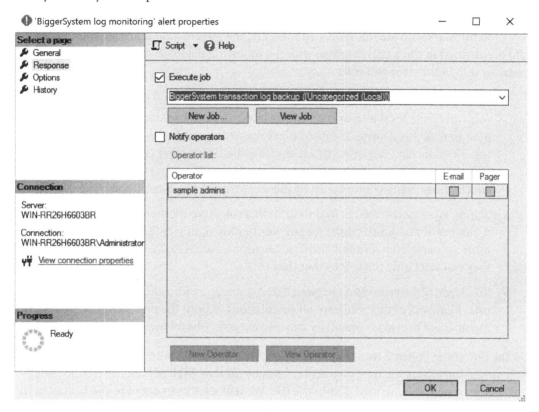

Figure 8.29 – The Response tab

From this moment, every time the transaction log of our BiggerSystem database becomes full, a transaction log backup is executed along with the regular scheduled execution.

SQL Server Agent security

As was discussed at the beginning of this chapter, **SQL Server Agent** is a service that logs itself into the host operating system. However, we should also take into consideration two more things about security – who is allowed to create jobs and what the user context of the executed job steps is. The following paragraphs explain how to properly secure **SQL Server Agent**.

SQL Server Agent security roles

SQL Server Agent is almost useless without jobs. As jobs execute a bunch of repetitive administrative tasks, such as backups, database consistency checks, and more, we should carefully control who is allowed to define jobs. Most jobs created in real-life scenarios are created by members of the sysadmin group, but sometimes the DBA is asked to allow job creation for users who are not DBAs. In this case, the job creation and execution rights are pre-defined in the msdb database with the following database roles, sorted from the weakest role to the strongest role:

- SQLAgentUserRole: This role is the least privileged role. Members of this role can create local jobs and schedules and will be the owners of created objects. Members of SQLAgentUserRole never can change the ownership of jobs. This is very important, because SQLAgentUserRole members cannot take the jobs of other owners. The second most important consideration is that job ownership affects the security context used by job steps during their execution.

- SQLAgentReaderRole: Members of this role have the same permissions as members of SQLAgentUserRole, but they also can view a list of jobs created by other owners. Even if members of SQLAgentReaderRole can view a list of jobs, they can start only those jobs that they own.

- SQLAgentOperatorRole: Now, SQLAgentOperatorRole is the strongest role. Members of this role have all permissions of both the previous roles, but unlike members of previous roles, they can also execute jobs owned by other users.

In the preceding bulleted list, I have briefly explained who is authorized to define jobs. The job ownership affects the user context that will be used by **SQL Server Agent** during the execution of each step defined within the job. We will see this in detail in the next section.

Job step security context

Each job step has a type assigned to it. The type could be a **T-SQL** job step or another job step type such as the exec command or PowerShell. The job step type in conjunction with job ownership determines the effectiveness of the user context used for the job step execution. The rules governing how **SQL Server Agent** sets the execution context differ for T-SQL job step types and all other job step types.

When the job owner is a member of the sysadmin server role, T-SQL job steps are executed in the context of the **SQL Server Agent**'s service account. When the job has an owner who is not a member of the sysadmin role, the job step is executed in the context of the owner's user account.

Let me explain with a simple example. The user is asked to create a job with just one step. The step will execute a stored procedure, checking some business rules in the AdventureWorks database. The user who creates the job is not a member of the sysadmin server role. This leads to the following configuration being required for successful job execution:

- The user must be at least a member of SQLAgentUserRole in the msdb database. This is needed to allow the user to create a job.

- The user must also be added as a user of the AdventureWorks database. This is needed to allow the user access to the AdventureWorks database.

- The user must have execute permissions to the stored procedure (or its covering schema) in the AdventureWorks database.

But what if the user, who is not a sysadmin member, wants to execute something other than T-SQL, that is, PowerShell or exec commands, as a job step? For sysadmin members, **SQL Server Agent** applies a similar rule; a job step other than a T-SQL job step is executed in **SQL Server Agent**'s security context. For all other job owners, a SQL Server Agent proxy must be created first. Let's see what a SQL Server Agent proxy is.

Using SQL Server Agent proxies

A SQL Server Agent proxy can be thought of as a placeholder identity used as a security context for job steps other than T-SQL job steps. We need a proxy in situations when a job is owned by a user who is not a member of the sysadmin server role. Also, proxies are used when a **SQL Server Agent** service account does not have permissions to access system resources such as file shares.

The proxy itself links to another identity object called a **credential**, which is defined within the SQL Server instance. At first, this linking from one SQL Server object to another may be confusing to the user, but it has its justification.

SQL Server uses credentials for more purposes. Credentials are defined on SQL Server as Windows (or domain) users that can be used for impersonation by other logins. In other words, SQL Server acts as a source of named identities for **SQL Server Agent**. When we are working with proxies, we must start with the creation of a credential object in SQL Server. Now we will walk through the creation of a local Windows user, a credential object, and finally a job owned by a non-administrator's SQL login. Then, we will test the whole thing.

Preparing a Windows user with PowerShell

Let's begin by preparing a Windows user with PowerShell:

1. First, we will prepare a local Windows user without elevated permissions using simple PowerShell commands (remember to run PowerShell as an administrator). The password will be set to Pa$$w0rd:

```
$password = Read-Host -AsSecureString
New-LocalUser -Name "Bob"  -Password $password
Add-LocalGroupMember -Group "Users" -Member "Bob"
```

2. Then, we will skip to Management Studio and write the following statement, which creates new credentials:

```
create credential Bob
with identity = '<computer_name>\Bob'
, secret = 'Pa$$w0rd'
```

Now we are ready to create a SQL Server Agent proxy.

Creating a SQL Server Agent proxy

The easiest option to create a SQL Server Agent proxy is to use dialogs in Management Studio:

1. In **Object Explorer**, expand **SQL Server Agent**, right-click on the **Proxies** node, and select the **New Proxy...** option as shown here:

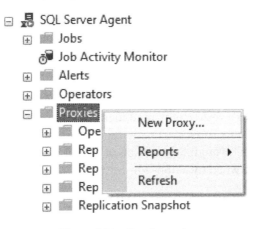

Figure 8.30 – Proxies node

2. In the opened dialog, fill in **Proxy name** (Bob), select **Credential name** (it will be Bob as that credential name was created previously), and select **Subsystem Operating system (CmdExec)**:

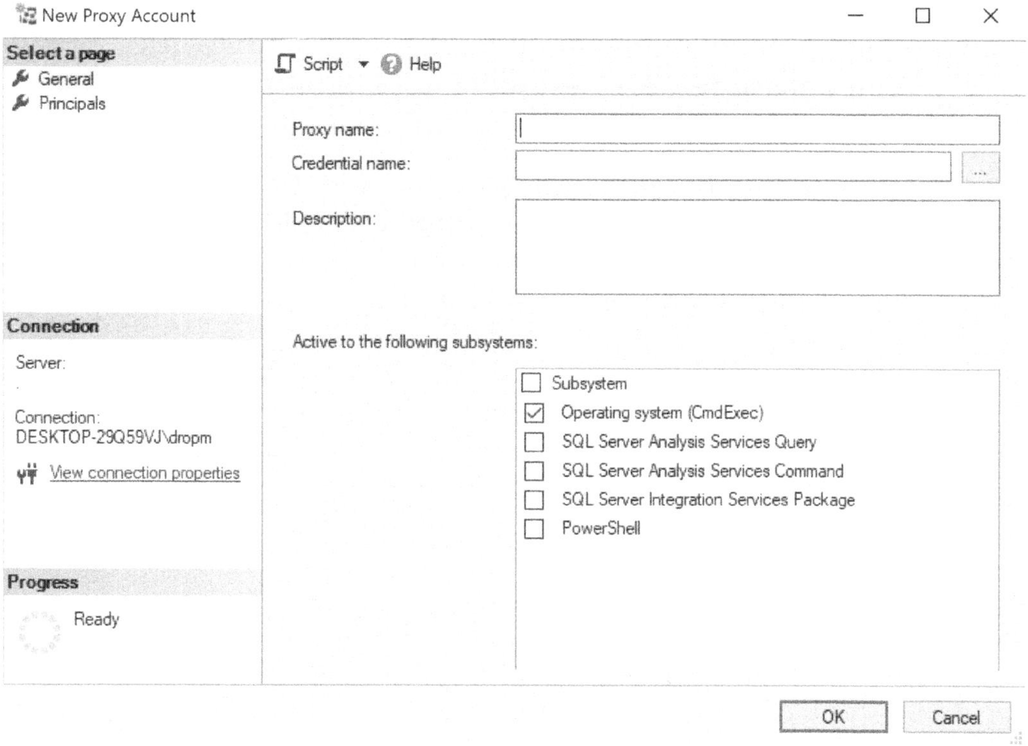

Figure 8.31 – New Proxy Account

3. Click **OK** and your proxy is ready to use.

Now, let's learn what **Subsystem** means. The proxy itself does not have permissions to an operating system and its subsystems. We must set proper permissions at the Windows user's level and we may also need to configure granulated permissions. This leads to more proxies being created for a particular task type. **Subsystem** helps to maintain granularity. In our example, the proxy with the name Bob will be allowed to execute operating system commands such as exe or bat files, but it will not be allowed to execute PowerShell commands. One proxy can be assigned to multiple subsystems.

Testing a SQL Server Agent proxy

When all the security objects are created, we can test the solution as follows:

1. First, let's create a non-administrative login who will be the owner of a newly created job. The following statement creates a login with the name Tom:

```
create login Tom with password = 'Pa$$w0rd', check_policy
= off
```

2. Now we will create a new job using the proper dialog in Management Studio. The following screenshot shows the filled **General** page of the dialog. Remember that the owner of the job was changed to **Tom**:

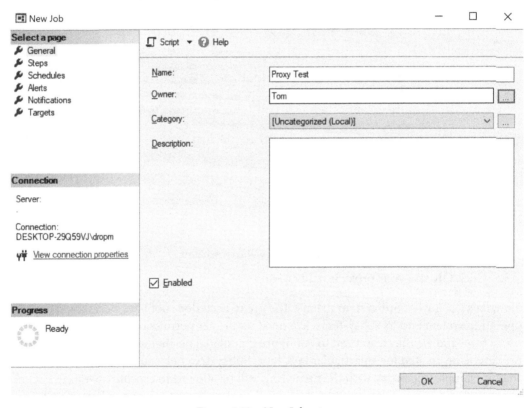

Figure 8.32 – New Job setup

3. Now we will create one job step as shown in the following screenshot. Remember that the **Run as** field points to **SQL Server Agent Service Account**, but if you create the job step and the job itself (two clicks on the **OK** button), no error or even warning will be shown to you:

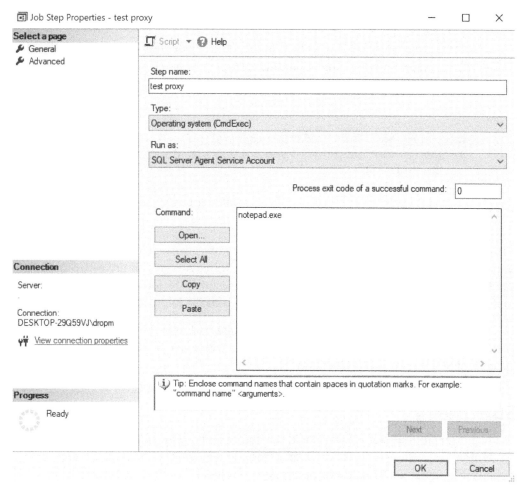

Figure 8.33 – Creating new job step

4. Now, let's find the newly created **Proxy test** job in **Object Explorer** and let's execute it. The job will fail and the message in the job history will be displayed as follows:

```
Non-SysAdmins have been denied permission to run CmdExec
job steps without a proxy account.  The step failed.
```

5. Because the job owner is not a member of the `sysadmin` server role, the job owner is not allowed to impersonate the **SQL Server Agent** service identity, as this is expected behavior. Now we will allow the `Tom` login to use the proxy called `Bob`:

```
exec sp_grant_login_to_proxy @login_name = 'Tom', @proxy_
name = 'Bob'
```

6. Now we can change the **Run as** field in the job step's definition to the name of the proxy. If you followed the names in this example, the name of the proxy is **Bob**.

7. Let's execute the job again. The result in the job history is very similar to the following:

```
Executed as user: DESKTOP-234uhVJ\Bob. The step did not
generate any output.  Process Exit Code 0.  The step
succeeded.
```

8. We can also explore the filesystem of our computer to see that a new folder called `mydir` is created on drive `C`.

The preceding walk-through showed all the security objects needed to create a **SQL Server Agent** proxy. Then, we created a simple job with a non-sysadmin owner and a `CmdExec` job step. When the context of the user executing the job step was improperly configured, the job failed. Then, we used our proxy and the job succeeded.

The security of **SQL Server Agent** is a very important part of SQL Server administration. Without good knowledge, we will run into troubles with failed jobs, or we will make our instance of SQL Server very vulnerable.

Summary

To imagine an administrator's world without automation is almost impossible. SQL Server provides a very comprehensive set of tools and techniques to use to achieve comfortable regular administration and reduce administration to non-regular monitoring or troubleshooting actions.

In the first part of this chapter, we went through **Database Mail** and **SQL Server Agent** setup. The main point here is to have **Database Mail** configured and **SQL Server Agent** running all the time when SQL Server runs.

In the second part, we looked at **Maintenance Plans**, a useful tool to create a basis for automatic SQL Server administration. We realized that **Maintenance Plans** are divisible into smaller subplans, which can be executed on their own schedules.

The third part of the chapter was dedicated to showing, by example, all the traditional objects maintained by **SQL Server Agent** – jobs, alerts, and operators.

The last part explained the security model of a job execution security context. We explained objects such as credentials and **SQL Server Agent** proxies, which ensure proper security settings for each job step.

We can say that most administrative tasks and responsibilities end up as planned jobs on **SQL Server Agent**.

Using **SQL Server Agent** makes a DBA's life easier as it allows the scheduling of regular tasks. But the prevention possibilities of **SQL Server Agent** against serious outages are limited. The next chapter will provide knowledge about the high-availability features of SQL Server to make a DBA's life even easier.

9
Configuring Always On High Availability Features

SQL Server high availability includes two main components called **Always On Failover Cluster Instances** and **Always On Availability Groups**. In this chapter, we will look at these two in depth and explore possible configurations for the SQL Server environment. Both features use **Windows Server Failover Cluster** (**WSFC**) functionality but have different methods of deployment.

WSFC is a server feature available on Windows Server, which allows the grouping of computers into a fault-tolerant cluster. In a case where one or more nodes fail, others will keep the service or application available.

Each Windows Server version brings new features to the WSFC feature and many of those can be beneficial for SQL Server deployment. Windows Server 2012 and 2012 R2 have brought many new enhancements and new features to WSFC, with a strong emphasis on the **Hyper-V** role used for virtualization. The main new features and improvements for these two versions of Windows Server in regard to WSFC include the following:

- Shared **Virtual Hard Disks (VHDs)**
- **Virtual Machine (VM)** drain on shutdown
- **VM Network Health Detection**
- **Cluster Shared Volume (CSV)** improvements
- **Active Directory (AD)**-detached clusters
- **Dynamic witness**
- The cluster dashboard
- Support for **Scale-Out File Server (SoFS)**
- **Cluster-Aware Updating**
- Integration of the **Task Scheduler**

Windows Server 2016 brings even more new functionalities to the **Failover Clustering** feature, enabling better management, scalability, and performance for the solution. Again, there are many features used by the **Hyper-V** role that are used for virtualization, including the following:

- **VM load balancing**
- **VM start order**
- **Cluster OS system rolling upgrade**

Other important features of Windows Server 2016 used in WSFC include the following:

- **Cloud Witness**: A new type of quorum that uses **Microsoft Azure**. Like any other quorum, **Cloud Witness** has a vote and takes part in quorum calculations. **Cloud Witness** uses **Microsoft Azure Blob Storage**, which can be configured for multiple clusters as a very cost-effective solution.

With Windows Server 2019, there are even more new features for **Failover Clustering**, which include the following:

- **Cluster sets**: This is a feature that allows you to increase the node count in a data center.

- **Azure-aware clusters**: WSFC is able to detect whether the systems are running in Azure as **IaaS VMs** and simplify the configuration by removing the need to add **Azure Load Balancer** to the deployment.

- **Cross-domain cluster migration**: You can now migrate WSFC between domains for easier consolidation.

- **USB witness**: Instead of a node or disk witness, you can use just a simple USB stick, ideally attached to a network switch.

- **Cluster hardening**: Communication between cluster nodes over SMB uses certificates for authentication.

- **Kerberos and certificate-based authentication**: Allows clusters running in infrastructures that have disabled the **NTLM authentication protocol** for enhanced security.

In this chapter, we will cover the following topics:

- Installing Windows Server Failover Cluster
- Configuring Always On Failover Cluster instances
- Configuring Always On Availability Groups

Installing Windows Server Failover Cluster

Like any other server role feature, WSFC requires careful planning before you begin the installation. There are many things you need to consider, including the following:

- The number of host nodes
- Network configuration
- Storage configuration
- Application requirements

WSFC is a server feature that can be added via the **Server Manager** GUI or via the command line. This feature will allow you to add several sub-features such as a **PowerShell module**, remote server admin tools for **Failover Clustering**, and so on. To install the WSFC feature via **Server Manager**, navigate to the **Add Roles and Features Wizard** and select the **Failover Clustering** feature as shown here:

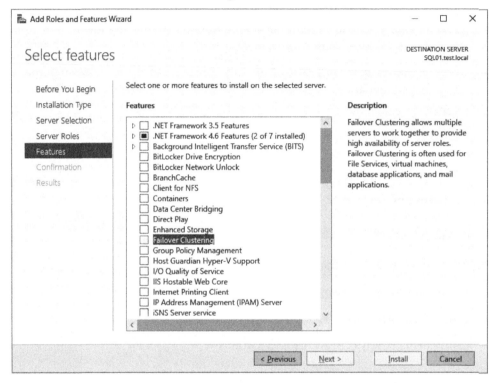

Fig. 9.1 – Installing the WSFC feature

Another option would be a PowerShell command line, where you can run the following code to install the **Failover Clustering** feature:

```
Install-WindowsFeature " Failover-Clustering","RSAT-Clustering"
-IncludeAllSubFeature
```

Once you finish the installation with PowerShell, you will see whether or not the installation was successful and whether a restart is required. In this installation, we have just added the **Failover Clustering** feature to the server and there's no cluster configured yet. That's very important to realize. You can deploy the feature with PowerShell using the following scripts:

Fig. 9.2 – Adding the WSFC feature via PowerShell

Both the **Server Manager** GUI and PowerShell can deploy this feature to multiple nodes at the same time. The maximum number of nodes that can form a cluster is 64, but usually, SQL Server clusters don't have that many nodes. There is also a big difference between SQL Server editions in regard to the cluster size supported. SQL Server Standard edition supports only two-node clusters, whereas Enterprise Edition supports the maximum number of nodes available in the OS.

Configuring Always On Failover Cluster Instances

When SQL Server is installed as a **Failover Cluster Instance** (**FCI**), it leverages the WSFC feature for high availability and disaster recovery. An FCI is made up of a set of physical servers that have a similar hardware configuration, operating system, patch level, SQL Server version, and components. They also share the instance name.

Once you have planned your Windows Server configuration, you can start the SQL Server installation process. In FCI installation, you have several choices, including installation via the setup GUI wizard, available in the installation media, installing with advanced options, or installing as an unattended setup via the command line. Here, we will use the GUI wizard to start the installation. To start the FCI installation, simply click on **New SQL Server failover cluster installation**, which will bring up the wizard to install the SQL Server cluster, as shown in the following screenshot:

Fig. 9.3 – SQL Server Installation Center

The setup program goes through an extensive validation process in terms of your environment and also examines the cluster and the validation of the cluster. You will need to select the features and instance name and configure the service accounts as with a regular installation. What you will need to configure differently will be cluster-specific information, such as the following:

- **SQL Server Network Name**
- **Cluster Resource Group**
- **Cluster Disk Selection**
- **Cluster Network Configuration**

The **SQL Server Network Name** is a **Virtual Network Name** (**VNN**) that is used as a connection point to your FCI. Connection to a VNN works regardless of the active node, and the IP address of the VNN always points to the active cluster node hosting the SQL Server services. The configuration can get a little complex if the cluster nodes are in different network subnets. If a failover occurs, the VNN is then updated with the virtual IP of the respective subnet for the active cluster node, as shown in the following screenshot:

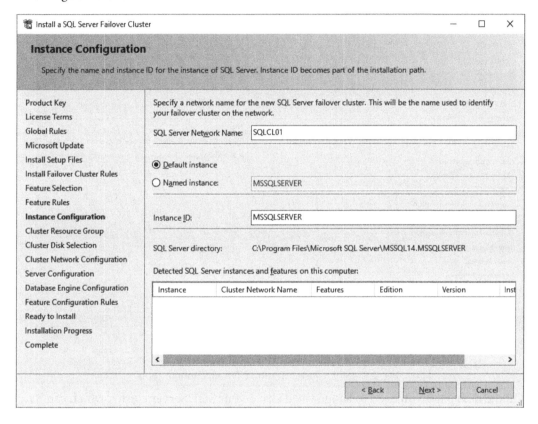

Fig. 9.4 – SQL Cluster Network Name configuration

The SQL Server **Cluster Resource Group** will be used to host SQL Server services that are installed on the failover cluster. You can either create the group in advance as an empty role in **Failover Cluster Manager** or the setup program will create a new one for you during the installation, as follows:

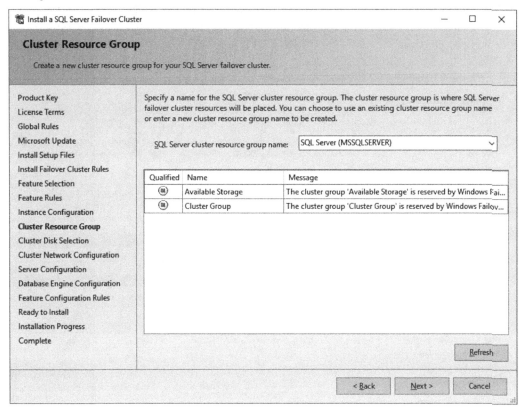

Fig. 9.5 – SQL Cluster Resource Group configuration

On the next page, you need to assign the disks to your SQL Server cluster, which can have a variety of configurations on Windows Server 2016 or 2019, such as the following:

- **Cluster volume**
- **Cluster shared volume**
- **Storage spaces direct**

The full disk configuration will usually be prepared by your Windows Server administrator based on your requirements. Based on the disks available, you will need to configure the critical folders for your SQL Server deployment, including the following:

- **Root files**
- **Data files**
- **Log files**
- **Backups**

As with standalone installation, you should follow the best practices for SQL Server storage, such as isolating the data and logging and backing up files. During the performance evaluation and requirement verification, you may end up creating more disks for the SQL Server deployment, such as **data drives**, **log drives**, **backup drives**, **tempDB drives**, and more. In such cases, you'll see more disks available for the cluster deployment:

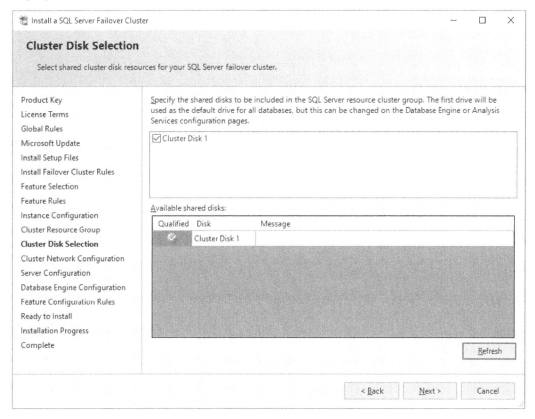

Fig. 9.6 – SQL Cluster Disk configuration

The **Cluster Network Configuration** page allows you to select the IP address for your SQL Server's virtual name. You can either choose to use **Dynamic Host Configuration Protocol (DHCP)** or assign a fixed IP address, as you can see in the following screenshot:

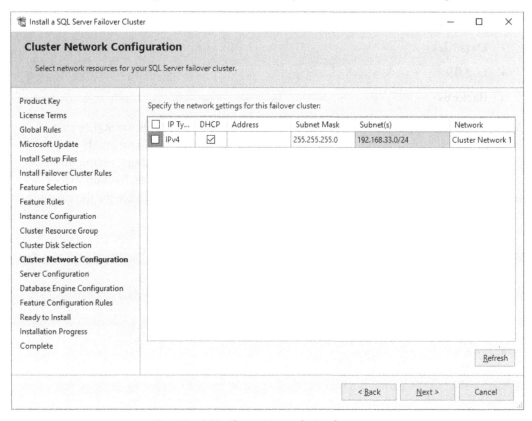

Fig. 9.7 – SQL Cluster Network Configuration

On the **Server Configuration** page, you will need to configure the SQL Server accounts. These accounts were discussed in *Chapter 4, Securing Your SQL Server*. Favorable choices for the cluster would be a domain account or a group managed service account. With SQL Server 2016 and 2019, you can also select the **Grant Perform Volume Maintenance Task privilege to SQL Server Database Engine Service** checkbox, which is important for the **Instant File Initialization** feature of SQL Server. This feature may have a performance impact on your SQL Server disk operations if not enabled. The screenshot for the **Server Configuration** page is as follows:

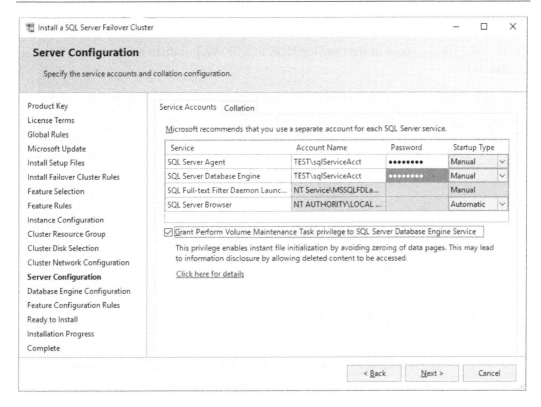

Fig. 9.8 – SQL Cluster Service Account configuration

On the **Database Engine Configuration** page, you will configure important server settings including the following:

- **Server Configuration**: Mixed mode or Windows mode

- **Data Directories**: Data files, log files, and backup folder

- **TempDB configuration**: Amount of files and their size

- **FILESTREAM** configuration

Once you get to the **Ready to Install** page of the setup program, you're set to start the installation. This installation will deploy the FCI to one of the cluster nodes.

Adding nodes to the SQL Server failover cluster

On the other node, you will start the installation with **Add node to a SQL Server failover cluster** as follows:

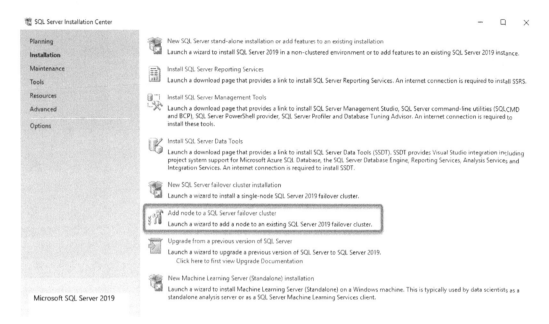

Fig. 9.9 – SQL Server Installation Center

The installation begins as in the regular SQL Server setup, but on the **Cluster Node Configuration** page, you can select the instance name and node to add to the failover cluster. On the next page, you will need to configure the networking settings and **Service Accounts** settings:

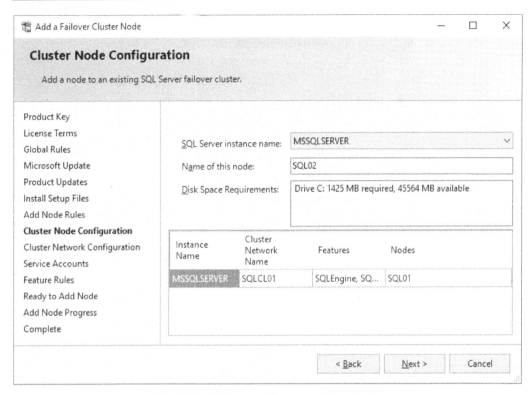

Fig. 9.10 – Adding a node to an existing cluster

Once you have prepared the installation, you can run the setup to add the node to the cluster that will install the SQL Server instance on this node. The SQL Server services will be configured to start manually on both nodes and their startup will be controlled by the **Failover Cluster Manager** tool.

Once the installation is finished, you can connect to your virtual SQL Server name, which you configured in the first cluster node installation, as shown in the following screenshot. You can then start working with your database server:

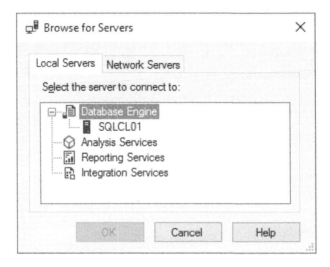

Fig. 9.11 – Connecting to SQL cluster

Now, the next step is to initiate a failover.

Initiating a failover

Once we have the SQL Server instance up and running with the failover cluster, it's protected by the WSFC feature and will automatically start on another cluster node upon failure. You can perform this failover manually via the **Failover Cluster Manager** tool.

You can use the WSFC console to move the role of your SQL Server to another node:

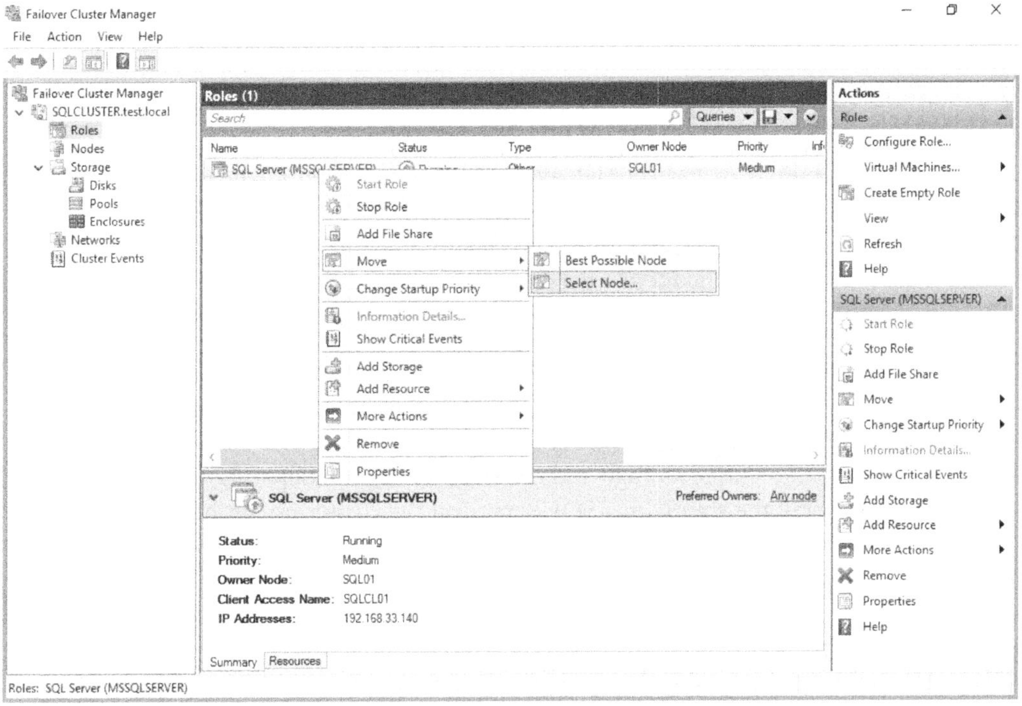

Fig. 9.12 – WSFC Console Failover initiation

Once you choose a node and where to move the role, the failover will reassign the resources from the currently active node to the other node. It will move disks, assign names, register IPs, and finally start the SQL Server services. In FCI, the services for a selected instance run only on one node and the other node or nodes are stopped. Only after a failover is moved to a newly selected active node are the services started on that node and stopped on all other nodes.

> **Note**
>
> This configuration is frequently referred to as an **active/passive cluster**, where one node is active (hosting the running services) and the other node is up, but all SQL Server services are stopped. Another configuration may be referred to as **active/active**, where both nodes are hosting SQL Server services that are started, but in this deployment, the two nodes are hosting two different instances. One instance is active on the first node, and the other instance is active on the other node, making both nodes the hosts and running SQL Server services.

Always On Failover Cluster Instances do require shared storage and are available with the Standard edition of SQL Server 2019. Let's now explore a different deployment option for Always On Availability Groups.

Always On Availability Groups

Always On Availability Groups is a high availability and disaster recovery feature that was introduced in SQL Server 2012. This feature, similar to Always On Failover Cluster Instance, requires WSFC to be configured on the nodes running on SQL Server. **Availability Groups** (**AGs**) work at a database level, where the FCI protects the whole instance.

We won't focus on WSFC anymore and will just use the common platform to deploy the SQL Server Always On Availability Groups in the following scenarios in the chapter. The WSFC configuration for **AGs** is simpler when compared to the FCI infrastructure since **AGs** don't require any shared storage and the storage solution depends on the node type. To utilize **AGs**, install the standalone SQL Server on the cluster nodes, but use the basic SQL Server installation, since the instances in AGs don't share the SQL Server VNN and IP, and are independent of each other.

Configuring Always On Availability Groups

Before we start configuring the **AGs**, we need to make sure all the prerequisites are met on the server, instance, and database levels. Databases for **AGs** need to do the following:

- Be user databases (no system DBs are allowed)
- Use a full recovery model
- Be read/write databases
- Be multi-user databases
- Have at least one full backup

There are several key terms that we need to define to be able to work with **AGs**. AGs itself is a set of user databases, which is considered a unit for high availability. These databases (or the **AGs**) fail over to other nodes of WSFC if there is an issue detected either at the server level or the database level. **Availability Replicas** is an instance of an AG hosted by an SQL Server instance. The replica maintains a copy of the databases that belong to the AG. The replica can be either a **Primary** replica or a **Secondary** replica. Different versions of SQL Server support a variety of secondary replicas.

Currently, up to eight secondary replicas can be created. The secondary replica can be a local SQL Server running in the same data center, a distant data center, or in Microsoft Azure (an Azure replica). The primary replica is the read-write instance of the availability database. The secondary replicas host a copy of the database, which may be configured for read-only access if required by the design.

To start the Always On Availability Groups configuration, you first have to verify that your SQL Server instances are properly configured to use WSFC for **Availability Groups**. To check the configuration, you can use the **SQL Server Configuration Manager** tool and check the properties of your SQL Server instance as shown in the screenshot:

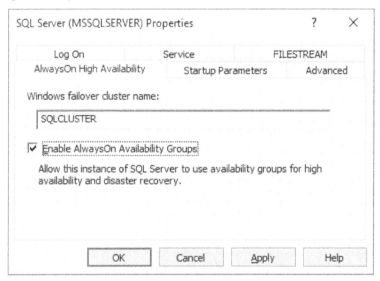

Fig. 9.13 – Configuration Manager Enable AlwaysOn Availability Group

Once you select the **Enable AlwaysOn Availability Groups** checkbox, you will need to restart your SQL Server service to see the effect of such a setting. The main expectation is to have a fully configured WSFC service. All nodes in such a cluster should run the same SQL Server version and edition and should use the same collation.

Creating an Availability Group

An AGs is a collection of databases you would like to host on the **Availability Replicas**. You cannot add any of the system databases to the AGs, so this works only for the user databases. The AGs can be created from **SQL Server Management Studio (SSMS)**, where you can also script out the whole configuration T-SQL script for future reference or larger deployments. In SSMS, navigate to **Always On High Availability** and start the wizard. Then, on the **Specify Options** page of the wizard, you have to enter the **Availability group name** as shown in the following screenshot. Remember that the group name can't be longer than 128 characters and should describe the group you are creating:

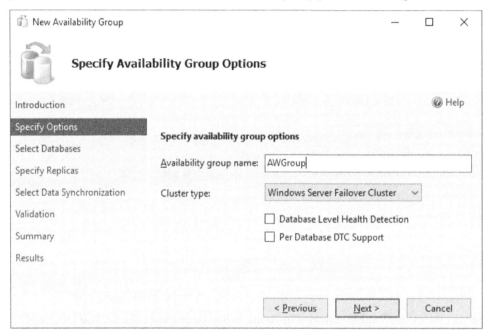

Fig. 9.14 – Creating an Availability Group

There are then three choices available for you when selecting a cluster type:

- **Windows Server Failover Cluster**: This type is used when SQL Server AGs are hosted on WSFC, a common solution for high availability and disaster recovery.

- **External**: This type is used when the **AGs** are managed by external cluster technology such as AGs on Linux with Pacemaker.

- **None**: This type is used when there's no cluster technology used for managing **AGs**.

Two more checkboxes are available for you to configure and we'll mostly focus on **Database Level Health Detection**. This option enables the failover of the availability group when the database status is no longer *online*. This health detection is applied to the whole availability group. So even if one database has issues, the whole group will fail over to another node in the cluster.

On the next page, **Select Databases**, you will select the databases you would like to add to the **AGs**. The wizard will perform several checks to verify whether the selected databases can be added to the group. If any of those checks fail, you'll see a warning describing what is required as shown in the following screenshot:

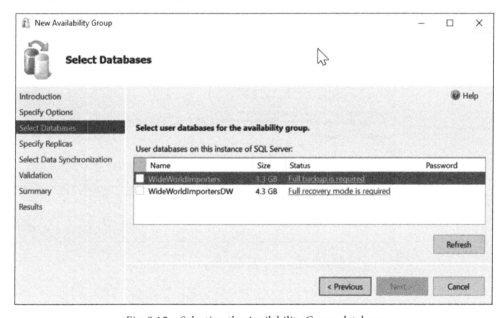

Fig. 9.15 – Selecting the Availability Group database

If your database or databases meet all the prerequisites, you can move on to the next page, called **Specify Replicas**. Here, you will configure all your nodes that are participating in hosting the availability group and configure additional features and options:

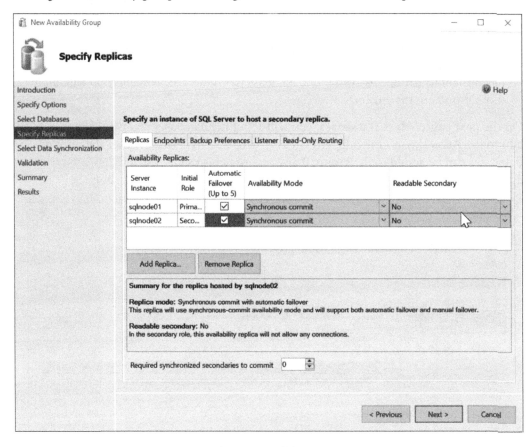

Fig. 9.16 – Configuring Availability Group replicas

You can see what server instances you have added to the configuration and their initial roles. You can configure one primary and up to eight secondary replicas for the database availability group. Next to **Initial Role**, you can see an important checkbox, which is used to select which instances take part in **Automatic Failover** configuration. Out of all the instances, you can select up to five that can be configured for **Automatic Failover**.

When you are choosing the **Availability Mode option**, you can choose between synchronous and asynchronous commit:

- **Synchronous Commit**: **Synchronous Commit** is a setting where the primary replica will wait to commit the transactions until they have been hardened on the secondary replicas. **Synchronous Commit** is required for the **Automatic Failover** option. Usually, **Synchronous Commit** will be the choice for servers or replicas that reside in the same data center and it is used as a high-availability option.

- **Asynchronous Commit**: **Asynchronous Commit** is generally used for servers in remote data centers for disaster recovery scenarios and for high-load systems, where the **Synchronous Commit** mode would be too slow. **Asynchronous Commit** does not have to wait and commits the transaction immediately.

The last column, **Readable Secondary**, is also very important. There are three options that you need to select from:

- **Yes**

- **No**

- **Read-intent only**

If **Yes** is selected, you can access the secondary replica for read-only and use the database for reporting purposes or any other read-only access. With the **Read-intent only** type of configuration, the replica is available only if the application specifies the **Application Intent property** with **ReadOnly** in the connection string.

In the next section, called **Endpoints**, you have to configure the **TCP** endpoints, which will be used for synchronization between replicas. The SQL Server Service accounts will be granted permission to connect to such endpoints. Notice that the **Port Number** is the same as the default **Mirroring** port **5022**. Using the **Encrypt Data** checkbox, you can also configure the encryption for the traffic between the nodes:

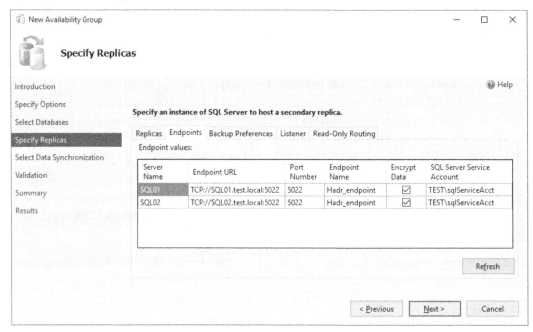

Fig. 9.17 – Availability Groups endpoint configuration

Once you have configured the endpoints, you can set up the **Backup Preferences** in the next section. Here, you can configure the preferences for the backup, and you have, again, several options to choose from:

- **Prefer Secondary**
- **Secondary only**
- **Primary**
- **Any Replica**

The following is a screenshot of specifying the replicas:

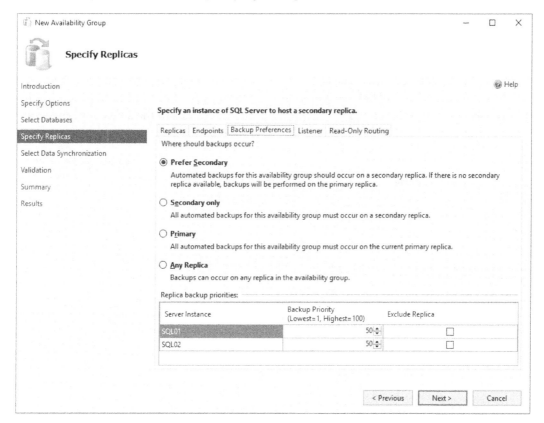

Fig. 9.18 – Availability Group backup configuration

When using **Prefer Secondary**, backups for the AG will occur on an available secondary replica. If there are more secondary replicas available, the replica for backup is chosen based on priority. Only if no secondary replica is available will the backup occur on the primary replica. Backups for large databases can consume a lot of system resources and having a backup on a secondary replica can offload this task from the primary node.

In the next section, you can configure a **Listener**. An Availability group **Listener** is an object that provides a set of resources to direct the client connection to the appropriate replica. This replica does not have to be the only primary one but can also be the secondary replica if the read intent is configured by the application connection string. This **Listener** works like a VNN, which we have already seen in FCI configuration. As such, the **Listener** can connect the client to the proper replica, without any need to know the server name. After any failover, you don't have to modify the connection properties in the application, since the **Listener** will point the client requests to the active replica:

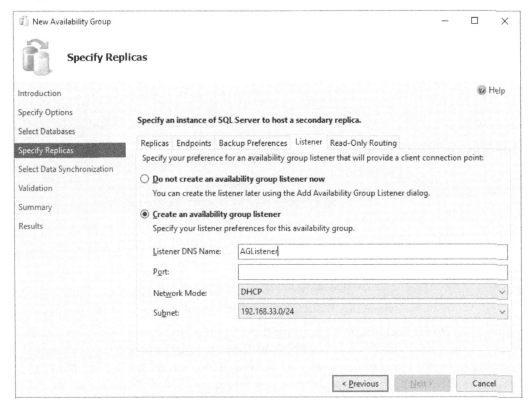

Fig. 9.19 – Availability Group listener configuration

To configure the **Listener**, you need to provide the DNS name, which has to be unique, and the network configuration consisting of the IP address and the port. The IP address can be configured as either **Static** or **DHCP** configured. The port number can be entered to configure the **Listener** to listen on a specific port, which then has to be configured in the application. If you want to use the default port 1433, ensure that there are no other services using the port, except the default SQL Server instance so it can be shared with the Availability Group **Listener**.

Once the **Listener** is configured, it will become a resource in the WSFC service, together with the VNN and IP address used for the connection to the listener:

Fig. 9.20 – Cluster resource view for Availability Groups

The last section can be used to configure **Read-Only Routing**. With this feature enabled, each replica will have a routing URL and list configured. Both the URL and list are configured on a per replica basis and each secondary replica has its own routing URL and routing list. The configuration can be performed either directly via the GUI or later on with the T-SQL script. **Read-Only Routing** works on a round-robin basis to distribute the read-only load among the secondary replicas.

Once you have configured all the replica options, you have to configure **Data Synchronization**. This configuration section has many options and you can choose from the following:

- **Automatic seeding**
- **Full database and log backup**
- **Join only**
- **Skip initial data synchronization**

The **Automatic seeding** option will create the database on all replicas and synchronize the databases between the primary and secondary replicas. There is, however, one strict requirement for **Automatic seeding**—database and log file paths have to be the same on all SQL Server instances that are configured as replicas in the **New Availability Group**:

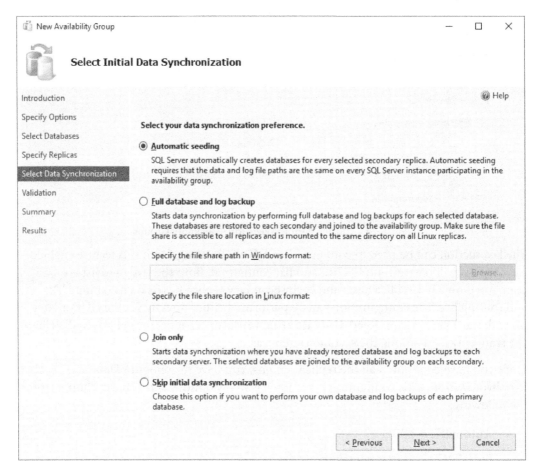

Fig. 9.21 – Availability Group data synchronization

Once you have entered all the options, you are ready to finish the configuration. The wizard will then create all required logins, endpoints, listeners, and databases on the replicas, initiate **Automatic seeding**, and join the nodes to the availability group. If the configuration is successful, you will have a working AG configured for your databases.

Failover and monitoring

During the configuration of each replica, there will be a new **Extended Session** event created and started to monitor the **AGs**. Information from these sessions is then used on the **Dashboard**, which you can open to view the basic information about your AGs, databases, and replicas:

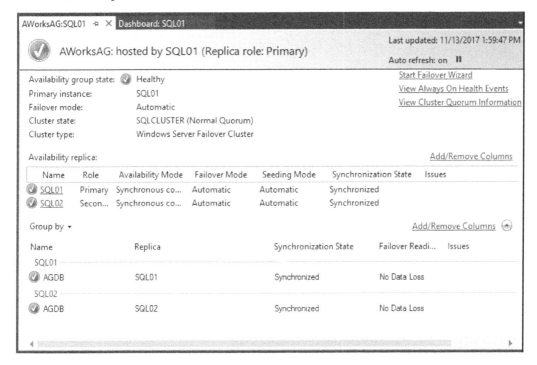

Fig. 9.22 – Health Dashboard for Availability Groups

You can check whether or not the databases are synchronized or if there are any issues detected. When displaying the health events, you can dig deeper into the state of the availability group.

To fail over between replicas, you should use the failover wizard available on the **Dashboard** or the menu item in SSMS. You can right-click the availability group in the **Always On High Availability / Availability Groups** section in **Object Explorer**:

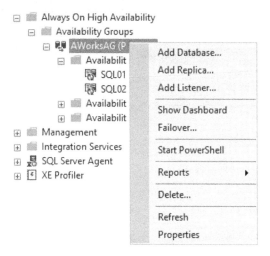

Fig. 9.23 – Failover initialization

Once you click **Failover...**, a new window will open where you can select a new primary replica based on the available replicas in your environment.

You can see which replicas are available and whether the databases are synchronized with those replicas:

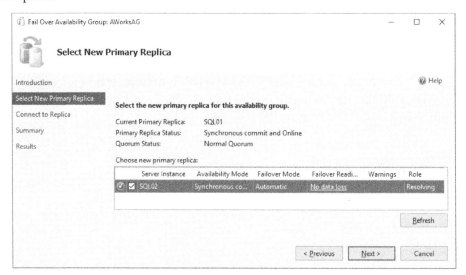

Fig. 9.24 – Choosing a replica for manual failover

When you select your new replica for failover, the wizard will initiate the failover and follow the required steps to swap the replica roles. In our scenario, we have only two roles, so the primary replica will become the secondary and the secondary will become the primary:

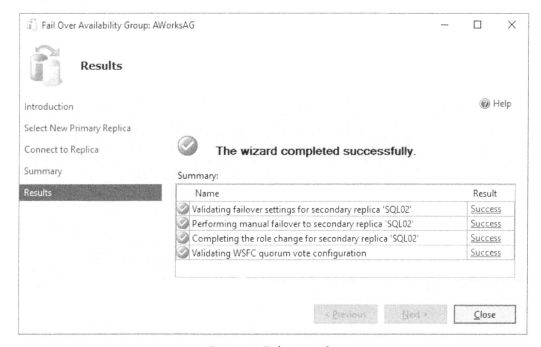

Fig. 9.25 – Failover results

On the dashboard, you can then see that the primary instance has changed to your selected replica, which you chose in the failover dialog window.

You can add more databases or more replicas to the existing AG. In SSMS, simply right-click **Availability Databases** in the **Availability Groups** section of SSMS as you can see in the following screenshot:

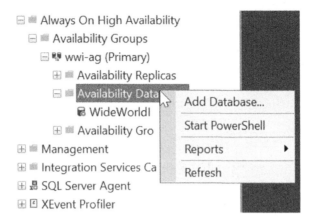

Fig. 9.26 – Add a database to Availability Group

Any database will be subject to checks as if you were creating brand-new **AGs**. In the following screenshot, you can see that one database is already a member of one of the **AGs** and several databases cannot be added until the prerequisites are met:

Name	Size	Status	Password
AGDB2	16.0 …	Meets prerequisites	
DWConfigurati…	16.0 …	Full backup is required	
DWDiagnostics	1.0 GB	Full recovery mode is required	
DWQueue	16.0 …	Full recovery mode is required	
WideWorldImp…	3.3 GB	Already part of this availability group	
WideWorldImp…	4.3 GB	Password required	

Fig. 9.27 – Checking prerequisites for a new database

After connecting to the replica(s) and choosing the data synchronization, the database will be added to one of the **AGs** as you can see in the following screenshot:

 ## The wizard completed successfully.

Summary:

Name	Result
Adding databases to availability group 'wwi-ag'.	Success

Fig. 9.28 – Adding a database to an Availability Group

This step can be achieved either with SSMS, T-SQL, or PowerShell, depending on your needs and the complexity of the environment.

If you decide to use PowerShell, the code for the task will be as follows:

```
Add-SqlAvailabilityDatabase -Path SQLSERVER:\SQL\SQLNODE01\
DEFAULT\AvailabilityGroups\wwi-ag -Database AGDB2
```

Let's now move onto **basic availability groups**, which were introduced in SQL Server 2016.

Basic Availability Group

Basic Availability Group are available in SQL Server 2016 and 2019 as a replacement for **Database Mirroring**, which has been deprecated since SQL Server 2012. Although **Mirroring** is deprecated, it's still available and is still being deployed in Enterprise environments. **Basic Availability Group** can offer you similar options to **Database Mirroring**.

A database can maintain a single replica in synchronous or asynchronous commit mode. The secondary replica is inactive and not accessible to users until there is a failover. The failover just swaps the primary and secondary roles between servers, causing the secondary replica to become the primary replica. **Basic availability groups** can even span the environment and you can configure hybrid scenarios with Azure.

There are several limitations to **basic availability groups**:

- Only one secondary replica.

- There is no read access on secondary replicas.

- There are no backups on secondary replicas.

- There are no integrity checks on secondary replicas.

- There is no support for adding or removing a replica to an existing **basic availability group**.

- Supports one availability database.

- Only Standard edition servers support the **basic availability group**.

- The **basic availability group** is not a part of a **distributed availability group**.

When you are configuring **basic availability group**, you need to select the **Basic Availability Group** checkbox. This checkbox is available only in the Standard edition and not in the Enterprise or Evaluation edition of SQL Server:

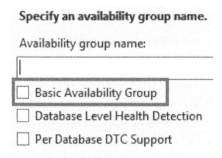

Fig. 9.29 – Creating a Basic Availability Group

Let's now move on to **distributed availability groups**.

Distributed Availability Groups

Distributed availability Groups are similar to the **basic availability group** and are a new feature in SQL Server 2016; they are also available in SQL Server 2019. Distributed availability groups are a new type of availability group that can span over two separate AGs. Those separate underlying AGs are configured on different server clusters (WSFC). These distributed availability groups are not configured within a cluster and do not configure anything in the underlying WSFC. There is a requirement that the underlying AGs must have a **Listener** configured.

This **Listener** will be configured as an endpoint URL for the distributed availability groups. The distributed availability groups have synchronous and asynchronous commit modes. However, the data movement is a little bit more complex, since only one database in distributed availability groups can accept the updates. There is a new role named **Forwarder**, which is a primary replica in a secondary availability group. The **Forwarder** receives transactions from a primary replica in a primary availability group and forwards transactions to the secondary replicas in the secondary availability group:

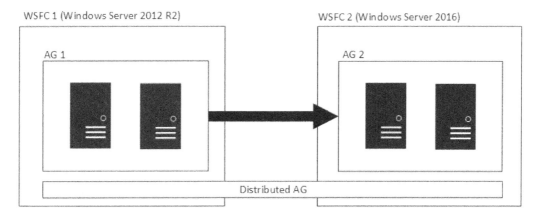

Fig. 9.30 – Distributed Availability Groups

The distributed availability groups are just SQL Server level configurations and they need to share the SQL Server version with the underlying AGs. However, the version of the OS for the two WSFC clusters can be different. So, one WSFC can run on Windows Server 2016 and the other can utilize the previous version of Windows Server 2012 R2. This is particularly useful when the two clusters are in different data centers and have different OS-level upgrade policies.

Summary

In this chapter, we have looked at two main features for high availability which can be used with SQL Server 2019. As both Always On Availability Groups and Always On Failover Cluster Instances are dependent on the WSFC feature, we went through the initial configuration of the failover cluster. As the failover cluster topic itself is quite complex, we have deployed a simple cluster with basic options. Usually, in large-scale environments, there will be a dedicated team to fully deploy and configure the cluster for the database administrator.

The FCI is an older approach, based on shared storage; it requires more complex cluster configuration. In business continuity planning, you need to consider your options for high availability at the storage and network level, too, since from an SQL Server and cluster perspective, shared storage can become a single point of failure. The deployment of FCI and **AGs** is different, so you need to plan carefully regarding which option you would like to manage in your environment. Each has different requirements for licensing. Availability Groups (except the basic option for one database) require the Enterprise edition of SQL Server in which a FCI can be hosted on SQL Server Standard edition.

In the next chapter, we will focus on in-memory OLTP technology and the performance improvements that in-memory OLTP technology can bring to your application.

10
In-Memory OLTP – Why and How to Use it

Performance is crucial for every system's success and it's the same for SQL Server. However, as data contention grows all over the world, the traditional method of continuous algorithm tuning and improving from version to version becomes an insufficient approach. Since 2010, Microsoft has been working on a completely new approach to data processing called **Hekaton**. The first version was present on SQL Server 2014 as the In-Memory **OnLine Transactional Processing (OLTP)** feature. It offers new frontiers for developers and administrators to design and maintain speedy applications and also break many limits of traditional disk-based data processing.

In this chapter, we will have a top-level overview of how the In-Memory OLTP architecture works and the requirements for its successful implementation. We will also look at how to create in-memory tables and how to enhance their performance with natively compiled stored procedures. Along with this, we will also explore some useful scenarios. As a **database administrator (DBA)**, we need to have detailed knowledge about In-Memory OLTP behavior. So, we will also learn a few simple techniques to monitor the memory-optimized part of our database. All of this will be covered in the following topics:

- In-Memory OLTP architecture
- Creating in-memory tables and natively compiled stored procedures
- In-Memory OLTP usage scenarios
- Monitoring In-Memory OLTP

In-Memory OLTP architecture

In-Memory OLTP is a feature of SQL Server that offers the option to create memory-optimized tables and natively compiled modules just like stored procedures. In-Memory OLTP utilizes a portion of memory up to a limit set by the given edition of SQL Server (for example, Enterprise Edition). The data of the memory-optimized tables is placed in memory. Transactions working with data in memory-optimized tables are controlled in optimistic row-versioning mode. Both properties – the memory utilization and optimistic transaction control – lead to a throughput in the database of up to 30 times greater. The adoption of In-Memory OLTP is quite easy from a developers's perspective as the development effort is not increased with new syntax. The traditional T-SQL approach has been kept by Microsoft to ease the adoption of the feature. Besides the simplicity of the development effort, In-Memory OLTP brings great performance benefits to the database.

The architecture of In-Memory OLTP on SQL Server is completely different from everything we have seen before on SQL Server. The authors of the solution proceeded from the assumption that everything that could be done on the disk-based part of the data engine was just an evolution of the data processing optimization, so some kind of revolution was needed. In this chapter, we will explain what In-Memory OLTP is, we will describe the top-level architecture, and then jump deeper into the details of In-Memory OLTP.

To see the benefits gained when using In-Memory OLTP, we need to consider the differences between two areas of work: data storage architecture and user request processing phases.

Data storage differences in In-Memory OLTP

Disk-based data is stored in classic files (`.mdf` or `.ndf`) and divided into small 8 KB parts called **data pages**. Those data pages are registered within other data pages called **Index Allocation Maps (IAMs)**. Other types of data pages are used for identifying things, such as, for example, which data pages have free space, and so on.

SQL Server uses all data page types to find out if the portions of data needed by SQL Server to fullfil user requests are already located in buffer cache. If data pages containing data used to process a query are not in the buffer cache, SQL Server moves the data pages to the buffer cache from the physical disk and then processes the buffered data pages as needed according to the user's request. Basically, we can experience two major issues:

- The first issue is the back-and-forth movement of data pages between the physical disk and the buffer cache, which incurs significant overhead.

- The second big issue occurs when data pages have to be protected against accidental reading or changing by concurrent sessions. Session isolation and protection invokes locking as a protective mechanism used by SQL Server to avoid situations such as non-repeatable reads, dirty reads, or phantom reads.

In-memory tables, on the other hand, use neither data nor locking architecture. Structures of in-memory tables are internally C-structures like application objects in other environments, and they are held in memory all the time when SQL Server is running. This omits the need for reading data from the disk when the data is required by a user request.

Even if it seems that in-memory tables are somehow similar to structured memory buffers, in-memory tables can be persisted on physical disks but in the form of sequential data saved into a dedicated filestream filegroup, also called a **memory-optimized filegroup**. The persisting is done by SQL Server outside of regular user request processing, so the performance from the user's perspective is not affected by it. SQL Server has two ways of handling the data durability of in-memory tables:

- **Full durable in-memory tables**: These tables are **Atomicity, Consistency, Isolation, Durability (ACID)** compliant, and when SQL Server is restarted, the table content is reconstructed from the memory-optimized filegroup.

- **Non-durable in-memory tables**: The content of such tables is lost when SQL Server is restarted. That's why this type of in-memory table is not ACID compliant.

Both types of in-memory tables have their purposes—some scenarios are mentioned in the *In-Memory OLTP usage scenarios* section of this chapter.

> **Note**
>
> ACID is an acronym of the four basic transaction properties: **Atomicity**, **Consistency**, **Isolation**, and **Durability**. This last property is broken when we use non-durable in-memory tables.

Another big difference is the mode of **concurrency control**. Records, or group of records, of in-memory tables are not locked. SQL Server uses row versioning for concurrency control. This means that every record in a certain in-memory table has two hidden columns called **Begin Timestamp** (BTS) and **End Timestamp** (ETS). When a record is inserted, the first version of the record is held with BTS containing the record time and ETS containing the special **infinity** symbol.

When the record is updated, SQL Server creates new version of the same record. The old version has the infinity symbol in ETS replaced by the transaction **timestamp value**, and the same transaction timestamp value is used in the BTS of the new record version. When the transaction is committed, the transaction timestamp is replaced by the actual timestamp value in both the old and new version of the record. The old version has ETS filled with the actual timestamp of the end validity, and at the same time the new version remains valid, with ETS set to infinity.

Old versions of records are removed asynchronously by the garbage collector, so row versioning does not invoke memory consumption growth.

We can summarize the comparison as shown in the following table:

	Disk-based tables	In-Memory tables
Data storage	Data pages saved to disk	C-structs held in memory
Data movement	Movement between disk and memory	No data movement
Concurrency control	Locks and latches, pessimistic concurrency	Row versioning, optimistic concurrency

Figure 10.1 – Comparison of disk-based and in-memory data processing

When the approaches from the preceding table are compared, In-Memory OLTP improves the performance of data storage and concurrency control up to ten times greater than that with disk-based processing. However, data storage and concurrency are not the only areas of improvement. Another area of improvement is **request processing** and we will explore that in the next section.

Request processing differences in OLTP

User requests processed in traditional disk-based processing are received by the data engine and then several steps are carried out before a result of the request is sent back to the session's output buffer:

1. **Parsing**: Parsing is a syntactical check of the request validity. The result of the parse phase is a syntactical tree.

2. **Binding**: Binding checks for existence, user permissions, and valid usage of objects used in the query. During this phase, the data engine reads the metadata of used objects.

3. **Algebrizing**: This process detects and substitutes logical operators that represent certain actions declared in the request (for example, WHERE predicates or JOIN operators). The result of this phase is called an algebrizer tree. The algebrizer tree is a prerequisite for the creation of the execution tree.

4. **Optimizing**: The optimization phase is probably the most complicated phase of request processing. SQL Server uses known metadata such as data types, indexes, statistics, and relative costs of operators used in algebrizer trees, and builds the execution tree. The optimization is highly affected by the state of the database, especially the timeliness of statistics.

5. **Compilation and execution**: When the query tree is optimized enough, SQL Server compiles the tree as an execution tree. The execution tree contains physical operators that are interpreted during execution by functions developed inside SQL Server's core. The execution tree is often cached into a memory section called the **procedure cache** so it can be reused.

This summary of user request processing was mentioned because we can now think of places where some performance enhancements can be done. From the preceding listed points, two areas are possible—optimizing and execution:

- When SQL Server optimizes a query, it uses more than 90 different factors or measures to recognize and create a good enough execution tree. The weights of those measures change slightly as versions of SQL Server are released and optimized algorithms adjusted. Nowadays, it can increase performance by a tenth of a percent.

- The second area of enhancement is the execution part of query processing. The optimization of functions interpreting physical operations over data has probably the same minor benefit as the optimization adjustments themselves.

In SQL Server 2014, natively compiled stored procedures were introduced. This first attempt covered stored procedures but in later versions the set of objects programmable in a natively compiled manner was expanded to include scalar functions and triggers. Yet, we still speak about natively compiled stored procedures.

A natively compiled stored procedure has some particularities and limitations because it is not interpreted as a traditional SQL statement, even though it is still written using the T-SQL language. When a natively compiled stored procedure is created, it's actually compiled into a set of C instructions and then, when called by a user, it's executed directly by the CPU without any additional overhead resulting from the necessity of optimization and compilation.

Comparing these two approaches of request processing—natively compiled versus traditional objects—we can see that using the natively compiled approach gives a performance improvement of up to twenty times greater than using the traditional approach.

As written in this and the previous sections, SQL Server has not one but two data processing engines now. The following section describes how those two parts of the data engine work together.

Cooperation between the disk-based and memory-based parts of SQL Server

In-Memory OLTP was incorporated into SQL Server as a second hidden engine, but from the client's perspective, nothing has to be changed. Let's explore the architecture depicted in the following diagram:

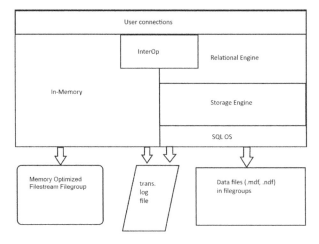

Figure 10.2 – In-Memory architecture

As seen in the preceding diagram, the top layer is called **User connections** and covers the rest of the engine, so users are connected in the same way. When a user sends a request, the **InterOp** component serves as a signpost for in-memory or disk-based processing. When the request is disk based, it's taken by the **Relational Engine** for parsing, binding, and optimizing. Then it's sent to the **Storage Engine**, which resolves the execution in cooperation with **SQL OS**. Data is persisted in traditional **data files** and transactions are logged in the transaction log file or **trans. log file**.

The **InterOp** component resolves parts of interpreted SQL requests using in-memory tables. When a user calls the natively compiled stored procedure, **InterOp** sends the request completely to the in-memory part and the request is processed in the way it was described in the previous section. Data is read by the natively compiled stored procedure. When the transaction is executed, SQL Server uses the same transaction log file for transaction logging. This feature covers transactional consistency across both the in-memory and disk-based parts of the database.

Both engines must share the same memory given the limits of the edition of SQL Server installed. For Enterprise Edition, the memory limit for In-Memory OLTP is 2 TB. For other editions, the In-Memory OLTP limit is computed as 1/4 of the memory limit of the other editions of SQL Server.

For example, let's look at the Standard Edition. Its memory limit is set to 128 GB, so the In-Memory OLTP could occupy an additional 32 GB of memory in each database where In-Memory OLTP is used. Make sure that sufficient memory is present on the OS because In-Memory OLTP is quite aggressive in its resource consumption. The following diagram shows what will happen when the memory of the OS becomes low:

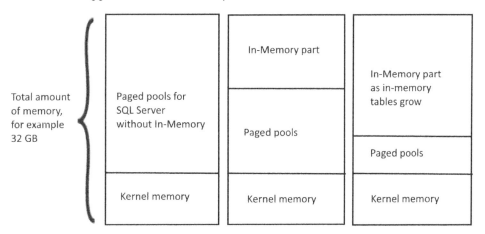

Figure 10.3 – How In-Memory OLTP impacts on memory consumption

When we look at the preceding diagram from the left to the right, we see how the memory consumption changes when In-Memory OLTP is used. We can see how the growing In-Memory part of memory steals memory from paged memory pools, and eventually, the In-Memory allocation could occupy almost all the memory dedicated to SQL Server.

In-Memory OLTP limitations

As explained in the previous section, in-memory tables have limits for memory usage determined by the given edition of SQL Server. But this isn't the only limit we have to keep in mind. There are many more limitations, and they are as follows:

- In-memory tables cannot have data types such as XML, geography, or geometry.
- In-memory tables cannot be indexed by full-text indexes.
- In-memory tables cannot be used in replications.
- In-memory tables cannot refer to disk-based tables by foreign key constraints.
- In-memory tables cannot use computed columns.
- In-memory tables are always bound to the memory-optimized filegroup, hence they cannot be placed into partition schemas.
- In-memory tables cannot be filetables.

Natively compiled stored procedures also have limitations. The biggest limitation of the natively compiled stored procedures is that they can only handle in-memory data, yet traditional SQL queries, stored procedures, or other objects can use both disk-based and in-memory data. Other limitations include the following:

- Transactions cannot be controlled – everything is closed to the atomic block.
- A lot of syntactical limitations are present, for example, common table expressions, cursors, temporary tables, the SELECT..INTO construct, and so on.

All these limitations have to be considered when we want to migrate some functionality of our databases to In-Memory OLTP.

At this moment, we know that In-Memory OLTP consists of tables intended for fast data contention, held in memory, and using the optimistic concurrency approach. We also know that natively compiled stored procedures, triggers, and scalar functions can handle data in in-memory tables. Taken together, both in-memory tables and natively compiled objects maintain very fast data access in situations when classic disk-based tables and T-SQL procedural objects reach their performance limits. In the next section, we will go through the procedure for setting up In-Memory OLTP on the server and the database.

Creating in-memory tables and natively compiled stored procedures

The previous section was about the top-level architecture of In-Memory OLTP. Knowing the architecture will help us get familiar with all the steps needed to set up the environment for In-Memory OLTP applications and to create objects within it.

In this section, we will create memory-optimized filegroups and then we will create some tables, indexes, and natively compiled stored procedures. All these tasks will be described in the form of walkthrough examples.

Preparing for In-Memory OLTP

The first step is to create a memory-optimized filegroup. The following screenshot shows you how to use the **Properties** dialog for the database, opened by a right-click on the database in **Object Explorer**:

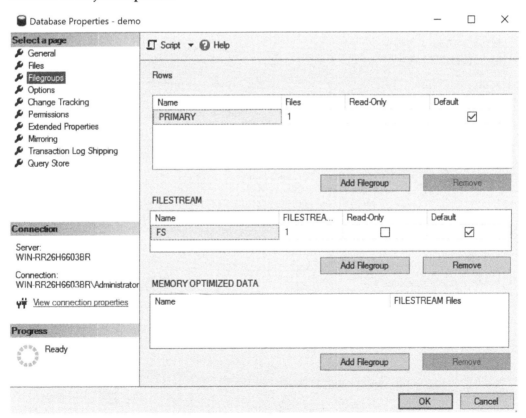

Figure 10.4 – Filegroups page of Database Properties window in SSMS

As seen in the preceding screenshot, the **Filegroups** tab is divided into three lists. The last list, labeled **MEMORY OPTIMIZED DATA**, is dedicated to creating the memory-optimized filegroup.

Every database can contain only one memory-optimized filegroup. So, when the filegroup is created by the **Add Filegroup** button, the button is disabled and no additional memory-optimized filegroups can be created. The second option we can use to create memory-optimized filegroups is to use a simple script as follows:

```
ALTER DATABASE [demo] ADD FILEGROUP [INMEM] CONTAINS MEMORY_
OPTIMIZED_DATA
GO
```

In the preceding script, [demo] is the name of the database to which we want to add the filegroup and [INMEM] is the name of the newly created filegroup.

Every filestream's filegroup must have at least one folder. So, the second step is to add a folder to the filegroup. The following screenshot shows the **Properties** dialog one more time:

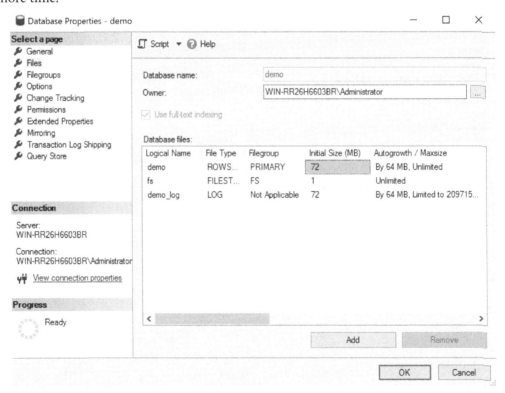

Figure 10.5 – Files page of Database Properties window in SSMS

In the preceding screenshot, the **Files** section is selected. By clicking the **Add button**, a new row is added to the **Database files** list and we have to fill in the following columns:

- **Logical name**: The logical name used for administrative purposes such as backup.
- **File Type**: This could be rows, a log, or a filestream. The last choice is the most suitable one.
- **Filegroup**: The name of the memory-optimized filegroup from the dropdown.
- **Path** (not visible on the screenshot): The path to an existing folder that will contain data persisted from the in-memory tables.

The second option is the following script:

```
ALTER DATABASE [demo]
ADD FILE
(
  NAME = N'inmem_file',
  FILENAME = N'F:\DATA\inmem'
)
TO FILEGROUP [INMEM]
GO
```

Here are some short explanations about the preceding script:

- `[demo]` is the name of the sample database.
- `inmem_file` is the logical name of the folder added to the filegroup.
- `F:\DATA\inmem` is the path to the folder containing the data.
- `[INMEM]` is the name of the memory-optimized filegroup.

After performing the steps described in this section, the environment is prepared, and we can start to create objects.

> **Note**
> Unlike other filegroups in the database, SQL Server does not support the removal of memory-optimized filegroups. For all of our experiments with In-Memory OLTP, consider creating a sample database first, because the only way to stop working with In-Memory OLTP completely is to drop the database.

Creating In-Memory OLTP objects

Two types of objects are created within In-Memory OLTP—tables with indexes and natively compiled stored procedures. Now we'll go through their creation.

Creating tables with indexes

The basic syntax for creating memory optimized tables is almost the same as when we are going to create disk-based tables, but we have to consider some extras:

- The index is created as part of the table creation.

- Clustered indexes are allowed.

In other words, we create indexes with CREATE TABLE or ALTER TABLE statements.

> **Note**
>
> In earlier versions of SQL Server, the ALTER TABLE statement was not allowed in an In-Memory OLTP environment. It was introduced in SQL Server 2016.

The syntax for creating a table is as follows:

```
create table Ratings_InMem
(
id int not null identity primary key
nonclustered hash with (bucket_count=1048576)
, UserId int not null
, MovieId int not null
, Rating tinyint not null
, Index ix_Users (UserId)
)
with
(
memory_optimized = on, durability = schema_and_data
)
```

As seen in the preceding script example, the base syntax is very similar to disk-based table creation. The exceptions are as follows:

- In-memory tables do not support clustered indexes. That's why the primary key is marked as `nonclustered`.

- Indexes are a part of an in-memory table; they are not created separately by the `CREATE INDEX` statement. The last row in the table structure shows us how to create the index. When indexes have to be changed, the `ALTER TABLE` statement is used.

- The `ON` keyword is used for placing a new disk-based table or disk-based index into the right filegroup and is prohibited from creating in-memory tables.

- The `WITH` keyword says that the table will be in memory. Its definition consists of the following:

  a) A `memory_optimized` option set to on.

  b) A `durability` configuration option. This option sets whether the table will be fully durable (this is the value `schema_and_data` as seen in the script; it's also a default value) or a non-durable table (the value is `schema_only` in that case).

Tables can be accessed via traditional interpreted T-SQL statements; otherwise, in-memory tables will stay separate from the rest of the database. Indexes in In-Memory OLTP are used completely the same way as in disk-based tables, but the index structures are different. Let's explain in-memory indexes in deeper detail in the following paragraph.

In-Memory OLTP indexing

In In-Memory OLTP, we work with three types of indexes:

- **Hash indexes**
- **Range** (or **BW-Tree**) **indexes**
- **Columnstore indexes**

Each of these preceding indexes plays a different role in In-Memory OLTP. In the following sections, we will learn about these three In-Memory OLTP indexes in detail.

Using hash indexes

Creating a hash index might be a point of confusion for developers or DBAs who are not familiar with the concept of hash indexes. A hash index itself is a sorted list of **hash values**. The list has a fixed capacity of **hash buckets**. The capacity must be declared during index creation and must not be changed later. The number of hash buckets should be greater than the estimated number of distinct key values stored in the table in the future. Hence, a good practice is to use the number 220 (1,048,576) as a basis for the estimation. In the CREATE TABLE statement, in the *Creating tables with indexes* section, we estimate that the number of records will not be greater than approximately 1 million. If we expect more than 1 million records, a good practice is to multiply by 220. One hash bucket can contain just one hashed value. When the number of hash buckets is underestimated, hash collision occurs, and the performance of the index decreases.

When a new record is being inserted into a table with a hash index, SQL Server calculates the hash value of the **index key** and places the hashed value to the proper position in the index. Because the index key values are hashed, this index serves the best for WHERE conditions with equality operator. That is why the hash index is usually preferred as the right index for the primary key. But we often need to search for ranges of records. For such cases, the range index works best. The following paragraph describes the usage of range indexes.

Using range indexes

Range indexes, sometimes also referred to as BW-trees, are very similar to the B-tree indexes we know from the disk-based parts of databases. A BW-tree has its own internal differences compared to B-trees, but we use BW-trees the same way as non-clustered B-trees designed on disk-based tables. As we can see in the CREATE TABLE example, the ix_Users index is just one more index without any additional properties. The ix_Users index is a BW-tree. BW-trees serve common WHERE conditions using relational operators such as *greater than* or for range seeks. Range indexes are very simple to create and very useful for many search predicates. But it does not solve big range scans nor aggregates. For analytically oriented queries, the columnstore index is the right option. Let's go ahead and examine it in the context of the In-Memory OLTP environment.

Using columnstore indexes

The third type of In-Memory OLTP index is the columnstore index. A columnstore index created on an In-Memory OLTP table is always a clustered index. Everything else works completely the same way as in disk-based tables. Columnstore indexes were described in *Chapter 6, Indexing and Performance.*

For some operations, using in-memory tables is very good to enhance performance when using natively compiled stored procedures. The next section shows you how to write such a procedure.

Natively compiled stored procedures

Natively compiled stored procedures are written in T-SQL. When such a procedure is created, it's saved into metadata and compiled into C. It makes natively compiled stored procedures very efficient, but the C compilation also causes a lot of limitations. Let's take a look at the following example:

```
create proc procNativeModification
  (@Id int
  , @UserId int
  , @MoveiId int
  , @Rating int)
with native_compilation, schemabinding, execute as caller
as
begin atomic with (transaction isolation level = snapshot,
language = N'English')
  if @id is null
    insert dbo.Ratings_InMem (UserId, MovieId, Rating)
    values (@UserId, @MoveiId, @Rating)
  else
    update dbo.Ratings_InMem
    set UserId = @UserId, MovieId = @MoveiId, Rating = @Rating
    where Id = @Id
end
go
```

This procedure does a very simple thing; when a record does not yet exist in the Ratings_InMem table, it's inserted. Otherwise, it's updated according to the key value provided in the @Id parameter.

Let's explore this as it differs from the regular stored procedures. The first syntax requirements for every natively compiled procedure are in the header. This declares that the procedure is natively compiled (the native_compilation keyword), and the procedure is also schema bound (the schemabinding keyword). The schema binding forces the writer of the procedure to use two phase names – Ratings_InMem (as a table name) and dbo.Ratings_InMem – inside the procedure. Also, a security context of the stored procedure's execution must be explicitly declared (the execute as keyword).

The body of the natively compiled stored procedure must be enclosed in an atomic block. As seen in the preceding code, it's traditionally the `begin .. end` block but it's marked by the `atomic` keyword. The atomic block has additional properties such as `language` and `transaction isolation level`. The `language` property affects which language will be used to translate any error messages that are raised. We can set the language to any of the languages supported by SQL Server. The `transaction isolation level` is always set to `snapshot` because it means that updates will be row versioned.

Natively compiled stored procedures cannot access disk-based tables, so when creating them we must keep in mind this limitation. If we still want to profit from the efficiency of these procedures, we have to migrate all tables used in transactions to the in-memory area.

Natively compiled stored procedures offer big performance gains and are suitable for cases when new transactions arrive frequently (for example, thousands of transactions every second) and when transactions are executed from many concurrent sessions.

At this moment, we know how in-memory tables and natively compiled stored procedures work together. In the next section, we will briefly describe how to monitor data contention in an In-Memory OLTP environment.

Migrating disk-based objects to In-Memory OLTP

Lots of systems were built a long time before In-Memory OLTP was born. As the data contention is growing, such systems enhance their performance but the traditional method of optimization, such as more indexes or hardware upgrade, fail. For these cases, Microsoft offers reports and wizards that help with the migration of tables and stored procedures to the in-memory environment.

The first question is which tables are suitable to be migrated to the In-Memory OLTP environment to improve performance. The second question is how expensive the migration could be. The migration of tables and stored procedures to the In-Memory OLTP environment has to be transparent to the applications using it; otherwise, significant effort will be needed to remake some part of the client applications due to the need for physical design changes on the database side. As was mentioned in the *In-Memory OLTP limitations* section, not all data types or constraint types are supported and sometimes it's hard to consider all of the limitations.

Both of these questions are answered by a report called the **Transaction Analysis Performance Overview**. This report is reachable via SSMS by right-clicking the database in **Object Explorer** and selecting this report from the list of reports. When opened, the report provides a signpost to any problems, as seen in the following screenshot:

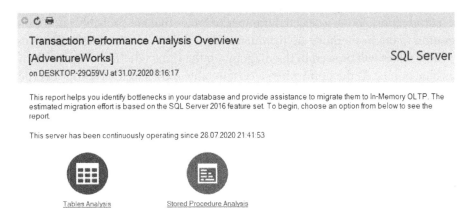

Figure 10.6 – Transaction Performance Analysis Overview report

When we want to inspect tables that are candidates for migration, we will click through the left option, labeled **Table Analysis**, and for migration candidates that are stored procedures, we will use the right link labeled **Stored Procedure Analysis**.

When using the **Table Analysis** link, a report called **Recommended Tables by Usage** will be opened as follows:

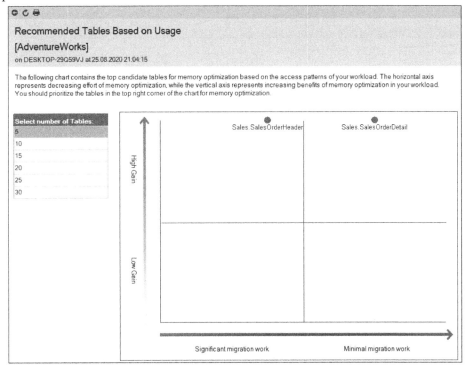

Figure 10.7 – Recommended tables for migration to In-Memory OLTP

The preceding report shows a selected number of tables that are probably good candidates for migration to the in-memory environment. The left table with numbers allows us to select how tables will be seen in the diagram on the right side. The diagram shows tables as blue points. At the point when a certain table moves to the top-right corner, the migration of the table is considered useful from a performance perspective and the effort needed for migration is relatively small. If tables are shown in the top-left corner, they are still heavy-loaded, and the migration effort will be substantial. Tables in the bottom half of the diagram are not good candidates for migration at all, because the migration effort tends to be big while the performance benefit is disputable.

When we need more detailed information about migration blockers, we can click certain tables in the diagram and a new report appears:

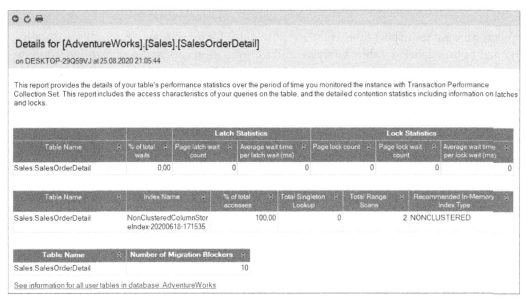

Figure 10.8 – Details of table usage

The preceding screenshot shows the details for the Details for Table Name report. It summarizes the actual wait statistics, which are good criteria for making decisions about migration (when more waits have been issued, it's a better idea to migrate the table) and it also summarizes existing indexes and the total number of potential migration issues. Unfortunately, this report does not show which issues have to be resolved prior to migration. We can try to find all the issues on our own. In this example, the three problems are as follows:

- **A clustered index created by the primary key constraint**: We have to create a non-clustered primary key.

- **A foreign key referring to another table**: Here, we have to decide whether we will migrate the parent table as well, or whether we'll drop the foreign key constraint.

- **A column of the xml data type**: This is the most serious issue because we must drop the column and save the data to another disk-based table; this action means effort for all client applications using this table.

The following screenshot shows the structure of the table in the **Object Explorer**:

```
☐ ⊞ HumanResources.JobCandidate
    ☐ ▦ Columns
        ⊶● JobCandidateID (PK, int, not null)
        ☞ BusinessEntityID (FK, int, null)
        ▤ Resume (XML(HumanResources.HRResumeSchemaCollection), null)
        ▤ ModifiedDate (datetime, not null)
```

Figure 10.9 – HumanResources.JobCandidate table structure preview

Once all roadblocks are removed, we can start the migration itself. It can be done by using a simple wizard. The wizard is accessed this way:

1. In the **Object Explorer**, spread the **Tables** node under your database.

2. Right-click on the desired table and from the popup menu, select **Memory Optimization Advisor**.

3. The wizard is open, so follow its steps.

The reports described in this section help us recognize which tables could benefit from being moved to the In-Memory OLTP.

At this point, we've got a firm grounding in the concepts, functionality, and operation of In-Memory OLTP has been explained. In the next section, we will explore some useful use cases.

In-Memory OLTP usage scenarios

The upcoming sections are going to show you some useful scenarios for In-Memory OLTP usage. The following sections are intended as walkthrough examples. We will work with a large amount of data in In-Memory OLTP, then we will change the scope to heavily updated data, and in the next exercise, we will add a system versioning feature. In the last example, we will merge OLTP and **Online Analytical Processing** (**OLAP**) workloads, two highly different areas of data manipulation, using In-Memory OLTP to make them work together efficiently.

Assignment of the user story sample

To provide a consistent use case, we will use an imaginary water management company. Such companies have geographically distributed networks delivering water across a whole region. The network has to be monitored constantly because the company has to be informed about every abnormality or disorder as soon as possible.

That's why there's approximately 100,000 sensors measuring the amount of water flowing through the network. Every sensor sends records with its own identification and measures the flow rate every 5 seconds. This means 20,000 simple transactions per second. This scenario is typical for In-Memory OLTP applications as the amount of transactions processed in regular disk-based OLTP increases the risk of locking conflicts.

The company also requested reports showing trends, history, and statistics about water flow rates over time:

1.   Our first example will resolve the amount of transactions by capturing all new information sent by the sensors using INSERT statements only, so it will work as a log.

2.   The second example will do the same task using INSERT or UPDATE statements.

3.   The third example will add the functionality to be able to show real-time information about the current state of the network.

As an ancient Chinese idiom says, even the longest journey begins with the first step. Let's start our journey with the first example now.

Example 1 – Inserting incoming data into in-memory tables

This first sample shows probably the most traditional method of data capture for production tracking or monitoring systems. It originates from traditional disk-based data processing. What we need is a table living in the in-memory environment and also a very simple natively compiled stored procedure to achieve the best possible performance. Let's begin!

1.   Our first code sample shows the table creation. We have to keep in mind that the database prepared for such tables must have a memory-optimized filegroup:

```
use Demo
go
create table SensorData
(
```

```
Id bigint not null identity primary key nonclustered
, SensorId uniqueidentifier not null
, RecordTime datetime2 not null default(sysdatetime())
, WaterFlowRate decimal(7, 2) not null
)
with
(
memory_optimized = on
)
go
```

The previous code sample shows the creation of a very simple table without indexes, except the primary key. For data handling, we need to develop a natively compiled stored procedure.

2. The creation script is shown in the following code block:

```
create procedure procAddSensorData
(
  @sensorId uniqueidentifier
  , @waterFlowRate dec(7, 2)
)
with native_compilation, schemabinding
as
begin atomic with (transaction isolation level =
snapshot, language = 'English')
insert dbo.SensorData (SensorId, WaterFlowRate) values (@
sensorId, @waterFlowRate)
end
go
```

As seen in the preceding code block, the procedure does only one action—it inserts a new record.

The first example seems to be ready to go live, but that's not true. We must consider the limitations of In-Memory OLTP with regards to the given edition of SQL Server, and we have to decide how much memory will be dedicated to in-memory tasks. That's why one more requirement needs to be fulfilled – we have to develop a retention policy.

3. The retention policy is simply the action of moving data from an in-memory table to a disk-based table. It could be done as in the following script:

```
use Demo
go
create table SensorDataHistory
(
   Id bigint not null primary key
, SensorId uniqueidentifier not null
, RecordTime datetime2 not null
, WaterFlowRate decimal(7, 2) not null
) on [primary]
go

create proc procMoveSensorData
   @recordsBefore datetime2
as
begin try
   begin tran
      insert SensorDataHistory (Id, SensorId, RecordTime,
WaterFlowRate)
      select Id, SensorId, RecordTime, WaterFlowRate
      from SensorData
      where RecordTime <= @recordsBefore

      delete SensorData where RecordTime <= @recordsBefore
   commit
end try
begin catch
   rollback;
   throw;
end catch
go
```

The previous script consists of two steps:

a) In the first step, a table called SensorDataHistory is created. This table will contain all historical data.

b) The second step is the creation of a stored procedure called procMoveSensorData. The procedure invokes regular explicit transactions controlled by the try..catch block.

The transaction takes data intended for deletion from an in-memory table and inserts it into a classic disk-based table, and then deletes the original records from the in-memory table. If any errors occur, all the action taken is rolled back correctly.

> **Tip**
>
> The `procMoveSensorData` procedure works with both in-memory and disk based-data; that's why it cannot be written as natively compiled. For better performance, the procedure could be rewritten into two procedures. The first one would copy the data to a disk-based table, with the second stored procedure nested into the first one—it could be natively compiled and could just delete data from the in-memory table. Transaction consistency will be kept by the first procedure.

4. The last step is to schedule the calling of the procedure, for example, every day. It's just two rows of code to be written into a job step. Let's look at the script:

```
declare @timeBefore date = getdate() - 1
exec procMoveSensorData @timeBefore
```

As seen in the preceding script, deletion time is computed as the current date and time minus one day. Then the procedure is executed. This example will move all the data inserted before yesterday.

Let's summarize how the assignment was satisfied:

*   Data was stored in a fast, lock-free structure so no conflicts nor waits were expected.

*   Data was moved from the in-memory environment to the disk to keep the environment healthy, but we made some extra effort to manage the retention policy.

*   Statistical reports were selected against the disk-based table with no attention paid to the constantly incoming data (data delays would then occur if not).

*   Real-time analytics were were queried from an in-memory table.

Given the third point, we have to find a better solution, and this solution will be provided in the next scction.

Example 2 – Updating data in an in-memory table

The previous sample involved big data contention with the need for a regular retention policy. This sample is going to start at almost the same point as the previous one:

1. Let's create an in-memory table similar to the previous one, as follows:

```
create table SensorData2
(
SensorId uniqueidentifier not null primary key
nonclustered
, RecordTime datetime2 not null default(sysdatetime())
, WaterFlowRate decimal(7, 2) not null
)
with
(
memory_optimized = on
)
go
```

As seen in the preceding script, the table does not need an extra Id column as a surrogate key (compared to the table from the first example) as every sensor is registered once. The rest of the table definition remains the same.

2. Bigger changes have to be done in the stored procedure's definition, as follows:

```
create procedure procUpdateSensorData
(
    @sensorId uniqueidentifier
    , @waterFlowRate dec(7, 2)
)
with native_compilation, schemabinding
as
begin atomic with (transaction isolation level =
snapshot, language = 'English')
    update dbo.SensorData2 set
      WaterFlowRate = @waterFlowRate
      , RecordTime = default
    where SensorId = @sensorId
    if @@rowcount = 0
      insert dbo.SensorData2 (SensorId, WaterFlowRate)
values (@sensorId, @waterFlowRate)
end
go
```

The preceding script creates new stored procedure called
`procUpdateSensorData`. This stored procedure tries to update a record
according to the parameters provided. If the record does not exist (a new sensor was
installed), then a new record is inserted. This conditional `insert` ensures that the
new sensor's data will be saved correctly.

This design does not cover the requirement for statistical reports as it overwrites
data time after time. Fortunately, SQL Server provides a feature called **temporal
tables**. The idea of temporal tables is to catch every data change done in a table
and save the changes to a separate table with the same structure. Aside from this
functionality, the T-SQL language provides the required syntax for querying the
original table with the possibility of time shifts as needed.

3. The following script shows you how to modify the table structure to start the
change capture:

```
alter table SensorData2
add
StartDate datetime2 generated always as row start,
EndDate datetime2 generated always as row end,
period for system_time (StartDate, EndDate)

alter table SensorData2
set
(system_versioning = on (HISTORY_TABLE = dbo.
SensorData2History))
```

The preceding script has two steps:

a) The first step adds two new columns that will set a range for record version
validity. Those columns must be of the `datetime2` data type and both columns
must have the `generated always...` adjective. Also, the `period for`
`...` is mandatory. Even though the first step modifies the structure of the
table, this kind of change is transparent to other database objects and client
applications, but the table is not a temporal table yet.

b) The second step is the moment when the data change capture is turned on.

> **Tip**
> The history table could be created as a standalone table with the same structure
> as the original table and bound to the temporal table feature later. It's good
> when a lot of changes are made because we can create the history table more
> precisely, for example, to other filegroup or even to a partition schema.

From now on, we can write simple queries against the in-memory table itself to retrieve current values, for example, to `select SensorId, RecordTime, WaterFlowRate from SensorData2`, or we can continue to write queries against the in-memory table but returning a state from the history table.

An example of such a query is shown in the following script:

```
select SensorId, RecordTime, WaterFlowRate
from SensorData2 for system_time as of '2017-02-11 00:00'
```

The preceding script will move us back to the time provided in the `system_time as of` clause. If we want to obtain a set of record versions for a given time range, we can use a similar query with a slightly different `system_time` clause.

An example of the query looks like this:

```
select SensorId, RecordTime, WaterFlowRate
from
SensorData2 for system_time between '2017-02-11 00:00' and
'2017-02-11 01:00am'
```

Temporal tables offer very comfortable ways of exploring changes in data over time.

Let's summarize this example:

- The data was stored in fast, lock-free structures so no conflicts nor waits were expected.

- The quantity of data was relatively small because the insertion of new records was dramatically reduced.

- We didn't need to manage the data retention policy.

- Statistical reports were selected using the `system_time` clause in the `select` statements so no data delay would occur.

- Real-time analytics were selected against in-memory tables.

This sample took us one step higher because of less memory consumption and natively created historization, so all points of assignment are fulfilled now. But the real-time analytics still are subject to improvement. The last example exercise will show you how to ultimately improve performance.

Example 3 – Improving real-time analytics

The previous examples relied on the performance ensured by memory storage. But if the degree of data contention is huge, it's a good idea to improve the read load and at the same time not let it affect the write load. In this example, we will just enhance the solution described in the previous section.

When we think of real-time analytics, we can imagine some kind of aggregation queries frequently issued by a client. As an example, we can use a regularly (and often) refreshed dashboard. Such dashboards or any other aggregate queries requested can often profit from `columnstore` indexes. SQL Server enables us to create `columnstore` indexes over an in-memory structure. The sample script looks like this:

```
alter table SensorData2 add index cs_SensorData2 clustered
columnstore
```

The only action we need to take is to improve is the querying of in-memory tables. The `columnstore` index is described briefly in *Chapter 6, Indexing and Performance*, as an object, which is very useful for analytical queries with long, full, and range scans.

As in the previous examples, we will summarize what was done:

- The data was stored in fast, lock-free structures so no conflicts nor waits were expected.
- The data was relatively small because the insertion of new records was dramatically reduced.
- We didn't need to manage the data retention policy.
- Statistical reports were selected using the `system_time` clause in the `select` statements so no data delay would occur.
- Real-time analytics were selected against in-memory `columnstore` indexes.

This third example showed us the complete functionality that we can use to create efficient and extremely powerful solutions.

The In-Memory OLTP feature brings great performance benefits to us, but the increased performance it delivers has its price. When working with In-Memory OLTP, we need to know how memory is consumed. The following section shows how to monitor In-Memory OLTP.

Monitoring In-Memory OLTP

As mentioned in the *Cooperation of disk-based and memory-based parts of SQL Server* section, memory consumption of the in-memory part of the database can be huge and aggressive. That is why it is necessary to monitor the amounts of memory occupied by in-memory objects regularly. The simplest way to obtain an overview of the memory usage of the in-memory environment is to use reports in Management Studio:

1. Right-click on a database in Management Studio and select **Reports** from the pop-up menu that appears.

2. Under the **Standard Reports** option, select **Memory Usage By Memory Optimized Objects** from the list of reports.

    The report shown by this option is depicted in the following screenshot:

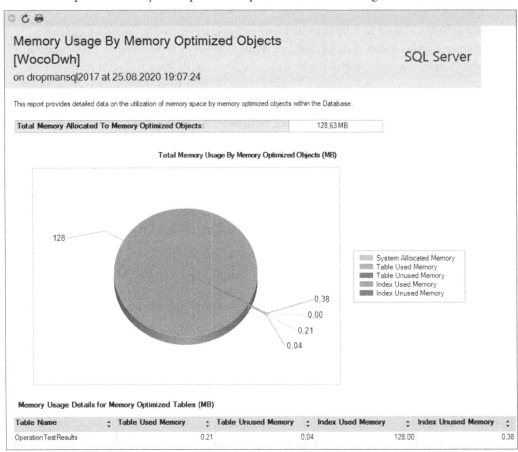

Figure 10.10 – Memory consumption report

The first row shows the total amount of memory consumed by objects created by the user. The diagram shows several sections of in-memory allocation such as tables and indexes. The table at the bottom of the report shows the size of each in-memory table within the indexes.

There are also internal objects used by SQL Server for internal purposes. For a better overview of the complete contents of the in-memory environment, we can use a **Dynamic Management View (DMV)** called `sys.dm_db_xtp_memory_consumers`. This DMV shows the parts of memory allocated to and used by objects.

3. To compare the result of query from `sys.dm_dm_xtp_memory_consumers` with the report mentioned in preceding image, we can write the query as follows:

```
select sum(allocated_bytes) / 1024 / 1024. as
TotalObjectsMemoryInMB
from sys.dm_db_xtp_memory_consumers
where object_id > 0
```

This query returns exactly the same number as in the **Total Memory Allocated to Memory Optimized Objects** field in the first part of the previous report.

4. In the same way, we can try to compute the numbers in the rest of the report. The following code is provided as an example:

```
select object_name(xtp.object_id) as ObjectName
    , iif(grouping_id(object_name(xtp.object_id), xtp.
memory_consumer_desc) > 0
        , 'TOTAL'
        , xtp.memory_consumer_desc) as MemoryConsumerDesc
    , sum(xtp.used_bytes) / 1024 / 1024. as
UsedMemoryByObjectInMB
    , sum(xtp.allocated_bytes) / 1024 / 1024. as
AllocatedMemoryByObjectInMB
from sys.dm_db_xtp_memory_consumers as xtp
group by grouping sets
(
    (object_name(xtp.object_id), xtp.memory_consumer_
desc)
    , ()
)
having sum(xtp.used_bytes) / 1024 / 1024. > 0
```

Let's explain the preceding code:

- It uses the same `sys.dm_db_xtp_memory_consumers` DMV. The `select` clause of this statement contains several columns.

- The first column is just `object_id` translated to the object name by the built-in `object_name` function.

- The second column consists of two nested functions:

  i) The first function used is `iif`. This built-in function is used here for the creation of a summary row description of the result set. The first parameter of the `iif` function tests the level of grouping. It uses the `grouping_id` function.

  ii) This second function, `grouping_id`, is very useful when an aggregate query is written with more combinations of grouping criteria, as seen in the `group by` clause. When the lowest level of grouping is computed on a certain record, the function returns zero.

  When a grouping column is omitted by SQL Server, in other words, when a higher level of aggregation is computed on a certain row, the function returns an integer value bigger than 0. In our case, the `grouping_id` function returns 3 when the total row is computed, otherwise it returns 0. The second parameter, called the true block, returns the word TOTAL when the grouping level is the higher one. The third parameter returns the `memory_consumer_desc` column when the `grouping_id` returns zero. Simply put, the second column shows the concrete memory consumer description or the word TOTAL.

- The third and fourth columns are the results of the aggregation. The third column shows the actual memory usage, in MB, used by all memory consumers individually, and the fourth column shows the memory allocated by the consumers.

The results of the query look like this:

	ObjectName	MemConsumerDesc	ObjectUsedMemoryInMB	ObjectAllocatedMemoryInMB
1	NULL	256K page pool	2.500000	2.500000
2	NULL	4K page pool	0.007812	0.015625
3	NULL	64K page pool	0.125000	0.125000
4	NULL	Database internal heap	0.058593	0.375000
5	NULL	Hash index	0.210937	0.210937
6	NULL	Logical Root table	0.003906	0.187500
7	NULL	Physical Root table	0.000976	0.062500
8	NULL	Range index heap	0.000976	0.625000
9	NULL	Storage internal heap	0.008789	0.562500
10	NULL	Storage user heap	0.005859	0.062500
11	NULL	Tail cache 256K page pool	38.500000	38.500000
12	Ratings_InMem	Range index heap	5.891601	6.937500
13	Ratings_InMem	Table heap	27.767578	28.000000
14	NULL	TOTAL	75.086914	78.664062

Figure 10.11 – Result from sys.dm_db_xtp_memory_consumers view

As seen in the preceding screenshot, SQL Server allocates and uses more memory objects than just tables and indexes. The actual memory consumed by the in-memory functionality of SQL Server is in a surrogate record with the TOTAL in the memory consumer description (MemConsumerDesc) column, and in the fourth column labeled ObjectAllocatedMemoryInMB. Its value is approximately double the **Total Memory Allocated to Memory Optimized** column of the **Memory Usage By Memory Optimized Objects** report.

> **Note**
> If you want to compare the values shown on the report with the values received by querying the DMV, add all values from ObjectAllovatedMemoryInMB for ObjectName to the Ratings_InMem value. You will obtain a value of 34.9375, which, when rounded up, is 34.94 MB. Now add on all the values from the bottom table of the report. You will get 34.94 MB. This means that the DMV calculates exactly the same data as the report shows, but in the report, memory consumers are limited to user objects.

Summary

This chapter provided a detailed overview of a very valuable part of SQL Server, called In-Memory OLTP. The biggest advantage is the in-memory nature of the solution; the biggest risk we need to consider is the memory consumption.

In the first section, we went through an architectural overview. We also compared different approaches to transaction handling for disk-based and in-memory data.

In the second section, we learned how to implement tasks that have to be done before implementing In-Memory OLTP, and then we created objects hosted by the In-Memory OLTP part of SQL Server.

In the third section, we saw how to apply In-Memory OLTP in real-world use cases. In this section, we went through the step-by-step usage of in-memory samples.

In the last and most important section, we saw how to monitor In-Memory OLTP. If we follow the techniques mentioned in the discussion on the topic of monitoring, we should never run out of memory.

As a conclusion, we can say that In-Memory OLTP makes significant advances in the performance of SQL workloads where the traditional approach of disk-based data processing reaches its performance limits. The In-Memory OLTP implementation is not difficult, so we can experiment with this feature easily.

The next chapter will explain another set of advanced scenarios, and the cooperation of an on-premises SQL Server with Microsoft Azure.

11
Combining
SQL Server 2019
with Azure

Microsoft Azure, as well as other cloud technologies, have been growing over the last couple of years and nowadays, they can cover every global, technical, or business need without compromise. When it comes to **Microsoft SQL Server**, we can provision it on-premises, but SQL Server can also be completely hosted in cloud environments. Nowadays, we see more hosting alternatives for SQL Server in Azure, and this sometimes leads to a point of confusion for on-premises DBAs. In this chapter, we will describe a set of server and serverless technologies offered by Azure for database hosting. We will also take an end-to-end and step-by-step look at some samples of several features, such as data files in Azure, backing up to URL, and managing backups to Azure. We will provide an overview of what's possible in Azure when manipulating data, and then we will go through some hybrid scenarios where we'll be combining on-premise instances of SQL Server with Azure.

In this chapter, we will cover the following topics:

- Beginning with technologies in Microsoft Azure
- Microsoft SQL Server 2019 and hybrid scenarios
- Quick overview of running SQL workloads in Azure
- Migrating SQL Server workloads to Azure

Let's get started!

Beginning with technologies in Microsoft Azure

Cloud technologies profit from the so-called **all independent** concept. This means many computers, disk arrays, server network switches, and many other elements (collectively called **nodes**) work in cooperation.

For example, when a node is not available, the rest of the nodes fully cover its absence. When this occurs, the whole system must be stable; otherwise, it could go down.

Building such an environment in-house leads to high expenses. Years ago, big players offered to provide fully supported services using the cloud concept. This has helped to reduce the expense of IT solutions because hardware and software are now maintained by the provider; the customer only pays for the operations of the feature itself, the performance level they need for the feature, and for the high availability level of the feature.

One of the most basic properties of most of the tenancies in Azure is the **pay-as-you-go** charging mode, which allows you to pause, stop, or completely remove features or technologies that are not needed. When new web applications, storage, whole Windows servers, or any other service is needed, it's usually just a few clicks away from the tenant. This pay-as-you-go concept supports the very good predictability of expenses of IT.

Microsoft also started to offer a huge cloud-based technology called Microsoft Azure. Nowadays, Azure covers all IT needs and also offers new technologies such as AI, IoT, data science tools, and so on. It's very hard to list all the technology offered by Microsoft, but a few include SharePoint servers, Active Directory in the cloud, and virtual servers with many operating systems and services on it. Last but not least, there is Office 365, which is perhaps the most popular cloud environment now. In addition, the scale of products and technology offered by Microsoft continues to grow, and every technology found in Azure continues to improve.

In the following sections, we will focus on data-related technologies such as Cosmos DB, Azure Data Factory, Azure SQL Database, Azure SQL Server, and Azure Synapse. In every section, a short example of these technologies will be provided. If you want to try them out for yourself, remember that you'll need an Azure account. If you don't have one, it's easy to create a trial account at `https://azure.microsoft.com/en-us/free/`.

Overview of data-related technologies in Azure

Microsoft Azure offers many options for storing data, depending on the format of the data (structured or non-structured), the source of the data (that is, LOB applications or IoT devices), the amount of data, and the speed of the data contention. The way data is processed is also very important to consider when the data engineer goes to select the right option or combination of options of data-related technologies in Azure. The following short paragraphs will help provide you with an introduction to the technologies hosted by Azure.

Storage Account

Storage Account is mostly intended to store unstructured data; that is, text files or images with no option to query the data directly. Storage Account is just a cover name for four types of containers:

- Blobs
- File shares
- Tables
- Queues

The most frequently used container types from the preceding list are **blobs** and **file shares**. Blob containers offer storage for unstructured files in something called a **flat namespace**. The flat namespace means that the blob containers do not support folders. A typical use case for blob containers is to store large amounts of data, such as text files, JSON documents, images, and so on. The blob container serves as cheap storage for data that will be processed in the future by other Azure resources.

> **Note**
> We will also use the storage account in the following section for backups and data file placement.

File shares are similar to blob containers. The main benefit of file shares is that they support the **Server Message Block (SMB)** protocol. This means we can use file shares as mapped drives in local devices.

At the time of writing, tables and queues are rarely used because new technologies, especially Cosmos DB, tend to be their successors.

Cosmos DB

Cosmos DB is defined by Microsoft as a **multi-API**, globally replicated **NoSQL** database with the **multi-write** option. But what does this definition mean for us?

Cosmos DB is a cover name for several NoSQL database types. These database types are listed here:

- **MongoDB API**: MongoDB is a document-based database. It works with JSON documents and it allows us to store **semi-structured**, possibly **nested** or **recursive**, data.

- **SQL API** (formerly known as **DocumentDB**): The SQL API is a competitor of MongoDB. Unlike MongoDB, the SQL API was developed by Microsoft for Azure only.

- **Cassandra API**: The Cassandra API is a **columnar** database. It stores data in a format comparable to **columnstore indexes**. It allows super-fast scan operations to be performed on open data stored in the Cassandra API.

- **Gremlin API**: The Gremlin API stores and maintains graph data. It allows us to define nodes and edges in any graph-based data.

- **Table API**: The Table API is quite similar to **relational databases** since it works with structures very similar to tables. Unlike relational databases, this API is still a NoSQL database, which provides more freedom to the developer. Like every other API in Cosmos DB, the Table API profits from the global scalability and super high throughput that is common to all Cosmos DB APIs.

Such NoSQL databases are used to store and manipulate JSON documents stored in collections. Typical use cases for such databases are online gaming, IoT data arriving in JSON format from many concurrent connections, or hot storage for data from mobile applications. Aside from Mongo DB and the Core API, Cosmos DB is also the host for the Gremlin API for graph processing and the Cassandra API for column-based databases.

Global replication with the multi-write option is a common feature of all the APIs hosted within Cosmos DB. This option allows us to configure more locations to which the same database is replicated natively by Azure. In other words, we are free of replication configuration as it's ensured by Microsoft. Hence, secondary replicas, as well as primary replicas, can be writeable. This follows two goals: high availability and improved responses from the database to distant connections.

Now, what about **NoSQL shortcut**? NoSQL shortcut or **Not-only-SQL** means that besides the client API, the Core API of Cosmos DB offers the **SQL-lite querying language** for manipulating data. Unlike SQL databases, NoSQL databases are not so widely known by developers, so the Azure portal offers you the option to download **SDKs** for `.NET`, `Node.JS`, and others with quick-start samples.

With that, we've seen that Azure is not limited to SQL solutions, but that we also need to move and transform data between data sources and destinations. For such purposes, Azure Data Factory is the right technology to use.

Azure Data Factory

Unlike blob storages and NoSQL databases (and the following SQL solutions), in Azure, **Azure Data Factory** (**ADF**) is an environment not for storing data, but for orchestrating **Extract-Transform-Load** (**ETL**) and **Extract-Load-Transform** (**ELT**) processes. **Orchestration** is a term used to describe the automated configuration, coordination, and management of data movements and transformations. In on-premises environments, we usually use **SQL Server Integration Services** (**SSIS**) or third-party tools such as **WhereScape** to define workflows or pipelines to coordinate which data, in which route, from which sources, to which destinations, and in which order should be moved and transformed.

For data movements and transformations, we can use the ETL or ELT approach. The ETL approach extracts data from one or more sources and then makes all the required transformations on the data before it is loaded into its destination. This approach is very common in traditional data warehousing projects. The ELT approach, on the other hand, extracts the data first but loads the extracted data into the destination before transforming it. The ELT approach allows you to fully utilize the capabilities of destination technologies such as **Azure Synapse** and **Databricks**.

Basically, ADF hosts an environment for pipelines. A pipeline can be compared to executable processes; it can be scheduled for execution, monitored, and troubleshooted, if needed. Each pipeline contains at least one activity. This activity could be a **copy activity**, which loads data from one connected service, such as SQL Database, to another connected service, such as a blob container, as a **flat file**. However, ADF contains many more activities.

Typically, we need to transform data; that is, aggregate it somehow, normalize the data, and so on. ADF has a set of activities dedicated to executing an executable script or object in the target data source. As an example, we can provide a **stored procedure activity** or an Azure Databricks notebook activity. In other words, ADF commonly utilizes the computation resources of other data-related technologies.

With that, we have understood some of the commonly used data-related technologies in Azure. However, as DBAs, our interest lies in SQL solutions. So, let's look at SQL databases in more detail.

Azure SQL solutions

In this section, we will go through some commonly used SQL technologies hosted within Microsoft Azure. Even if we are oriented mostly toward SQL technologies, the following section can also be used to prepare DBAs to become more familiar with the Azure portal, so this knowledge can be used when you're working with all the all the resources offered by Azure.

Understanding Azure SQL Database

In simple terms, Azure SQL Database is a typical relational database that behaves like a database without a SQL Server instance. However, this isn't the case, because the database is hosted in a SQL Server cloud environment in the form of a **partially contained** database.

This database containment can be used on-premises as well. The partially contained database is a SQL Server database that has some server level properties inherited by itself. That's why such databases are also called **self-contained databases**. Using self-contained databases on on-premise SQL Server instances enables DBAs to create users with passwords. This bypasses traditional authentication and authorization models, as described in *Chapter 4, Securing Your SQL Server*.

The user with the password is the kind of user that is not authenticated by a SQL Server instance, but is authenticated directly by a certain database. This could be very useful for scenarios such as hosting web databases or having some database often being migrated between more server instances.

Starting with the Azure portal

Everything in Azure is done through a web application called the **Azure portal**. It can be found at `https://portal.azure.com`. We will visit it often throughout the next few sections. If you have never used Microsoft's web technologies before, you'll need to create a new **LiveID** account. By doing this, you will be signed in with your LiveID or with an organizational account. Azure portal provides an initial dashboard, and this is where the work starts. The following screenshot shows how to get oriented in the Azure portal:

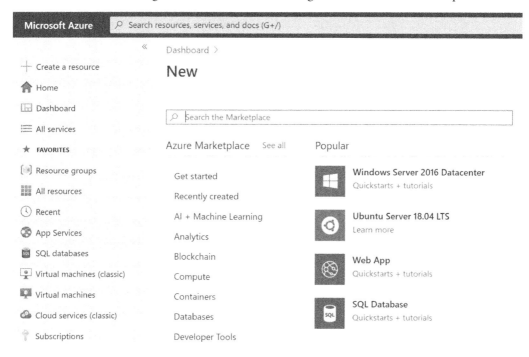

Fig. 11.1 – A selection of new resources in the Azure portal

When the Azure portal is accessed, it shows a dashboard in the main area and a set of the most popular features that can be requested. When you click on the **New** link in the top-left corner, a screen with a more complex set of features and technologies appears.

These sets can be filtered by categories, but sometimes, it's easier to just type the feature name into the search box at the top of the screen.

For example, let's write the word `database` in the search box. Several options will be shown, such as **Azure Database for PostgreSQL** or **Azure Database for MySQL**, but the **SQL Database** label will also appear. When **SQL Database** is selected, the previous screen will disappear and be replaced by a screen for Azure SQL Database creation. The following screenshot shows this screen:

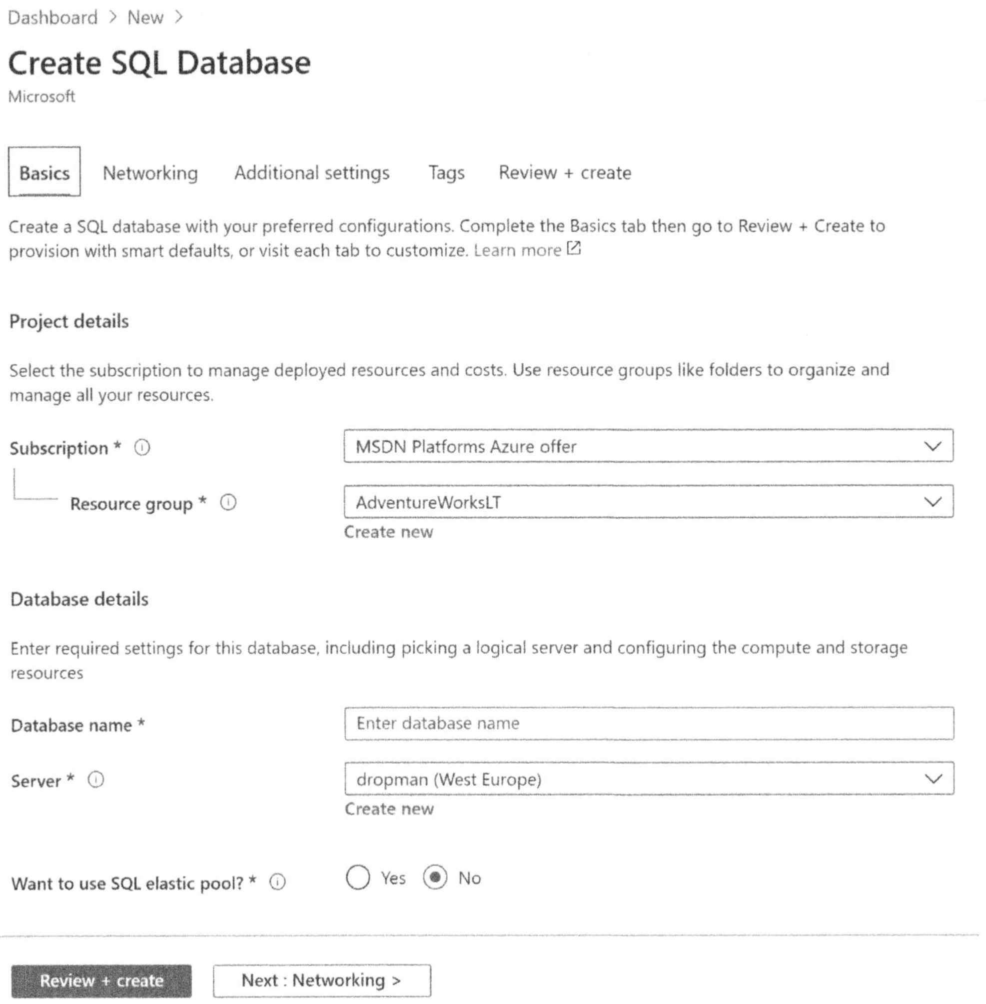

Dashboard > New >

Create SQL Database
Microsoft

| Basics | Networking | Additional settings | Tags | Review + create |

Create a SQL database with your preferred configurations. Complete the Basics tab then go to Review + Create to provision with smart defaults, or visit each tab to customize. Learn more ☑

Project details

Select the subscription to manage deployed resources and costs. Use resource groups like folders to organize and manage all your resources.

Subscription * ⓘ   MSDN Platforms Azure offer   ⌄

    Resource group * ⓘ   AdventureWorksLT   ⌄
                           Create new

Database details

Enter required settings for this database, including picking a logical server and configuring the compute and storage resources

Database name *   Enter database name

Server * ⓘ   dropman (West Europe)   ⌄
                           Create new

Want to use SQL elastic pool? * ⓘ   ◯ Yes ◉ No

[Review + create]   [Next : Networking >]

Fig. 11.2 – The Basics blade of Azure SQL Database creation

From here, we can fill in all the property information for the database being created. In the next section, we will learn how to create a complete and ready-to-go-live Azure SQL database.

Creating an Azure SQL database

In the previous section, we focused on basic orientation in the Azure portal. Now, we are going to continue with creating an Azure SQL database. The creation of an Azure SQL database starts with the screen shown in the preceding screenshot.

Let's describe the fields shown on this screen one by one:

- **Subscription**: A subscription is an account for payments and invoicing. One login can have more than one subscription.

- **Resource group**: This is an organizational unit, not a SQL Server! One resource group can hold all the resources that belong to the same solution or application.

- **Database name**: You just need to enter the name of the new database here.

- **Server**: The server property is not about creating a new instance of SQL Server. Instead, it provides the following:

  a) The first part of the name, which is used as a server name when connecting to Azure SQL database. The link is always in the `selectedservername.` `database.windows.net` form. This name must be unique within all of Azure. If the name already exists, a red exclamation mark will be shown; otherwise; a green tick will be shown.

  b) The geographical location of the newly created database (for example, Western Europe, West Central US, and so on). Select this property with care; a database created in a location that's a long distance away slows down the response time dramatically due to network latency.

  c) Admin login and password: It's not `sa` login actually; when comparing with on-premises SQL Server, the login to Azure SQL Database behaves more like a `dbo` user.

- **Want to use SQL elastic pool?**: When the answer is **Yes**, we can set fixed pricing for a group of databases that are created within the same elastic pool. This helps when each of the databases in the same elastic pool has its peak hours at a different time. The pricing unit in elastic pools is **elastic DTUs (eDTUs)**. If we want to control pricing for just one database (or the database has more or less constant load), the answer to the question is **No**.

- **Compute + Storage**: We have to pay according to the type of database we need. Nowadays, we have two pricing/performance options: **Database Transaction Units (DTUs)** and **vCores**. When the pricing tier is set to DTU, we are going to consume DTUs; the unit is composed of memory consumption, CPU consumption, reads and writes, and the maximum storage amount. For example, the cheapest database has five DTUs with 2 GB maximum storage and is about $5 per month. The most expensive database is 1,000 DTUs with 1 TB maximum storage, but it's more than $800 per month. This property can be changed at any time. So, if you are not sure how expensive the database should be, start with cheaper settings and when needed, add more resources, DTUs, storage, or a combination.

  DTUs are hard to estimate properly. That's why the second option, called vCore, is also available. When DBAs come from on-premise environments, they are used to think in numbers of CPUs and the amount of memory. vCore is a unit that is basically the maximum number of virtual CPUs used for a certain database. Unlike in on-premise environments, in Azure, the number of vCores we are going to utilize is going to be two or three times smaller.

- **Additional Settings**: The following fields are present on the **Additional Settings** tab:

  a) **Data source**: This drop-down list offers three values:

  i) **None**: New blank database prepared for content provision.

  ii) **Sample** (`AdventureWorksLT`): Database containing sample data about a non-existing company called Adventure Works.

  iii) **Backup:** Database recreated from the existing backup of the same or other Azure SQL database.

  b) **Collation**: Default database collation. This property is the same as in on-premises databases.

When all the properties have been filled in, we can check the **Pin to dashboard** checkbox. This pins the database on the dashboard and is useful for providing an overview or stating when the database settings are visited. The last action could either be **Create**, for immediate creation of the database, or the **Automation option** link. The **Automation option** link generates a full JSON description of the newly created database. This helps when resources are created or configured in Azure by using **Azure Resource Manager** for provisioning the automation of different resources. Clicking the **Create** button starts the database creation process. It lasts a couple of minutes and then a new screen appears, showing an overview of the database. This overview is shown in the following screenshot:

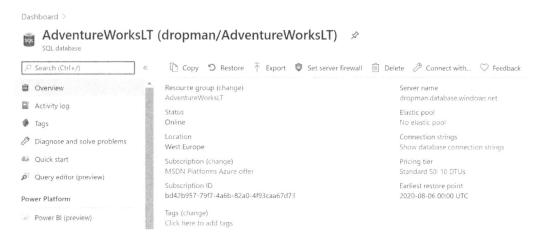

Fig. 11.3 – Overview blade of an existing Azure SQL database

There are a lot of options that can be configured here, but going into them is beyond the scope of this book.

When connecting, a user must provide their server name and database name since they are not going to connect to a real SQL Server, but an alias created for them. The database name is needed so that Azure knows which database will authenticate the user. We can find this information on the **Overview** blade, as shown in the preceding screenshot.

Nowadays, Azure SQL databases provide almost the same feature set as on-premise databases for basic SQL operations but with one important exception. Even if they are hosted on the same server (and let's keep in mind that the term *server* means the alias of a whole group of SQL servers maintained by Microsoft), they are the accessible points for connections. That's why it's not possible to combine more databases in one connection. In other words, the USE database_name command is not allowed against Azure SQL databases, and statements can only be executed against the database that the user is already connected to.

As we start working with Azure SQL Database, we will experience more limitations in this database compared to an on-premises SQL Server. For up to 100% compatibility, Azure offers an alternative to Azure SQL Database called Azure **SQL Managed Instance**. In the next section, we will look at the main differences between Azure SQL Database and Azure SQL Managed Instance.

Comparing Azure SQL Database and Azure SQL Managed Instance

As we explained in the previous section, Azure SQL Database is the best option for a standalone database with OLTP data contention; that is, a database serving as data storage for a simple e-shop. But in many cases, we have information systems with more databases being used together. Here, we can use **Service Broker** or speed up data contention using **In-Memory OLTP**.

Azure SQL Managed Instance is a SQL solution that allows us to work with the complete SQL Server feature in cloud without the need to maintain the underlying operating system and the instance of SQL Server itself. Azure **SQL Managed Instance** can be taken as a group of related databases, containing a full set of system databases such as msdb, that removes all the limitations that are experienced in Azure SQL Database. Azure **SQL Managed Instance** combines all the known features from on-premises SQL Server with the instance configurations fully maintained by Microsoft.

The decision of using Azure SQL Database or Azure **SQL Managed Instance** is often confusing and painful for newbies, so let's explore a few of the limitations and use cases for these two resources with the help of the following table:

Feature	Azure SQL Database	Azure SQL Managed Instance
T-SQL abilities	Full stack with an exception of USE statement	Full stack
Cross-database queries	Not possible	Fully supported
Optimistic concurrency	Turned on by default	Turned on by default
Database mail	Not possible	Fully supported
Service Broker	Not possible	Fully supported
In-Memory OLTP	Not possible	Fully supported
Backups	Managed by Azure	Fully supported as explained in Chapter 3, Backup and Recovery

Fig. 11.4 – Azure SQL Database and Azure SQL Managed Instance limitations and use cases

The preceding table does not contain all the differences, but it will help you decide which resource to utilize in different cases. Simply put, if we just need a basic T-SQL workload, such as a small database for storing the data of a web or desktop application, Azure SQL Database tends to be the strong enough but still cheap solution. On the other hand, when we need several cooperating databases maintaining data for more complex information systems, possibly with asynchronous data processing (Service Broker), super-fast telemetry data processing (In-Memory OLTP), or other, more sophisticated, features, Azure **SQL Managed Instance** will ultimately cover our needs since most of our instance's configuration details will be fully maintained by Microsoft.

Even if we have the option to provision Azure **SQL Managed Instance**, we still want to easily migrate our on-premises SQL Server environment to the cloud. That's why, in the next section, we will focus more on Azure SQL Server.

Understanding Azure SQL Server

Azure SQL Server hosts databases in the cloud in a completely different way. It is a regular virtual machine that has SQL Server installed on it. A good point to note here is that administrators are completely aware of the high availability of the machine itself. On the other hand, we have one more SQL Server instance and it's completely up to the DBA to maintain it correctly in the form of database checks, rebuilding indexes, or configuring security, as described in *Chapter 6, Indexing and Performance*, and *Chapter 8, Automation – Using Tools to Manage and Monitor SQL Server 2019*.

Azure SQL Server breaks the limitations of Azure SQL database because it's a regular instance of SQL Server. Let's consider some other properties of Azure SQL Server:

- Azure SQL Server could be incorporated into an **Active Directory** when the Active Directory has to be hosted in Azure as well.

- Azure SQL Server is a better option than Azure SQL database when we need a highly available machine with more databases for **Line-of-Business** (**LOB**) applications.

- The performance of the machine can be set through its price level.

- Azure SQL Server can serve as a secondary replica for AlwaysOn. This is really good because we can spread our **availability groups** outside organizations in case of physical disaster.

In the next section, we will create a sample Azure SQL Server.

Creating a sample Azure SQL Server

The creation of Azure SQL Server starts in the Azure portal in the same way that we described in the previous section. When it comes to finding the correct option, we need to use SQL Server 2019 as our search term, because SQL Server 2016 and SQL Server 2017 are already offered. Azure portal will show a list of many options, but basically, we need to decide between three editions of SQL Server:

- Enterprise
- Standard
- Web

When we've made a choice, we will be asked for the **deployment model**. The deployment model decides whether we will create a resource (a virtual machine, in our case) that exists independently of other resources or whether we wish to group more resources together logically. The deployment model can be either of the following:

- **Classic**: The newly created resource is independent.
- **Resource Manager**: Resources can be grouped together. This is useful when provisioning some solution using more resources, such as SQL Server, web applications, and other resources together. This is a newer option and one of the enhancements it brings is the possibility of using an SSD disk for storage.

The process of creating an Azure SQL Server consists of several steps. The first step for virtual machine creation is shown in the following screenshot:

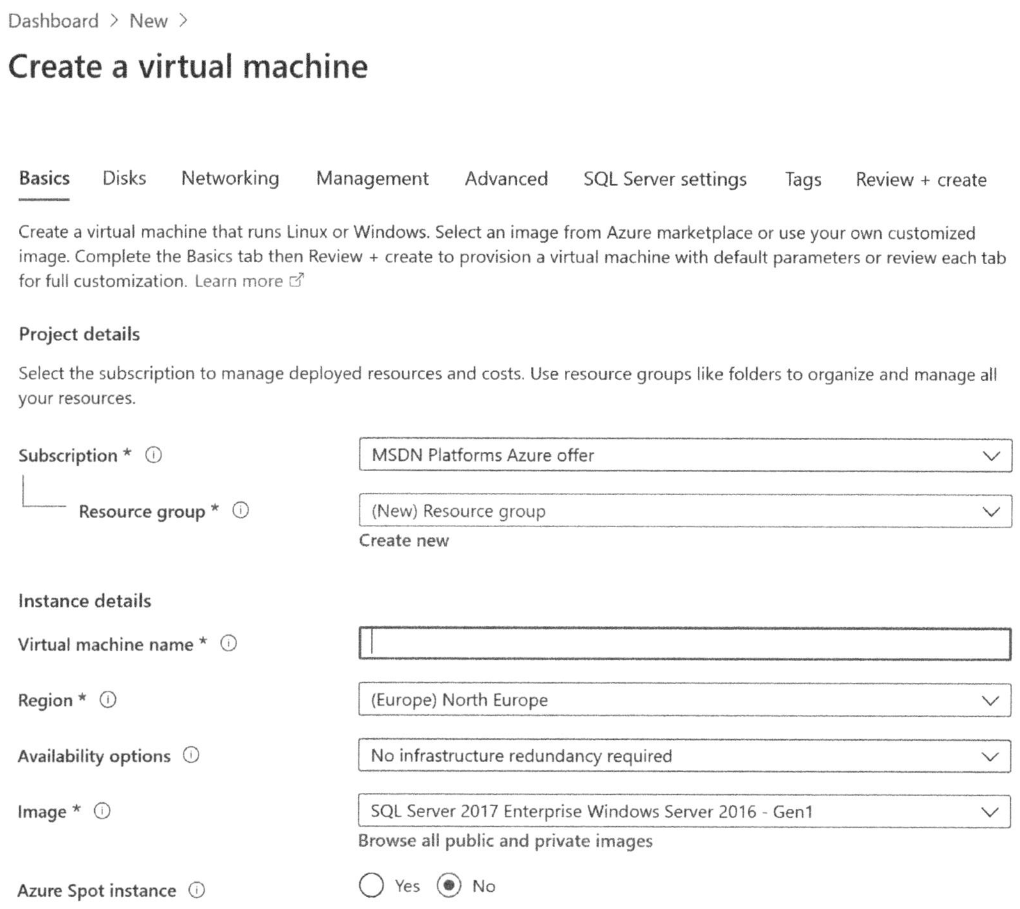

Dashboard > New >

Create a virtual machine

| Basics | Disks | Networking | Management | Advanced | SQL Server settings | Tags | Review + create |

Create a virtual machine that runs Linux or Windows. Select an image from Azure marketplace or use your own customized image. Complete the Basics tab then Review + create to provision a virtual machine with default parameters or review each tab for full customization. Learn more ☐

Project details

Select the subscription to manage deployed resources and costs. Use resource groups like folders to organize and manage all your resources.

Subscription * ⓘ

> MSDN Platforms Azure offer ⌄

    ⌐ Resource group * ⓘ

> (New) Resource group ⌄
> Create new

Instance details

Virtual machine name * ⓘ

> [|]

Region * ⓘ

> (Europe) North Europe ⌄

Availability options ⓘ

> No infrastructure redundancy required ⌄

Image * ⓘ

> SQL Server 2017 Enterprise Windows Server 2016 - Gen1 ⌄
> Browse all public and private images

Azure Spot instance ⓘ

    ◯ Yes   ◉ No

Fig. 11.5 – Azure SQL Server creation

Let's describe some of the properties in the **Basic** tab:

- **Subscription**: This field is used to configure from which subscription the virtual machine will be charged by Microsoft.

- **Resource group**: The server can be added to an existing resource group or it can occupy its own.

- **Virtual Machine Name**: This is just the name of the newly created virtual machine.

- **Region**: Geographic location of the new server.

- **Availability options:** We can configure a redundancy for our newly created virtual machine to keep it more available in case of failure.

- **Image**: This option allows us to select the type of the underlying operating system.

Apart from the properties explained in the preceding list, we must also set up the following important properties placed on the **Basic** tab (not visible in the screenshot):

- **User name**: The name of the administrator of the server who will be able to connect the server through a remote desktop.

- **Password** and **Confirm password**: The password of the administrator user. It must be at least 12 characters long.

Even if we can use all the other properties with their default values, it is recommended to go through all the tabs.

After doing this, we're provided with a summary and need to confirm all the properties we set during the previous steps. Then, the creation process starts, and we just have to wait a couple of minutes until it's finished. During the creation process (and this is true for all newly created resources), we can leave the portal running and return to it later.

When the server is created, we can start to use it. In the next section, we'll learn how to use Azure SQL Server.

Using Azure SQL Server

Once the virtual machine has been created, a dashboard is shown in the Azure portal, as follows:

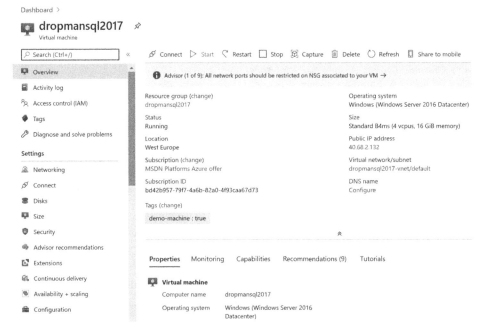

Fig. 11.6 – Overview blade of Azure SQL Server in the Azure portal

The dashboard contains a set of configuration properties on the top part and diagrams showing CPU or network utilization, as well as disk utilization on the bottom part. There are two main controls on the dashboard. The first is the **Connect** button on the top toolbar. When it's clicked, an RDP configuration file is downloaded, and we can access the virtual server over our remote desktop using the username and password we set in the first step of the creation process. When we are connected to the server, we can configure the operating system and SQL Server services. The remote desktop does not contain **Management Studio**, but we can install it.

The second control can be in the right-hand column of the configuration properties and it is the **Public IP address** of the server. This is useful for accessing SQL Server via Management Studio from outside the virtual machine.

> **Note**
>
> Azure SQL Server comes installed with a full feature set and with default settings at the instance level. After provisioning in the Azure portal is finished, review the Service Manager services and instance properties in Management Studio first, as we mentioned in *Chapter 1*, *Setting Up SQL Server 2019*.

Azure SQL Server is a good option for larger LOB applications as a secondary replica in AlwaysOn groups, and it can also serve for reporting or traditional analysis via Analysis Services. But for data warehouses with really big contention, Microsoft prepared a special resource called Azure Synapse. We'll look at this in more detail in the next section.

Azure Synapse

Data warehouse workload means a very big database with a lot of range or full scans. Against it, everything must be subject to the response time. Azure Synapse, formerly known as **Azure SQL Data Warehouse**, fulfills these requirements through its complex design.

The following screenshot shows the architecture of Azure Synapse:

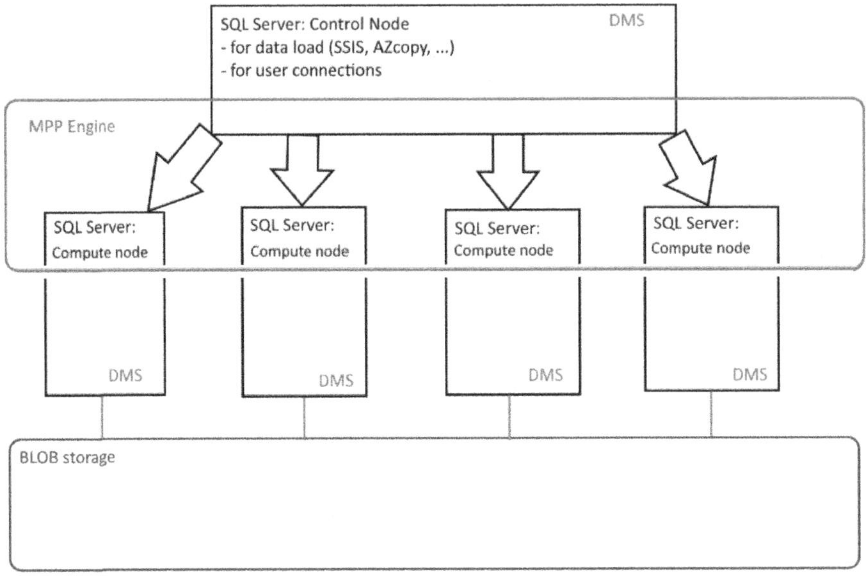

Fig. 11.7 – Azure Synapse high-level architecture

The only point of contact with Azure Synapse is a SQL Server instance called **Control Node**. Control Node responds to user requests and also receives incoming data during ETL executions. The Control Node itself plays the main role in the distribution of load between compute nodes. Every **compute node** is a SQL Server instance holding part of the data that was loaded into Azure SQL Data Warehouse. The amount of compute nodes could be up to 60 SQL Servers; that's why everything is done via **massively parallel processing** (**MPP**). The MPP engine is **Polybase**.

Polybase is a technology with two usage purposes:

- It controls MPP processing.

- It enables a connection to be made between relational databases and Hadoop applications such as **HDInsight** (also present in Azure).

- The second generation contains a fully integrated **Apache Spark** environment.

The Polybase topology can be installed in on-premise as part of SQL Server Enterprise Edition, but this is beyond the scope of this book.

The last part of every node in Azure Synapse is **Data Movement Service** (**DMS**). This feature starts to work when data that's used in the same query is not stored together in one node.

Creating an Azure Synapse instance

The creation of Azure Synapse is also done through Azure portal. The best search term to use when creating a new resource is **Azure Synapse**. Once found, the resource type's creation by an administrator is started, and a screen with several properties appears, as shown in the following screenshot:

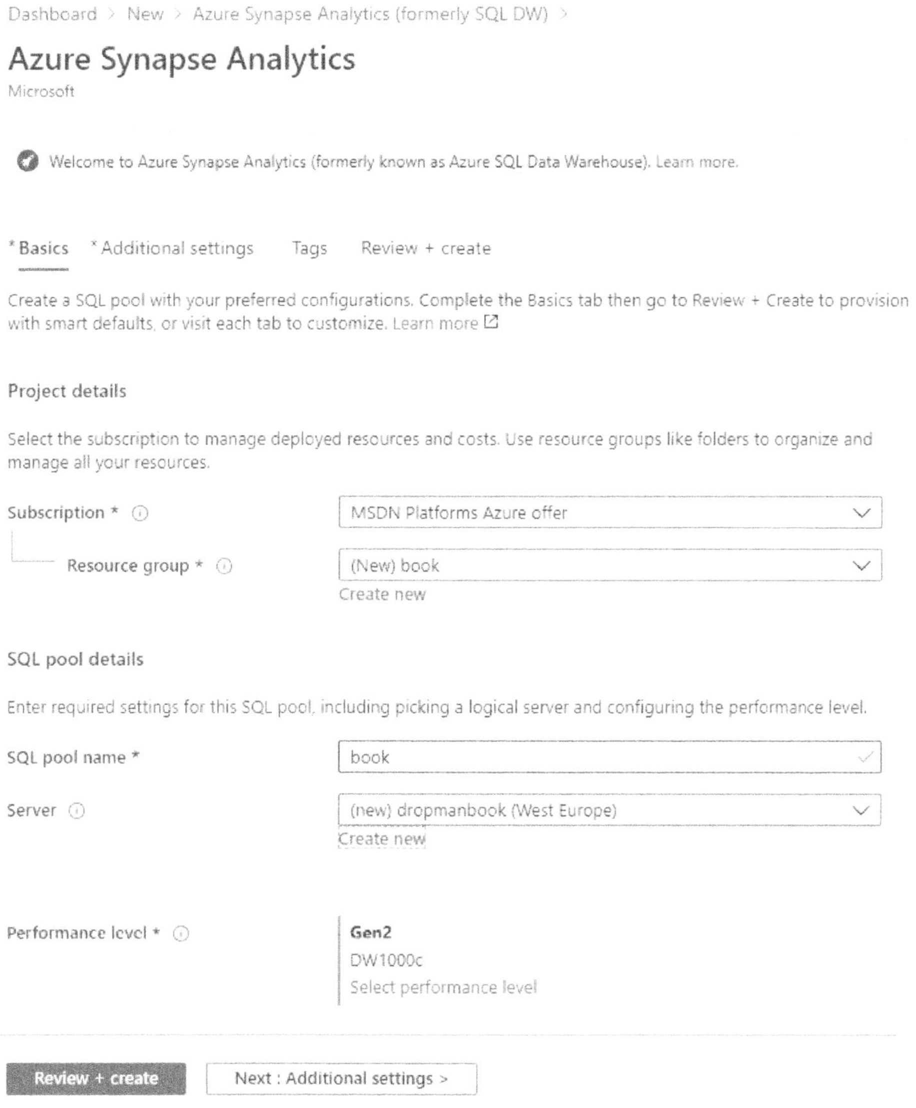

Dashboard > New > Azure Synapse Analytics (formerly SQL DW) >

Azure Synapse Analytics
Microsoft

⦿ Welcome to Azure Synapse Analytics (formerly known as Azure SQL Data Warehouse). Learn more.

* Basics   * Additional settings   Tags   Review + create

Create a SQL pool with your preferred configurations. Complete the Basics tab then go to Review + Create to provision with smart defaults, or visit each tab to customize. Learn more ⌕

Project details

Select the subscription to manage deployed resources and costs. Use resource groups like folders to organize and manage all your resources.

Subscription * ⓘ	MSDN Platforms Azure offer ∨
Resource group * ⓘ	(New) book ∨
	Create new

SQL pool details

Enter required settings for this SQL pool, including picking a logical server and configuring the performance level.

SQL pool name *	book
Server ⓘ	(new) dropmanbook (West Europe) ∨
	Create new
Performance level * ⓘ	**Gen2**
	DW1000c
	Select performance level

[Review + create]   [Next : Additional settings >]

Fig. 11.8 – Azure Synapse Analytics creation blade

All the properties shown in the preceding screenshot, such as **Database name** and **Resource group**, are self-descriptive. The **Select source** property, which can be found on the **Additional settings** page, enables the creation of a blank database that's been prepared for a new schema and ETL data load, a sample database, or a database from (Azure) backup. The **Performance level** option in **data warehouse units** (**DWU**) is quite complicated and consists of three parts:

- **Search/aggregation**: I/O-intensive and CPU-intensive types of operations.

- **Read**: I/O-intensive types of operations.

- **CTAS**: This shortcut creates a table via select I/O-intensive operations and provides us with a way to load data into the data warehouse from non-relational data sources. It also shows us how to archive a data warehouse data from the relational database in a non-relational destination.

The computation formula, when using the preceding factors, is not publicly documented. But as the number of DWUs we need grows, the more expensive the Azure Synapse service will become. The expense of Azure Synapse is probably its biggest and only disadvantage!

When the Azure Synapse instance has been created, an overview is shown, along with a summary of the basic properties. Now, we can connect to the Azure Synapse instance using any common tool, such as SQL Server Management Studio, or we can use the quick start options that have been placed in the left navigation menu, as shown in the following screenshot:

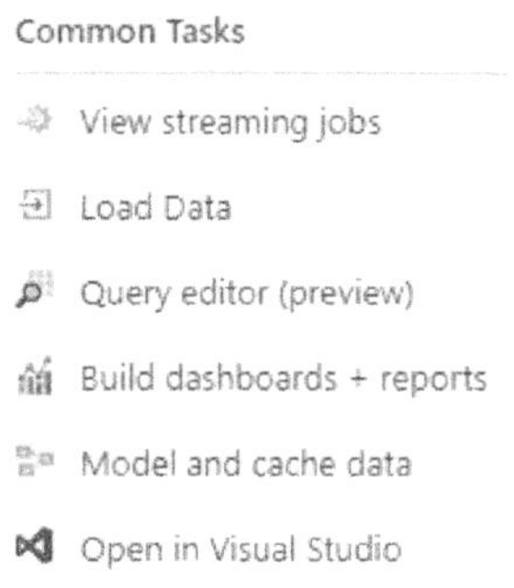

Common Tasks

-ʘ View streaming jobs

⬔ Load Data

♪⁴ Query editor (preview)

ⓜ Build dashboards + reports

🖳 Model and cache data

🔌 Open in Visual Studio

Fig. 11.9 – Navigation options for Azure Synapse

As seen in the preceding screenshot, there's a lot of possibilities with Azure Synapse, such as starting to load data, access to built-in monitor, or connect to it using Power BI.

When using Azure Synapse, a few more things need to be considered. This information is summarized in the next section.

Using Azure Synapse

Azure SQL Data Warehouse was designed to support a huge amount of big read operations and full scans. That's why the physical design of tables has three extra differences compared to common SQL Server databases:

- **Storage**: Storage means the internal structure of each table. Basically, the storage could be a columnstore, a clustered B-tree index, or a heap index.

  a) By default, every table stored in Azure Synapse is a clustered `columnstore` index.

  b) Clustered B-tree indexes are also supported and must be explicitly defined upon table creation.

  c) Heap indexes are also supported and must be explicitly defined upon table creation.

- **Table geometries**: As a massively parallel technology, every table is distributed across all compute nodes. This distribution can be solved in three modes:

  a) **Round-robin**: Default mode of distribution. The control node distributes data randomly and evenly across all compute nodes.

  b) **Hash**: The non-default mode of distribution based on a user-defined hash key. This mode of distribution can lead to so-called data skewness (data is not spread across all nodes evenly).

  c) **Replicated**: Replicated table topology is good for small tables. Each table is placed in every storage node of the Azure Synapse instance.

- **Statistics**: Azure Synapse does not support auto create and auto update statistics.

We must also consider not using defaults in several cases:

- **Small tables**: These should be heaps or clustered B-tree indexes (Microsoft thinks of small tables stored in Azure Synapse when they have less than 100,000,000 records).

- **Dimension tables with selective random searches**: These tables should be clustered B-tree indexes.

- **Tables joined often together**: When these tables are distributed randomly in round-robin mode or are not distributed by the same hash key, the data movement service is forced to move data from one instance of the compute node to another to put the data of joined tables together. We should minimize the work of the data movement service. This is why hash distribution is the best practice in these circumstances.

In addition to the issues listed here, an ETL developer has to know that Azure Synapse does not create and update column statistics automatically. When a table is loaded, column statistics must be created or updated manually using the CREATE STATISTICS or UPDATE STATISTICS command.

In this section, we learned about Azure SQL technologies and other data-related technologies, such as Data Factories and serverless Cosmos DB storage. Now, let's move back to on-premises environments and learn how to utilize hybrid SQL Server scenarios.

Microsoft SQL Server 2019 and hybrid scenarios

While the previous section showed several clear Azure deployments of SQL Server, SQL Server is traditionally hosted on-premises. As data contention grows over time, administrators face the challenge of handling the increased storage space needed for data or for backups, as well as **Recovery Time Objectives (RTO)** and **Recovery Point Objectives (RPO)**.

Migration to an Azure environment is not always easy or possible. That's why Microsoft incorporated many enhancements in SQL Server to help DBAs succeed when facing these situations. In the following sections, we will go through these enhancements and show you how to use them. Every section contains appropriate situations for using them and also a detailed description of their implementation.

In the next section, we will explore the first hybrid scenario: data files in Azure.

Data files in Azure

Data files in Azure is a topology in which SQL Server runs on-premise or as an Azure VM. The metadata of user databases is stored in its master database, but the files of these user databases are hosted in Azure blob storage. This feature is useful in scenarios where a database is often migrated between instances or we want to divide the instance and the data. This topology also benefits from the ability of snapshot backups, which will be mentioned at the end of this section.

First of all, an Azure Storage account has to be created. This can be done in the Azure portal, as shown in the following screenshot:

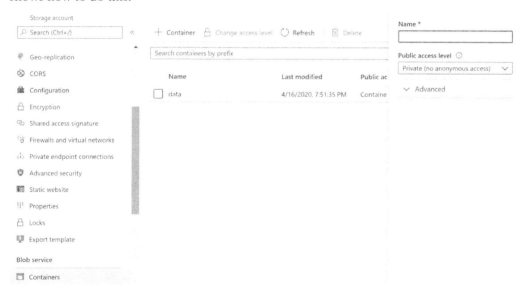

Fig. 11.10 – New Azure Storage account creation in the Azure portal

We must fill in several properties, such as name and placement, for the **Storage account** option. After doing this, the Storage account will be prepared and empty.

Now, we have to go into the Storage account and create a **container**. A container is a physical place for placing files; we can think of it as a folder. The following screenshot shows how to do this:

Fig. 11.11 – How to create new container within Azure Storage

The container has a name and a **Public access level** property. This should be set to private, as shown in the previous screenshot. Once the container has been created, an access policy should be created for it with at least **Read**, **Write**, and **List** permissions. Delete permissions are preferred if you will be dropping a database later. The access policy is created in the Azure portal, at the container level.

In the previous steps, the cloud storage was prepared automatically. In the next few steps, we will prepare other security prerequisites for using data files in Azure. SQL Server needs to be authenticated against certain containers. This is done by a server credential. This credential needs to have a secret created for the container in Azure.

Azure portal does not help to correctly create the secret. Fortunately, a free and often used tool called **Microsoft Azure Storage Explorer** solves this issue in the Azure portal. **Microsoft Azure Storage Explorer** is a desktop application and is shown in the following screenshot:

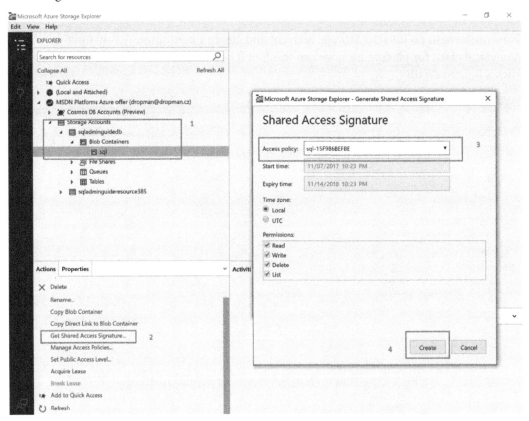

Fig. 11.12 – Where to find Shared Access Signature

As shown in the preceding screenshot, once connected, **Microsoft Azure Storage Explorer** shows all the storage types that can be created within the Azure subscription. However, let's stay focused on the highlighted places. They have been numbered for better orientation:

1. After the connection, we have to expand the **Storage accounts** node – a certain storage account (**sqladminguidedb**, in our example) – to **Blob Containers**, and then we'll see a container being created in the Azure portal (its name is **sql** in our example). Alternatively, we can create one by right-clicking on the **Blob Containers** node.

2. When the **sql** container is selected, the bottom part appears with two tabs: **Properties** and **Actions**. The **Properties** tab is shown by default. The **Actions** tab contains a set of links for certain actions. Here, we have to click **Get Shared Access Signature**.

3. When the **Get Shared Access Signature (SAS)** link is clicked, a dialog is opened for SAS creation. In this dialog, we have to select the access policy we created for the container in Azure portal.

4. When the access policy is selected and the **Create** button is clicked, the dialog window is changed and shows the newly generated SAS.

    This new dialog is shown in the following screenshot:

Fig. 11.13 – SAS in Storage Explorer

The field shown in the red rectangle contains the complete SAS that will be used in the next step. Your query string will differ from the one highlighted in the preceding screenshot. You must also copy the whole string, even if just a portion of it is shown in the highlighted field. We have to copy it before closing the dialog.

> **Note**
>
> The Azure portal also contains an SAS link, but on the Storage account level only. It's too high level and when used for credentials, it does not work! An SAS on the container level must be created.

Once the SAS has been created, we can switch to Management Studio and create the credential. It's not a database scoped credential; it's created in the `master` database. The script for this is as follows:

```
use master
go


create credential [https://sqladminguidedb.blob.core.windows.
net/sql]
with
identity='SHARED ACCESS SIGNATURE',
secret = 'sv=2017-04-17&si=sql-15F986BEFBE&sr=c&sig=4d*********
************3D'
go
```

Let's dive deeper into the preceding script:

- The credential's name has to be a complete link to the container. In our example, the base link to the Storage account is `https://sqladminguidedb.blob.core.windows.net` and the container's name is just `sql`.

- The `identity` property, along with the `SHARED ACCESS SIGNATURE` value, constantly informs SQL Server that this is the credential that's used for Azure container access.

- The `secret` property contains the query string that was generated in the previous step. Keep in mind that the leading question mark must not be there.

Now that all the prerequisites have been completed, the last thing we need to do is create the database. The script for database creation is identical to any other database creation script. The following script creates a database with files placed in Azure:

```
create database FilesInAzure
on
(
name = 'FilesInAzureData',
filename = 'https://sqladminguidedb.blob.core.windows.net/sql/
masterfile.mdf'
)
log on
(
name = 'FilesInAzureLog',
filename = 'https://sqladminguidedb.blob.core.windows.net/sql
/logfile.ldf'
)
go
```

Once the database has been created, we can go back to **Microsoft Azure Storage Explorer** or to the Azure portal and we will see that the necessary files have been created in the container.

Creating databases with files placed in Azure Blob storage is the same for on-premise and Azure virtual machines. From on-premise instances, a worse response time could be issued when the internet connection being used is not capable enough, but when combining an Azure SQL Server VM with data files in Azure, the response is very good. The only limitation is that such a database cannot be bigger than 1 TB.

Using data files in Azure offers a very good feature called **snapshot backup**. In the next section, we will learn about all the hybrid backup types, as well as about the snapshot backup. Keep reading!

Backups in Azure

In this section, we will learn how backup operations can be executed and place backup files directly in Azure. Using this approach provides several advantages:

- Backup files are stored reliably due to native Azure data redundancy.
- Backup files are highly accessible from around the world. This helps with database migrations.

- The cost of on-premise storage is always higher than Azure Blob storage.

- Depending on the backup scenario, restoration can be done extremely quickly.

Managed backup to Azure

Managed backup to Azure is probably the first feature of SQL Server that profits from cloud technologies. However, we can back up databases locally and plan backup strategies by jobs created on **SQL Server Agent**. Managed backup to Azure offers an automated way of performing regular backups to Azure blob storage. It is a very good option for backups because we don't need to maintain local storage. We only have to pay for the amount of space consumed in Azure. Managed backup to Azure was introduced in SQL Server 2012 as a fully automated way of doing backups. Since then, managed backup to Azure has been enhanced. Nowadays, we can set our own time schedule for backups or we can back up on demand whenever we need to.

When using managed backup to Azure, the following prerequisites must be fulfilled:

- An Azure blob container must be created.

- An SAS must be generated for the container.

- Credentials must be created in SQL Server.

All three prerequisites were described in the previous section, so here, we will create a managed backup to Azure. The following screenshot shows **Object Explorer** in Management Studio:

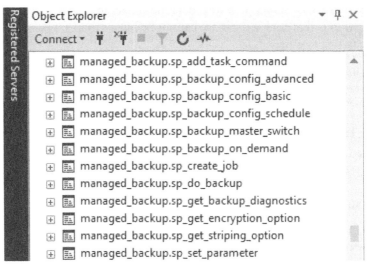

Fig. 11.14 – Stored procedures involved when maintaining managed backups

The preceding screenshot shows some of the stored procedures that are created in the `msdb` database in the `managed_backup` schema. A full description of all stored procedures is available at `https://docs.microsoft.com/en-us/sql/relational-databases/system-stored-procedures/managed-backup-stored-procedures-transact-sql?view=sql-server-ver15`, but for now, let's look at a simple example. We'll use the `demo` database and the Azure Blob storage container from `https://sqladminguidedb.blob.core.windows.net/bck` here. We want to back up the database demo with a default schedule and we also want to keep backup retention for 7 days. The following script shows the solution to this:

```
-- credential has to be created
create credential [https://sqladminguidedb.blob.core.windows.
net/bck]
with
identity='SHARED ACCESS SIGNATURE',
secret = 'sv=2017-04-17&si=bck-15F9EE*****************Fdw%3D'
go


-- procedure managed_backup.sp_backup_config_basic is executed
to setup and start backups
exec msdb.managed_backup.sp_backup_config_basic
  @database_name = 'demo'
  , @enable_backup = 1
  , @container_url = 'https://sqladminguidedb.blob.core.
windows.net/bck'
  , @retention_days = 7
go
```

The preceding script shows the credential's creation, and then the `managed_backup.sp_backup_config_basic` procedure is executed. Let's explore the parameters of this procedure:

- `@database_name`: Basically, this is the name of a certain database. This can be set to `NULL`, and it means that all the databases, including system databases (except the `tempdb` database), will be backed up.

- `@enable_backup`: This parameter is just switched; when it's set to `1`, the backup process starts, while when it's set back to `0`, the managed backups are stopped.

- `@container_url`: The URL to the Azure Blob storage container.

- `@retention_days`: The number of days that backups will be kept for in the Azure Blob container. The default (and the longest retention) is 30 days.

When we want to stop all managed backups to Azure, there's another procedure we can use. The following code shows how to stop all managed backups to Azure at once:

```
exec msdb.managed_backup.sp_backup_master_switch @new_state = 0
go
```

Restoring a database from a managed backup to Azure is done in the same way we described in *Chapter 3, Implementing Backup and Recovery*. When the database is in a **simple recovery model**, just one full backup is used to restore and recover the database. When the database is in at least a **bulk-logged recovery model**, the database can be restored and recovered to its most recent state.

Managed backup is mostly an automated mode of database backup. Another option is to use backup to a URL, which will be described in the next section.

Backup to a URL

Compared to managed backup to Azure, backup to a URL is just a regular backup. It's exactly the same as every other regular backup, as described in *Chapter 3, Implementing Backup and Recovery*. The only exception is that we don't use DISK, but URL, as a backup device. Also, we need the credentials for access to the Azure blob storage. Let's use a database called SimpleDemo, which we want to back up using Azure blobs as backup storage.

First, we need to create some credentials with a shared access policy for the container. The same procedure was described in the previous section. Then, we need to write the following statement:

```
backup database SimpleDemo to url = 'https://sqladminguidedb.
blob.core.windows.net/bck/simpledemo.bak'
with init
```

With backup to URL, we can establish any backup strategy using any backup types according to our backup needs.

When restoring the database, the restore procedure and statements are exactly the same. Again, the only exception is the device type. The following script shows how to restore the SimpleDemo database from a URL:

```
restore database SimpleDemo from url = 'https://
sqladminguidedb.blob.core.windows.net/bck/simpledemo.bak'
with recovery
```

As shown in the preceding script, as we already mentioned, the only difference between the restores described in *Chapter 3, Implementing Backup and Recovery*, is that the `RESTORE` statement is `restore... from url = 'https://...'` instead of `restore ... from disk = 'L:\...'`.

In the next section, we will explore how to use the backups and restores of database files that are already stored in Azure Blob storage.

Snapshot backups

In *Chapter 3, Implementing Backup and Recovery*, we described the process of point-in-time recovery for a database. It contains the restore in sequence, from the full backup to the differential backup (if it exists), and then from all transaction log backups in sequence. This process is time-consuming and affects the RTO negatively.

When we want to ensure the best possible RTO, we can use **backups with file snapshots**. This type of backup is possible for databases whose files have been placed in Azure Blob storage. Backups, when executed, create pointers to snapshots of files. This is very fast and efficient. Backups must also be placed in Azure blob storage. From a DBA's perspective, backups are backups to URLs, as we described in the previous section.

Using backups with file snapshots allows us to recover a database to a certain point in time by using just two backups. That's why there's no need to go through all the regular processes we described in *Chapter 3, Implementing Backup and Recovery*.

From a DBA's perspective, a snapshot backup is a regular backup to a URL. The only prerequisites are as follows:

- To have credentials for access to Azure blob storage
- To have the files of the database placed in Azure blob storage
- To have a database in a **full recovery model**

Let's use a database called `FilesInAzure`. This database has its files in Azure blob storage and the database has set a **full recovery model**. We want to use file snapshots for our backup. The first backup has to be a **full database backup**. The sample script for this is as follows:

```
backup database FilesInAzure to url = 'https://sqladminguidedb.
blob.core.windows.net/bck/FilesInAzureFull.bak'
with file_snapshot
```

The `file_snapshot` backup option shown in the preceding script makes all the difference between regular backups and snapshot backups in Azure.

The same option is used in a **transaction log backup** statement. Let's look at the following script:

```
declare @url nvarchar(255) = 'https://sqladminguidedb.blob.
core.windows.net/bck/FilesInAzureLog_'
set @url = @url + convert(sysdatetime, 'yyyyMMddhhmm') + '.bak'
backup log FilesInAzure to url = @url
with file_snapshot
```

The preceding script has one extra feature: it computes a filename for consequential log backup files to keep each log backup in its own file. The `declare` statement in this script is just a variable declaration and initiation with a constant part of the device path. The `set` statement adds a date and time as a formatted string, and a file extension is also added to the `@url` variable.

When we need to perform a database restore, we need to have three backups:

- The full backup
- The last transaction log backup for when we want to restore the database to the most recent point in time
- The first transaction log backup after the time of failure

Let's consider the `FilesInAzure` database. This database has files in Azure blob storage and it is also regularly backed up to a URL. Let's say we need to restore the database because we have encountered an error in data. The following script shows the process of recovering from this:

```
restore database FilesInAzure from url = 'https://
sqladminguidedb.blob.core.windows.net/sql/FilesInAzureFull.bak'
with norecovery, replace

restore log FilesInAzure from url = 'https://sqladminguidedb.
blob.core.windows.net/sql/FilesInAzureLog_201711082300.bak'
with recovery, stopat = '2017-11-07 03:00pm'
```

From the preceding script, SQL Server recognizes which backups must be restored. The restore and recovery process is then very fast, and the database has minimal possible downtime.

Quick overview of running SQL workloads in Azure

In the world of growing cloud solutions, we shouldn't consider that this is the end of a DBA's job; rather, we should be prepared to adopt the cloud in the future. This section highlights several considerations that are useful for further cloud adoption. We will explain the differences between three aspects of SQL workloads regarding on-premises and Azure environments. We will talk about licensing, SLA, disaster recovery, and regular database maintenance in detail.

Licensing

Every software product needs to be licensed properly, and this is completely true for SQL Server as well. In on-premises environments, we need to know how SQL Server will be provisioned as a standalone instance on virtual machines, or in an **active-passive** versus **active-active** failover cluster.

In the cloud, licensing has different rules. The most important aspect is the type of resource hosting to be used. As you may recall, we have three options for resource provisioning in the cloud:

- **IaaS**: **Infrastructure as a service**. A typical case for IaaS is a virtual machine with a SQL Server instance installed on it.

- **PaaS**: **Platform as a Service**. As an example, we can show Azure SQL Database or Azure **SQL Managed Instance**.

- **SaaS**: **Software as a Service**. This resource hosting type is not typically used for data processing technologies, but as an example of a technology that tightly cooperates with a data platform. **Azure Stream Analytics** is an Azure resource that is used to read stream messages from **Event Hubs** or **IoT Hubs** (which are actually other SaaS resources transform the data, and finally store the data in a target storage such as blobs, Cosmos DB, or even SQL databases. The definition of the Azure Stream Analytics job is just one SQL (called **ASA SQL**) query. The query processor and other components are all maintained by Microsoft.

The preceding list is very important to determine shared responsibility. Every resource, every service or application, is developed, deployed, and maintained throughout its lifetime. In on-premises environments, the responsibility for each phase of the resource life cycle is completely on local developers, network administrators, security experts, but also on DBAs. In cloud environments, the responsibility is shared between the cloud provider and the customer. As the resource hosting type is growing from IaaS to SaaS, the portion of responsibility is moved from customers to the cloud provider site.

But what does this mean for SQL workloads in Azure? When SQL databases are hosted within a virtual machine in Azure, the license of the underlying operating system, as well as the license of the SQL Server, is up to the customer. By the way, when a new SQL Server virtual machine is provisioned as a new resource in Azure, the blade in the Azure portal contains a configuration where a license key can be added, if the customer has one. This saves approximately 33% of operational expenses in the future.

On the other hand, with PaaS hosting, we do not care about license keys because we are not hosting a whole instance of SQL Server –just a database or a group of databases.

So, how can we conclude this paragraph? It is not difficult to recognize that even if IaaS hosting is quite easy, the first step in cloud adoption is to move the workload to PaaS hosting as soon as possible. This is because it moves the licensing part of the responsibility to Microsoft.

Shared responsibility also affects another criterion – the **Service License Agreement (SLA)**.

SLA

The SLA promises the availability of resources in a timely manner to users. Usually, we describe the SLA level in terms of a percentage. In common information systems, we will have 1-day outages (planned or unplanned) in a year. Here, the SLA can be calculated as 1 – 1/365. The result of this formula is approximately 99.73 % availability of the information system during the year. In Azure, every resource has its SLA determined by Microsoft. The SLA of each resource can be increased or decreased using built-in features. For Azure SQL databases, the SLA starts at 99.9 %, depending on the pricing level, zone redundancy, and geo-replication. Details of the SLA for Azure SQL databases can change over time, so the best way to ensure you have what is needed for the desired SLA level is to follow this link: `https://azure.microsoft.com/en-us/support/legal/sla/sql-database/v1_4/`.

The whole SLA is calculated from partial SLAs of all the resources that form the information system. The availability formula is quite simple. It multiplies all the partial availabilities, and the result is the overall availability of the information system.

The availability of a database ensures that the service will be accessible to users. Even if the service is still running, data could be corrupted. In the next section, we will see the options for recovering corrupted data.

Disaster recovery

Except Azure SQL Server, which is an IaaS resource, Azure offers **automated backups**. The configuration process for automated backups is simple. The following screenshot shows the **Manage Backups** blade in the Azure portal:

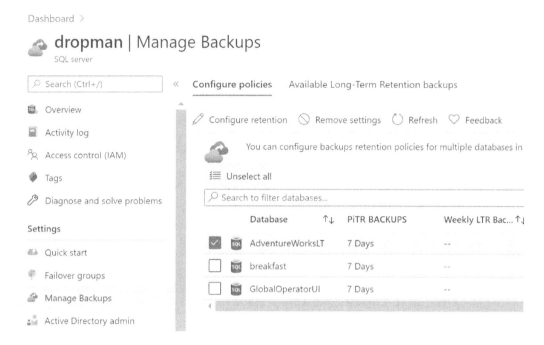

Fig. 11.15 – How to configure automated backups using the Azure portal

On the blade shown in the preceding screenshot, we can select one or more databases. Using the **Configure retention** button, we can configure how many days the automated backup will be available for. The time range is between 7 and 35 days. We can also configure the **Available Long-Term Retention backups** option. The LTR backup can be used to restore a database to a certain state (that is, the first day in a month).

Restoring a database is a very simple task using the Azure portal. When we recognize that the database needs to be restored, we can simply visit the database in Azure portal and use the **Restore** button, as shown in the following screenshot:

Fig. 11.16 – Starting a database restore using the Azure portal

The preceding screenshot shows a part of the **Overview** blade of the **AdventureWorksLT** sample database. When the **Restore** button is clicked, the **Create SQL Database – Restore database** blade is opened. This blade allows the DBA to select which backup will be used for recovery. The following screenshot shows this blade:

Dashboard > AdventureWorksLT (dropman/AdventureWorksLT) >

Create SQL Database - Restore database
Microsoft

Basics   Review + create

Project details

Select the subscription to manage deployed resources and costs. Use resource groups like folders to organize and manage all your resources.

Subscription ⓘ   MSDN Platforms Azure offer   ∨

└── Resource group ⓘ   AdventureWorksLT   ∨

Source Details

Select a backup source and details. Additional settings will be defaulted where possible based on the backup selected.

Source Database   AdventureWorksLT

Select source   Point-in-time   ∨

Earliest restore point   2020-07-03 00:00 UTC

Restore point (UTC)   07/10/2020   📅   11:07:00 AM

ⓘ Choose a restore point between earliest restore point and latest backup time which is 6 minute before current time.

Fig. 11.17 – The Restore database blade in the Azure portal

As shown in the preceding screenshot, the database can be recovered to a certain point in time or it can use an LTR backup when it is selected with the **Select source** drop-down control.

By comparing on-premises and PaaS Azure disaster recovery tasks, we can see that using PaaS database hosting makes a DBA's life easier. Disaster recovery is not only a task – we must also maintain the content of the database. In the next section, we will learn how to keep data defragmented, how to check for the consistency of data, and how to perform other common tasks.

Regular database maintenance

The common myth is that when PaaS database hosting is utilized, many common issues simply go away. Unfortunately, this is not true. Let's recall the common tasks that should be maintained by a DBA:

- Index defragmentation
- Statistics recompute
- Consistency checks
- Performance monitoring and tuning

For all these tasks, we can go back to *Chapter 8, Automation – Using Tools to Manage and Monitor SQL Server 2019*; everything from this chapter will work in Azure SQL database, as well as in Azure **SQL Managed Instance**. There is no difference between the two. Also, monitoring tools such as **Extended Events** or **dynamic management objects** are almost the same. Compared to on-premise environments, we can use the **Automatic tuning** feature in Azure.

Automatic tuning is based on pretrained machine learning models, which are used to estimate index creation or removal, as well as the option to force a plan if the same query has had two or more execution plans generated for it and some of the plans are not optimal. In the Azure portal, we can visit the database where we would like **Automatic tuning** to be turned on. Here, we will see the blade that's shown in the following screenshot:

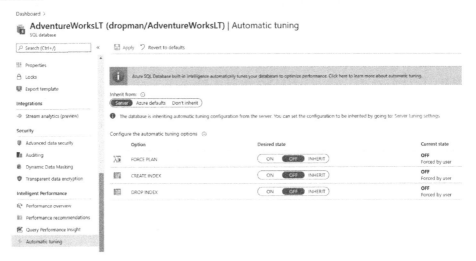

Fig. 11.18 – How to turn on the Automatic tuning feature in Azure portal

As shown in the preceding screenshot, we can turn on three parts of Automatic tuning – Force plan, Create index, and Drop index. Automatic tuning simplifies performance tuning in many cases and is very helpful for customers who are not experienced with performance monitoring and tuning. Even if we utilize the Automatic tuning feature in Azure when the database or client applications are not designed well, Automatic tuning will yield performance problems and it will not resolve them completely.

In this section, we explored many aspects of SQL databases already hosted in Azure. However, many organizations have their databases hosted in on-premises environments as well. In the next section, we will look at the basics of migrating databases to Azure.

Migrating SQL Server workloads to Azure

Every migration project is very complex, and this is the same for migrating our on-premises resources to the cloud. We can combine many techniques and recipes, but we will only pay attention to three resources and tools for database migration. Basically, we need to ask questions such as, where should we start the migration? How can we prepare for the migration in terms of pre-migration steps? The following sections will answer these questions, and more.

Using Azure Database Migration Guide

Azure Database Migration Guide is a website that contains detailed wizards for the whole migration process, from the preparation steps until the final check for the quality of the migrated data. The site can be found at `https://datamigration.microsoft.com/`. On the home page, as shown in the following screenshot, we are shown many possible data sources that can be migrated to Azure:

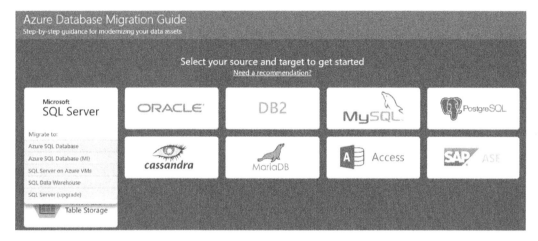

Fig. 11.19 – Home page of Azure Database Migration Guide

In the preceding screenshot, we can see that the migration supported by Microsoft is not only from SQL Servers to the cloud, but that Microsoft also supports many other data sources that can possibly be migrated to the cloud. Each tile in the preceding screenshot contains popup menus showing different ways to migrate. In the preceding screenshot, we can see that SQL Server workloads can be migrated to Azure SQL Database, Azure SQL MI, and so on. Clicking the right destination for the migration redirects Azure Database Migration Guide to the specified topic and provides a step-by-step recipe that will help us succeed with the migration. Besides the required network configuration, we can use the following tools for migration:

- SQL Server Migration Assistant
- Data Migration Assistant
- Azure Database Migration Service

We will look at these tools in the following sections.

Using SQL Server Migration Assistant

SQL Server Migration Assistant (SSMA) is a tool that is offered by Microsoft for free. A typical scenario for SSMA is when we have a heterogenous database environment and we are going to decommission a data processing workload from another database engine to SQL Server. This is why the SSMA can be downloaded as the following alternatives:

- SSMA for Access

- SSMA for DB2

- SSMA for MySQL

- SSMA for Oracle

- SSMA for SAP ASE

Before migration, we should know what the type of the source data is. We will download and install the proper alternative of SSMA from this URL: `https://docs.microsoft.com/en-us/sql/ssma/sql-server-migration-assistant?view=sql-server-ver15`. SSMA maintains migration projects. After installation, we need to create a new project using the **File – New Project** option from the upper application menu. The dialog for this will look as follows:

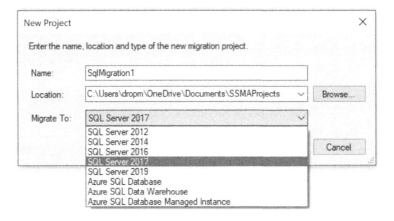

Fig. 11.20 – Creating a new migration project in SSMA for Oracle

The preceding screenshot was taken from SSMA for Oracle and it shows all the possible target SQL alternatives. As we can see, the SSMA allows us to migrate data to SQL Server (or Azure SQL databases), but it does not allow us to migrate databases to any database engine.

Once the project has been created, we will follow the upper toolbox, as shown in the following screenshot:

Fig. 11.21 – Using the SSMA toolbox

Let's go from the left to the right of the preceding toolbox. We will connect to the Oracle schema and then we will connect to the empty target SQL database. When both connections are successful, we can generate a report showing all the differences between Oracle and SQL Server objects and source code; that is, non-migratable Oracle stored procedures and so on. When an object, typically stored procedures, or functions cannot be migrated, the SSMA estimates the effort needed to rewrite the object's code. This is a very useful feature of SSMA because it helps to plan the time and expenses needed to migrate a certain Oracle schema to SQL Server.

The table structures can be migrated using the **Convert Schema** button. This feature will generate a migration script that can be executed on the target SQL Server. Last, but not least, when the schema is created on the target machine, we can execute data migration.

SSMA can be used in both on-premise to on-premise migration and for on-premise to Azure migration. When we have smaller databases already hosted by an on-premise SQL Server and we want to migrate them to Azure, we can use a helpful migration tool called Data Migration Assistant.

Using Data Migration Assistant

Data Migration Assistant (DMA) is another useful tool and can be downloaded from `https://www.microsoft.com/en-us/download/details.aspx?id=53595`. Unlike SSMA, DMA can be used just for migrations between SQL Server and Azure SQL data solutions. When the DMA is started, the following screen will appear:

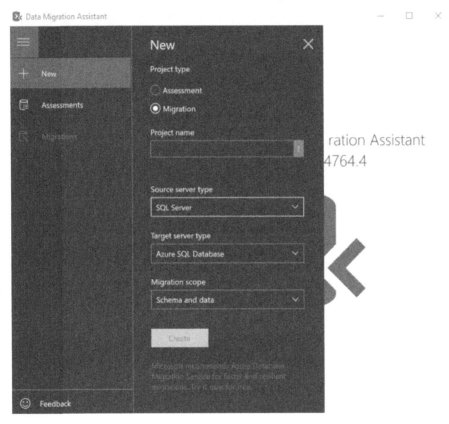

Fig. 11.22 – Home screen for DMA

As shown in the preceding screenshot, we will create a named project with **Assessment** or **Migration**. While **Assessment** just assesses the compatibility between the selected source and target, **Migration** actually moves data from the source to the target.

Once the project has been created, the rest of the migration process is a wizard that works in the following manner:

1. Configure source connection.

2. Configure target connection.

3. Select objects from the source database.

4. Generate migration script.

5. Deploy the schema.

6. Migrate data to the schema.

The preceding recipe allows us to migrate the database in parts. We do not need to migrate the database as a whole. This is very useful for scenarios where we have the migration planned as more phases or we can just test the migration.

DMA is used mostly for one-time migrations, but if we want to migrate data incrementally and if we want to automate the migration tasks, we can use one more tool that's fully managed by Azure. This tool is Azure Database Migration Service. Let's see what it entails.

Using Azure Database Migration Service

Unlike the other tools we've described so far, **Azure Database Migration Service (DMS)** can't be installed; instead, it is an Azure resource. It intends to fully maintain repeatable migration of on-premises data to the cloud. The following screenshot shows how to create a DMS instance:

Create Migration Service

Basics   Networking   Tags   Review + create

Azure Database Migration Service is designed to streamline the process of migrating on-premises databases to Azure. Learn more. ☒

Project details

Select the subscription to manage deployed resources and consts. Use resource groups as you would folders, to organize and manage all of your resources.

Subscription * ⓘ	MSDN Platforms Azure offer ⌄
Resource group * ⓘ	(New) book ⌄
	Create new

Instance details

Migration service name * ⓘ	book
Location * ⓘ	West Europe ⌄
Service mode * ⓘ	(Azure Hybrid (Preview))

Fig. 11.23 – Creating a DMS instance using the Azure portal

As shown in the preceding screenshot, the creation process is very straightforward. The tricky part is that the DMS is not open to the internet. This means it can only connect to a dedicated **VPN** or **ExpressRoute** (see `https://docs.microsoft.com/en-us/azure/expressroute/expressroute-introduction`). Hence, we need to ask our network administrator to establish the connection between our Azure subscription and on-premises data center. In other words, the DMS will not work.

While the DMS instance is being created, we can start to define the migration tasks using the Azure portal. We will work in a similar way to how we worked when using DMA. We will create a new project and then define the activities containing the source, the target, and the portions of the source database to be migrated. Once we've done this, we can execute partial migrations and monitor their behavior.

All these data processing disciplines are still evolving, and we must change our mindset and prepare for new challenges brought to us by the cloud. Moreover, there are other great resources in Azure we can discuss, but for now, we will continue focusing on the SQL solutions available to us. However, with cloud technologies here to stay, we should be prepared for more technologies being used in more scenarios for streams of data, data generated globally, and so on.

Summary

Microsoft offers a complete yet ever-growing cloud ecosystem for data processing in Azure. In this chapter, we explored all the possible SQL Server and SQL database scenarios. Although there are other technologies, such as Data Factory for ETL processes, machine learning for building predictive models and analytics, and so on, these technologies and features are beyond the scope of this book.

In this chapter, we summarized various scenarios for a data platform that had been placed in the cloud. The first of them, Azure SQL database, is provided as a service for hosting isolated databases. The second option we looked at was Azure **SQL Managed Instance**, which ensures 100% compatibility with an on-premise SQL Server. The last option we looked at was the very powerful Azure Synapse service, which is used to maintain and load balance a massively parallel data warehouse to fulfil the most demanding performance requirements.

After this, we looked at different hybrid scenarios that combine on-premises instances of SQL Server with Azure technologies. At the start of this section, we created an on-premise database and placed its files in Azure blob storage. The sub-sections following this described several backup and recovery scenarios that profit from the almost bottomless storage capacity provided by Azure.

Finally, we provided a brief overview of how to maintain Azure SQL solutions, as well as how to migrate SQL databases to Azure to profit from what's on offer from Microsoft Azure.

In the next chapter, *Chapter 12, Taming Big Data with SQL Server*, we will dive into the principles of how to combine big data with the traditional SQL approach of data manipulation.

12
Taming Big Data with SQL Server

In this last chapter, we will work with data outside of SQL Server. We will introduce technologies that can be used to access external data that also have capabilities that are used for big data processing. One of the newest features of SQL Server 2019 is known as Big Data Clusters, which combines the workload of SQL Server, scalable storage filesystems, and the Spark engine using containers managed by Kubernetes. This will take us away from the common relational data approach we are used to in SQL Server.

In this chapter, we will cover the following main topics:

- Big data overview
- Accessing external data with PolyBase
- Explaining the SQL Server Big Data Clusters architecture and deployment
- Working with a SQL Server Big Data Clusters workload

Let's get started!

Big data overview

Big data has garnered an immense following in the data industry and with SQL Server's entry, it is a new ball game altogether! In this chapter, we will explore the big data phenomenon, along with the part SQL Server plays in it.

Big data processing brings several challenges. The 5Vs of big data present those challenges:

- **Volume**: This represents the quantity of the data. Just imagine that, during 2020, the digital universe is expected to reach the size of 40 ZB (zettabytes). The challenge here is to store, replicate, and consume such a huge volume. The next year, the volume will be larger again.

- **Veracity**: This represents the quality of the data, which can vary greatly. Not every information system or source of data produces the same quality data. Data can be incomplete and have missing information or it can be inconsistent, and while processing such datasets, you must implement the data cleansing process to overcome such challenges.

- **Variety**: This represents the nature of the data – text, images, video, or audio. The days of simple text data organized as a relational table are long gone. With the release of machine learning and AI, you can easily analyze image, text, audio, and video to get metadata from such sources. This data can be used for further analysis. The challenge here is to process the nature of the data correctly.

- **Velocity**: This represents the speed of the data generation process, which is also related to real-time data. Although the datasets can be small, the influx of data generated by IoT devices and sensors can be very fast, which represents another challenge for such data processing.

- **Value**: This represents the information that can be extracted from the data. The fact that we have access to data does not necessarily mean we can extract valuable information. This overlaps with veracity, where the data quality is not sufficient.

As there are numerous challenges when it comes to big data processing, and there is no easy approach to building a system for ingesting and analyzing big data. We'll dive into several topics to discover how SQL Server can help with big data processing.

Each year, businesses are being challenged to ingest, store, and analyze more data than ever before. Such large datasets require scaled storage that's ready for such workloads and a proper processing infrastructure capable of delivering the results in a fast-paced world. With the increase of computing power, electronic devices, and accessibility to the internet, more data than ever is being produced, collected, and transmitted. Organizations have recognized the power of data analysis but are struggling to manage the massive amounts of information they have. There are numerous industries facing such challenges, including, but not limited to, the following:

- Finance

- Healthcare

- Manufacturing

- Retail

Next, we'll look at how to access external data with PolyBase.

Accessing external data with PolyBase

PolyBase has been available in SQL Server since SQL Server 2016, where it introduced the concept of data virtualization. With SQL Server 2019, PolyBase has been greatly enhanced with numerous features and provides support for more data sources, including the following:

- SQL Server

- Oracle

- HDFS

- MongoDB and others

Outside the common SQL Server deployments, the actual first release of PolyBase was available with **Parallel Data Warehouse** (a SQL Server workload available as **Analytical Appliance**) and **Azure Synapse Analytics** (formerly known as **Azure SQL Data Warehouse**).

PolyBase is a technology that helps you deliver data virtualization. Simultaneously, data virtualization allows you to access data from the original location without any need for data movement. Instead of moving the data from the source and importing the data into a central location for analysis, the data is simply retrieved through a query.

In the following diagram, you can see what data sources can be accessed with PolyBase. Many of these data sources don't require any specific libraries or drivers to work, although there may be exceptions, such as SAP HANA, that do require proper ODBC drivers to be installed on the system:

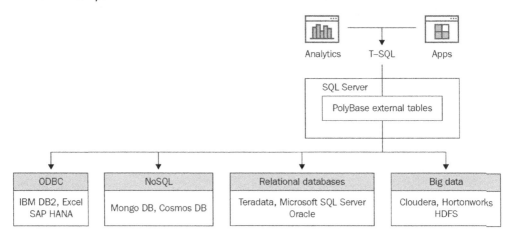

Fig. 12.1 – PolyBase data virtualization access

Now, let's look at the use cases for PolyBase.

PolyBase use cases

There are numerous cases for PolyBase usage, as follows:

- **Loading**: PolyBase can be used for data loads, which omits its data virtualization capability, where the data can be loaded into SQL Server from various data sources. You can use external systems such as Hadoop to perform **Extract-Transform-Load** (**ETL**) to cleanse the data before it's loaded into the database or data warehouse.

- **Interactive Query**: If the data stays in the original data source, you can use Interactive Query to access external relational or semi-structured data for processing.

- **Data aging**: If the data is getting old and you would like to move the data to cold storage for storage optimization purposes, you can leverage the **Hadoop distributed filesystem** (**HDFS**). With PolyBase, the data remains accessible for querying while it's being moved to cold storage.

With PolyBase, data is exposed as an external table. This is based on a file format (it could be any of `csv`, `gzip`, `parquet`, and so on) with a proper data source. In the following sections, we'll learn how to install PolyBase and create external tables for it.

Installing and configuring PolyBase

The PolyBase feature can be installed as an additional feature for your SQL Server instance. You can select not only PolyBase, but also **Java connector for HDFS data sources**. With HDFS, there's the option to use pushdown functionality, which improves the performance of external data access. For such instances, PolyBase uses **MapReduce**, which must also be available on the Hadoop cluster, together with **Yet Another Resource Negotiator** or **YARN** (a resource management and job scheduling daemon). If Java is already installed on the system with a proper version, SQL Server will detect it and won't install a new JRE. As a matter of fact, PolyBase can only be installed on a single instance of your SQL Server.

In the following screenshot, you can see the PolyBase feature, with **PolyBase Query Service for External Data** and **Java connector for HDFS data sources** being selected for the installation:

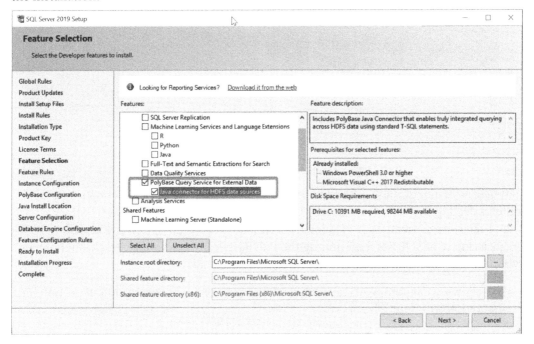

Fig. 12.2 – Installing PolyBase

If you do choose to install the PolyBase feature, you will need to configure PolyBase as another step of the installation wizard. Here, you have to choose whether PolyBase should be installed as a standalone or scale-out group, as shown in the following screenshot:

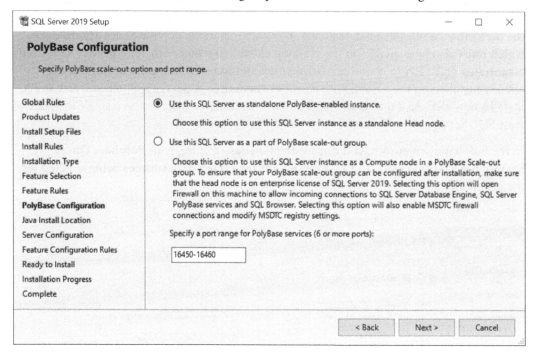

Fig. 12.3 – PolyBase scale-out group configuration

PolyBase scale-out groups are used to overcome performance bottlenecks on single-node systems dealing with massive datasets. Usually, data is stored in Azure Blob Storage, a Data Lake storage account, or Hadoop. A scale-out group is an option if you wish to create a cluster of SQL Servers running the PolyBase feature for increased throughput and performance by scaling out and parallelizing the workload.

In the following diagram, you can see the architecture of a PolyBase scale-out group configuration with multiple servers:

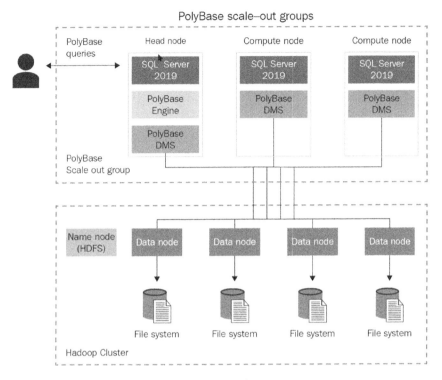

Fig. 12.4 – PolyBase scale-out groups

In such a configuration, we have two different PolyBase nodes running with SQL Server 2019 – a **Head node** and a **Compute node**. The Head node is used for user interaction and receives submitted queries. Compute nodes then assist in query processing the external data stored in the **Data node**. While there's always only one Head node, you can have multiple Compute nodes in your PolyBase scale-out group. Each Compute node runs a **PolyBase Data Movement Service** (**DMS**), which is responsible for two data flows – between the **Compute node** and the **Head node** and between various **Compute nodes** and HDFS. When you use a PolyBase scale-out group, all the nodes need to follow a set of rules:

- All nodes must be members of the same domain.

- All nodes must use the same service account for PolyBase installation.

- All nodes need to run the same version of SQL Server.

- Network connectivity is open between the nodes for the selected ports for the scale-out group.

As shown in the following screenshot, you must provide an **Account Name** for the **SQL Server PolyBase Engine** and **SQL Server PolyBase Data Movement** services. If you're using scale-out groups, this account needs to be the same on all nodes:

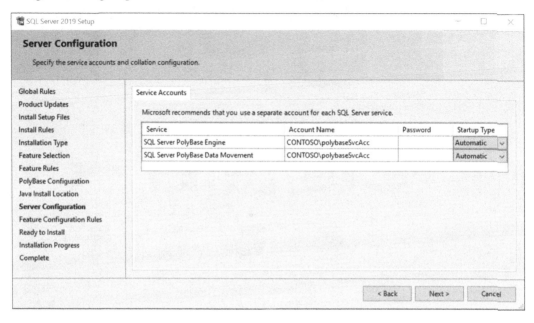

Fig. 12.5 – PolyBase service account configuration

Once the setup is finished, firewall rules are automatically created for the PolyBase engine based on the configuration – a single node or scale-out group. These rules are only created if the **Windows Firewall** is running. If the firewall service is stopped, no rules will be created. If your environment is using a third-party firewall solution, you have to implement the firewall rules yourself. From the range of ports provided in the PolyBase configuration setup dialog, PolyBase uses the first six available ports.

Once PolyBase has been installed, you also have to enable PolyBase with T-SQL. In **SQL Server Management Studio**, you will need to run the following script to enable this feature:

```
exec sp_configure 'polybase enabled', 1
GO
RECONFIGURE
```

Using PolyBase to access external data

Accessing external data using PolyBase enables you to query data in various data sources outside of SQL Server. Based on the external data source, you have to configure your PolyBase instance so that it uses the proper connectivity type. This can be achieved with T-SQL, as shown in the following example:

```
sp_configure 'hadoop connectivity', 7
GO
RECONFIGURE
GO
```

There are several connectivity type values you can choose from:

- 0: Disable Hadoop connectivity
- 1: Hortonworks HDP 1.3 on Windows Server
- 1: Azure blob storage (WASB[S])
- 2: Hortonworks HDP 1.3 on Linux
- 3: Cloudera CDH 4.3 on Linux
- 4: Hortonworks HDP 2.0 on Windows Server
- 4: Azure blob storage (WASB[S])
- 5: Hortonworks HDP 2.0 on Linux
- 6: Cloudera 5.1, 5.2, 5.3, 5.4, 5.5, 5.9, 5.10, 5.11, 5.12, and 5.13 on Linux
- 7: Hortonworks 2.1, 2.2, 2.3, 2.4, 2.5, 2.6, 3.0 on Linux
- 7: Hortonworks 2.1, 2.2, and 2.3 on Windows Server
- 7: Azure blob storage (WASB[S])

Once this connectivity has been configured, you must create two security objects – a master key and a database scoped credential. MASTER KEY is used to encrypt the credential secrets. If there's no master key in the database, you can create one with the following T-SQL:

```
CREATE MASTER KEY ENCRYPTION BY PASSWORD = '<strong password>'
```

Once the master key has been created, you can configure DATABASE SCOPED CREDENTIAL, which is used for authenticating to the external data source. The database scoped credential is only available in the database where it was created. If you want to access the external resources from another database, you'll need to create the scoped credentials again.

We will use the following script to create the database scoped credential for accessing the Azure Blob Storage account. With Azure Blob Storage, the WITH IDENTITY field is not used for authentication, which means you can put any value in this field:

```
CREATE DATABASE SCOPED CREDENTIAL AzureStorageCredential
WITH IDENTITY = 'user', Secret = '<azure_storage_account_key>'
```

Once the database scoped credential has been used, two more objects are required – the file format and the data source. These can be found in **SQL Server Management Studio**, as shown in the following screenshot:

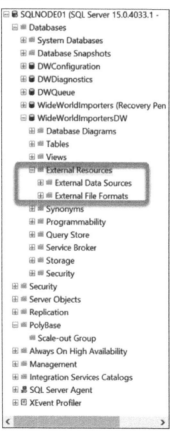

Fig. 12.6 – External Resources

There are three constructs required for accessing external data via PolyBase, as follows:

- External File Formats
- External Data Sources
- External Tables

External File Formats are used to define the structure of the data. In this example, we will use a CSV file stored in Azure Blob Storage. We will use **External File Formats** to define the formatting. There are several file type options available:

- Delimited Text
- Hive ORC
- Hive RCFile
- Parquet
- JSON (this file format is only available with an Azure SQL Edge deployment)

The external file format also defines the delimiter text for delimited files, the date format if there's a date stored, and so on.

Let's create an external file format for our example with the following T-SQL code:

```
CREATE EXTERNAL FILE FORMAT TextFileFormat
WITH (
      FORMAT_TYPE = DELIMITEDTEXT,
      FORMAT_OPTIONS (FIELD_TERMINATOR ='|', USE_TYPE_DEFAULT =
TRUE)
)
```

The preceding code creates a file format for a delimited text file (CSV file) where the columns (called fields in the definition) are split by the | character. Other very common options for termination are space ' ', tabulator \t, and many others.

Based on the file type, you can also use compression. For text delimited files, you can use GZIP compression, but for the compression and data retrieval process to work properly, the file needs to have a .gz extension.

Once the file format has been defined, we also need to configure the data source. For the data source definition, we will need the credential that was created in the previous sample code. With Azure Blob Storage, we have to provide a proper address that includes the name of the storage account – in this example, it is `polybasedemo2019`. Also, in the storage account, you need to create a container to store the blobs – in this example, the name of the container is `data`. There are several locations available that have proper location prefixes based on the external data source. The most common are as follows:

- `wasbs`: For Azure Blob Storage
- `hdfs`: For Cloudera or Hortonworks platforms
- `sqlserver`: For SQL Server
- `odbc`: For any generic connection with a proper driver installed

You can find the documentation for creating the external data source at the following link. It also provides the full list of location prefixes: `https://docs.microsoft.com/en-us/sql/t-sql/statements/create-external-data-source-transact-sql?view=sql-server-ver15`.

We will use the following code to define the external data source with the previously created credential. The location of the files will be based on your available storage account:

```
CREATE EXTERNAL DATA SOURCE AzureStorage with (
      TYPE = HADOOP,
      LOCATION ='wasbs://data@polybasedemo2019.blob.core.
windows.net',
      CREDENTIAL = AzureStorageCredential
);
```

Once all the external resources have been defined, we can finally create the external table. An external table is the definition of the data stored in the external data source; no data is stored in SQL Server, just metadata. An external table is mapped to the external data store definition for the real location of the data.

Let's see what the data looks like in the Azure Storage Account. In the following screenshot, you can see one text file formatted as a CSV file. We will query this by using a combination of an external table, a file format, and a data source:

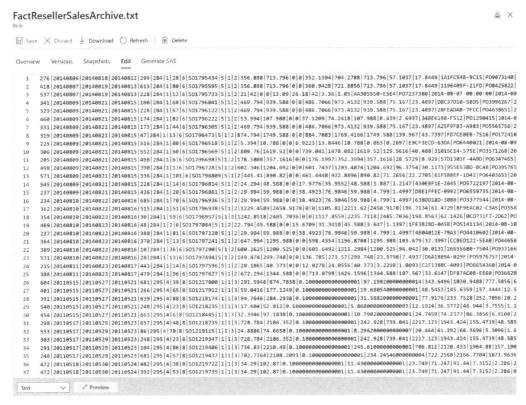

Fig. 12.7 – File structure in Azure Storage Account

To create an external table, use the following T-SQL script:

```sql
CREATE EXTERNAL TABLE dbo.FactResellerSalesArchiveExternal (
    [ProductKey] [int] NOT NULL,
    [OrderDateKey] [int] NOT NULL,
    [DueDateKey] [int] NOT NULL,
    [ShipDateKey] [int] NOT NULL,
    [ResellerKey] [int] NOT NULL,
    [EmployeeKey] [int] NOT NULL,
    [PromotionKey] [int] NOT NULL,
    [CurrencyKey] [int] NOT NULL,
    [SalesTerritoryKey] [int] NOT NULL,
    [SalesOrderNumber] [nvarchar](20) NOT NULL,
    [SalesOrderLineNumber] [tinyint] NOT NULL,
    [RevisionNumber] [tinyint] NULL,
    [OrderQuantity] [smallint] NULL,
    [UnitPrice] [money] NULL,
    [ExtendedAmount] [money] NULL,
```

```
        [UnitPriceDiscountPct] [float] NULL,
        [DiscountAmount] [float] NULL,
        [ProductStandardCost] [money] NULL,
        [TotalProductCost] [money] NULL,
        [SalesAmount] [money] NULL,
        [TaxAmt] [money] NULL,
        [Freight] [money] NULL,
        [CarrierTrackingNumber] [nvarchar](25) NULL,
        [CustomerPONumber] [nvarchar](25) NULL,
        [OrderDate] [datetime] NULL,
        [DueDate] [datetime] NULL,
        [ShipDate] [datetime] NULL
)
WITH (
        LOCATION='/',
        DATA_SOURCE=AzureStorage,
        FILE_FORMAT=TextFile
);
```

The way we create the external table is nearly the same as creating a regular table in the database. The major difference here is the addition of the location, data source, and file format. The LOCATION parameter is used for defining the folder structure in the proper container on your Azure Storage Account. In this case, this container is your external filesystem.

To query this external table, you can use the regular SELECT statement. The following T-SQL code will retrieve all the rows and a filtered set of rows:

```
SELECT * FROM dbo.FactResellerSalesArchiveExternal -- returns
all rows from CSV file
```

```
SELECT * FROM dbo.FactResellerSalesArchiveExternal -- returns
filtered set of rows
WHERE SalesAmount > 1000;
```

Although the table is external, it can be used with all the tables in the database with operations such as JOIN. This provides you with a great opportunity to combine your relational data with semi-structured data stored in external files.

While working with an external table, you can also create statistics on the table columns for better optimization, such as pushdown operations. Pushdown operations work with Hadoop data sources, where SQL Server can initialize the **MapReduce** job to retrieve the rows that match the filter predicate in the query. This can save significant time for performing operations on large datasets with proper filters. Pushdown operations can be used with the following:

- A subset of rows
- A subset of columns

To enable pushdown operations with Hadoop storage, you need to edit the `yarn-site.xml` file in the installation path of your SQL Server. To do this, go to the SQL Server 2019 path, `C:\Program Files\Microsoft SQL Server\MSSQL15.MSSQLSERVER\MSSQL\Binn\PolyBase\Hadoop\conf`, and edit the `yarn.application.classpath` property.

> **Information**
>
> More information about the pushdown configuration can be found on the Microsoft documentation website at `https://docs.microsoft.com/en-us/sql/relational-databases/polybase/polybase-configure-hadoop?view=sql-server-ver15#pushdown`.

Explaining the SQL Server Big Data Clusters architecture and deployment

SQL Server **Big Data Clusters** (**BDC**) is a piece of technology – a combination of three distinct services – available in the latest release of SQL Server. The BDC combine SQL Server, **Apache Spark**, and the HDFS filesystem to store data. All three components run in the **Kubernetes** environment. These three components run side-by-side to provide you with the capability to process and analyze big data, as well as combine a relational workload with a big data workload.

The BDC heavily rely on numerous open source technologies, which are used together for deploying, maintaining, and monitoring the solution.

BDC deployment is based on a full installation of SQL Server 2019 running in a container based on a Linux OS image, orchestrated via the Kubernetes engine. You can use various Kubernetes environments, such as the following:

- **Azure Kubernetes Service (AKS)**
- **Azure Red Hat OpenShift (ARO)**
- **Red Hat OpenShift**
- **Multiple machines**

Once Kubernetes has been configured, you can deploy BDC with the **azdata** utility. The great benefit of deploying via Azure Data Studio or the Python deployment script available with BDC is the automatic configuration of your Kubernetes environment. You're only responsible for choosing the virtual machine sizes for your node pool. However, you can have **Kubernetes (K8s** for short) deployed and configured in advance, though the full deployment and configuration of K8s is outside the scope of this book.

In the following diagram, you can see the three components of BDC running as a **Kubernetes pod**:

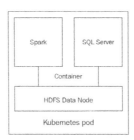

Fig. 12.8 – Big Data Clusters components

SQL Server BDC can leverage the PolyBase feature to access external data without any need for data movement. This enables you to fully utilize the data virtualization feature.

Deploying Big Data Clusters

There are several ways to deploy BDC. Let's explore the UI-based method with **Azure Data Studio**. **Azure Data Studio** is a cross-platform utility used to manage **Azure Data Solutions** such as Azure SQL Database, Azure Synapse Analytics, and SQL BDC. You can also manage on-premises SQL Servers; however, SQL Server Management Studio offers a more feature-rich experience for management. At the time of writing this book, **Azure Data Studio 1.19.0** is the latest version. Keep in mind that Azure Data Studio is updated monthly, so your experience may be different.

In the following screenshot, you can see the welcome page for Azure Data Studio, along with the option to deploy a server. This deployment can be used to deploy the following:

- **SQL Server on Windows**
- **SQL Server container image**
- **SQL Server Big Data Cluster**

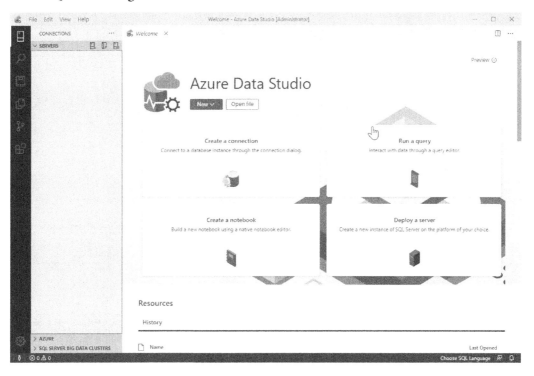

Fig. 12.9 – Azure Data Studio

To deploy BDC, you will need additional tools such as **kubectl**, **Azure CLI**, and **azdata**, all of which **Azure Data Studio** can detect. If these tools are not installed, **Azure Data Studio** can automate the installation by clicking on **Install tools**. In the following screenshot, you can see the installation process for the tools required for BDC deployment:

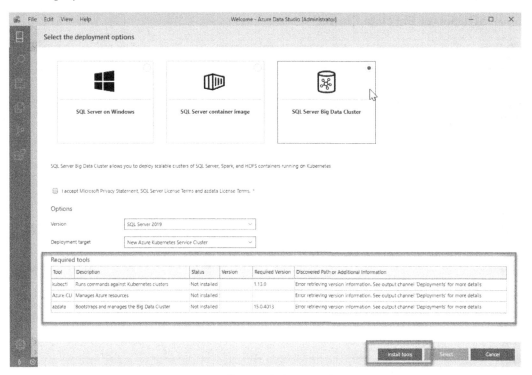

Fig. 12.10 – Installing tools for BDC deployment

Once all tools have been installed, you can choose the target for your deployment. You can deploy BDC to any of the following options:

- **New Azure Kubernetes Service Cluster**
- **Existing Azure Kubernetes Service Cluster**
- **Existing Kubernetes Cluster (kubeadm)**

The only version of SQL Server you can choose for deployment is the 2019 version. However, if you are deploying SQL Server on Windows, you can deploy SQL Server 2017. When you're deploying BDC, **Azure Data Studio** allows you to choose a deployment profile. There are two default profiles available – **dev-test** and **dev-test-ha** – that provide high availability on the SQL Server Master node, as shown in the following screenshot:

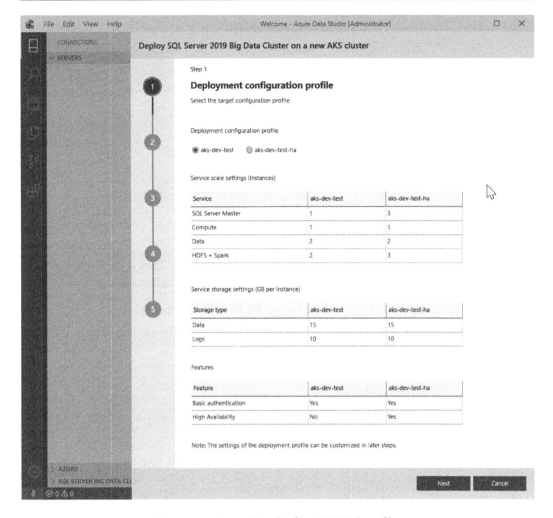

Fig. 12.11 – Azure Data Studio AKS BDC profiles

once you've selected a profile you need to enter some details about your Azure subscription, such as the following:

- **Subscription id**
- **New resource group name**
- **Location**
- **AKS cluster name**
- **VM count** and **VM size** for your node pool

These options can be seen in the following screenshot:

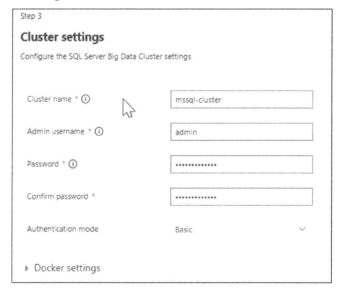

Step 2

Azure settings

Configure the settings to create an Azure Kubernetes Service cluster

Subscription id ⓘ	Use my default Azure subscription	View available Azure subscriptions
New resource group name *	bdc	
Location *	eastus2 ▼	View available Azure locations
AKS cluster name *	mssql-20200703183016	
VM count *	5	
VM size *	Standard_E8s_v3	View available VM sizes

Fig. 12.12 – Azure Settings for BDC deployment

Once you have entered these Azure settings, you need to enter the settings for the cluster, as shown in the following screenshot:

Step 3

Cluster settings

Configure the SQL Server Big Data Cluster settings

Cluster name * ⓘ	mssql-cluster
Admin username * ⓘ	admin
Password * ⓘ	••••••••••••
Confirm password *	••••••••••••
Authentication mode	Basic ⌄

▸ Docker settings

Fig. 12.13 – BDC cluster settings

Once the BDC cluster settings have been entered, you have to provide the required **Service settings**, which would include scaling, port numbers, and storage classed for each of the components of the BDC deployment, as shown in the following screenshot:

Fig. 12.14 – Azure Data Studio Service settings

The individual components under the **Storage settings** section are part of the architecture of BDC. Let's learn a little more about them:

- **Controller** is a service (control plane) used to manage BDC. During the deployment, once the **azdata** tool has created the controller, it takes control and deploys the remaining parts of the BDC.

- **Storage pool** (**HDFS**) is used for reading data from HDFS storage for various file types, such as parquet, CSV, and so on.

- **Data pool** uses Kubernetes pods for data caching. It is used to ingest data from **Spark jobs** and **SQL queries**.

- **SQL Server Master** is a SQL Server instance in the BDC architecture that provides numerous services, such as the following:

  a) Connectivity

  b) Query Management

  c) Metadata and user database

  d) Machine Learning Services

In the final dialog of **Azure Data Studio**, you can generate a notebook that can be executed on your local machine. The notebook contains all the commands required to build the BDC in Azure, as per your configuration. Once all the steps in the notebook have been completed, BDC is deployed to the Azure Kubernetes Service, as shown in the following screenshot from **Azure Data Studio**:

Fig. 12.15 – Notebook used to deploy BDC

You will also be presented with numerous endpoints that were created during the deployment phase. You'll need those endpoints to perform operations and manage your BDC infrastructure.

Working with a SQL Server Big Data Clusters workload

While working with BDC, you can combine two types of data — data stored in relational databases that's hosted by SQL Server and data stored in HDFS that's hosted by data nodes.

The BDC team has provided a sample script that will load data into your BDC deployment, both for your SQL Server workload and HDFS. You can use this script to populate your environment with usable sample data for experiments.

One of the possible approaches to this is to directly query the data stored in the **Data node** with the external table approach, as shown in the *Using PolyBase to access external data* section. The major difference here is that the external data source can be hosted on the Storage pool. To configure such a data source, use the following query:

```
CREATE EXTERNAL DATA SOURCE SqlStoragePool
     WITH (LOCATION = 'sqlhdfs://controller-svc/default')
```

Considering we have a CSV file stored in the Storage pool, as shown in the following screenshot, we can create the external table and query the data:

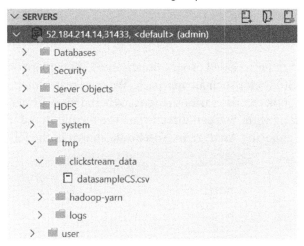

Fig. 12.16 – HDFS explorer with Big Data Clusters

One of the great features of Azure Data Studio is the **HDFS** node, which allows you to explore the data stored within your BDC deployment on the HDFS filesystem on the Storage pool. You can not only explore, but also upload, manage, and preview the content of the data on the HDFS node.

Let's create an external table that we can query later:

```
CREATE EXTERNAL TABLE [clickstream_data_table_csv]
(
     "NumberID" BIGINT ,
     "Name" Varchar(120) ,
     "Name2" Varchar(120),
```

```
    "Price" Decimal ,
    "Discount" Decimal ,
    "Money" Decimal,
    "Money2" Decimal,
    "Company" Varchar(120),
    "Type" Varchar(120),
    "Space" Varchar(120)
)
WITH
(
    DATA_SOURCE = SqlStoragePool,
    LOCATION = '/tmp/clickstream_data',
    FILE_FORMAT = csv_file
)
```

The very same data can be accessed programmatically. Let's explore one more option we have in Azure Data Studio for such an approach. We can create notebooks for working with data. This notebook can use various languages based on your needs, experience, and the data you're working with. You can directly analyze the file stored in HDFS by right-clicking the file and choosing **Analyze in Notebook**, shown in the following screenshot:

Fig. 12.17 – Azure Data Studio notebooks

Once you've clicked on **Analyze in Notebook**, a new notebook will be created, and you can choose the kernel and the connection to use. The following kernels can be used to work with the notebook:

- **SQL**

- **PySpark**

- **Scala**

- **R**

- **Python**

- **PowerShell**

Once the notebook is connected to your controller instance, you can run your code and get proper results from the CSV file, as shown in the following screenshot:

Fig. 12.18 – Using PySpark to access CSV files

Using such a kernel requires that you install the proper libraries on the workstation where you're using **Azure Data Studio**. Luckily, **Azure Data Studio** can install all the required dependencies.

In this sample, PySpark was used, which is a Python API for Spark that's used for exploratory data analysis, machine learning, and ETL for big data processing. You can also use PySpark with another great tool for big data processing called Azure Databricks.

You can use code to further enrich the data with machine learning as there are numerous packages available, as well as numerous other Azure services for machine learning and artificial intelligence.

Summary

With this chapter, we have concluded our journey of the SQL Server 2019 Administrator's Guide. We began this journey by looking at planning and installation before moving on to security, backup, and high availability. After that, we looked at more advanced topics such as Azure and BDC deployment.

Through this journey, we have learned how to install and upgrade SQL Server, gained the required knowledge to secure our server in terms of principals, permissions, and various encryption types, and also learned how to plan and implement High Availability and Disaster Recovery technologies such as AlwaysOn Availability Groups, AlwaysOn Failover Cluster Instances, Log Shipping, and many others. Apart from this, we have also learned how to plan a restore strategy and plan our backup routine accordingly. After this, we learned how to use various tools to troubleshoot the performance of the server, as well as how to use advanced features to improve the performance and scalability of the system using in-memory technology and column store indexes. Moreover, we are now aware of how to leverage Azure for SQL Server workloads and how to deploy BDC.

Finally, with this chapter, we have achieved our aim of covering all the aspects of SQL Server 2019 from an administrative point of view.

Other Books You May Enjoy

If you enjoyed this book, you may be interested in these other books by Packt:

Introducing Microsoft SQL Server 2019

Kellyn Gorman, Allan Hirt, Dave Noderer, Mitchell Pearson, James Rowland-Jones, Dustin Ryan, Arun Sirpal, Gregory Woody

ISBN: 978-1-83882-621-5

- Build a custom container image with a Dockerfile
- Deploy and run the SQL Server 2019 container image
- Understand how to use SQL server on Linux
- Migrate existing paginated reports to Power BI Report Server
- Learn to query Hadoop Distributed File System (HDFS) data using Azure Data Studio
- Understand the benefits of In-Memory OLTP

Mastering Azure Machine Learning

Christoph Körner, Kaijisse Waaijer

ISBN: 978-1-78980-755-4

- Setup your Azure Machine Learning workspace for data experimentation and visualization
- Perform ETL, data preparation, and feature extraction using Azure best practices
- Implement advanced feature extraction using NLP and word embeddings
- Train gradient boosted tree-ensembles, recommendation engines and deep neural networks on Azure Machine Learning
- Use hyperparameter tuning and Azure Automated Machine Learning to optimize your ML models
- Employ distributed ML on GPU clusters using Horovod in Azure Machine Learning
- Deploy, operate and manage your ML models at scale
- Automate your end-to-end ML process as CI/CD pipelines for MLOps

Leave a review - let other readers know what you think

Please share your thoughts on this book with others by leaving a review on the site that you bought it from. If you purchased the book from Amazon, please leave us an honest review on this book's Amazon page. This is vital so that other potential readers can see and use your unbiased opinion to make purchasing decisions, we can understand what our customers think about our products, and our authors can see your feedback on the title that they have worked with Packt to create. It will only take a few minutes of your time, but is valuable to other potential customers, our authors, and Packt. Thank you!

Index

X

Y